The Parent's Guide to
TEENAGE SEX
and PREGNANCY

The Parent's Guide to

TEENAGE SEX
and PREGNANCY

Howard R. and Martha E. Lewis

ST. MARTIN'S PRESS • New York

Copyright © 1980 by Howard R. and Martha E. Lewis
All rights reserved. For information, write:
St. Martin's Press, Inc. 175 Fifth Ave., New York, N.Y. 10010
Manufactured in the United States of America

Design by Dennis J. Grastorf

Library of Congress Cataloging in Publication Data

Lewis, Howard R
    The parent's guide to teenage sex and pregnancy.

    1. Sex instruction. 2. Youth—United States—
Sexual behavior. 3. Pregnancy, Adolescent—United
States.   I. Lewis, Martha E., joint author.
II. Title.
HQ56.L334   649'.65   79-27439
ISBN 0-312-59660-X

FOR DAVID AND EMILY
OUR CHILDREN AND CONSULTANTS

Contents

Authors' Note

This is intended to be the most useful, complete book for parents about adolescent sexual intercourse.

In researching and writing it, we sought to fill a need that we became aware of as our own children approached puberty. Like you, we want to prepare and protect our vulnerable youngsters—who at once are too young and too old, know both too much and too little, need our help even while resisting it.

Innumerable books purport to teach youngsters about sex. But, we found, few are realistic. And none are genuinely helpful to mothers and fathers, the forgotten figures in the crises of sexual maturing.

As parents, we had lots of questions, beginning with: What do we need to know about present-day teenage sexual activity? What information and advice should we impart to our youngsters? How can we talk to our children freely and frankly about sex, in ways they'll understand and accept? How are we likely to react to our children's emergence as sexual beings?

As medical writers, we set about finding the answers. Our research soon revealed that, for concerned parents, the topic of children and sex takes in much more than aspects of intercourse. This book, then, is one of three.

Here we deal primarily with teenage heterosexual intercourse and its ramifications. We survey the so-called sex revolution, and suggest how you might counter the pressure on your children (boys as well as girls) to have intercourse before they're ready. We report what specialists advise you pertaining to sexual dysfunctions, cohabitation, and promiscuity. We cover how you can help your youngsters avoid venereal diseases and unwanted pregnancy. And, if you do face the problem of pregnancy, we provide you with practical information about how to proceed in respect to each of your options.

A related book, also completed, is *How To Raise Sexually Healthy Children*. There we deal with the ways you can healthfully influence even a very young child's psychosexual development. We discuss how to handle problems concerning a youngster's physical and emotional development. We take up the issues of masturbation and dating. We go into detail about responding to youngsters' sexual contacts with members of their own sex, ranging from normal same-sex play to homosexuality as a lifelong preference.

The third book in this series, in progress, is *Sex Crimes and Your Child.* This deals with the problems posed by obscene telephone calls, voyeurs and exhibitionists—and with the traumas of molestation, rape and incest.

On these pages, we address ourselves to you, whom we presume to be a parent. We often refer to the plural "your children," "your adolescents," "your youngsters"—not only because most families have more than one child, but also because we thereby can use the unisex "them" instead of the general but masculine "him." We reserve "him" and "her" for when we explicitly want to talk about a child of a particular sex.

Throughout this book we take the position that you are an essential source of sexual knowledge and guidance for your children. But how can you express important scientific findings and psychological insights? In keeping with the practical intent of this book, we offer suggestions as to phrasing. Please don't regard them as a script, but adapt them to your conversational style and family relationships.

Our interviewees were promised anonymity, so all names and other identifying details of parents and young people are disguised. In constructing readable anecdotes from journal reports, we often assign a name to such designations as "Patient 5" or "one 16-year-old Caucasian female." Any similarity to the real name, of course, is sheer coincidence.

You may want to read more about teenage sexuality. At the end of the book you'll find an alphabetical list of the most useful source material we consulted. We especially recommend the journal *Medical Aspects of Human Sexuality.* Besides articles on a great variety of sexual subjects, each issue offers a large number of brief replies by specialists to questions posed by physician-readers. We draw on many of these replies, but have refrained from citing them lest we overload our bibliography.

Like anyone who works in the field of human sexuality, we are indebted to the outstanding pioneers, who tend to be referred to in abbreviated form. "Kinsey" thus designates Dr. Alfred C. Kinsey and his associates, whose surveys *Sexual Behavior in the Human Male* and *Sexual Behavior in the Human Female* launched a new era in dealing with sexual activity as it actually is, irrespective of myth and dogma. "Masters and Johnson" refers to Dr. William H. Masters and Virginia E. Johnson, whose physiological studies produced *Human Sexual Response* and whose treatment program for sexual dysfunction was reported in *Human Sexual Inadequacy.* "SIECUS" means Sex Information and Education Council of the United States, a bastion of good sense and helpful material. "Planned Parenthood" refers to the organization in its several forms (local groups, Planned Parenthood Federation of America, Planned Parenthood-World Population); aside from its contraceptive programs, Planned Parenthood is a clearinghouse for useful information and sexual statistics.

Our special thanks to the scores of youngsters and parents who shared their experiences with us; to our agent Betty Marks; to our editor Marcia Markland; and to our research assistant Jill Stanton.

Howard R. and Martha E. Lewis
Shady, New York

Part I

YOU AND YOUR CHILD'S SEXUALITY

A REVOLUTION in sexual attitudes is threatening your children with emotional distress, pregnancy, and venereal disease. Your youngsters almost certainly wish you'd give them information and advice about sex. Without your help, they're likely to remain sexually ignorant and in danger. Yet your children's teens are likely to be a difficult stage in your own life—a little-discussed period marked by fear of aging, anger, jealousy, sexual tensions. Learn to talk with your children about sex in ways that will make you and them more comfortable, and help them be sexually responsible.

• •

Chapter 1

Your Sexualized Teenager

What you need to know as a parent of an adolescent in the Eighties.

- PETER AND CAROL know they should tell their youngsters about sex. But they don't know what to say, or how to say it. Nor have they much confidence in their facts and opinions.
- Len is disturbed over fears and fantasies he has concerning his adolescents' sex lives. His once-placid family is now in turmoil over his teenagers' behavior.
- Marian and Hank think their 16-year-old Jennifer is too young to have sex. They're worried that she'll be pressured into it, for they've read that half of youngsters between ages 15 and 19 engage in sexual intercourse.
- Bart and Stella are justifiably proud of John, 15, a star athlete and model student. Neither they nor John realizes he has gonorrhea, one of over a dozen venereal diseases that are epidemic among teenagers.
- Elizabeth and Niles never thought they'd favor abortion. But 17-year-old Ginger confesses she's been having intercourse, using withdrawal for contraception. Now she's three months pregnant and wants to keep the baby, the choice of 9 out of 10 teenage mothers.
- Lou finds 19-year-old Ken sobbing in his room. The boy reveals his greatest secret: He's a virgin. The few times he's tried to have intercourse, he's been impotent.

YOUR CHILDREN'S SEXUAL EMERGENCE

This sampling of problems illustrates something you already know too well: Your children's sexual development can cause difficulties for you as well as for them. Inevitably, a child's sexual emergence confronts you with important, difficult questions—about your course of action, your values, and your attitudes toward sex.

Little has been written on the emotional crises that parents go through during a youngster's adolescence. Your child's becoming a sexual being can be fraught with psychological significance for you. This can be an important and difficult stage of your life, but few parents comprehend the emotional depth charges it may set off within their psyches.

A child's sexual emergence can make you worry over your own aging, and can raise in you the unconscious specter of death: "A new generation is coming of age. I am getting older and closer to the end of my life." Your child's maturing can cause you sexual jealousy. It can make you possessive and overprotective. It can reveal in you unexpected anger and resentment. It can arouse sexual tensions—and guilt over reactions wrongly presumed to be abnormal.

Parents are typically unprepared for the conflicts raised in them by a child's physical maturing. One result of such struggles is often reluctance to discuss sex with a child.

As a loving parent, you need to tell your children much more about sex than you almost certainly now do. For their well-being, and your own, you need to provide them with accurate, detailed information on sexual matters. Moreover, you must offer them guidance to help them develop into sexually secure, competent adults.

Contrary to what many parents believe, youngsters do *not* get such instruction in school or from books. They get the bulk of their supposed knowledge from friends. Most teenagers are hazardously ignorant about essential sexual matters—and urgently wish their parents would tell them more.

By talking with your children about sex, you make it more probable that they'll have a healthy attitude—physically, emotionally, and socially—toward sexuality. Teenagers whose parents discuss sex with them are more likely to avoid premature intercourse, and when they do engage in intercourse, are more likely to use contraceptives and prevent venereal disease.

THE NEW MORALITY AND YOUR FAMILY

Your tasks as a parent are made no easier by the so-called sex revolution. You must know what this seeming upheaval in morals entails, what its effects are likely to be on you and your children, what behavior you can realistically expect or enforce.

Like many conscientious, loving parents, you might be at sea with the much-vaunted "new morality." Chances are you don't want to be prudish. You have no nostalgia for Victorian standards. But you sense that your children are in danger of having sexual involvements earlier than is good for them.

You could be recognizing an actual hazard. Although biologically teenagers are able to conceive children, psychologically they are often much like children themselves. Few adolescents can envision the possible results of premature sexual activity. Most have great gaps in their knowledge about sexuality, contraception, and venereal disease. Rare are the youngsters who are prepared for the effects an intense sexual relationship can have on themselves and their partners, on their school and family life.

Despite the likelihood that adolescents will be injured by yielding to peer pressures about sex, parents often surrender their rightful role as honest, sympathetic guides. The years of experience and insight that you have can be invaluable for your children, who have only an immature concept of cause and effect. But mothers and fathers commonly fear they're ignorant and out-of-date. They're often at a loss over how to deal with new sexual standards and the problems they can cause.

Like many parents, you may feel that traditional moral supports have deserted you. Community standards have assumed less importance as families become increasingly mobile. Religious values have largely loosened their hold. Institutions once held in respect are now in disrepute. Your youngsters know that our nation can be involved in an immoral war, government officials can lie, a President can be a criminal.

Political assassination and terrorism have become commonplace. The economic future is shaky. Nuclear catastrophe looms as a grim possibility, if not from war, then from a radioactive accident.

And even while the traditional anchors are giving way, your youngsters are engulfed by yet another source of instability: an adolescent subculture that promotes sex irrespective of the individual's needs or desires. Your children are coming of age in a society steeped in sexuality to a degree unimaginable when you were their age. Movies are sexually explicit. Sexually oriented books and periodicals are everywhere. Television programs and commercials abound with titillation.

No wonder your children get the message that independent judgment about sex is outdated.

TO BE A PARENT IN THE EIGHTIES

What does it take to be a parent in the erotic Eighties? You must be able to show your youngsters that premature sex has negative emotional and physical consequences. You need to help your youngsters ascertain when they are ready for the responsibilities and joys of a mature physical relationship.

If your children do engage in intercourse, they may find it disappointing. Your good advice can help overcome sexual problems. Cohabitation is an increasingly popular living arrangement among young people. You should know how to address yourself to it. You may also need to deal with adolescent promiscuity, often a sign of emotional disturbance for boys as well as girls.

Your children are at great risk of contracting one or more of the many venereal diseases rampant among teenagers. You can give your children advice on how to avoid them, recognize them, treat them. These diseases are considerably more serious than your children probably realize—and can cause sterility, insanity, cancer, and death.

Most teenagers who have intercourse don't use proper contraception, and are at great risk of pregnancy. You need to know the pros and cons of the various types of birth control, and how to counsel your children on their use. You won't be encouraging sexual activity if you give advice on birth control. But be prepared for the resistance your teenagers might have toward using contraceptives.

IF PREGNANCY OCCURS

Nearly 3 in 10 teenage girls who have premarital intercourse become pregnant— a conservative estimate of 700,000 a year.

If your daughter becomes pregnant, or your son faces fatherhood, you should be equipped to deal with the alternatives.

You'll need to be aware of the emotional crisis your teenage daughter faces when she suspects she's pregnant. Your whole family may well require professional help in accommodating to the situation and making the proper decision.

If your daughter opts for abortion—the choice of 300,000 girls each year—she should know what emotional consequences to expect, and where to find good counseling and support. You and she will want to know what the procedure involves, where to get safe, low-cost abortions, what the future medical effects may be.

If your daughter carries to term, you'll need to know how to help her reduce the special health risks pregnant teenagers face. Without proper prenatal care—and 7 in 10 pregnant teenagers receive *no* care in the first three months—she faces more complications during her pregnancy. Her infant is more likely to be born prematurely, and also more likely to suffer mental retardation, epilepsy, and other birth defects.

Your daughter may need your help in deciding whether to keep the child she's delivered or give it up for adoption. You can provide her with the pros and cons of each alternative.

It's likely she'll want to keep the baby, with unrealistic expectations. Then you must provide practical information about the myriad problems she and her child may face. Compared with older first-time mothers, teenagers are more likely to abuse their children. You'll also need to give her tips on ways to improve her education, finances, and social life.

You should know about adoption: how to ease the trauma of separation; how to go about choosing an agency; how the child may fare; what the future may hold for both parents and child.

Marriage is a consideration when teenagers are about to become parents. About 100,000 a year enter hasty marriages, which are typically short-lived. Teenagers who marry as a result of pregnancy tend to be undereducated and impoverished for the rest of their lives. With or without pregnancy, your teenage son or daughter may be contemplating marriage. Your good counsel can help them avert a disaster.

The following chapters will help you cope with these and a multitude of other sex-related problems that might arise as your children journey toward adulthood.

Chapter 2

Teach Your Children About Sex

They want you to—for they're likely to be ignorant and in danger.

IF YOUR CHILDREN are like most youngsters, they wish you'd tell them more about sex. Only with your sexual instruction and guidance are they likely to be well informed and properly directed.

Teenagers typically feel a great need for reliable sex information, which they want to get from their parents, but seldom do. Adequate school sex education programs are virtually nonexistent.

In the absence of authoritative sources of sexual knowledge and advice, children generally turn to their friends. For most youngsters, sex education largely consists of exchanging misinformation with equally ignorant peers. Adolescents thus remain plagued by sexual misconceptions that can cause them emotional and physical distress.

"I WISH I COULD TALK TO MY FOLKS"

The U.S. Commission on Obscenity and Pornography has found that by far most adolescents it surveyed would like to learn more about sex from their parents. The Commission asked the youngsters in effect, "Check from which sources you'd welcome sex information." Mothers are a preferred source for nearly 90 percent of the youngsters; fathers, a preferred source for 80 percent.

Merilee Inman, an obstetrical nurse, has queried high school students in Arizona about their sources of sex information. A typical comment, from a young man: "I learned a lot of sex stuff in school, but I sure wish I could have talked to my folks about it." The desire to talk with parents tends to increase as adolescents grow older and acquire sexual experience.

If you're a father, your children are likely to especially appreciate your participation in sex talks. "Mothers alone provided much more sex information than did fathers," reports nurse Inman. Both boys and girls told her they'd prefer to have sex information come from both parents rather than just their mothers.

RULE OF SILENCE

Parents themselves widely feel that they're shortchanging their youngsters on sex instruction. "Do parents provide sufficient information to their children on sex?" asked Dr. John A. Conley and Robert S. Haff of the University of Illinois. "No," replied 7 out of 10 mothers and fathers—and 6 out of 10 teenagers.

Although youngsters love and respect their parents, communication generally breaks down when sex comes up. In Anaheim, California, over 50,000 high school students have taken a sex education program in which they describe their earlier sources of information. Fewer than 10 percent of the boys and girls have had discussions with their parents or other responsible adults who could help them accept sex as normal and natural.

In New Jersey, some 6 out of 10 surveyed high school students told researchers, "I can't discuss sex freely with my parents." Added 4 out of 10 girls and 2 out of 10 boys: "I've never really discussed sex with my parents."

Social psychologist Robert C. Sorensen studied the sex experiences of a nationwide sampling of teenagers. Fully 7 out of 10 boys and girls told Dr. Sorensen that they and their parents do not talk freely about sex. "In fact," observes Sorensen, "most adolescents are at a loss to know what their parents want them to know about sex."

Fathers seem consistently reluctant to engage in sex talks. Sandra Potter and Herbert Smith discovered that no more than 2 percent of the girls ever received sexual information from their fathers. Dr. Lester A. Kirkendall, editor of *Sex in the Adolescent Years* and director of the American Humanist Association, finds that almost half of surveyed fathers believe, "I'm not qualified to give my children a comprehensive understanding of human sexuality"—and thus deprive their children of an adult male point of view.

When communication is lacking, you are unlikely to find out what your kids actually believe about sexual matters. They may not share some—or any—of your views. The boys in the New Jersey sampling were nearly evenly divided among those who agreed with their parents about sex, those who agreed only in part, and those who disagreed altogether.

Similarly, don't confuse your youngster's silence with assent. Some 6 out of 10 teens confessed this stratagem to psychologist Sorensen: "My parents think that I pretty much agree with their ideas about sex, and I don't say anything that would make them think different."

COUNTING ON THE SCHOOLS?

You might be relegating your children to sexual ignorance if you're counting on their schools to provide them with sex education.

A decade or so ago, sex education seemed like an idea whose time had come. Schools across the country introduced special courses variously labeled "sex education," "life science," and "family life," some beginning as early as kindergarten. Today, many people assume the issue is settled and sex education is generally available in the classroom. It's not. Widespread opposition to sex education has pretty well halted the movement dead in its tracks. As a practical matter, your children will be old grads before schools offer meaningful sex instruction—if they ever do.

Only a few youngsters get any sex education at all. A mere six states (Hawaii, Kentucky, Maryland, Michigan, Missouri, and North Dakota) and the District of Columbia require family life or sex education as part of the public school curriculum. A National Institute of Education survey of principals of junior and senior high schools reveals that only a little over a third of their schools offer sex education courses. One state, Louisiana, forbids such courses.

Several states, such as California, have an extensive written curriculum. If put into effect, such programs can provide essential basic information. But what actually gets taught depends on the community, school, and teacher. The mere possibility of controversy tends to limit the implementation of a program.

Thus, even if your youngsters do take a sex education course, chances are they're not learning as much as you'd like them to know. Teaching children the "plumbing" details of how their bodies work is a good start. But merely a knowledge of anatomy doesn't help youngsters deal with their sexuality or with social pressures from peers. Yet the great majority of school sex education programs teach little more than where babies come from.

Many neglect to do even that. A survey of school districts shows that 1 out of 3 so-called sex education courses do not teach human reproduction. The same number fail to take up adolescent changes or venereal disease. Even more ignore the anatomy of the genitals and such important sociosexual concerns as dating, necking, and petting. Nearly half fail to mention nocturnal emissions or masturbation, major worries for many young people. Six out of 10 don't cover prostitution.

Even less frequently discussed is the most pressing subject of all: birth control. Contraception is touched on in only 39 percent of school sex education programs. Indeed, in some areas teaching about contraception in public schools is illegal.

Sex education programs either leave out or barely mention the extremely common problems of impotence and frigidity, according to a survey of high school principals by Dr. Charles E. Reed of Central Michigan University. Similarly neglected are the subjects of homosexuality, promiscuity, and pornography. Also virtually unmentioned are issues relating to marriage, including topics couples should discuss before marriage, and problems of sexual adjustment in marriage.

UNINFORMATIVE BOOKS

Many youngsters get most of their sex information from books sold for the sexual instruction of adolescents. You may be tempted to buy such a book to give your children. Youngsters commonly share them with friends who similarly seek to educate themselves. At the University of North Carolina at Greensboro, Dr. Carrie Lee Warren and Richard St. Pierre find that books constitute the most important source of sex information for over a quarter of surveyed students. Books rank second in importance only to friends, and substantially more important than parents or school courses.

The best of these books can be valuable adjuncts to your children's sex education. But most such books are extremely unlikely to teach your youngsters what they want or need to know.

Thirty-one widely used books have been analyzed by Harvard researchers Drs. Judith S. Rubenstein, Fletcher G. Watson, and

Howard S. Rubenstein. The investigators started off by asking a sampling of ninth graders: "What specific sexual subjects are you most interested in learning about?" The teenagers' areas of greatest concern: venereal disease, birth control, and sexual intercourse. Next most desired are discussions of love, pregnancy, and enjoyment of sex. Then come the topics of abortion and sex offenses. Last of the youngsters' top ten are discussions of prostitution and of guilt about sex.

How do the books stack up against adolescent interests? The researchers find that 20 percent of the books fail to mention sexual intercourse. Of the books that do discuss intercourse, over 90 percent give it deficient treatment. Or the books discuss either the physical or the emotional aspect of intercourse, but not both. Or they glut the discussion with clinical detail that obscures major concepts.

Similarly, 25 percent of the books fail to discuss pregnancy. Some 30 percent neglect to mention love, 40 percent ignore venereal disease, and 50 percent say not a word about birth control, abortion, or guilt about sex. About 55 percent say nothing on enjoyment of sex or on prostitution.

The scientific information in the great majority of these books is further compromised by the authors' moral stance, which detracts from a realistic, objective approach to teenage sexuality. The Harvard investigators describe only 20 percent of the books as "Impartial," which they define as providing biological and psychological information on sexual intercourse without comment on the context in which it should be performed. An example of an impartial presentation: "Intercourse means that a man's penis is inserted into a woman's vagina. During intercourse, semen passes from the penis to the vagina." In this discussion, the people are referred to as "man" and "woman," not "husband" and "wife." There is no judgment about people being married before having intercourse.

If your youngsters are turned off by preaching, they're likely to resist what might be valuable in 80 percent of the books. The researchers find 30 percent of the books to be "Christian Moral," expressing the view that sexual intercourse should be reserved only for marriage as shown by Christian teachings.

Fully half the books are "Moral," though secular. These generally describe sexual intercourse as chiefly a physical and spiritual act between husband and wife. In this view, sexual intercourse should be reserved for marriage. Some Moral books allow unmarried intercourse for mature adults, but never for teenagers.

Extreme examples are what the investigators call "Fig-leaf Moral" books, which totally ignore the genitals. One such book—described on its jacket as an "anatomy book" for "children who are curious about their bodies"—has detailed discussions and drawings of every system of the body except the sex organs.

SHARING IGNORANCE

Your children's main sources of sex information are likely to be their friends, who generally know as little as they do.

Most of the Arizona youngsters interviewed by nurse Merilee Inman got their first sex instruction during grade school. "The source was described as 'dirty' talks with friends or reading sexually oriented magazines with friends."

Over 60 percent of a sampling of boys in a northeastern high school told investigators Madelon Lubin Finkel and David J. Finkel that they learned about intercourse and reproduction from other kids. Some 37 percent were informed by male friends, 18 percent by female friends, 8 percent by brothers. Parents were sources of sex information for under 15 percent.

New Jersey high school students were asked, "From whom did you first learn about sex?" "From friends," replied 80 percent of the boys and 50 percent of the girls. Significantly, 60 percent of both boys and girls reported they were dissatisfied with what they'd learned so far about sex.

Small wonder. If your youngsters are like most, their areas of sexual ignorance are as vast as the Grand Canyon. They may seem sophisticated, but chances are it's only surface sophistication. Indeed, the more sexual experience an adolescent has had, the less likely is he or she to know facts about sexuality.

Obstetrician-gynecologist Takey Crist of the University of North Carolina at Chapel Hill administered a questionnaire on sexual anatomy to six hundred women students. Among the young women who were sexually relatively inexperienced, 80 percent correctly answered half the questions. Nine percent got all the answers right.

The sexually active women scored much lower. Only 59 percent could correctly answer half the questions. None could answer all. Over 25 percent could not answer any.

One conclusion from several such studies: The more adolescents know factually about sex, the more realistic they are in their sexual expectations and activity. They tend to be more discriminating in their premarital relations. They understand the process of conception. They favor the use of contraceptives.

Conversely, sexually active teenagers tend to know the mechanics of intercourse—but little of its relationship to pregnancy or disease. Similarly minimal is their understanding of birth control, menstruation, masturbation, oral sex, and homosexuality. Often they oppose the use of contraceptives.

How much your youngsters may need to learn about sex is reflected in the thousands of appeals for sexual advice received each month by *'Teen* magazine. Most of the magazine's readers are girls between 12 and 17. Many are evidently unprepared for their emerging womanhood. One wrote *'Teen:* "I'm 13 and have a terrible problem. I have HAIR on my private parts!" Another, unaware that adolescents are normally preoccupied with sex, expressed a fear of being abnormal. "I think about sex more and more. I have these feelings and dreams . . . is something wrong with me?"

To teenage girls, boys often present serious problems. "How do boys and girls differ regarding sexual attitudes?" "How do you know when a boy is just using you?" Intercourse is a frequent worry. "I don't feel ready to have sex. How can I say 'No' to my boyfriend without losing him?"

The subject of pregnancy abounds in confusion. "At what age is a boy capable of making a girl pregnant?" "Can you get pregnant if you have sex standing up?" "Is it possible to get pregnant without actual intercourse?"

Young men are no better informed about their sexuality, to judge from the anonymous calls received by New York's Community Sex Information telephone service. A common worry of boys who call: "How often should you masturbate? Can it be harmful?" Another frequent concern: "How long is the average penis? What can I do to make mine bigger?" Yet another urgent problem: "How can I stop myself from getting erections in public?"

Even bright, upper-income teenagers need basic information on a wide range of sexual topics. In Illinois, students at suburban Evanston High School were given the chance to question a medical expert about human sexuality. Among their queries: "What's an orgasm?" "What's the difference between erection and ejaculation?" "How does a girl know if she's pregnant?"

If your children are like those in Evanston, they have a lot of questions about birth control. "What is contraceptive foam and how does it work?" "When should a girl start using birth control pills?" "Where can a minor get reliable contraceptives?" They're likely to be aware of potential psychological problems. "Is it emotionally bad for a teen to have sexual intercourse?" They also want to know about VD, about oral sex, about homosexuality.

Such questions don't disappear with your youngsters' graduation from high school. Unless properly instructed and guided, college students remain sexually ill-informed and confused. At the University of North Carolina at Greensboro, Dr. Carrie Lee Warren and Richard St. Pierre gave students a multiple-choice quiz on human reproduction. More than one-third of these college students did not know the meaning of ovulation, did not know the basic function of the contraceptive pill, did not know how the sex of a baby is determined, did not know the umbilical cord is attached to the placenta, and did not know the name of the medical specialist concerned with the care of pregnant women. "All of these missed questions point out a gross lack of information about some basic concepts of human sexuality," comment the researchers.

Imagine the sexual misinformation, they add, that must fog the minds of adolescents who are younger or less schooled.

What sexual subjects do college students feel a strong need to know about? At the beginning of a course in human sexuality, reports Dr. Peter Scales of Syracuse University, over two hundred students were asked to write anonymously on an index card the one question they'd like answered during the semester. About a fourth of the students were concerned about contraception. "Can a girl who is still a virgin use a diaphragm?" "How safe is it to use foam and a rubber together? How safe is the rhythm method?" Large percentages of students also asked about orgasm, sexual techniques, oral or anal sex, and sexual dysfunction (mainly impotence, premature ejaculation, and frigidity).

DISTRESS SIGNALS

Lack of information can cause your children sexual anxieties. At the University of Houston, psychologist James Leslie McCary has asked students to submit questions they'd like him to cover in his lectures on sexuality. Dr. McCary has collected and analyzed more than 100,000 queries representing areas of college students' greatest sexual concern. At a northeastern women's college, psychiatrist Lyon Hyams made a similar study of over one thousand questions submitted by students at his lectures. From their analyses, Drs. McCary and Hyams detect recurrent themes of psychosexual distress, largely due to the young people's ignorance of pertinent sexual facts.

One common group of fears is related to personal injury and death. Young women are often apprehensive about the safety of all contraceptives. While their concern about the Pill may be justified, their anxiety extends unrealistically to the use of foam, diaphragms, and condoms.

Although it will be several years before most coeds have children, pregnancy frequently causes them anxiety. They fear damage to the infant. "How do brain injuries occur at birth?" They worry about injury to themselves. "If labor is prolonged, what are the dangers to the mother?" "Does sexual intercourse have any effect on the pregnancy?"

Sexual activity in general raises fears of physical harm. "Can the penis penetrate the muscle at the entrance of the womb?" "Could it be possible that the penis is too wide to fit in the female?" "Can petting below the waist harm your internal organs?"

Considerable emotional distress can result from your children's sexual misconceptions. Psychiatrist Arnold Werner of Michigan State University has written a health column, "The Doctor's Bag," appearing in fifty college newspapers. More than half the questions deal with sex. Many betray worries over sexual myths.

Penis size comes in for grave concern. Young men whose penises seem small when limp commonly avoid shower rooms. Many boys contemplate buying a vacuum pump, a diabolical-looking apparatus, to help them gain an inch or two. Often a young man is sure he's deformed because his erection, of normal shape, is not ramrod straight. "It takes the shape of a banana. . . . I am sure there is something wrong with me."

Oral sex arouses a variety of needless fears. Girls worry they can become pregnant if they swallow semen. One young man asked, "Is the accidental ingesting of contraceptive foam hazardous to my health?" Dr. Werner says he was tempted to reply, "It would be an effective means of preventing oral pregnancies." Then he realized a great many people might think he was serious.

Myths about intercourse and contraception can lead directly to pregnancy. Many young people have a mystical belief in the efficacy of withdrawal, or in the supposed protection afforded by certain days of the girl's menstrual cycle. Some believe that if the boy drinks a lot of alcohol, the sperm will be too drunk to find the egg.

One of the most prevalent misconceptions is that a girl cannot become pregnant if she doesn't have an orgasm. Naive? Of course, and also woefully inconsiderate of the girl. But imagine the distress you'd feel if, out of ignorance, your son or daughter were one of the youngsters described in this letter to Dr. Werner:

"Over a period of about three months my girl friend and I have had sexual intercourse about fifteen times. In all of these encounters, she claims never to have had an orgasm of any kind. With this in mind, we use no protection. Now she is pregnant! How?"

Chapter 3

Your Own Growing Pains

Expect fear of aging, anger, guilt, jealousy, sexual tensions.

YOUR CHILDREN'S ADOLESCENCE is likely to be a highly charged period for you as well as for them.

Their reaching puberty can trigger emotions in you that you didn't know you had. Thereafter, as your teenagers mature physically, emotionally, socially, you might reveal further attitudes that surprise you. Conflicts can erupt unexpectedly—within yourself, between you and your youngsters, even between you and your spouse. Communication, needed more than ever, may break down.

Most books and articles about adolescence focus on the youngsters: their physical and emotional health, their transition from the playworld of childhood to the responsible community of adults, their problems and their needs. Rarely touched on is the parent's side of the process.

Yet you are very much affected by your teenagers' upheavals, suffering through them with pains that may go back to your own childhood. Moreover, as an active adult, you are hardly on ice. During the years of your children's adolescence, you are going through much developing of your own.

You too are in flux, for your thirties, forties, and fifties are dynamic ages. They are marked by personal growth, by constant learning and adjustment, by inevitable family and job crises—all compounded by your relationships with children who are in a state of rapid change. Any of this can influence how you respond to your teenagers' sexual development, and how they in turn react to your response.

Your children's sexual awakening can thus present a distinct, difficult stage of your life. Understanding this seldom-discussed phase in your life cycle can help you get through it with a minimum of discomfort. Here are some problems that parents of adolescents often need to confront within themselves:

WORRY OVER AGING

Your children's adolescence catches you at a vulnerable age. By the time your youngsters begin entering their teens, you are likely to be in your thirties or forties. From dealings with younger friends and colleagues, you may already have sensed that you are a member of an older generation. But this truth is brought home to you literally when your first child reaches puberty.

A postpubescent youngster is no longer your little boy or girl. Rather, that child is a young man or woman capable of sexual activity, indeed of making you a grandparent. Your adolescent is an inescapable reminder of your middle age.

"Living in a culture that has glorified youth, this can be quite an emotional shock," comments psychiatrist Helen R. Beiser of the Abraham Lincoln School of Medicine at the University of Illinois. The shock is not softened by signs of your physical aging. Gray hairs appear. Facial muscles sag. Excess weight becomes ever more tenacious. Illnesses take their toll.

Mothers might find it especially difficult to adjust to a daughter's maturing. Even a loving mother with a good marriage may resent her daughter's vigor and attractiveness. This glowing aliveness can contrast painfully with the mother's sense of lost youth and fading sex appeal. Notes Dr. Beiser: "It is a rare woman who can sincerely welcome her daughter into puberty."

Fathers likewise might begrudge a son's adolescent vitality. By the late thirties or early forties, men commonly start to slow down. You get tired more easily, unable to play or work as hard or as long. On the job, your younger competitors seem ever brighter, more alive, greater and greater threats to your position and prestige. In bed, you detect a slowing of your sexual response, a diminishment in the number and quality of your orgasms. Thus, despite your paternal pride, you may not wholeheartedly enjoy your son's increasing physical abilities. With each passing year, they seem to come at the expense of your own strength and manhood.

However strong your marriage, your child's adolescence brings growing pains to you and your spouse as a couple. You have lost the small child you once cherished. So too have you lost the confident expectations and unjaded hopes you had when your youngster was little. Comments University of Michigan psychologist Elizabeth Douvan: "The emerging adulthood of one's children must at some level register as the signal of one's own decline."

JEALOUSY

You might find yourself becoming sexually envious of your teen-agers. Think twice if a youngster complains, "You're not allowing me enough privacy." Parents may inspect their children's rooms, open their mail, and wish to be told the details of their social life. This behavior can conceal jealousy of a child's burgeoning sexuality.

A mother may seek a physician's care as a result of her stress over a daughter's development. "When sexual jealousy is strong, she might have a gynecological or dermatological complaint or seek plastic surgery to improve her appearance," reports psychiatrist Beiser.

At the opposite extreme is the supposedly enlightened mother who floods her daughter with sexual information. Long before the girl wants the instruction, she may be told in detail about intercourse. When she begins to menstruate, her mother may introduce her to contraception.

Seemingly, this excessive sexual instruction suggests that the mother is not jealous. "However," observes Dr. Beiser, "often an unconscious hostility is operative." Without being conscious of her motives, the mother might be seeking to sabotage her daughter. "The mother senses that this push toward early sexual activity may actually interfere with the development of mature sexual and interpersonal relationships."

A mother's jealousy can be aroused by her husband's attention to their maturing daughter. Psychiatrist Silas B. Coley of the University of North Carolina School of Medicine tells of twelve-year-old Julia, who became an avid horsewoman and the constant riding companion of Harold, her father. They left out the mother, Doris, who became consumed with jealousy toward Julia.

"I'm furious, anxious, depressed," Doris told Dr. Coley. At thirty-nine, she was feeling inadequate, and was worried over her age and health. Dr. Coley helped her see that her personality could lead her to being scapegoated by Julia and Harold. Doris overcame her jealousy, and grew to enjoy horse shows and riding.

POSSESSIVENESS

With your children's entry into adolescence, you might struggle with an irony of parenthood: Your success as a parent enables your young to become self-sufficient.

Many parents feel this as a loss. In exchanging a child for an adult, for a person who can leave you and live independently, you are largely deprived of your role as a parent. Such roles help you define yourself as a person. Ask yourself, "What am I?" Chances are you'll soon list that you're a mother or a father.

Parenting is likely to be among your most important activities. With love, in acceptance of your role as a parent, consider how many things you do every day in connection with your children. Think how you shape your hours around them. Contemplate how much thought and emotion you devote to them. Feel the satisfactions you get in nurturing your young.

Then sense what a hole would be left in your life if your children no longer needed you. "When the child pulls out of the family—at least emotionally and perhaps also geographically—the parents are left with their parenting needs and behaviors dangling," observes psychologist Elizabeth Douvan. "They need to parent and they need the parent role as one of their self-defining elements. But there is no longer a child to receive the parenting, no longer a reciprocal to their parent role."

A child's early teens mark the beginning of this transition for the parent. Ideally, suggests Dr. Douvan, a parent could say to an adolescent: "You need to have freedom to explore and form yourself outside the bounds of the family. I will give you this freedom, this distance. I will also grant you new recognition as an autonomous being. What you need from me has changed. That you need something remains."

Ideally, too, a parent could accept that adolescent sexuality can be a declaration of independence. Dr. Roger W. Libby, while at Syracuse University's Institute for Family Research and Education, urged parents to show their willingness "to let go that part of their children which no longer belongs to them [and] to nurture that part of their children that needs proof of parental concern and loving kindness."

But few parents are so ideal. Psychiatrist Helen Beiser has seen mothers develop psychosomatic illnesses over a daughter's assertions of independence. Frustrated over losing control of her daughter, a mother may have headaches or arthritic pains. If she feels that her daughter's growing up or moving away from home is a threat to her own usefulness as a woman, she might get depressed or become unusually susceptible to colds and other virus conditions. A significant part of any mother's medical history, observes Dr. Beiser, is the state of her relationships with her children.

Single mothers are especially likely to resist a girl's growth, warns psychiatrist Myrtle LeBow of the University of Southern California Medical School. "If the mother does not remarry, she may feel the need to devote her life to her children and therefore resents her adolescent daughter's move toward independence and her preference for her boyfriend over her." Some widows or divorcees, lonely for male companionship, encourage the daughter to bring her boyfriend to the house. They then try to take the young man over. Dr. LeBow counsels such a mother "to find a life of her own, not to live vicariously through her daughter."

A father may suffer his teenager's separation from the family even more acutely. Children's gestures of autonomy often come as a ruder shock to their father than their mother. If she has been in charge of the kids' upbringing, she has seen day-to-day many expressions of growth. He has not.

Moreover, a child's move toward independence often comes at a time when many men take stock of their lives. "Is this all there is?" a father might be asking. His teen's pulling away can deepen his void, worsen his despair. Cautions psychologist Douvan: "The combination of disappointment in work and loss of control of the child can precipitate a crisis . . . which in turn can lead to the dissolution of the family."

OVERPROTECTIVENESS

Your wish to protect your children continues long after they reach puberty.

Much as you'd like to, you recognize that you can't completely safeguard your adolescents from the physical and emotional hazards they face in moving toward adulthood. To a great measure, you know, your teenagers must negotiate these pitfalls for themselves in their own way.

Nonetheless, you might realistically view your youngsters as endangered by their idealism and lack of experience. You may fear that your son or daughter will be seduced into a relationship that will end in heartbreak, if not pregnancy. In response, you may almost instinctively be training your teenagers to make independent judgments about their sexuality.

During a child's early adolescence, most parents provide firm limits and guidelines. By the time the youngster reaches 15 or 16, the parents are ready to give increasing freedom—and their child is prepared to accept greater and greater responsibility. "In this way," notes the Reverend Thomas Edwards Brown of SIECUS (the Sex Information and Education Council of the United States, Inc.), "they try to help their adolescent to move progressively from strong dependence on external parental controls to increasing reliance on his own judgment and internal controls."

But some parents are not up to their children's level of readiness. They establish arbitrary rules. They give too much advice. They put the child through an inquisition after every date.

Parents anxious about aging might try to keep an adolescent a baby, in an attempt to cling to their own youth and vigor. Unconsciously, they may fear that as a child matures, they lose their hold on life itself. They may hope to forestall the passage of generations that marks their getting closer to death, and in an attempt to freeze time, they often attempt to protect the teenager as they would a younger child.

A father is particularly likely to be overprotective of his adolescent daughter. He may remember his own early sexual exploits, which he now recognizes were exploitation. A mother may be caught in the middle between her overprotective husband and her resisting, if not rebelling, daughter. Often the mother fights to get her daughter increasing freedom: to visit friends, stay out late, dance, date, whatever.

Fathers often want schools to stand *in loco parentis*, in place of the parents—a role that colleges have to a considerable extent abandoned. When a girl is ready to go off to college, her father may fear, "She's not emotionally ready." Observes psychiatrist Raymond Babineau of the University of Rochester School of Medicine: "More likely this is a projection of his own fears concerning her sexual behavior and his struggle to 'keep her safe' under his behavioral controls."

Dr. Babineau describes such a father as resisting his daughter's maturational task of separation/individuation: the need for young people to go off on their own and develop their own personalities. An important milestone in this process often occurs when children depart for college or move away from home, as much as it may pain the father.

You may well derive much pleasure from reliving your adolescence through your youngster's activities. Parents commonly want their children to be charming, happy, and have lots of friends. This is generally a healthy impulse. But some parents push their teenagers. Many normal girls are sent for psychotherapy because their mothers feel they are not "popular enough." Dr. Helen Beiser spoke to one such mother. "She herself had been a shy and unpopular adolescent and had married late and without love. Such mothers burden their daughters by their own need to be socially successful."

Parents often have a schedule in mind of what's "normal" for a teenager's maturation. If your aspirations are unrealistic, you are likely to fear that a child is "backward." You may worry, "He's not interested in girls," or, "She stays home all the time."

In fact, teenagers vary enormously in their readiness for social and sexual relationships. Every child's development is unique, subject to such widely divergent influences as the youngster's personality, biochemistry, interests, experiences. Long periods of isolation suit many adolescents. Just as an adult may enjoy bouts of privacy, so too a youngster can enjoy stretches of being alone, the better to engage in fantasy and other solitary pursuits.

ANGER

Brought up in a more restrictive era, you may resent the looser standards that seem to govern your youngsters. At the psychiatry department of the State University of New York at Stony Brook, Dr. Ann Welbourne has noted that parents are often reluctant to discuss sex with a child because they feel "angry that today's youngsters know a lot about sex, and are cool and comfortable with their sexuality."

A child's sexuality might be used as a weapon in arguments between the parents. Notes psychiatrist Helen Beiser: "When serious marital difficulties exist, a father may use his adolescent daughter, as well as other women, to make his wife miserable."

Dr. Beiser tells of Harriet, who came for treatment because she was constantly shouting at her 11-year-old daughter Sue. The girl took on more activities than she could handle, and didn't finish her schoolwork or household chores. "I nag her to get things done and often do things for her, which I hate," said Harriet.

Almost every evening after Sue went to bed, Frank, the father, visited her in her room for a long talk. Not only was Frank interfering with discipline, but he was also fanning the flames of Harriet's jealousy, and treating Sue like a small child who needed comforting in order to sleep. Harriet recognized this. But, because she felt like such a bad mother, she held her tongue.

At last, as a result of treatment, Harriet herself stopped treating Sue like a little girl. She let Sue take responsibility for limiting her activities to what she could comfortably finish. Harriet insisted that Sue's bedtime be enforced, and that Frank stop his provoking after-hours talks.

SEXUAL TENSIONS

Your children's sexual maturing is likely to arouse in you strong sexual reactions.

Psychiatrist Sol Nichtern of New York Medical College believes that children are part and parcel of their parents' sex lives. For one thing, observes Dr. Nichtern, your sexual behavior is influenced by all your relationships within your family, including those with your children. "The child is not only the product of the sex act, but also may determine significant parental sexual attitudes." Any feelings your children generate in you—love, pride, joy, frustration, resentment, guilt—can affect you sexually.

For another thing, you are likely to act in the hope that your children will fulfill your aspirations, sexual and otherwise. "My child will be what I can never be," you may unconsciously resolve. "My child will achieve what I can never achieve." Thus you might shape their sexuality.

Your sexual aspirations are powerful determinants of what you communicate to your children. How masculine should they be? How feminine? How aggressive? How passive? How should they show love? You give such instruction to your children long before they become sexually active. But you may be unaware of what you are teaching them by word and example. Then you are likely to be upset if they put into effect your unconscious lessons.

Thus Stella, who'd had to work from an early age, wanted her daughter Kathy to be "dainty" and "ladylike," a supposed sign of Stella's success as a provider. But Stella's behavior shouted, "Get yours!" She, but no one else, was surprised when Kathy became a gold digger—sexually manipulative, and about as ladylike as a Sherman tank.

Deep in your psyche, concludes Dr. Nichtern, your feelings about your children and about sex are inseparable. The psychological drive is often essentially the same, even though whom and how you love is expressed differently in sex and child-rearing. Your sexual and parental attitudes thus tend to be consistent. A giving lover will generally be a giving parent. A cruel lover, a cruel parent. An abusive parent, an abusive lover. A demanding parent, a demanding lover.

Your children's sexual emergence is likely to cause you anxiety. Prudishness permeates our culture, so your own upbringing is likely to have had antisexual overtones. From infancy on, you may have been inculcated with the attitude that sex organs and their functions are inherently dirty, unsightly, and sinful. Few parents feel free enough about their own sexuality to be comfortable with sexual activity in their children. A typical reaction to a child's sexual exploration is alarm, often followed by punishment.

Your anxiety may be worsened if your child's sexual development gives new urgency to sexual problems in your marriage. Husbands and wives are often out of touch with their sexual feelings. Sex goes underground—until a child's sexual maturation makes the subject hard to ignore. Advises psychologist Sol Gordon of Syracuse University's Institute for Family Research and Education: "Parents should recognize that before they can communicate freely with their children, they must be able to talk freely about sexuality with *each other* and to develop sensitivity to their own feelings."

In your marriage, you and your partner can start by sharing your responses to such questions as, "Am I satisfied with our sexual relations?" "Are we able to express the affection we feel for each other?" "How has our sex life changed since we were married?"

Husbands and wives can thus get in touch with their sexual attitudes. "Such talks can make them aware of their own selves, and more open to their partner's needs," comments Dr. Gordon. "By discovering what is pleasing to themselves—never mind what the books say!—they can understand and eventually become more comfortable with their own sexuality."

GUILT

Guilt as well as anxiety is likely to burden parents who are sexually aroused by their children. You've been infixed with the taboo against incest since early childhood. Society regards sexual abuse of your children as a loathsome perversion, thus parents often feel discomforted when they sense they are having incestuous thoughts.

In fact, such thoughts—without overt acts—are a little-discussed aspect of normal parenthood. Sexual fantasies concerning your children are likely to crop up repeatedly, even when they're babies. When your children are as palpably sexual as they are in adolescence, you may have frequent erotic sensations stirred by them.

Parents who misinterpret such feelings as "abnormal" or "incestuous" can be reassured by psychiatrist Milton M. Berger. "They need to be informed that they are not abnormal or bestial persons, as these reactions are more common than uncommon and even perhaps universal."

Dr. Berger, who teaches at Downstate Medical Center in Brooklyn, warns against believing that you can control your sexual feelings through your intellect. Many parents expect that they can keep themselves from having erotic sensations toward their children. They're often disturbed when feelings arise in them "which emerge from their innermost being and which are not amenable to consciously willed control."

Of course, except in rare instances, the fantasies stay just that: harmless flashes of thought.

Most parents who do have sexual sensations, and even desires, for their children find that the capacity to control their behavior is well within their power. They are thus far from ever making moves of a sexual nature toward their youngsters. Despite their guilty fears, they commit nothing that can be remotely called incest.

Your physical contacts with your children do change, however, because of their sexual maturing. A problem you face is to keep sex and love neatly segregated. This is no easy trick. You've been accustomed over the years to a relationship of closeness, affection, and tenderness with your child, a relationship uncomplicated by sexual conflicts. Now, all of a sudden, this physical pleasure that you've taken for granted is disrupted by the intrusion of sexuality. Remarks psychologist Elizabeth Douvan: "The tickling, the sitting on Daddy's lap becomes overcast with a hint of danger, conflict, the need for controls where none previously needed to be invoked."

Children often sense this, and make the first move toward separation. Writer Shelley Steinmann List recalls: "For years I would go to the movies and sit between my mother and father and hold each of their hands. A ritual. A warm thing. But when I got to be about thirteen I started pulling away from my father, suddenly uncomfortable, uneasy. And he would be hurt and confused that his little girl was rejecting him. I couldn't identify the feelings, and neither could he."

If you're the mother of a son, you're likely to be taken aback by your little boy's sudden emergence into a sexually provocative young man. Since you're the first woman in his life—and, in his eyes, safe— he may practice his sexual wiles on you: speaking breathily into your ear, pitching his voice to a seductive tone. While such flirtations go on, many mothers feel a glow—who can resist the attentions of a suitor, even if he's your own 15-year-old?

Inevitably, your son's courtship of you ends. Then you're likely to feel the natural pains of abandonment, followed by pangs of jealousy and resentment as he turns to girls his own age. This too soon passes. And you can reward yourself with the satisfaction that, in a way you probably did not expect, you helped your son mature into a man comfortable with women. Fathers often have special problems in respect to their daughters' sexual development. An ideally mature father looks forward to his daughter's maturation on all levels. Observes psychiatrist Milton Berger: "He tends to be pleased and shares his joy with her over her normal development and can comment on her attractiveness as a sexual female."

But a father frequently experiences discomfort as his daughter sexually matures. At the same time, he may feel guilty over inhibitions he puts in his daughter's way. His daughter is no longer *his* cute, lovable, adoring, and adorable little girl. Instead, she is moving toward becoming an independent human being whose sexuality is now obvious to the world. Concludes Dr. Berger: "She is now of interest to males other than her father."

A major adjustment may face a father whose daughter has been a great lap-sitter, hugger, and kisser. Her sexual development may now make such physical intimacy too sexually stimulating. "He must now learn to maintain closeness and touch his daughter in ways that may be less gratifying," advises Dr. Berger. "He moves toward a more mature kind of intimacy, which leaves individual physical boundaries and privacy more clearly delineated."

Chapter 4

How to Handle Sex Talks

These tips ease discussions—and promote sexual responsibility.

WHEN YOU TALK with your children about sex, you help them be more responsible in their sexual behavior.

Staff members of Syracuse University's Institute for Family Research and Education have completed a review of studies on the effects of sex education. The major findings of a wide range of investigators:

- Teenagers whose parents discuss sex with them tend to delay their first intercourse longer than youngsters whose parents avoid sex talks.
- When these better-informed teenagers do have intercourse, they are more likely to use contraceptives.
- The more sex information youngsters have, the less likely they are to suffer a pregnancy or venereal disease.

Candid discussions with you can also help your children develop a healthy attitude toward sex. Psychiatrist Stuart M. Finch of the University of Arizona Medical School was asked, "What is the best way to prepare maturing boys and girls for sexual experience?" Dr. Finch described the young person whose preparation has been ideal: "As his natural curiosity about sex and procreation produced questions, they have been answered truthfully and in an age-appropriate way. . . . The 'best' is an emotionally mature set of parents with a comfortable attitude about sex, and a willingness to answer the child's questions appropriately and honestly. Other approaches [such as school sex education courses] only try to make up for a lack of this and are really only second best."

[30]

Conversations with you about sexuality can improve your youngsters' skills at sexual communication. By talking freely with your children about sex, you train them to be open about sexual matters. This can liberate them in their relationships with the opposite sex. By being able to express themselves easily, they are less likely to be embarrassed or misunderstood. Your loving give-and-take with them about sex may encourage them to be similarly sensitive and responsive in their sexual activity.

"Adolescents often make mistakes as they try to communicate with the opposite sex both verbally and in actual sexual behavior," note psychiatrist Gordon D. Jensen of the University of California at Davis and Professor Mina Robbins of the California State University School of Nursing at Sacramento. "They are less likely to get into trouble if they have someone whom they trust, who accepts them as they are, who is knowledgeable about sex, and who will take time to talk with them. Under these conditions, most adolescents are willing to talk freely, and such encounters are refreshing and rewarding."

Many parents find that straightforward discussions of sex open up other areas of communication as well. When you provide sexual information and guidance, you hand down wisdom from one generation to the next. You fulfill the traditional role of a parent in a way your children are likely to cherish.

Your teenagers, moreover, need you to acknowledge their sexuality. Adolescents strive for autonomy, when they will be responsible for their own behavior, including their sexual activity. Through sex talks you give recognition to their sexual development. Implicitly you tell them, "I approve of your coming of age." You encourage their maturing, the supportive act of a loving and successful parent.

A parent's silence about sex, however, is likely to be interpreted by the teenager as rejection. "You do not accept how I am." Lack of parental support can make sexual maturing even more difficult for adolescents. If sexually deserted by their parents, they must often suffer their sexual heartbreak and confusion alone. Psychiatrist George H. Orvin of the Medical University of South Carolina warns against being "too timid" or "too uninvolved" in your children's development. Your silence can send them a "highly significant message" that you don't care.

Adolescents also need parental acknowledgment of their sexuality so they need not conceal it and feel guilty. To relieve their guilt, teenagers often make a show of their sexual activity, seeking to provoke an argument. "Young people benefit more from disagreement as a form of acknowledgement than they do from the pretense that they have no sexual behavior at all," reports psychologist Robert C. Sorensen from his survey of teenage sexuality. "Young people puzzle over this absence of acknowledgement and sometimes become angry when they can secure no parental reaction, even as their sexual conduct becomes more blatant."

There is extensive communication about sex even in families where the subject is never discussed. Most basic sexual information comes to youngsters from their parents. Children learn their deepest lessons by example. Their attitudes toward sex are not so much taught as caught.

Wittingly or not, parents may rebuff a child's attempts at sexual communication. Silence, a frown, a stilted reply—a youngster doesn't have to get a telegram to be told, "You don't talk about sex." The child often receives related messages as well: "Sex is dirty." "Sex is a no-no." "Sex is a mystery, and we're not giving you any clues." The veil of mystery and scent of the forbidden can make extreme sexual behavior all the more attractive to teenagers. If angry enough, some use sexual acting out as a weapon against their parents.

BARRIERS TO COMMUNICATION

Parents often believe their children are "too young" to know about sex. This belief can persist to an advanced age, and is picked up by the youngsters. Fully 42 percent of surveyed 13- to 15-year-olds told psychologist Robert Sorensen, "I don't talk about sex with my parents because their attitude is that I'm too young to know anything."

Dr. Roger W. Libby, while at Syracuse's Institute for Family Research and Education, called this parent attitude "generational chauvinism," leading to a communications gap "complete with hostilities, conflicts, deadly silence, and evasiveness."

Parents may read or hear about teenage sexual activity and be so shocked that they don't try to communicate with their children for fear of what they might discover. For many parents, denial takes the form of an ostrichlike attitude. They give virtually no information or advice about sex, as if not acknowledging their child's sexual development will make it disappear. Two out of three of the nonvirgin teenagers interviewed by Sorensen said, "My parents know about my sexual activities, but act as if they don't know." One girl told Sorensen that a boy lived in her bedroom for several months. "My mother never asked me anything about it."

Many parents are shy about discussing sex because of feelings carried over from their own childhood. "Sex is bad," they may have learned from their parents. Believing their children to be innocent, they seek to shelter them from corruption. "Sex is dangerous" is a similar lesson learned at a parent's knee. What parents, so convinced, wouldn't try to protect their children from sex? Unfortunately, such sheltering teaches children to fear sex as much as their parents do.

Parents often worry, "Talking about sex will put ideas into my child's head. It will be overstimulating and encourage sexual activity." Specialists find that the opposite is true. What your children want to know about sex corresponds closely to what they need to know. Sexual ideas are already in their heads. Their unanswered questions may be causing them anxiety.

Nor, in discussing sex, are you giving your children tacit approval to be permissive. Youngsters can make sharp distinctions between knowing and doing, between factualism and propriety, between what is possible and what is right for them. Indeed, an important part of your sex talks is making those distinctions clear. In sex education, guidance is as important as information.

Don't worry about telling your children too much about sex. From your teenager's point of view, you can hardly tell enough. Sex is exciting, and permeates an adolescent's body and surroundings. Everything you tell teenagers to help them deal with their sexuality is almost certain to hold their interest and be helpful.

If you are reluctant to talk about sex with your children, you are hardly alone. Sex talks come with difficulty to most parents for fundamental reasons: Not only are open sexual relations in a family unacceptable—the taboo against incest is deeply rooted in the unconscious—but the typical family desexualizes its relationships for the sake of day-to-day comfort.

"Family discussions of sexuality in general are more limited than many writers would have the anxious parent believe," observes psychiatrist Christopher H. Hodgman of the University of Rochester School of Medicine and Dentistry. "Even though easier conversational treatment of sexuality between the generations appears to be the rule these days, it is usually brief; families cannot tolerate much more."

In the face of your children's pressing need for sex education, how can you overcome such a barrier? Every family is different, of course. Children move toward sex at different speeds. Parents are concerned over different problems. Adolescence is marked by transition and conflict.

Thus there are no rigid rules or ready-made formulas. But you can apply to sex the time-tested principle accepted in other areas of education: Equip your youngsters with the sexual knowledge and attitudes that will enable them to make intelligent decisions. To help you do so, here is advice drawn from authorities on how to handle sex talks:

The Earlier You Start, the Better

To teenagers the world can turn sexual overnight. One day your child may have random curiosity about sex but little personal concern. The next day everyone in your youngster's class may be atingle over something sexual. Menstruation, masturbation, breasts, erections, dating, kissing, intercourse—these issues can be stressful to the adolescent encountering them close-up for the first time.

If you've prepared your children over several years, they have a good chance of taking such problems in stride. Your early teaching can stand your teens in good stead during the inevitable periods when they are withdrawing from you. Just when you may feel your adolescents most need your sexual counseling, they are likely to be making themselves unavailable to your information or advice.

Indeed, their sexual behavior is one means by which they achieve their separation from you. So make them ready while they're receptive to your guidance. Moreover, it's usually easier to discuss such risks as venereal disease and unplanned parenthood early, before a youngster is deeply involved in a sexual relationship.

There's no timetable governing what sexual facts should be provided at which age. As a rule of thumb, if a child hasn't started asking sexual questions by age 4 or 5, look for occasions to bring the subject up.

Take the Initiative

Well-intentioned parents often boast, "We let our kids know they can talk to us anytime they want." Alas, children often are reluctant to volunteer what concerns them in sexual matters. They often fear how their parents will react to their raising the topic. So they typically wait for conversations their parents never initiate. Adolescents are likely to be shy about approaching you with specific sexual questions, although they find many issues disturbing: masturbation, intercourse, and homosexuality, among dozens of others.

To open up discussions, seize "teachable moments," occasions when your youngster is likely to be receptive to sexual information or guidance. Opportunities abound to give simple, honest explanations.

You can find teachable moments in TV shows you watch with your children. Many dramas and comedies feature sexual situations. There are frequent documentaries on VD, abortion, and the like. So, too, can you initiate talks beginning with movies, articles, books. Indeed, give your adolescent this book to read. One of its purposes is to serve as a starting point for precisely such discussions.

Be alert to teachable moments emanating from your child's own experiences. Pubic hair sprouts. Breasts bud. Menstruation starts. A growth spurt occurs. Underarm odor develops. Each such physical change makes it timely, thus interesting, to expand your youngster's sexual knowledge.

Also be aware of how your children's friends are maturing. "Arlene is developing breasts" is a way to bring up a topic related to a girl's maturing. You can proceed to biological consequences with, "Physically Arlene will soon be able to have babies." You can introduce issues of emotions and responsibility: "What do you think about kids Arlene's age getting pregnant?"

Expect to Say Some Things Again

Teenagers often block out sexual information because they're frightened by it. From earliest memory, the tones in which parents and other adults discussed sexuality may have led the child to believe that sex is sinful, dirty, wrong. Thus children frequently repress sexual knowledge. Their unconscious tells them, "You can't be guilty if you don't learn."

When you need to repeat sexual facts, reassure your child that this is tough stuff to understand. Such complex issues are not resolved easily or lightly, and certainly not all at once.

Around puberty—from about 9 to 13—youngsters are often like newspaper reporters. They typically want to know scads of details: who, what, when, how, and—perhaps most important to them— why. Most youngsters this age do not feel ready for sexual activity. Yet they sense that it is coming, and wish to prepare themselves with as much information as possible. Even when they've been given information about anatomy, physiology, and reproduction, the onset of puberty heightens their interest and awareness.

Information that they only partially understood or incorporated at an earlier age takes on new meaning during adolescence. A penis penetrating the vagina begins to mean something more pertinent to their own lives; it's no longer merely the academic method of "how a baby is made." Some youngsters begin to date and to hear of peers who have had sexual experiences.

Older teenagers need your most sensitive answers. Generally, they've become aware of the hurts and hazards that can accompany sexuality. They want to know about relationships and love. They're concerned with the mechanics surrounding sexual intercourse: when to approach it, what to do. They're interested in birth control.

Help Your Child to Trust You

Let your youngsters know that you'll never use against them anything they reveal to you about their sexuality.

At a meeting of the American Association of Sex Educators, Counselors and Therapists, a panel of ten white middle-class boys and girls, ages 15 to 17, revealed a deep mistrust of their parents. "Kids are afraid to share their feelings with their parents," said Olivia. "You're afraid of what they're thinking about you."

"Parents are too close to you," added Kevin. "You don't want to expose too much." Scott observed, "You don't know what judgments they'll make of you." Declared Melissa: "You don't want them to feel they have a weapon."

The panelists burst forth with this advice to parents: "You have to show your kid that he can trust you." "You shouldn't throw in a person's face something he did or something he doesn't know." "You shouldn't say, 'Oh, oh, Daddy's little girl shouldn't know that.'"

Fifteen-year-old Alan said he had no problems discussing sex with his parents. "I was three or four when they first told me about intercourse. I thought it was so weird I put my hands over my ears and ran out of the room." Later on, he realized his notion about how babies are made couldn't quite work. "I thought that I got swallowed on a piece of toast and that's how I got into my mother's belly." He asked his parents. They told him again about intercourse. Since then, he's had free and easy exchanges with them about sex.

All the other youngsters on the panel wished that they could talk to their parents about sex, but felt that they could not. "The parent has to make the first move," urged Craig. Concluded Andrea: "You have to know that you'll be received, that your parents will accept you."

When you talk sex with your youngsters, use humor if that's your style. But take their sexual concerns very seriously. Never make fun of any misinformation or area of ignorance.

Self-consciousness is epidemic among adolescents. A teenager may be obsessed with how to approach a certain member of the opposite sex: what to wear, how to act, what to say. Your youngster may have heard some bizarre "fact" about sex from a friend—and be terrified that it might be true.

In many cases, such worries may strike you as trivial; they aren't. Adolescents regard them with the utmost gravity, and might be terribly embarrassed over their need to ask. It takes great courage for youngsters to bring the issue up with their parents. If their concerns are met by laughter, they find it hard to forgive.

In your efforts to build trust, resist trying to be your children's pal. Almost certainly they want you as a parent, not a friend. They need your authority and expertise. Besides, in the same way that your children have a right to be young, you have a right to be a mature adult. You won't be comfortable for long pretending you're a teenager, and your youngsters will sense your strain.

Don't use kids' slang either. It sounds phony to youngsters when an adult talks in their code. Anyway, you're likely to get it wrong—it changes fast.

Keep It Casual

Avoid lectures. A long speech suggests to youngsters that they're being spoken at, not to. They turn you off accordingly. Instead, welcome informal, spontaneous exchanges.

Your child often needs time to assimilate new information and clarify fresh attitudes. In general, be brief, and leave the door open for a further conversation very soon. Families frequently talk for several days about a trip, a purchase, an event. The subject of intercourse or molestation or gonorrhea can similarly come up as often as necessary.

Expect questions to come up at odd moments. Conversations are often easiest when both you and your youngster are driving somewhere, doing a job together, or engaged in some other activity that makes the sex talk incidental.

Let anyone participate. Sex is a heterosexual topic. Valuable contributions can be made by either a mother or a father, a sister or a brother. Also have an age mix, recommends psychiatrist Christopher Hodgman. Younger children can be introduced early to matters that their older brothers and sisters had to wait years to hear.

At the same time, provide opportunities for a parent to talk alone with a child. Ideally, a father or a mother can talk with any of their children with equal ease. It rarely works out that way. Make time for private conversations with a youngster whom you're more comfortable with, or who's more at ease with you.

Answer the Question That's Asked

Take a question at face value. Reply factually. Only then ask, "What's aroused your interest?"

Resist jumping to conclusions. If your daughter wants to know, "Are birth control pills dangerous?", don't assume she's asking because she wants to take them. Teenagers have a strong urge to file away all sorts of sexual information, which they may or may not ever use.

Your assumptions can scare off your youngster. Social worker Mary G. Garfield and pediatrician Joan E. Morgenthau tell of Paula, who encouraged her daughter Erika, "Talk to me anytime you want." Erika's friend Mindy had missed her period, so one day Erika—herself a virgin—asked "How can a person tell if she's pregnant?" Paula's unfortunate reply, "Are you pregnant?" made Erika so upset that she stopped coming to Paula for advice.

If a question's not clear, ask, "In what way?" or "How do you mean?" Often a youngster wants only an answer to his question and perhaps a little bit more. But his parent, having lain in wait, pounces with a tedious explanation of the facts of life.

Don't hesitate to check your youngsters' understanding, or you and they may be misled. Psychiatrist Gordon Jensen and nursing professor Mina Robbins remember a 17-year-old boy who was asked, "Do you and your girl friend use contraception?" "Oh, yes, every time," he replied. Not until later did he mention his supposed method: "I or my chick squeeze the base of my penis so that I don't have any sperm."

If you sense that behind your child's question there's a deeper question, probe with caution. Fear of embarrassment or disapproval may account for why the real question wasn't asked. You might draw it out if you indicate that you respect your youngster's interest. Try a response like "I'm glad you brought that up" or "That's important to explore."

You may suspect what's troubling your youngster. One way to open up a subject in a nonthreatening manner is to show that you recognize—and approve of—any facts your child has already acquired. You can make your discussion less threatening by introducing it with a statement that suggests that your youngster's concerns are universal or normal. "Many people are told . . ." "Most kids think that . . ." "A lot of young people worry that . . ." Avoid using the word "abnormal." It's translated to "wrong" or "bad" by teenagers who desperately want to be "normal."

Some parents overidentify with their teenager's sexuality. They regress back to their own adolescence and covertly encourage sexual behavior such as they had, or missed out on. The youngster may not be ready for such activities. Psychiatrist Sol Nichtern of New York Medical College recalls a 13-year-old girl who asked her mother a casual question about sex. In response the mother bought her a contraceptive.

Yield If You Meet Resistance

Your efforts to discuss sexual matters can be frustrated by your children. You might be told, "I already know everything I need to know." Your youngster may assume a glazed look, or change the subject, or flee from your presence.

Rather than pursue the topic (or child), merely say, "Let's talk about it another time." If you force the topic, your youngsters will sense your tension. They are likely to feel pressured, and may become ever more resistant to including you in their sex education.

You may merely need to wait for a more propitious moment. Your youngster might have had a hard day at school, or have been bugged by friends, or be on the downside of an adolescent mood swing. You may have had problems with each other. After a day of bickering about many things—neatness, clothes, manners, God knows what— you can hardly expect to sit down and have a heart-to-heart talk about sex.

You may also need to follow your teenager's agenda rather than your own. A girl may be worried about menstruation, a boy about wet dreams. Until that pressing problem is resolved, the youngster will probably not be able to handle another sexual subject, however vital you feel it is.

To reduce the likelihood that you'll meet resistance, scrupulously respect your child's privacy. Parents often fear that a teenager who doesn't want to talk about sex is abnormally inhibited. In fact, it's generally normal for adolescents to cling to their budding independence.

Teenagers typically have a strong urge to protect their privacy, part of the growing sense of self that is essential to their emotional maturing. Fully 6 out of 10 teenagers interviewed by psychologist Robert Sorensen said, "I don't talk to my parents about my sex life because I consider it a personal subject and nobody's business but my own." Even teenagers who reported talking with their parents about sex rarely discussed their own experiences.

Your youngsters are likely to react defensively if they feel you're being intrusive. Teenagers tend to be extremely touchy about their private lives. They often resent parental comments, however inoffensive or well-intentioned. A remark like "Oh, good, he wants to take you out" can reduce a girl to tears. "I think she really likes you" can send a boy up a wall.

Some parents are overly curious about their children's sex lives. They press their youngsters for details of what the children know about sex, what they do on dates, how often they masturbate. Angry over such invasions of their private lives, teenagers commonly build around themselves walls of noncommunication—evasiveness, silence, lies—to keep their parents out.

Indeed, prying parents can impede a youngster's maturing and incur a rebellion. Dr. R. C. Marohn of the Illinois State Psychiatric Institute warns that an "intrusive parent who reads diaries or insists that teenage children share all their secrets" seriously interferes with the separation-individuation process by which teenagers grow toward independence. "Adolescents may then 'rebel' in an attempt to preserve their own autonomy and . . . to achieve separation." This often is not so much a rebellion against authority, but rather a "new self attempting to declare his or her independence."

Parents whose children shut them out of sex talks often feel guilty over having "repressed" their youngsters at an earlier age. "I smacked Joey's hand when he took out his penis," they may recall. "I punished Karen when I found her playing doctor."

True, such incidents, especially if repeated, can make a child cautious about demonstrating sexual curiosity. Nonetheless, a worried parent can easily overestimate the importance of a few incidents. Furthermore, your child may be reluctant to have sex talks with you because of attitudes picked up outside the home. A sharp reaction from a neighbor or teacher can convince a youngster that it's "not nice" to show an interest in sex to any adult, especially a parent. This barrier is reinforced if your child's playmates are furtive about sex, treating it as a subject only to be giggled about among other kids.

A child's attitudes toward sex are shaped over many years, by countless cues from a multitude of sources. Psychotherapist Thomas Edwards Brown reassures you: "Children are more powerfully influenced by the human warmth, affection and sensitivity they have felt from their mother and father than by the anxiety, hostility or insensitivity which occasionally emerge from even the best of parents."

Use the Proper Terms

Father Eugene M. Kennedy, a professor of psychology at Loyola University, calls sex a "language which people must learn together in order to communicate with one another." By giving the correct names for parts and functions of the body, you aid your children in gaining sexual information. You also help them to share their feelings about sexuality.

The following words convey generally clear meanings: penis, vagina, hymen, clitoris, vulva, menstruation, nocturnal emission or wet dream, sexual intercourse, petting to climax, climax or orgasm. Similarly acceptable words are breasts, nipples, testicles, semen, erection, ejaculation, masturbation, oral sex, anal sex, condom or rubber, panties.

Few parents or children use these words often, notes Dr. Gerhard Neubeck of the University of Minnesota Family Study Center. To free yourself from any disturbing qualities the terms have for you, recommends Dr. Neubeck, say the words out loud and listen to yourself. "Repeating dozens of times penis, vagina, nipples, panties, rubber will begin to desensitize you."

Employ these words freely in talks with your children. Youngsters who are comfortable with proper terminology have a medium for gaining additional knowledge. They can participate in ever more sophisticated conversations. They can understand the scientific language of books. They can discuss sex openly and with dignity. They can express their emotions and assert their wishes in sexual relationships. They can thereby enhance tenderness, pleasure, and responsibility.

By contrast, in many homes children learn early that sex talk is dirty talk. They are thus discouraged from learning and using words in the sexual realm. This denies them verbal tools for understanding sexual acts and their consequences. In sexual relationships, their inability to communicate can lead to exploitation, to chance-taking, to feeling unfulfilled and used.

The typical teenage couple has sex sessions in embarrassed silence. Some of them feel loving. Some plan the next move. But the plans are rarely mutual plans, for the youngsters cannot talk about sex.

"Keith and Kathy can talk about other kids, their parents, movies, dances, classes, dates, clothes," observes Dr. Gerhard Neubeck. "However, with each other they cannot talk about their sexual adventures." Their decisions are made not by deliberation but by locomotion. "At last Kathy feels she has gone too far. . . . Keith would ask her what he should order for her at the drive-in, but he did not ask her if she wanted to have intercourse."

In discussing sex with your children, refrain from using supposed euphemisms. It's just as easy to teach "penis" as it is "flower," "ding-a-ling," or "noodle." A vagina can be a "vagina" right off, instead of a "thing," "private," or "down below." Babyish terms are nonwords, a form of verbal static that blocks a child's sexual communication.

They deprive youngsters of a vocabulary to increase their understanding. Not knowing the proper words, they can be impaired in sexual relationships.

What's more, euphemisms carry an implied message: that sex is too special and secret to be spoken of in ordinary language. The subject is thus made mysterious and obscure, often destructively. The English novelist E.M. Forster recalled that his penis was called his "dirty." The word, and the attitude it reflected, helped make him a sexual cripple.

Nor should you take the opposite tack. Instead of being excessively delicate, some parents introduce their children to sex using what most middle-class people regard as obscenities. A family's routine use of street language puts a burden on children. Often they don't know when not to use it. Outside the home—in school or in friends' homes—a vulgarity is likely to arouse an angry reaction. This can make the child feel shame about not only the word but the part of the body or sexual act it refers to.

A child brought up with only obscenities can be trapped in an obscene attitude. Four-letter words degrade sexuality. They are aggressive words, forcing their way into people's consciousness. They can give a child the feeling that sex is intrusive and hostile.

Give an Accurate Picture

Be prepared to dispel myths. Adolescence is rife with sexual folklore, much of it hazardous. Innumerable girls have become pregnant because they got the reproductive cycle backward—they believed they could get pregnant only while menstruating. Teenagers are often mystified when they get VD, explaining, "But right afterward I took a shower."

A teenager may confidently tell you that females ejaculate, and males menstruate. Boys are commonly under the impression that they can produce only a limited amount of semen over a lifetime. A boy may worry himself sick when he "uses it up" by masturbating "too much." A lot of girls similarly torture themselves about kissing. They think it can get them pregnant.

When you scotch a myth, make a point of not pooh-poohing your child's problem. "Instant reassurance should be avoided," counsels psychiatrist Charles W. Davenport of the University of Michigan

Medical School. It can make your youngsters feel their concerns are unimportant.

For your sex talks to be most useful, be frank. Make no bones about the reality behind a word. For example, abortion is often described only as "termination of a pregnancy." Let your teenagers know that it involves the destruction of the fetus. You'll be giving them a reasonable basis for making a decision. Chances are they'll appreciate your leveling with them.

Parents who repeat myths, or who "protect" their children from hard sexual truths, confuse their youngsters and risk discrediting themselves. You also skate on thin ice if you distort facts to influence your teenagers' behavior. You're likely to lose your audience if you pass on falsehoods like "A girl can't use the Pill until she's over eighteen" or "A boy can get arrested if he makes a girl pregnant." Your subsequent statements, however accurate, may be doubted, even ridiculed. As it is, you may start out with a credibility gap. Over 2 out of 3 teenagers interviewed by psychologist Robert Sorensen feel they understand more about sex than do most older people.

Some parents mistakenly avoid sexual discussions because their child may ask questions they can't answer. A large part of the problem, believes sociologist John Petras of Central Michigan University, is that parents often expect too much of themselves. They feel they must be *thoroughly* knowledgeable about sex before they have a discussion with a child. Declares Dr. Petras: "This seems to be the only area in which parents place such a burden on themselves."

Few adults have been provided with any formal instruction about sex. Indeed, it's a rare parent who has a clear overview of sexuality. Moreover, parents are often intimidated by the so-called sexual revolution, fearing their own experiences and views are out of date. A survey by Dr. Lester A. Kirkendall of The American Humanist Association finds that less than one father in ten feels qualified to give his children a comprehensive understanding of sex and human relations. Their lack of information makes many parents conclude they have no useful guidance to offer their teenagers. Others become defensive. They argue that the standards of their day were superior, often because those are the standards they understand and feel comfortable with. Their arguing obstructs communication with youths who know only the standards of their own day.

In sex talks, you don't have to be an expert. If you don't have an answer, say so. No one has all the answers, particularly about sex. Increasing your sexual knowledge is a good idea, if only to expand your own sexuality. Read and think and talk more about sex. This book is intended to help you brush up on your sexual facts.

Face Up to Your Inhibitions

Your personal discomfort is a great deterrent to your talking about sex with your children. Any embarrassment you feel is hard to hide. Unknowingly, you may change your facial expression or body carriage. Your voice may become tight or high-pitched. You may rapidly repeat phrases, and press your youngster to learn the "correct" facts about sex. Such involuntary signals can prompt your child to steer clear of the subject.

Parents who come from restrictive backgrounds are sometimes more liberated intellectually than they are emotionally. You might say the right thing, but if you don't feel it, it's likely to ring false to your children. They may get a mixed message, which provokes anxiety. "Do you mean yes or no?" they may wonder. "Is this good or bad? What's your real feeling?"

Listen to yourself as you talk about sex. Become aware of the attitudes you bring to sexual discussions. Do you detect shame? fear? anger? aggressiveness? Your feelings may have been long buried, emerging only when you confront a sexual issue with your child. Parents often get a double shock when they see their youngster behaving sexually. One shock is over the behavior. The other is over their reaction to it.

Watch for responses that reveal your shyness over sex. You may dodge sexual questions with replies like "I'm busy now" or "Other people are around." You may ask your youngster to wait for an answer, then forget to give it.

How to overcome difficulties you may have discussing sex? Practice. Engage in conversations about sexuality with your spouse, family members, friends. Become comfortable speaking about the sexual organs as parts of the body like any other. Get used to talking of sexual behavior as the normal activity it is.

When you talk with other parents, verbalize your feelings and expose yourself to probing. Then sift things through. "It's amazing what can happen when adults talk together," remarks psychiatrist Martin Symonds of The American Institute for Psychoanalysis. "It's a tremendous comfort to learn that your situation and your reactions are not unique, that other parents battle with their kids, come to an impasse, are often filled with despair." Talking out your thoughts about sex can help you unearth the feelings that gave rise to your inhibitions.

Another way to ease your self-consciousness: Become active in a community organization that deals with sexual issues. Join a local chapter of the Planned Parenthood Federation. Help out at a hospital VD clinic. Work at an abortion counseling center, either pro or anti. Take a shift at a hot line, many of whose calls may be appeals for sexual help. You're likely to find that sexuality soon becomes ho-hum.

Some parents, no matter how they try, cannot overcome their inhibitions. Fine. Tell your children, "I'm not comfortable talking about that"—and urge them to get instruction and advice from other reliable sources.

Make information available to your youngsters. Display reading material on your family bookshelf, and invite your children to pick it up any time they feel inclined. Some well-run, realistic sex education courses are conducted by schools, churches, and community agencies. Help your youngsters sign up for them.

Even more important, encourage your child to find another sensitive adult who can act as a confidant, instructor, and adviser. When parents feel uneasy discussing sex, youngsters often reach out elsewhere: to a friend's parent, a teacher, a church leader, a co-worker, a neighbor, a physician. Your child and the older friend may worry that you're jealous, so reassure them both that you're glad your youngster has someone to talk to whom you can trust. Such grown-up friends can help your youngsters develop better relationships with adults, including yourself.

"Adolescents need contact with satisfied and effective adults, both inside and outside the family," comments psychologist Elizabeth Douvan of the University of Michigan. "And sometimes the parent-child relationship needs an intervening third person who can mediate and interpret the parties to each other."

Be Discreet About Your Sex Life

When children are told about sex, they sometimes ask about their parents' activity. A specific discussion of what you do in bed is likely to prove discomforting for both you and your youngsters. So, for a satisfactory response to such questions, consider giving answers that are positive in tone but only general in detail.

If your child asks if you have intercourse, you might reply, "Yes. People who love each other usually do." If asked for specifics—"How often?" "What do you do?"—you can say, "That varies with how we feel." If you're caught short for an answer, consider replying, "That's an interesting question. I want to think about it." If you don't wish to answer, you can often say, "Most people feel that's personal."

Few parents feel comfortable in relating their sexual biographies to their children. The taboo against incest is so strong that, in the depths of the subconscious, an alarm is likely to go off. The parent may feel sexually seductive, with consequent embarrassment and guilt.

At the same time, don't untruthfully deny your sexual activity. Some parents needlessly worry: "What effect will it have on the children to know we have sex? Won't it shock them? Won't they lose respect for us?"

Such parents are often ashamed of their sexuality. They may have picked this shame up from their own parents. Chances are they felt compelled to hide their sexual activities from their mothers and fathers. Now they groundlessly feel a need to seem asexual to their children.

A full disclosure of your sexuality is not likely to be welcomed by your children. Youngsters often find it difficult to think of their parents as sexual beings. One 16-year-old girl was shocked when her mother announced she was pregnant. The girl confessed, "Somehow, I just didn't think of Mother as doing that!"

Teenagers generally prefer to believe that their parents have no personal interest in sex. Research by sociologist Ollie Pocs of Illinois State University shows that all categories of youth significantly underestimate their parents' sexual activity. Some youngsters were so upset by the thought of parental sex that they couldn't complete Professor Pocs's questionnaire.

"In youth's perception, even parents in their forties have little if any sex life," reports Pocs. About 40 percent of youngsters believe that their parents "never" have intercourse or have it only a "few times a year." Over half estimate that their parents have intercourse once a month or less.

The incest taboo may provoke such anxiety that some teenagers can't tolerate images of their parents engaging in sex. Youngsters also widely believe that older people are sexless, adds Pocs. In part, this results from stereotypes put forth by the media which are reinforced by parents' reluctance to talk about sex or show open affection. An adolescent may further reckon as follows: "Only youth have fun. Sex is fun. So sex is for youth. For married people, sex is for having children only."

There are further hazards to sharing your sexual history with your children. You may be unwittingly setting up a model that your children feel they must emulate. This can put pressure on them, and work against their own sexual needs and wishes. The converse is no less sticky, notes psychiatrist Paul L. Adams of the University of Miami School of Medicine. Parents may have more limited sexual experience than their children. "The son is a little embarrassed to discern that his father is by no means a virtuoso. . . . Fathers can rarely purvey either a real or idealized sex life that can cut the mustard for their sons."

Indiscretion can be especially hazardous if a parent is having sex outside the marriage. Psychologist Robert Sorensen finds that many adolescents suspect their parents are committing adultery. The youngsters resent the parent's hypocrisy, and mistrust the parent's behavior toward them as well. They become unable to differentiate between the parent's good advice and bad advice. One 17-year-old boy told Sorensen: "What could my dad say to me, considering what he had been doing? Oh, I think he's right, but who is he to say it?"

Explain Your Moral Position

One sexual dilemma your teenager is likely to face is: "What do I do with what I know? What things that were wrong for children are now all right for me?" Having learned salient facts of biology, your teenagers may be sexually knowledgeable. But they also need to be sexually responsible, and so must your guidance.

Unless your children know your moral position, they might be adrift in a sea of conflicting values, with results that neither you nor they may like. "Adolescents grow very rapidly and erratically, and need a solid point of view to push against," comments psychiatrist Martin Symonds of the American Institute for Psychoanalysis. "In all the children in trouble that I've seen, one thing stands out: Their parents are not providing the anchorage, the support, the guidance they need."

Early on, as you give your children sexual information, put it in a moral framework. In matters other than sex—social behavior, schoolwork, clothing, food—you tell your youngsters what is appropriate. In a similar way, you can explain the circumstances in which you consider sexual relations appropriate. You can emphasize the value of their being selective, of choosing carefully the time and the partner. You can make clear your standards on such issues as virginity, contraception, pornography. Thus, along with a healthy acceptance of sexuality, you can instill in your children sexual values.

In the intensely personal area of sexuality, no one is better qualified to guide your children than you are. In essence, the message you want to get across to them is this: "Here is what I feel are the proper standards of behavior about sex. I love you, and I want you to benefit from my experience and observations. I hope they'll help you make the best decisions on your own. Don't accept my beliefs just because I'm your parent. But please consider them carefully and discuss them with me further."

Your declaring your values is likely to directly influence your child's behavior. In guiding your adolescent, you have a secret weapon: Parental approval and disapproval carry a lot of weight with teenagers, even if they don't always act that way. Often they're fearful over what they've gleaned from friends and the media. They may therefore try out on you all sorts of ideas they pick up.

Teenagers, when uncertain what to do or think, commonly watch the reactions of grown-ups they love. How you respond helps put your youngsters' latest bit of information in perspective. They may seem to reject most of what you say. But they remember it. Typically, they test their friends' beliefs against your opinions. If you exert no coercion, if they have no reason to rebel, they may well adopt your position.

To be most convincing, state explicitly what you feel. If your stance is unclear, you're likely to leave your youngsters confused. They may believe you have no opinions on the matter. Or they may labor under the misapprehension that no clear-cut position is possible.

Use "I" language to express your beliefs: "I believe . . ." "It's my opinion that . . ." "My feeling is . . ." "I worry when . . ." "It upsets me that . . ." These state your position in the proper context, emanating from inside you. By contrast, avoid "you" language: "You seem . . ." "You think that . . ." "You have no . . ." "You're always . . ." Such phrasing rarely describes how they see themselves, and so is likely to make them defensive.

"I think that dress you're wearing is too short" is a simple statement of your opinion. But "You look like a floozy in that dress" is an attack on your daughter. "I" language tends to invite discussion. "You" language usually provokes arguments. Speak your mind as another human being, not as a judge.

Explain your reasons. If you're against abortion, for example, say so—and tell why. If you believe in abortion, help your child to understand your concept of the role it plays in a mature approach to sexuality.

Resist talking down or moralizing. Elizabeth Canfield, a family planning counselor and sex educator at the University of Southern California Student Health Service, has come up with a list of "Frequently Heard Phrases Guaranteed to Turn Off Adolescents." Among them: "When you get older you'll understand." "Because I say so." "Oh, it's just puppy love." "We're very progressive, but . . ." Some teens find "I trust you" to be especially pernicious. Complains one teenager: "Parents don't trust you to live the way you want to. If they say, 'I trust you,' they mean, 'I trust you to take *my* values and live the way *I* want you to live.'"

Offer compromises and alternatives. Refrain from giving directives like "don't," "you should," "you must." Normal adolescents, seeking separation from parents, often deliberately behave contrary to their parents' wishes.

"If you are too constricting, you run the risk of the adolescent becoming even more rebellious in his fight for self-expression," warns psychiatrist Martin Symonds. "Avoid ultimatums like, 'If you see that boy again, don't come home.'" Orders and threats may serve only to drive your teen further in the wrong direction. To translate your values into behavior, advises Dr. Symonds, tell your children what you would like from them. "Say, 'I'd like you to do so and so,' or, 'I wish you would . . .'" By giving your teenager some choice, you have a much better chance of getting cooperation. You are providing guidance, but aren't forcing the youngster to defy you in order to feel free.

Be sure you and your spouse are in agreement over rules. When you don't feel the same way, iron out differences between yourselves so you can set forth a joint policy. Adolescents need consistency and harmony. "I don't think it matters which decision is made, so long as there is one," comments Dr. Symonds. "What does matter is that there is no undermining, no playing off one parent against the other, no father saying, 'If it were up to me, I'd say okay, but your mother doesn't want you to do it.'"

Explore Your Youngster's Values

Expect to modify your views after looking at sex from your teenager's perspective. A good, probing discussion is your best response to children's age-old accusation, "You're old-fashioned. Those standards are all changed now."

Talk to your youngsters about how they feel about their bodies. What does sex mean to them? When do they feel it's right to have intercourse? How have they arrived at their feelings?

Seek to understand where your teenagers are, what influences they're exposed to, how different they are from when you were young. Ask how you can help them to respect themselves and get the most out of all aspects of their life, including their sexual experiences. Get their suggestions about what you can do to keep the channels of communication open between you and them, and to earn their love and respect.

You may find that you and your youngsters agree far more than you disagree, and that you can comfortably adopt at least some of their beliefs. Accept that changes in attitudes and behavior are inevitable since you were in your teens. They may not be your preferences. But seeing them clearly can help you deal with your anxieties, and those of your children.

Parents are generally more conservative than adolescents in sexual attitudes. For example, parental preference remains strongly on the side of chastity for their daughters. If you continue to believe your children should be virgins until marriage, let them know that those are your feelings. They deserve to know where you stand, and may welcome the support your opinion provides.

Facing up to the generation gap is also only realistic. In truth, you're not likely to throw your children out of the house if they don't act in accord with your wishes. There's a vast difference between what most parents prefer in their children and what they can accept. Most parents come to believe the truism that you can't force your morals on someone else, not even your own children.

You do, however, have a right to have your opinions respected by your youngsters. "Parents need not be ashamed of their own values or apologetic about the stance they have decided to take and with which they feel comfortable," note social worker Mary Garfield and psychiatrist Joan Morgenthau. "It is better to be honest about one's views than to espouse liberal attitudes which one does not really feel."

To prevent unnecessary conflicts, resist rising to your children's bait. Teenagers often seek to shock their parents. Some flaunt real adventures of themselves or their friends. Others embellish limited experience. Many permit their parents to suspect far more sexual activity than is true—including many virgins, who presumably could reassure their parents simply by telling the truth.

Regard such contrariness as an attempt at independence. Forbear. "Don't make an issue of everything that your adolescent says or does," counsels psychiatrist Martin Symonds. "Don't react to everything. Don't listen too intensely, ready to challenge."

But do listen. A 16-year-old high school honor student put it this way: "Even though parents say they will listen and nod their heads in agreement as you talk with them, they are not really listening. They don't agree with you or they don't care about what you say. They are against you and not with you."

Parents often become anxious when confronted with their teenagers' alien values. In their anxiety, parents may be eager to do all the talking, to explain, to give advice. Thus when your teenager is talking, refrain from interrupting or changing the subject. Resist breaking in with a parental putdown like "Stop fidgeting!" or "Sit up straight!" Your goal is to keep your youngsters speaking their minds about sex, so hear them out.

In the eyes of teenagers, merely your willingness to sound out your youngsters sets you apart from most other mothers and fathers. "Parents offer advice based on the recollections of their own adolescent sexuality, but they are largely ignorant of what sexuality is like for adolescents today," summarizes psychologist Robert Sorensen. "Such parents, however, often believe they have good rapport with their children."

Only a third of the teenagers surveyed by Sorensen believed they shared the same sexual values as their parents. Most teenagers weren't sure about this, partly because sex was discussed so little that they really did not have a clear definition of their parents' attitudes.

One parental attitude that often does show through is disapproval. Many adolescents told Sorensen they have a sour time at home because their parents view them as sexual beings with no morals, only physical desires and inability to love. To avoid arguments, youngsters may seek an unspoken conversation truce. Over half told Sorensen, "When talking with my parents about sex, I try to tell them only what I think they can accept."

Put Sex in Perspective

Help your youngsters see that sex is just one part of their lives and that it's bound up with feelings in general. Adolescents, by dint of their experience, lack perspective. They often believe (and worry) that the way they are now, they'll be always. They don't know what life actually offers, and so tend to be unrealistic in their expectations.

By contrast, as an adult, you've been through the fire. Your experience with sex has almost certainly made you more realistic about it than you were as a teen. Here are some insights you might pass on to your children:

- Keep relationships paramount. Let your sexual behavior match your emotional commitment. The right degree of sexual activity will leave you and your partner aglow with good feelings. Too much or the wrong kind of sex is likely to be cold, manipulative, and boring.
- Emphasize affection. Sex is far more than the mechanical act of a penis going into a vagina. It's trusting. It's caring. It's giving. It's opening your feelings to another person, and being received in return. Sometimes the best physical way to express your present stage of spiritual joining is by just holding hands.
- Be patient. You can be so busy with other involvements— including growing up—that you have no time or energy for a sexual relationship. Think of yourself as getting ready for the right time and person. There's no "normal" age for when you should have your first date, kiss, intercourse.

- You don't have to be pretty or handsome. Or clever, or a good dancer, or well-built. Or anything else but yourself. In real life, nice ordinary people can enjoy sex—and find other nice ordinary people to enjoy it with.
- Sex isn't always such hot stuff. Sometimes it's great. Most times it's enjoyable. Many times it's disappointing. The trick is not to expect too much from it.
- Have no ulterior motives. All your doubts will remain if you try to use sex to prove you're desirable, or get attention, or hold on to someone. Sex is best when it matters least.
- Don't feel guilty over sexual thoughts, however "perverted" you may fear they are. They're harmless. So are masturbation, and sex play with members of your own sex—both extremely common in adolescence. Punish yourself with guilt only if you hurt someone else, and then don't do it again.
- Plan ahead for intercourse. You can control your sexual activity. "Getting carried away" not only is baloney but can cause the personal disaster of pregnancy. If you're not ready to use contraception, you're not ready for intercourse.
- You're as bad as a germ if you spread disease. At the first suspicion of VD, get to a doctor or clinic. You owe that consideration to yourself, your family, and anyone who has sex with you.

Part II

RELATING TO INTERCOURSE

A SURVEY of the sex revolution shows that, although most parents disapprove, possibly half of all teenagers have intercourse on occasion. Girls and younger adolescents lead the increase. To prevent your children from having intercourse before they're ready, help them resist pressures. For their lifelong enjoyment of intercourse, impart these hints for sexual pleasure, and these remedies for major dysfunctions. You may encounter cohabitation or promiscuity. If your youngsters live with someone, if they're sexually indiscriminate—here's what you need to know.

• •

Chapter 5

Surveying the Sex Revolution

Although most parents disapprove, possibly half of all teenagers have intercourse on occasion. Girls and younger teenagers lead the increase.

"I DON'T EXPECT to be a virgin when I marry," says 18-year-old Heather, a high school senior. "But I don't want to sleep with a guy unless I love him and I feel he loves me. I guess my religion has something to do with this decision, and my parents too. I feel sex is too important to treat casually."

Says 19-year-old Julia, a college sophomore: "Rod and I started sleeping together recently, after we'd been going out for several months. We love each other and plan to marry when he graduates next year. He's the only boy I've slept with, and I'm glad I do. Sex is a very nice part of our relationship."

"I slept with my boyfriend when I was fifteen," says Betsy, now 17. "We'd been dating for about a year, and it seemed like the natural thing to do. Now I make it with a boy if I like him. Sex is a lot of fun. It makes us both feel good. And it's no big hassle when we break up."

Says 18-year-old Kevin: "I know it's old-fashioned, but I still believe that sex and love and marriage should all go together. I'm hoping to find a girl who feels the same way."

These youngsters represent the great range of sexual activity and attitudes among today's teenagers. Just where your youngsters fall on this continuum is likely to be causing you considerable concern. If you're like most parents, you frown upon your teenagers' engaging in intercourse before marriage.

Adults largely disapprove of premarital sex, finds the National

Opinion Research Center's General Social Survey. According to the NORC poll, fully 39 percent of parents of teenagers feel that premarital sex is "always wrong." An additional 14 percent believe that it is "almost always wrong."

On the other hand, you may hold an equally firm minority view. In the NORC sampling, 28 percent of parents feel that premarital sex is "not wrong at all." The remaining 19 percent believe it is only "sometimes wrong."

If you're a mother, you're likely to be considerably more opposed to premarital sex than your husband. Almost half of the surveyed mothers of teenagers—48 percent—feel that premarital sex is "always wrong." Only 29 percent of the fathers so condemn it. At the opposite end of the scale, a mere 19 percent of the mothers feel that premarital sex is "not wrong at all." A substantial 38 percent of the fathers hold this relatively permissive view.

All your worries may be compounded if you've been frightened by tales of the teenage sex revolution.

WHAT REVOLUTION?

In 1938, Lewis M. Terman—a forerunner of Kinsey in sex research—predicted that by 1960 the female virgin at marriage would be virtually extinct.

The failure of Terman's prediction should make everyone wary of overestimating the pace of sexual change. Even so, many parents your age are under the impression that there's been a turnabout in adolescent sexual activity since their own teenage years. Whereas in your day teenagers were supposedly chaste, today's adolescents are widely thought to copulate like rabbits.

In the minds of many adults, this constitutes a "sex revolution." Of course, it would be revolutionary if sexual behavior so greatly altered in but a single generation. But what's actually occurred is a moderate increase in intercourse among some teenagers, added to activity that was previously unrecognized.

The teenagers of your generation were hardly all virgins, but the prevalence of their intercourse was not generally realized. Seemingly all at once, the public has been made aware of the whole amount, which in fact consists of not only the recent rise among some groups, but also the levels that were always there. What seems like a revolution in behavior is actually a revolution in awareness.

Previous generations paid lip service to chastity before marriage. But Kinsey and his associates found that this idea was honored in the breach as much as in the observance. Of the almost six thousand married women interviewed by Kinsey's staff, half had engaged in intercourse before marriage. Ninety percent of the men had done the same. Other surveys conducted several decades ago reported similar findings. Thus, premarital intercourse among young people has been extremely common for at least as long as sex surveyors have been asking about it.

Sociologist Phillips Cutright of Indiana University believes that most parents are victims of the "myth of an abstinent past and a promiscuous present." Dr. Cutright dismisses the notion that "a generation of roundheeled teenagers is currently involved in a sexual revolution," even though the myth of widespread teenage promiscuity has "engaged the . . . prurient envy or blind rage . . . of many adults."

Cutright reasons that the startling, and much-publicized, rise in out-of-wedlock births to teenagers has colored the picture most people have of adolescent sexuality. "The fact that the teenage illegitimacy rate continues to increase," he notes, "is considered prima facie proof of increased sexual activity of revolutionary proportions." In essence, the typical parent reads the newspapers and concludes: "If so many more teenage girls are getting pregnant, there must be at least that much more intercourse, right?"

"Wrong," contends Cutright. There's been much less increase in adolescent intercourse than the rise in teenage motherhood suggests. "The extent to which young unmarried people are sexually active today may not have increased very much, after all."

Many of today's teenage pregnancies, he shows by statistical analysis, are due to the fact that girls are able to conceive younger. Menstruation now begins at an average age of about 12½, as opposed to 13½ in 1940. Girls generally reach their mature level of fertility two and a half to three years after they start menstruating. Thus the average girl now faces maximum risk of pregnancy as early as 15 instead of as late as 16½.

Cutright calculates that merely a one-year head start in menstruating has resulted in over 30 percent more 15-year-old girls being able to have babies. They would therefore have a large increase in their pregnancy rate even if they had intercourse no more frequently than in 1940.

Furthermore, notes Cutright, today's teenagers are generally in better health than the adolescents of previous generations. This has reduced the number of miscarriages, and has accordingly increased the number of out-of-wedlock births. Increasing it still further is the population explosion, which has produced a disproportionately large number of adolescents, and has thus made the occurrence of teenage pregnancy ever more visible.

The rise in adolescent pregnancy has forced society to confront the existence of teenage sexuality for the first time. In former generations, fewer young girls having intercourse were fertile, thus their pregnancy rate was low. Observes Cutright: "A society in which few girls can become pregnant before age 17 does not need to be deeply concerned over the 'problem' of teenage illegitimacy, no matter how prevalent teenage sexual activity may be. Indeed, such a society can afford to close its eyes to the existence of such activity. . . . If there are few consequences (illegitimate births), the behavior may be safely ignored, and even denied."

Denial of adolescent sexuality was long the norm in popular culture. One example will suffice: The movies mirror national attitudes. Consider, then, the difference in the public concept of teenage sex as mirrored in the *Andy Hardy* movies of the Thirties and Forties and, say, the Seventies' *Saturday Night Fever*. It is the difference between a chaste kiss climaxing the film and a throwaway "blow job" in the back seat of a car.

Neither image is true to life for most teenagers, though their parents—who formerly could take comfort in the *Andy Hardy* myth— cannot help but be frightened for their youngsters after watching *Saturday Night Fever*. This film, and others like it, are indicators of another type of sex revolution that's taken place. A real one. A revolution not in behavior but in *attitudes*.

There's been a marked shift toward the openness with which sex is discussed in public. Much of the notion of a revolution in sexual behavior flows from what Paul H. Gebhard, an associate of Kinsey, calls the "terrific amount of verbalization about sex." Drs. Isadore Rubin and Lester A. Kirkendall, authors of *Sex in the Adolescent Years*, note:

Never before in our history or in the history of any country has there been so much talk about sex—on our campuses, in all our mass communications media, in our pulpits, in fact whenever literate (or illiterate) citizens or worried parents get together. Any newspaper editor knows how easy it is—merely by deciding to play up prominently some details of crimes that are always occurring—to create a "crime wave." In just such a way has a "sex revolution" in behavior been created.

The touting of teenage sexual behavior has misled not only adults but also young people. Adolescents are driven to conform with the behavior of their peers, or at least with their image of that behavior. Caution Drs. Rubin and Kirkendall: "There is a danger that many teenagers, fed by a steady diet of the 'sexual revolution,' will come to feel that they are in some way unusual if they have not had sexual intercourse."

One study in Britain showed that "a large number of boys (25 percent) and quite a few girls (13 percent) were driven towards their first experience for reasons that can best be summed up by the word curiosity." Warnings in the press and "handwringing by important people" have backfired, observes researcher Michael Schofield. "Some adolescents [get] the impression that the average teenager is sexually experienced, and some of these boys and girls must have wondered why they were exceptional and whether they were missing something."

There's also been a marked shift in attitudes among Americans in general about premarital sexual behavior. Sociologist Ira L. Reiss of the University of Minnesota summarized the following trends:

- There's a greater belief in male-female equality and a swing away from the "double standard."
- More men and women are accepting premarital sexual intercourse by women. Fewer women are feeling traditional repression.
- "Sex-with-affection" is gaining increasing acceptance. Marriage need not be a couple's intention—an emotional commitment is seen as sufficient reason for engaging in premarital intercourse.

Such liberalization of sexual standards has led to concrete changes affecting adolescents: Regulations concerning behavior in student dormitories have been abolished or considerably eased. Students have moved out of college dorms into their own apartments. College health services are dispensing contraceptives to students, married and unmarried. Prestigious national medical organizations are encouraging doctors to prescribe contraception for sexually active minors without parental consent.

Not surprisingly, less-restrictive attitudes have become the norm among young people. Pediatrician Joan E. Morgenthau and Natalie J. Sokoloff of the Mount Sinai School of Medicine cite a nationwide survey of college students that finds that almost two-thirds of the students feel it is all right to have sex "when any two people consent" or "when a couple have dated some and care a lot about each other." Only one-fourth of the students did not believe in premarital sex. Another study shows that 70 percent of college students clearly approve of premarital intercourse.

These reports from the 1970s reflect a change in attitude from the 1960s. Studies in the Sixties indicate a lesser acceptance of premarital intercourse among high school and college students, and certainly a much lower acceptance of premarital intercourse by women as well as men. Sociologist Ira Reiss found that only 26 percent of the youngsters he interviewed in the Sixties believed that intercourse was all right whenever people consent or like each other.

This more liberal attitude is not necessarily followed by a change in behavior, note Mount Sinai's Morgenthau and Sokoloff. "It is not uncommon for a teenager to express this attitude: 'I believe it's all right for my friends to have sex; I just don't believe it for myself.'" One social researcher they cite suggests: "Both sexes are more lenient in their attitudes about what is permissible heterosexual behavior for companions than for themselves."

Conclude Morgenthau and Sokoloff: "People are more permissive in their attitudes about other people's sexual behavior as well as more 'open' about their own . . . ; it is not that what they are doing is so vastly different."

GRAINS OF SALT

All sex studies need to be taken with several grains of salt. Sex surveys are often flawed by samples that are too small. Or they may be unrepresentative, and thus limited as to their uses. A major study of teenage sexuality by psychologist Robert C. Sorensen shows some pitfalls facing a serious sex researcher.

Following established procedures, Dr. Sorensen started out with a representative group of 2,042 households. These families had 839 youngsters between the ages of 13 and 19. Ideally they'd have given a sampling applicable to the U.S. teenage population as a whole. However, the parents of 331 youngsters refused to let their children be interviewed. In addition, despite having parents' approval, 115 boys and girls declined to participate. Thus Sorensen lost 53 percent of his original sample. Presumably, most were sexually conservative, inclined to resist questions about intimate behavior and attitudes. This left a large remainder of youngsters who evidently were sexually less restricted than adolescents at large.

Further, Sorensen added to his sample eighteen youngsters who'd ordinarily belong in a nationwide study of teenagers. They represented "invisible" adolescents, the large population not residing with their families but living in reformatories, military barracks, communes, and crash pads. The catch is that such youngsters tend to be more sexually experienced than teenagers who stay at home supervised by their parents.

Because of such weighting, Sorensen's ambitious effort, *Adolescent Sexuality in Contemporary America,* is widely thought to overstate teenage sexual experience. This is the sort of statistical snafu that gives pollsters nightmares—yet is a perpetual hazard of teenage-sex surveying.

There are also major problems with interviewer bias. Few adults are comfortable talking with youngsters about sex. Many interviewers don't like teenagers, or—equally bad—over-identify with them. Moreover, in sex surveys, an interviewer who seems salacious or shocked ("You did *that!*") will discourage meaningful responses.

Questionnaires pertaining to teenage sex are especially difficult to draft. For example, how should a researcher refer to "intercourse," when many youngsters not only never use the word but rather charmingly misunderstand it? In a discussion aimed at the social scientists who read *Journal of Marriage and the Family,* sociologists Arthur M. Vener and Cyrus S. Stewart of Michigan State University describe their problems in translating "coitus" for an adolescent survey:

> Many terms exist for the notion of coitus (e.g., "sexual intercourse," "balling," "fucking," "screwing," "making-it," "laying," "dorking," and "decking"). Some had to be rejected on the basis of propriety, others

were rejected because of their provinciality, and still others were rejected because younger children were unable to understand them. . . .

Several youngsters felt certain that they had had "sexual intercourse." Under intensive probing, it was discovered that these young children believed that sexual intercourse referred to socializing with the opposite sex.

Ultimately, Vener and Stewart decided on "going all the way"— "despite the fact," they add, "that many thought it to be somewhat archaic."

In addition, teenagers are rarely the most reliable respondents. They are seldom at ease discussing sex, compounding an axiom of social research: The more emotional the issue, the less objective the reply. They frequently have trouble relating to an adult interviewer. They are easily bored, and are wont to let impulse, embarrassment, and wishful thinking dictate their replies. There is no way of knowing whether the misstatements balance each other out. Are youngsters who exaggerate their experience offset by those who admit to nothing?

Sex researchers have a further handicap in reaching a teenage population. High schools are the institutions affording the most direct access to large numbers of adolescents. But school administrators are reluctant to let a sex surveyor in the door. Administrators explain, "People are going to protest that this survey falls outside the school's province and invades the privacy of minors. We don't need the headache." Researchers are therefore widely barred from the efficient mass contact that is needed to draw the most accurate picture of teenage sexuality.

Nonetheless, some statistical studies of adolescent sexuality meet rigorous sampling criteria. They also pass at least two tests suggesting that their general conclusions are largely correct. Their findings tend to check each other out, although specific figures are rarely identical. And their results tend to be confirmed by the real-life observations of physicians, psychologists, guidance counselors, and other qualified professionals.

Even with such statistical validity, there is room for a final caveat: You cannot necessarily apply any of these findings to your youngsters' behavior. To begin with, your children are not averages but individuals. It is the individual's experience, combined with many others, that dictates the "norm." The so-called norm does not describe the individual, or even give fair odds as to what any one person is or is not doing.

Further, your children are subject to extremely local influences—their immediate family and peer group—which may or may not be statistically typical. In a predominantly white, middle-class high school in a Western town, Shirley L. Jessor and Richard Jessor found that students seem to major in sex. More than half the girls lose their virginity before graduating, a much higher figure than reported elsewhere. By contrast, in a private school outside of Philadelphia, there is little dating among the students and practically no intercourse.

So much for the numbers game. Here, then, is what the most relied-on studies of the last decade show about teenage sexual intercourse:

Possibly Half Are Nonvirgins

Perhaps the most quoted national estimate comes from the U.S. Bureau of the Census Current Population Survey: Of the roughly 21 million young people in this country between the ages of 15 and 19, more than half—some 11 million—are estimated to have had sexual intercourse: almost 7 million young men and 4 million young women. In addition, one-fifth of the nation's 8 million 13- and 14-year-old boys and girls are believed to have had intercourse.

These estimates, however, are probably high. They come too close to Robert Sorensen's findings for his national sampling, which is believed to be atypically nonvirginal. Fifty-two percent of the adolescents Sorensen surveyed had intercourse at least once. An eighth of these had intercourse by the time they were 12. About a quarter had 7 or more partners.

Most researchers conclude that rates of sexual intercourse among teenagers are much lower, especially among middle-class whites. Psychiatrist Daniel Offer and his colleagues, in interviewing normal adolescent boys from a well-to-do Illinois community, found that only 10 percent of the boys had experienced sexual intercourse by the end of the junior year of high school. In a poll of 23,000 high school student leaders and high achievers, those reported as having experienced sexual intercourse amounted to 22 percent of boys and 19 percent of girls, about 1 in 5 youngsters.

Sociologists Arthur M. Vener and Cyrus S. Stewart of Michigan State University surveyed 1,972 Michigan junior and senior high school boys and girls. The youngsters surveyed were white and from upper-working-class to upper-middle-class families. No more than 33 percent of the boys and 22 percent of the girls reported "going all the way" at least once. Only about 20 percent of the boys and 9 percent of the girls had had more than one partner.

The typical teenager from such a background evidently has not yet begun deep involvement with the opposite sex. While about two-thirds of the youngsters necked ("prolonged hugging and kissing"), only about half the students reported even light petting, which the researchers define as "feeling above the waist." Heavy petting ("feeling below the waist") was experienced by less than half the boys and about a third of the girls.

A similar survey in Illinois studied the sexual activity of 2,064 white adolescents ages 14 through 17. The study—conducted by Patricia Y. Miller and William Simon of Chicago's Institute for Juvenile Research—took in nineteen thousand households statewide. It embodied a diverse population of city, farm, and suburban teenagers, and is claimed to be representative of the nation as a whole.

Miller and Simon's findings refute the proposition that there have been major increases in sexual intercourse among adolescents. In their total sample, they found only 14 percent of the boys and 13 percent of the girls had engaged in intercourse. Even after they excluded younger teenagers (the 14- and 15-year-olds) they still found that intercourse had been experienced by only 21 percent of the boys and 22 percent of the girls.

Girls Show the Greatest Increase

In their Illinois study of whites, Patricia Miller and William Simon detect a "sexual revolution in terms of *who* has experienced sexual intercourse." They note from their sample that girls are approaching the rate of nonvirginity usually demonstrated by boys—"which may, in fact, constitute a revolution with far more profound implications for social life."

Drs. Melvin Zelnik and John F. Kantner of the Johns Hopkins University School of Hygiene and Public Health conducted two surveys five years apart, sampling four thousand never-married white girls ages 15 through 19. The first study showed that 23 percent had experienced sexual intercourse. The second, half a decade later, revealed a jump to 32 percent. A comparable sampling of two thousand black girls also showed a rise—from 52 percent to 62 percent.

A rise in intercourse among middle-class white high school girls was also shown in the Michigan samplings of Arthur Vener and Cyrus Stewart. Whereas their later study found 22 percent of girls to be nonvirgins, a similar survey three years earlier reported only 16 percent. The percentage of girls having had more than one partner likewise rose from 6 percent to 9 percent.

The proportion of college women engaging in intercourse has risen dramatically in recent years, after remaining fairly stable for decades. Kinsey and his associates reported that in the 1940s a mere 20 percent of 19- and 20-year-old college women had experienced intercourse. Fifteen years later, the figure was virtually the same. Kinsey found that the higher a young woman's social class, the less likely she was to engage in premarital intercourse.

That's no longer true. Sociologist Ira Reiss has offered compelling evidence that in generally liberal settings there is a link between social class and premarital sexual permissiveness: persons from higher social classes have more sexual intercourse. At universities—where "liberal" values, as Reiss defines them, are generally upheld—the positive relation between social class and permissive premarital sexual behavior is widely found. Dr. Andrew Sorensen of the University of Rochester School of Medicine and his colleagues theorize that a new middle class comprised largely of professionals and managers has emerged since the early 1950s. The children of this group appear to have a more liberal philosophy that, on campuses, may be producing a link between social class and sexual permissiveness.

In the late 1960s and early 1970s, researchers began to report that significantly larger numbers of college females were engaging in intercourse, estimated at between 39 to 45 percent. Now the proportion is thought to be even larger. Psychologist Robert M. Oswalt of Skidmore College in Saratoga Springs, New York, did a random sampling of 10 percent of the female student body. His conclusion: "Sixty-five percent of the total sample of female college students are not virgins." He calls this occurrence of intercourse by young women "markedly higher than the earlier studies . . . which were conducted from the 1940s to 1970."

Dr. James W. Croake, professor of marriage and family counseling at Virginia Polytechnic Institute and the State University at Blacksburg, reports a similar sexual activity among college students. Most freshmen are 18 and sophomores are 19. "During the freshman year about 40 percent of the males and 35 percent of the females are nonvirginal. By the sophomore year this rate probably jumps to about 65 percent for the males and 60 percent for females with little percentage increase through the senior year for either sex."

At Skidmore, psychologist Robert Oswalt tracked the increase in nonvirginity as young women proceeded through school. He found that intercourse had been had at least once by 42 percent of the freshmen and 55 percent of sophomores (plus 77 percent of juniors and 87 percent of seniors). Of all the nonvirgins, 30 percent had experienced intercourse before they entered college. Thereafter 31 percent lost their virginity during their freshman year, 25 percent as sophomores (followed by 12 percent as juniors and 2 percent as seniors).

Boys' Activity Is Largely Unchanged

In contrast to the increase in sexual intercourse by girls, the rate of nonvirginity for boys seems to have been remarkably stable over the last few decades. Sociologists Arthur Vener and Cyrus Stewart of Michigan State University and David L. Hager of Grand Rapids Junior College compared the boys in a study of Michigan teenagers with a study of middle-class teenagers reported by Glenn V. Ramsey in 1943. Ramsey's sample showed that, at age 14, sexual intercourse had been experienced by 20 percent of the boys. Some 30 years later, Vener and his colleagues detected nearly the same number, 18 percent. At age 16, Ramsey reported, 30 percent of his sample had experienced intercourse. Vener found a similar 28 percent. At 17 and older, Ramsey found, 33 percent had had intercourse—the identical number discovered by Vener.

For another study, Vener and Stewart waited three years—and revisited one of the Michigan communities they had surveyed. The sociologists found a 20-percent rise in boys' incidence of sexual intercourse—from 28 percent to 33 percent. Girls over the same period showed nearly twice that rate of increase.

In Patricia Miller and William Simon's large-scale study of Illinois teenagers, they detected an actual decline in boys' sexual intercourse, as compared to earlier studies. They speculate that white high school boys are having less intercourse for the following reasons:

- Their communities are more homogeneous along social-class lines, making it more difficult for them to recruit "bad girls" for sex. Boys seeking intercourse are "under pressure to recruit partners from among their peers."
- Coming from the same social group, boys are more likely to have friends in common with a sex partner. "They can now more significantly fail or look foolish."
- There's a swing away from "innate gender differences." Boys may have less need to demonstrate their manhood through intercourse.
- Intercourse may be "less critical for the maintenance of peer esteem." The boy may impress his friends by other means made possible by "growing affluence and the plethora of youth culture gadgets and fads."
- Girls, while more willing to have intercourse, require an emotional commitment from a partner. This "prompts a reluctance in the male who is inept at expressing his sexual needs within an emotional relationship." The boy therefore has "unresolved difficulties in placing his sexuality in more complex social relationships."

Teenagers Begin Intercourse Younger

It appears that more teenagers are starting intercourse at earlier ages. In the Michigan study of middle-class youngsters, sociologists Vener and Stewart compared their current results with a similar study of three years before. A larger percentage of the current 16-year-olds, both boys and girls, engaged in intercourse.

Vener and Stewart found the most striking increases among younger teenagers. The picture they draw is this: Of current 15-year-old girls, 24 percent had had intercourse, compared to 13 percent three years earlier. Among 15-year-old boys, 38 percent were nonvirgins, as opposed to 26 percent three years before.

Intercourse by 14-year-olds showed a similar large increase. Of current 14-year-old girls, 17 percent had had intercourse. Three years ago: 10 percent. For 14-year-old boys, 32 percent were nonvirgins, in contrast to 21 percent three years before.

Girls in particular seem to be starting sex earlier. The Johns Hopkins survey suggests that four years earlier only 3 percent of 15-year-old girls would have reported, "I'm not a virgin." Currently, fully 9 percent would make that statement—triple the percentage.

At Skidmore College, psychologist Robert Oswalt observed this decrease in age at first intercourse among his female college population. "It appears that the age of first intercourse is occurring at an earlier age even in this circumscribed sample," he remarks. Four years before, 38 percent of the freshman class were nonvirgins, compared to the current figure of 42 percent.

In Robert Sorensen's study, weighted toward those who've had intercourse, 13 percent of the nonvirgin adolescents (17 percent of the nonvirgin boys and 7 percent of the nonvirgin girls) had first sexual intercourse at the age of 12 or under. Of all nonvirgin adolescents, 73 percent of the boys and 56 percent of the girls had had sexual intercourse by age 16. Only 16 percent of the nonvirgin girls and 3 percent of the nonvirgin boys waited until they were 18 or 19 years old before they had first intercourse.

Sorensen's sampling is useful for showing what are likely to be maximum figures. Based on his results, the percentage of nonvirgins experiencing first intercourse at various ages is probably at most as follows:

Age at First Intercourse	All Adolescents (%)	All Boys (%)	All Girls (%)
12 or under	7	10	3
13	8	11	5
14	8	11	5
15	11	11	12
16	8	7	10
17	4	7	3
18 or 19	6	2	7
Total nonvirgins	52	59	45
Total virgins	48	41	55
	100	100	100

They Have Intercourse Infrequently

"Sexually active" teenagers are rarely very active as far as intercourse is concerned. The phrase "sexually active" is a poor euphemism to begin with—it suggests that the only form of sexual activity is intercourse.

For most nonvirgin teenagers, sexual intercourse is an irregular activity. "The picture is not one of rampant sexuality," report Johns Hopkins University's Melvin Zelnik and John Kantner. Fully 38 percent of the nonvirgin girls in their study had had no intercourse at all during the month before they were questioned. In that month, 30 percent had had intercourse once or twice, and 18 percent three to five times. Only 14 percent had intercourse six or more times. By contrast, nine times a month is averaged by married couples where the wife is under age 25.

An American Public Health Association Study found similarly low rates of frequency. Fifteen percent of nonvirgin boys and girls had not had intercourse in the preceding three months.

In a study of nonvirgin teenage boys, Madelon Lubin Finkel of New York University and David J. Finkel, anthropology professor at Adelphi University, report that "sexual activity appears to be sporadic." In the week before the survey, the mean frequency of sexual intercourse was less than once. More than half did not have sexual intercourse in the week prior to the survey—"a typical week," most report. In the previous month, the boys reported an average rate of intercourse of only 3.6 times.

Indeed, so low is the frequency of intercourse that some teenagers who are classified as "sexually active" have had only one experience of sexual intercourse. The Youth Values Project is a study of one thousand New York City adolescents. Teenage interviewers were hired to explore why youngsters don't use birth control. Of the so-called sexually active teenagers, fully 10 percent of the girls and 9 percent of the boys reported having had intercourse just once. In addition, 30 percent of the nonvirgin girls and 26 percent of the nonvirgin boys said they'd had sex only "a few times."

They Have Few Partners

The majority of nonvirgin teenagers are not promiscuous. On the contrary, they seem extremely sparing in their number of sexual partners.

At least 3 out of 5 nonvirgin girls told Zelnik and Kantner they'd had only one partner ever. Of those who'd had intercourse in the month prior to the interview, over 9 out of 10 had relations with just one partner. Only 16 percent of whites, and 11 percent of blacks, had had four or more partners since they began having intercourse.

What about as a girl gets older? Typically, her total number of partners increases, but not by much. For whites, 70 percent of 15-year-olds had had only one partner. By age 19, one partner remained the total experience of 50 percent. For blacks, there were more partners earlier but fewer later: 65 percent of 15-year-olds had had only one sex partner compared to 56 percent of 19-year-olds.

Psychologist Robert Oswalt of Skidmore reports much the same degree of sexual selectiveness among college women. "Although our results indicate that the incidence of female college student premarital intercourse has increased, promiscuity has not," he comments. Seventy-four percent of the coeds in his study had had intercourse with only one or two partners. (Forty-seven percent were still having intercourse with their first partner.) Only 9 percent have had sex with three partners, and less than 5 percent had had intercourse with more than eight partners.

Similarly, Vener and Stewart's Michigan study confirms that few teenagers have many partners. Of nonvirgins, nearly half the boys and over 6 out of 10 girls report only one partner. Conversely, only 3 percent of the girls and 14 percent of the boys had experienced sex with seven or more partners. Boys were more likely than girls to have had intercourse with more than one partner. But the great majority of the boys, 73 percent, reported experience with three partners or less.

The Michigan investigators called attention to an interesting finding: Relatively few very early adolescents—age 13 and younger—had had intercourse. But they tended to be involved with a greater number of partners than were older nonvirgins. Fully 60 percent of the experienced 13-year-old boys had had two or more partners. Among 17-year-old boys, only 49 percent had been so involved. For girls the figures were even more striking: Among 13-year-olds, 63 percent had had two or more partners—compared with only 30 percent for 17-year-olds.

"Apparently," reason the investigators, "if a young adolescent is able to transgress traditionally proscribed behavioral codes regarding premarital coitus, he is less likely to [require] sex with affection, and therefore is less guilt-ridden when experiencing coitus with a number of partners."

Most Intercourse Takes Place at Home

If your teenagers are having intercourse, they're likely to have it most often at home. In the Youth Values Project, 61 percent of the nonvirgin girls and 47 percent of the boys had sex in their own home or in their partner's home. Teenagers who report they have sex most often in their own homes tend to come from families in which parents worked during the day.

The study also finds that home is the site for intercourse even for teenagers who believe their parents would be very upset if they found out. "Anticipated anger from parents did not deter respondents from taking risks and having sex at home," the study reports.

And for college girls? At Skidmore, Robert Oswalt asked about the location of a girl's first intercourse. Forty-seven percent occurred at the college dorm, either the girl's or her partner's. Other locations were the young man's home or apartment (25 percent), the home of the girl's parents (10 percent), a friend's apartment (4 percent). Only 3 percent went to a motel.

INDICATORS OF INTERCOURSE

What kind of youngsters have intercourse in their teens? Among the clues found by social researchers:

No college aspirations. If a 16- or 17-year-old girl did not plan to go to college, Patricia Miller and William Simon found in Illinois, she was two and a half times more likely to be a nonvirgin than a girl who was college-bound. A noncollege-bound boy was twice as likely to have had intercourse as a boy with college plans.

A serious relationship. Half the nonvirgin girls, both black and white, told Melvin Zelnik and John Kantner of Johns Hopkins that they'd had intercourse only with the man they intended to marry.

The tendency of a couple to have intercourse before they marry each other seems to be on the rise. Sociologist Phillips Cutright of Indiana University analyzed statistics available for pregnant brides and found them on the increase by 10 percent. Cutright concludes the sexual revolution appears to be confined to an increase in intercourse among "girls involved with males who will become their husbands."

Intercourse during engagement seems the norm irrespective of college plans. Miller and Simon polled 16- and 17-year-old girls who were engaged. Intercourse was experienced by 50 percent of those who were college-bound, and 70 percent of those with no college plans. Similarly, girls who were going steady were about four times as likely to have had intercourse as girls who merely went out with a group.

Single-parent households. The Youth Values Project in New York found that 68 percent of girls and 77 percent of boys who lived with a single parent were nonvirgins. By contrast, sexual intercourse had been experienced by 51 percent of girls and 66 percent of boys from two-parent families.

Indeed, the study found, economic status and race or ethnic group made little difference in predicting whether or not a teenager had had intercourse. The strongest predictor was the number of parents in the household.

Alienation from parents. Miller and Simon found that teenagers were less likely to have had intercourse if they had more involvement with their parents—playing and shopping with them, talking with them, wanting to be like them.

In particular, boys who were very involved with their parents—and very uninvolved with friends—were least likely to have experienced intercourse. Conversely, boys with a high degree of peer involvement had a high rate of nonvirginity, all the more so if they had little to do with their parents.

Nonvirginal girls do not show the same involvement with friends. "Historically, the peer group has provided support, if not pressure, for the male's expression of his sexuality," note Miller and Simon. For girls the opposite has been true. "The peer group functions for the female to foster a positive valuation of romantic love." Thus girls generally get little support from friends for casual sex, and nonvirgin girls are more likely than nonvirgin boys to have weak peer-group ties.

Weak religious belief. "Religious institutions are committed to securing conformity to a system of ethics which usually proscribes premarital sexual experience," note Miller and Simon.

Consistent with earlier studies, they found a sharp rise in experience with intercourse as religious belief declined. Nonvirginal youngsters were about three times as likely to describe themselves as "not at all religious" than as "very religious."

The continuing resistance of religious youngsters to premarital sex discredits "another instance of social mythology," Miller and Simon conclude. The "much touted liberalizing" of the church has not in fact "disturbed the [negative] association between religious commitment and premarital sexuality."

Chapter 6

Before They're Ready

Help your children resist premature intercourse. Free them to say no.

"I DON'T EVEN have a boyfriend. But I had myself fitted for a diaphragm. I had to feel that in some way I was part of it all."

With this confession, 17-year-old Elena tried to express to M.I.T. psychotherapist Thomas Cottle her confusion about contemporary sexual mores. Your own children may share Elena's bewilderment. They may be casualties of the sexual revolution. Pressures in virtually every corner of your teenagers' world may propel them toward premature, and possibly harmful, sexual involvement.

The professed morality has come full circle since you were a teenager. In your adolescent years, girls who weren't virgins weren't "nice." Now it's the virgins, male and female, who are amiss—or so it appears to many of them.

Your children may be worried that there must be something wrong with them because they have not yet had intercourse. Terms like "the new morality," "sexual freedom," "free love" are used so blithely that your teenagers may be embarrassed about their own doubts. "If everybody's doing it," they may reason, "then I must be a freak to hesitate."

At Yale, Joyce Maynard as a virgin was considered a curiosity. Relates the young author of *Looking Back*,

For about three weeks last winter, I had two roommates instead of one—the girl in the bottom bunk and her friend, who made our quarters especially cramped because, in addition to being six feet tall with lots of luggage, he was male. We slept in shifts . . . the awkwardness was always there (those squeaking bedsprings), as it was for many girls I knew, and many boys.

One surprise Joyce got was that

it wasn't my roommate but I—the one who slept alone, the one whose only pills were vitamins and aspirin—I was the embarrassed one. How has it happened, what have we come to, that the scarlet letter these days isn't A, but V?

Virginity, has become not a flower or a jewel, a precious treasure for Prince Charming or a lovely, prized and guarded gift, but a dusty relic—an anachronism. Most of all, it's an embarrassment.

Your teenagers are likely to find that the burden of shame has shifted to those who are not willing to have sex. To many contemporary young people, the virgin is on the same team with sensible orthopedic shoes. "It's pretty awkward for a student here to admit that he or she is a virgin," observes Mary Saxe, a social worker at UCLA's student health service. "Around here," says a Barnard sophomore, "you either sleep with someone you may or may not like, or else you are lonely. We haven't been liberated at all if we are being *forced* to sleep with people."

The new morality your children face is as tyrannizing as the relative puritanism you grew up with. Comments Dr. John H. Wilms, director of mental health services at Purdue University Student Hospital: "Sexual liberation is often a cultural mandate, and as such is sometimes actually more confining than liberating."

Dr. Richard V. Lee of the Yale University School of Medicine contends that the youth rebellion against the old morality has transformed sex into an ideology.

To my mind, this new sexual ideology is as dictatorial and cruel as Victorian prudery. It unites the expectation of easily attained sexual competence and gratification with a cavalier disregard for some of the undesirable side effects of sexual activity.

It has used easier contraception, legal abortion, and surer diagnostic and therapeutic methods for venereal disease as arguments to make virginity irrelevant. It refuses to accept virginity as a reasonable way of life. In short, it allows no choice—it's liberation or nothing. And our sexual liberation does not include the freedom to say "no."

SOCIAL PRESSURES

A sex-saturated society may push your youngsters toward engaging in premature intercourse. Dr. Ira L. Mintz of the Columbia University Psychoanalytic Clinic reports the feeling among many young people that they are not yet ready for sex, yet they soon discover that society expects them to embrace the new "freedom."

Any pressure your high schooler feels toward early intercourse is likely to be stepped up at college. Many youngsters first entering college are struck by a pervasive sexual atmosphere. Coed dorms are common. Regulations often permit men in women's rooms twenty-four hours a day. "I went to Freshman Orientation my first day at college," recalls 18-year-old Sharon. "One of the first things they told us was where to get contraception and abortions. It was clear I was *expected* to need such services."

Joyce Maynard recalls entering Yale and encountering the sexual mores of the older students.

> The pressure is really on at college. I'm looking back now to . . . the beginning of my freshman year. What I should remember is my first glimpse of my college campus, freshman assembly, buying notepads and textbooks and writing my name and my dorm on the covers. Instead, my memory of September blurs into a single word: sex. . . .
>
> Ask a friend how things were going and he'll tell you whether or not he'd found a girl. Go to a freshman women's tea or a Women's Liberation meeting and the talk would turn, inevitably, to contraceptives and abortions. Liberated from the restrictions imposed by parents . . . we found ourselves suddenly sharing a world not with the junior high and the ninth grade, but with college seniors and graduate students—men and women in their twenties. Very quickly, we took on their values, imitated their behavior and, often, swallowed their pills.

College can overwhelm your youngster with this pervasive sexuality. Reports psychoanalyst Ira Mintz: "One college girl said she was in a constant state of turmoil because of the sexual activity she could not help but hear through the dormitory wall." Another felt panicky in the face of all the sexual freedom. She was unable to buckle down and study until she moved to an all-girl dorm. Some students drop out, without realizing that their poor grades and general discomfort are part of their sexual confusion.

"Many college students sense they are not ready for a mature sexual relationship but are pressured into one," concludes Dr. Mintz. "They have little or no protection—no curfew behind which to take refuge, no college rule that may be invoked without loss of face."

EXPECTATIONS OF DATES

"Lately I feel very confused and almost drained of everything I think is right," an 18-year-old girl wrote to *Seventeen* magazine.

> The other night I found myself *apologizing* for not going to bed with Jim, a guy I recently started going with. I had to practically fight him off. I felt very prudish and embarrassed when I tried to explain that I liked him a lot but that I was still a virgin and wanted to remain one till I married. He really couldn't believe it. He just sat there and stared. He said he really wasn't mad and we left it at that, but I do like him and I know the situation will arise again. What should I do? His simple solution is "Change!" But it's not that easy.

Your daughter may find herself in similar quandaries. Confused by the notion that virginity is now old-fashioned, she may be shamed into acquiescence. If she's received a traditional feminine upbringing, she may be especially vulnerable to such pressure. She may see as part of her femaleness the obligation to meet the needs of others. She may believe that the most important aspect of her body is its attractiveness to males. She may have been taught that it's feminine to be passive and follow the male's lead. The typical teenage girl, says Elizabeth J. Roberts of the Project on Human Sexual Development was "raised to think that 'sex' is something that happens to her, something she should not or cannot make decisions about." Psychiatrist Karem J. Monsour of the Counseling Center at Claremont Colleges in California found that of twenty college women who had abortions, fully seven said they always or usually felt "obligated" to engage in intercourse.

Your daughter may feel compelled to comply because the boy represents to her that he has an overwhelming "physical need" for sex. Tell her this is baloney. "Explode the myth of the male's desperate need and his terrible suffering if he is denied," advises psychiatrist William J. Gadpaille of the University of Colorado Medical Center. Your daughter can give a pushy date this sound physiological advice: "Go home and masturbate."

Another pressure on your daughter may be an implied threat that refusing intercourse will cost her the relationship. "Many youngsters enter upon sexual intimacy prematurely for fear of losing their boyfriends," observes psychiatrist Sheila Klebanow of New York Medical College, New York City. "They are afraid to say no." Complains Tara, a high school senior: "What girls want most is to go out and have a good time. By sophomore or junior year they get the idea, if I don't say yes, then a guy won't ask me out."

In a round table, teenage girls describe the sexual pressure they feel from dates. Says Ava: "I have found extremely few boys who aren't into a thing with girls just for the *sex* of it. To me, it seems pretty sad that boys can't picture girls as anything but sex partners and status symbols." Joanne agrees: "It's sort of like whatever you can get for the night.'" Comments Arlene: "I don't like it when all the guy wants to do is see how far he can get. . . . My girl friend said her guy broke up with her because she wouldn't do anything but 'hold hands' with him."

Sometimes the tables are turned, and your son may feel sexually pressured by dates. Chances are, when you were a teenager, a boy would expect a girl's parents to be waiting up for her at the prescribed hour. All he could expect would be a good-night kiss. "Since this would often be all he could handle comfortably," says psychiatrist Clarice Kestenbaum of St. Luke's Hospital Center in New York City, "he would usually experience great relief hidden behind his complaint at not being able to 'get more.'"

Now social convention may make it easier for him to get more, a prospect that may fill him with anxiety. What's more, many girls no longer accept a passive role, waiting for the boy to make the first sexual overture. A girl interested in a boy may now make the initial move herself. "I'd kiss him goodnight if it didn't look like he was going to give me a kiss," one high school sophomore told Dorothy M. Place, who studied the dating experience of adolescent girls. Another said: "If I went out with a guy and he didn't kiss me, I'd say, 'Gee, don't I get a good-night kiss?'"

If your son feels anxious and pressured at the prospect of more sex than he bargained for, he may be thoroughly unnerved when a girl presses for sexual intercourse. Psychiatrist John Wilms of Purdue tells of Michael, a shy, conservative college freshman who came to the emergency room after taking a drug overdose. "He was panic-stricken about his masculinity after a humiliating encounter with a sexually ambitious, 'liberated' woman, and was totally unprepared and impotent when *she* asked *him* first!"

SEXUAL FASCISTS

Warn your teenagers that their friends may be what psychologist Albert Ellis calls "sexual fascists." Your children's peers may be intolerant of anyone who does not have intercourse. Adds psychologist Eugene M. Kennedy of Loyola University: "Today a great many people are speaking about sexuality and telling everybody else how they should lead their sexual lives. People are intensely vulnerable in the area of sexuality; it is easy to intimidate them."

Yale's Dr. Richard Lee tells of a 17-year-old freshman we'll call Janice. She was doing well academically. She had a 19-year-old boyfriend, Ezra, whom she liked a lot. But Ezra was pushing her to have sexual intercourse. She was reluctant, she told Dr. Lee, "to go all the way."

She was not ready, she said. Not because she feared sex or pregnancy or her parents' disapproval. Rather, she felt that sex would interfere with her life as a student, with her plans for herself, with her studies, her freedom. "She did not want to be tied down," says Dr. Lee. "And she felt sex should be a commitment."

But Janice's most anguishing problem, Lee discovered, was the attitude of the other girls in her dormitory. She had talked about Ezra and she had explained her reservations, expecting support from her peers. Instead, she had been hurt to find them abrasively scornful of her virginity.

"Our conversation centered about how she could cope with the attitude of these girls with whom she was living more than how she could cope with her boyfriend's insistence on sex," notes Lee. Talking seemed to help, and a few weeks later, she reported that life as the "virgin queen" in her dormitory was rather unpleasant, but tolerable. She told Dr. Lee she could handle the scorn of her girl "friends" and was continuing to date the young man, whom she still liked very much.

Then one morning Lee received a tearful phone call from the girl: "My girlfriend Della told me that she'd just seduced Ezra. And he confirms it." Janice was terribly shaken, but still liked the young man so much she didn't want to break off with him. For several weeks, she vacillated between deciding to go to bed with him or never see him again.

Finally, Janice decided there was no solution. She decided to leave the university.

Comments Dr. Lee: "If she had found support among her girlfriends, she might have decided differently. But they were brutally unhelpful. In fact, they seemed to relish her distress. Her choice of virginity had made her an outcast. She came to recognize that her openness about her feelings had made her doubly vulnerable."

Your own adolescents may be subjected to the sort of peer pressure for intercourse that Janice experienced. Friends may tell your children: "You're not a real woman until you've had sex." "What kind of man are you if you've never been laid?" Psychiatrist Sheila Klebanow observes that "young people may be encouraged by their more sexually sophisticated friends to become sexually intimate before they are ready since this is presented as the 'in' thing."

Your son is almost certain to feel pressure from other boys to be sexually successful. In some circles, this means as much sex as young and as frequently as possible. The typical teenage boy, observes Elizabeth Roberts of the Project on Human Sexual Development, is "encouraged by his peers to be goal-oriented and to succeed at all costs, even in the bedroom." Your son's sexual athleticism may be an extension of his drive to win in sports. Boys often equate sex with "scoring." The male body is something to perform with, to use to prove masculinity. A boy not ready for sex is derided as a "loser." With girls he "strikes out."

It's almost as likely that your daughter will experience the same sort of pressure from her girl friends as your son from his friends. A high school senior told reporter Alice Lake: "A girl who isn't a virgin will talk to a girl who is and make her feel out of place, make her think, 'Maybe I'm not doing the right thing.' With a lot of kids, it's not so much that they want to do it, but that it's the thing to do." Joyce Maynard reports insidious coercion. "Though individuality is officially admired, 'peer-group pressure' . . . is very real when it comes to sex. Other girls assume a friend's sexual experience."

Gynecologist David Chapin, consultant to a coeducational boarding school near Boston, suspects that when it comes to bragging about sexual exploits, "the girls' locker room has replaced the men's; it is now girls who feel they have to go each other one better." Dr. Malkah Notman of Boston finds that inexperienced college girls, embarrassed by their virginity, often pretend to experience what they haven't in order to be included with the "in" group. Among pregnant teenagers Dr. Notman found a number who engaged in sexual relations because they were tired of being teased by peers and called names because they were still virgins.

Even if your youngsters don't experience actual teasing about their virginity, a push toward premature intercourse may spring from their adolescent impulse to pattern themselves after a model. Psychiatrist Irving H. Berkowitz of the University of California Medical School in Los Angeles reports that he has heard only occasionally of direct pressure from friends to engage in sex. "More often girls who were suggestible, unsure, and wished to emulate a sexually more active and/or popular girlfriend were thus indirectly pressured by peer example."

If your teenager is feeling pushed by friends to engage in intercourse prematurely, recommend a change of friends. True, much of the youth culture in general is sexually oriented. But it's their individual circles of friends that make the crucial difference in your children's sexual attitudes and behavior. Some groups engage in intercourse as the norm. Others of the same age are just beginning to play kissing games.

From a study of over one thousand students at twelve U.S. colleges, sociologist James J. Teevan, Jr. of the University of Western Ontario has determined the influence of friends: If your teenagers perceive their friends to act in a sexually permissive manner and to have "lots of sex," they will also be sexually permissive and engage in intercourse. But if your children perceive their friends as having little sex experience, then they are about three times more likely to remain virgins.

PRESSURES FROM PARENTS

Beware of ways in which you may be putting sexual pressure on your children. Observes psychoanalyst Ira Mintz: "Too many [parents] . . . actually push their children into premature sex."

Not unheard of are parents who explicitly encourage their teenagers to engage in sexual intercourse, feeling that it will help them avoid sexual problems in later life. Reports psychiatrist Clarice Kestenbaum: "Some parents have come to believe that early sexuality will be a 'liberating' experience—one that will minimize the kind of sexual 'hang-ups' suffered by the parents as a result of their more repressive childhood experience."

In most cases, more subtle influences are at work. Parents can unconsciously or inadvertently edge their children toward early sexual activity. Psychiatrist James F. Masterson, Jr. of Cornell University Medical College warns that parents who are either permissive or rigid each fail to respond to the individuality of the adolescent and "thereby instill a lot of hostility." Some parents have repressed their own urges to act out sexually, notes Dr. Masterson. "This type of parent obtains vicarious satisfaction by unconsciously provoking the adolescent to act out or express these urges for him or her." The teenager is placed in a situation where "on the one hand his individuality is being frustrated, which produces hostility, and on the other hand he is being provoked to express this hostility through sexual channels." The child thus uses sexual behavior to express hostility as well as to assert individuality. "The adolescent's potential for sexual fulfillment in later life can be seriously damaged by this use of sex."

Sons are likely to be more pressured toward early sex than daughters. Fathers, particularly, may give their sons the impression that to be a man involves sexual intercourse early and often. If you or your spouse convey to your son your expectation that he ought to be out there scoring, you're putting an extra burden on an already pressured youngster.

You may inadvertently put such pressure on your son. One father, believing that his 15-year-old son might soon start sleeping with girls, provided the boy with contraceptives and lectured him on how to use them. "Though for some 15-year-olds this might be quite helpful, this man's son was frightened by his father's advice," comments psychotherapist Thomas Edwards Brown of SIECUS. "The boy was just beginning to date, and the wide discrepancy between his actual sexual experience and his father's implicit expectations caused him considerable anxiety over his adequacy as a man."

If you're a father, you may be tempted to introduce your adolescent son to sex by taking him to a prostitute. This European tradition is not a good idea. Pediatrician Murray Kappelman of the University of

Maryland School of Medicine believes that "this age-old practice can have very negative emotional and physical effects upon an emerging adolescent." You can't tell from his external development just when your son is emotionally ready for sexual intercourse. Making this suggestion too early is pressuring him, with possible damaging emotional effects.

Further, Dr. Kappelman points out, the first sexual experience is often both hesitant and imperfect in technique and execution. "To be guided through this initial experience by one's own parent with expectations of success can be a devastating experience emotionally."

In addition, the introduction of the adolescent into sexuality through a prostitute puts sex into the totally physical realm, devoid of friendship and affection. Observes Dr. Kappelman: "This is the antithesis of what we should be attempting to teach our adolescent population."

Ironically, you may be putting a form of pressure on your children if you are overly restrictive about dating behavior. Long before a teenager is thinking of anything more intimate than a kiss, some parents become obsessed with fears of intercourse. Parents sometimes develop exaggerated fears about the sexual experiences of their adolescents. They worry that their children will act out the wild fantasies they themselves had during adolescence.

If your rules are too strict, your youngsters may go overboard to escape them. Psychologist Daniel A. Sugarman tells of 17-year-old Anne, the only child of older parents who stifled her with rules. She had to report home immediately after school. Dating was out of the question.

"Unable to persuade her parents to loosen their restrictions," recalls Dr. Sugarman, "she stole away from home and hitchhiked to a neighboring city." Her first pickup took Anne to a motel. Nine months later she gave birth to his baby. Reflects Dr. Sugarman: "Anne proved that she was, at least physically, grown up. But she paid a high price for winning an argument."

Your suspicions are a form of expectation. Some adolescents feel a need to fulfill their parents' fantasies. Promiscuous girls often reflect: "If I'm going to be treated like a whore, I'll act like one."

Seventeen-year-old Caroline says, "My mother just assumes I'm going all the way with my boyfriend, although I'm not. Her reaction is, 'Don't tell me about it. I don't want to know.'" It will be easy for

Caroline to slip into a premature sexual relationship with her boyfriend, since her mother has set the stage for it. Caroline, further, need not be concerned about her mother's reaction. By assuming premature intercourse to be a fact, Caroline's mother has lost her influence to prevent it.

Psychoanalyst Ira Mintz tells of the "enlightened" parents of a 15-year-old girl we'll call Alice. Afraid that Alice and her boyfriend would soon engage in intercourse, the parents made an appointment for Alice to go to a gynecologist and get birth control pills. "As it turned out, the girl was hesitant," reports Dr. Mintz. "She didn't really want to take this big step." She talked to her boyfriend and asked him if she should take the pills, hoping that he would say no. It was clear to Dr. Mintz that while the girl had insisted that she must have sexual freedom, she didn't really want all that much freedom. "She did not want to take the pills," Dr. Mintz says. "Even more strongly she wanted to have her mother and father tell her that she was too young to start having sexual intercourse and that they did not want her to start."

Indeed, if your youngsters ask your advice about whether or not they are old enough to have sexual intercourse, they're almost certainly hoping you'll say no. "For most adolescents the act of asking permission is a clear message that they are not emotionally ready and want their mothers to say 'no,'" comments psychiatrist Clarice Kestenbaum. "When an adolescent is genuinely ready for sexual intimacy he or she no longer feels the need of expressed parental permission."

WHY NOT

"I spend half an evening trying to explain to a guy why not," says 17-year-old Barbara. "Then afterward I ask myself—well, *why not?*"

Be prepared to help your youngsters answer this question. In view of the enormous pressures toward early sex your children may have to contend with, they may well look to you for solid reasons against succumbing to sexual activity they're unprepared for. Without explicit guidelines from you, their confusion may make them easy prey.

Don't fear that your sexual standards are old-fashioned and irrelevant to your children. "I am worried about the intimidation of sincere and intelligent parents and physicians by the 'sexual revolution,'" says Yale's Dr. Richard Lee. The new sexual mythology would have you believe that adolescents know more about sex than their parents, that they live in the best of all possible sexual worlds. Dr. Lee warns that if you're snowed by this, you may exclude yourself from helping your youngsters become "sexually competent, happy adults," and from your essential task of destroying "harmful myths and egregious oversimplifications."

In counseling your children to hold off on intercourse until they're ready, emphasize the positive reasons for them to be patient. Dr. Deane William Ferm, chaplain of Mount Holyoke College, wanted to convey to his college-freshman daughter Sue how he and her mother feel about sex, love, and marriage. To the extent you agree with Dr. and Mrs. Ferm, pass on to your children what he tells Sue in this open letter:

> Sex should add a beautiful dimension to a person's life. It is neither cheap nor dirty. But sex is far more than the physical pleasure derived from the act itself, although that is a large part of it.
>
> We believe that sexuality is the total involvement of two people who are in love. We don't think that sex and love should be separated. We are convinced that it is the relationship of love which enriches sex— not that sex should initiate the relationship. . . .
>
> Intercourse is one of man's most intense experiences, and should ideally be shared only with the one you choose to love the most and who loves you equally.

Chaplain Ferm expressed his worry over sexual experimentation before marriage. For how long—and with how many partners— should such sex-sampling take place? He suggests to Sue that intercourse be preceded not by marriage but by engagement.

> The surest road to happiness is for this experimentation to be confined within the vow to love and cherish and honor—within the promise to marry . . . rather than the marriage ceremony. It is naive to think that the wedding night should mark a radical change in the physical intimacy between two loved ones. This abrupt switch can often promote unnecessary tensions that compound the problems of adjustment to married life.
>
> Once the promise to marry and share dreams for the future is made, a man and woman can often experience a deepening fulfullment of their

love in their sexual intimacies. Such a gradual sexual adjustment may make the early stages of married life that much more harmonious and wonderful.

In stating your moral viewpoint, absolve your children in advance if they stray from it. By so doing, you're likely to save them untold guilt. Dr. Ferm acknowledges that Sue may not follow her parents' advice:

> You may think it quite proper to engage in intercourse under circumstances beyond our suggested limits. If you do so decide, . . . we would not want you to feel guilty. . . . Do not feel ashamed that you have acted contrary to what society (often hypocritically) demands, or to what your church and parents have suggested.
>
> Society, church, and your parents are as fallible as you are in their judgments of right and wrong. You must make your decision as best you can, and then hold your head high.

Present your children with realistic, relevant advice. Teenagers often complain that their parents' arguments for preserving virginity are lame. It's not sufficient to tell your youngsters merely that you prefer they remain chaste. Observes psychiatrist Beverley T. Mead of Creighton University School of Medicine: "When parents cannot present an argument any better than 'don't do it because I said not to,' they deserve to lose their argument, and with the modern adolescent they probably will, sooner rather than later."

In talking to your youngsters, you're likely to find that many traditional arguments for maintaining virginity cut no ice with them. Sixteen-year-old Amy argues with her parents: "Why do you even mention the possibility of pregnancy in the age of the pill? It's a whole new world today. We don't have any of your generation's hang-ups about sex. As long as you have a meaningful relationship with a boy, sex is fine. After all, no one is going to get hurt!"

Your adolescents may share Amy's assumption that having sexual relationships is natural, acceptable, a form of recreation. Reports psychologist Robert C. Sorensen: "Sexual behavior to many adolescents in our study—despite the ambivalence that often goes with it— is simply a lot of fun. Physical pleasure, love, beauty—with an earthiness and humanity to go with them—*are* fun." In probing teenage attitudes about sex, Dr. Sorensen finds that over two-thirds of his sampling agree that anything two people want to do sexually is moral, as long as they both want to do it and it does not hurt either one of them. A majority of all adolescents are unwilling to agree that sexual activities are immoral because society is opposed to them.

Your daughter may similarly reject the double standard you were brought up on: that premarital virginity is desirable for girls but not boys. "My parents expect women to be virgins at marriage," more than 3 out of 4 surveyed students told Professor Eleanore Braun Luckey of the Department of Child Development and Family Relations at the University of Connecticut. Professor Luckey concludes that "parents cling to the double sex standard, in that the majority of them did not expect boys to be virgin at marriage."

With considerable justification, your daughter may reject such classic arguments for virginity as: "Nice girls don't do it," "Boys never respect girls they have sex with," and "Men want to marry virgins." Those arguments are largely untrue among your children's peers. Psychologist Robert Sorensen found in his study of adolescents that fewer than 4 in 10 younger boys and fewer than 3 in 10 older boys feel, "I wouldn't want to marry a girl who isn't a virgin." Only about 1 in 3 adolescents believe, "A girl who goes to bed with a boy before marriage will lose his respect."

Psychiatrist Richard M. Sarles of the University of Maryland School of Medicine discovered that among boys between 15 and 19 there is not a "strong requirement for female virginity." The boys agree, "I'd lose respect for a girl who has a reputation for sleeping with just anyone." But what if a girl has had sexual relations, but has *not* acquired a "reputation"? Then, finds Dr. Sarles, there's "no loss of respect for her."

If your youngsters do refrain from sexual intercourse, it is not likely to be from moral or religious conviction. In Dr. Sorensen's study, the three major reasons given for never having any sexual experiences, in the order agreed by all virgin adolescents, are: "Because I'm not ready for it," "Because I haven't met a girl/boy who I would want to have sex with," and "Because I haven't met a girl/boy who wants to have sex with me."

Psychiatrist Beverley Mead finds some adolescents are more thoughtful and mature than most of their peers. They resist opportunities for premature sexual activity for one or more of the following reasons:

- They want to avoid any worry about pregnancy, venereal disease, or possible damaged reputation.
- They believe sexual involvement creates an intensity of personal and interpersonal feelings that may be very difficult to manage.
- They don't want their behavior to reflect adversely on their families and their parents.
- They fear it might be disappointing and cause resentment.
- They don't want to be a sucker for somebody's line and don't wish to take advantage of somebody else.

But even if your youngsters are so mature and hold such strong convictions, they may still fall prey to doubts in the face of "sexual freedom." What reasonable arguments can you offer to help counteract these pressures? Here's what you can tell your children to help them resist premature sexual involvement:

"You Face Medical Risks"

Disabuse your children of the myth that the pill and other contraceptives eliminate the risk of pregnancy. For a variety of reasons, many teenagers use contraceptives inconsistently, improperly, or not at all (see Chapter 10, "Protect Them from Pregnancy"). The result: hundreds of thousands of pregnant teenagers each year.

Over a dozen venereal diseases (Chapter 9, "Diseases from Sex") pose an increasing hazard to your teenagers—VD is spreading fastest in their age range. Your youngsters may be ignorant of the possible consequences of sexually transmissible diseases, which include severe pain, permanent injury, even death. For your daughter, an especially worrisome risk is cancer of the cervix. On the basis of epidemiological studies, obstetrician-gynecologist James A. Sebastian of the University of Minnesota-Duluth School of Medicine concludes: "Intercourse before the age of 18 predisposes to cervical cancer."

"You Have the Freedom to Say No"

Remind your children that today's new freedom also means they are free *not* to do something. If it means choosing to have intercourse when that seems right, it also means choosing to remain a virgin if that's what's best now. "Privacy—and freedom—can be maintained only by disregarding the outside pressures," advises Joyce Maynard. "Freedom is choosing, and sometimes that may mean choosing not to be 'free.'"

Real independence, tell your youngsters, means growing up according to their own needs and desires, not those of other people. Urge your children not to borrow their decisions, but to make up their own minds—to resist being pressured into intercourse they are not ready for merely because it's what other people are doing. Conformism is never a good basis for personal growth, and sexual conformism is no exception.

Assure your children that anyone worthy of their affection will honor their decisions about sex. "Girls should feel that boys will respect and appreciate a girl who knows her own mind," says sociologist Lester A. Kirkendall. Indeed, the boy may be grateful rather than scornful when a girl asserts her right to maintain her virginity. "Males are also caught up in a cultural confusion about what they *ought* to ask for and what they should *expect* to receive," notes Dr. Richard F. Hettlinger, professor of religion at Kenyon College in Gambier, Ohio. "Many of them will respond with relief to a woman who is sure enough of her own sexual integrity to put the record straight."

Your son—if he chooses to remain a virgin—should have the confidence that he is free to make this choice, and that his decision will be respected. In fact, his body may make the choice for him, in a way that can prove agonizing. No male can will an erection, and tension is lethal to one. If your son yields to pressure and tries to force himself to have intercourse, he is likely to be impotent.

"*How* do I say no?" is a question your children may ask you. "A student came to me recently in distress because she didn't feel ready for intercourse but hated to hurt her male friends by refusing them," reports Dr. Hettlinger. "She found it very difficult to explain that her choice had nothing to do with her respect for the man concerned."

Eunice Kennedy Shriver, executive vice president of the Joseph P. Kennedy, Jr. Foundation, which is concerned with teenage pregnancy, visited a group in Baltimore. She observed that the girls showed no interest in human biology, infant care, the physiology of childbirth. "Then the teacher asked: 'Would you like to discuss how to say no to your boyfriend without losing his love?' All hands shot up."

Let your teenagers know that it often takes far more courage to say no than to say yes. It's the difficult confrontations that put your child's character to the severest tests. Tell your youngsters that when they say no to sexual advances, they need offer no explanations, apologies, or excuses. They have an absolute right to govern how they are going to use their bodies. Your son or daughter can say gently but firmly: "I don't want to."

Dr. Hettlinger suggests that a kind way to bow out of sexual involvement is to say, "I appreciate the offer, and I really enjoy being with you; but at this juncture I'd rather share a conversation than my bed with you."

Caution your children against getting embroiled in an argument. Arguing suggests they may be persuaded. They should likewise avoid physical skirmishes. If a boy grabs your daughter, advise her to vent an angry "*No!*" and pull away. That will probably reduce his ardor. If she plays at struggling, the physical contact may arouse the boy further. He can interpret it as a signal that she really wants more body contact than she's admitting.

Your daughter may be pressed with the line, "If you really loved me, you'd sleep with me." An apt reply: "If you really loved me, you wouldn't pressure me to do something I'm not ready for." Indeed, that line should make your daughter question the relationship. Is it as manipulative and as one-sided as the boy's statement suggests? Is he so blind to her wishes, to the ephemeral nature of adolescent relationships, to the desirable linkage between emotional commitment and sex?

Suppose she's told, "Everyone is doing it." She can respond: "Terrific! Then you won't have any problem finding someone else."

"Virginity Is Perfectly Normal"

It may seem absurd to have to assure your youngsters that there is nothing wrong with maintaining virginity through their teenage years. But virginal youngsters, especially as they enter their late teens, are likely to feel that they're deficient.

"Must I have intercourse to be considered normal?" is a question that Dr. James Toolan, a psychiatric consultant at Bennington College and Marlboro College in Vermont, is asked with increasing frequency, often by girls. Psychiatrist John Wilms of Purdue tells of Rachel, who came to the student health center complaining of fatigue and worrying that she had mononucleosis. "I've lost my appetite," she told him. "My weight has dropped. I'm depressed. I can't sleep. I'm irritable and anxious. Sometimes I take my friends' tranquilizers."

In talking to Rachel, Dr. Wilms put his finger on her major concern, which probably accounted for her array of physical symptoms. "She feels rather abnormal or even defective . . . because she is not sexually active with one or more male friends as her sorority sisters report that they are."

Your children may be influenced by the notion that virginity is a psychological hang-up. Dr. Richard Lee of Yale finds that many young people have the "knowledge" that "if you don't have intercourse, you'll go crazy." Another great fear of virgins is that they're sexually abnormal. "Girls worry that they're . . . frigid or won't have enough practice when the right time comes," reports Dr. Sol Gordon of the Institute for Family Research and Education. Your virginal children's friends may suspect them of being homosexuals. Your youngsters indeed may fear that they are.

Joyce Maynard describes the campus speculation about the girl who remains a virgin.

> Her very refusal is scrutinized. People don't talk much about who's on the pill or who's sleeping together, but there's endless speculation about who isn't. 'What's the matter with her?' they ask. Is she frigid? Lesbian? Big-brother types offer helpful advice, reasoning that if she isn't interested in them except as a friend, something must indeed be wrong with her. Her abstinence, in short, is fair game for everyone.

While your daughter may feel uneasy about her virgin state, it's your son who's likely to suffer most. Inexperienced males commonly question their own potency and masculinity.

"Virginal males are the forgotten youth of our society," observes sociologist Lester Kirkendall. In years of interviewing virgin boys, Dr. Kirkendall has found that most—even those who were virgins by choice—were uneasy about their state. These comments were typical: "You wonder a lot of times if you're really normal." "You feel as though you're losing out on something." "You feel a little embarrassed or ashamed about it sometimes."

Kirkendall finds that most virgin boys dislike being in bull sessions in which their male friends get to comparing notes on sexual experiences. In such a situation, the virgin boy is almost always on the defensive. A few will say they are sexually inexperienced if asked directly. Otherwise they try to keep that fact under cover. "Unless I have to," one boy told Kirkendall, "I say nothing about my sexual behavior."

To avoid embarrassment, your son may adopt the tactic of silent withdrawal. "I just sit back and listen," says Albert. Gil reveals this strategy: "I try to sit a little back to the outside of the group. You aren't so easily seen there, and are less likely to be asked a direct question."

Or your son may manufacture experience. "I can tell as good a story as the next one," declares Joe. Keith proclaims, "I figure that half the others are lying, so why shouldn't I get in the game. After all, you do want to be one of the group."

Your son may discover how to maintain a mysterious silence, or to smile knowingly at the "right time," thus leaving the impression that his knowledge is very comprehensive. One boy informed Kirkendall: "I've just found a faint, knowing glance or wink at the right time gets you the reputation of being 'a pretty sly fox.'"

If your son's virginity becomes known, he may have to withstand considerable ribbing. Friends may offer to fix him up, implying, "If you really have what it takes, you won't have to remain a virgin for long." Your son may experience rough treatment in his associations with older men. "This is particularly true when boys do summer work with all-male groups, for example in factories, mills, on the docks, and with road gangs," reports Dr. Kirkendall. One boy told him: "They make you feel there is something wrong if you aren't trying to see how much sex you can get." Another said: "I worked on a road crew last summer, and all I heard all summer long was, 'Why don't you try it, son? You don't know what you're missing.'"

Unless he has a close friend who has also decided on temporary chastity, your virgin son may feel he has virtually no support. Kirkendall found that the parents of the boys he talked to were generally unaware of their son's suffering. But, Kirkendall finds, your virgin son may desperately need your endorsement of his choice. Help your son find words for his decision to abstain from intercourse, advises Kirkendall. "More than anything else these boys need to understand clearly the reasons for the pattern they have chosen. They are often unable to voice any reasons, or to voice them clearly, or to defend them if they are attacked."

Your son's virginity may result from his good character. Point out that he remains a virgin out of decency and consideration. Notes Kirkendall: "Many boys remain virgins because they cling to a feeling that fair play must underlie good relationships. They feel that somehow virginity is a matter of fairness, but ordinarily they cannot make it clear just how."

If your children ask, "Is my virginity normal?", they almost certainly are unprepared for sexual involvement. Psychiatrist James Toolan advises that you help your son or daughter to realize that the "age of initial sexual experience is not nearly as crucial as psychological readiness."

Let your youngsters know in no uncertain terms that—statistically and otherwise—virginity is absolutely "normal." Young people who want to remain virgins need reassurance that "because they don't want sexual involvement they are not queer, frigid, or abnormal," comments Dr. Lee. "Those young people who aspire to remain chaste need as much encouragement that their choice is healthy and of value as those who choose sexual liberation." Also tell your children that losing virginity by no means shows that a person is now grown up. A penis in a vagina does not automatically confer adulthood to either partner.

Your children also need reassurance that they are by no means alone in their virginity. Help your youngsters see that a conspicuous group of sexually active teenagers may make it appear as if "everyone is doing it." That's simply not true. While sexual activity among teenagers has indeed increased in recent years, a very large number of teenagers refrain from intercourse, especially those of the middle class.

Point out, too, that a lot of what's proclaimed as sexual experience is actually hot air. Finds Dr. Toolan: "Youngsters of both sexes sometimes brag about their sexual experiences even though they may be virgins." Dr. James Croake, professor of marriage and family counseling at Virginia Polytechnic Institute and the State University at Blacksburg, has discovered that college girls often attempt to give their friends the impression that they were more sexually active than was actually the case. Virgins would purchase contraceptives and leave them on the dresser in their dormitory rooms.

Help your children recognize that virginity in and of itself is not the real issue. "Exploitive, self-centered, injurious use of sex as contrasted to a meaningful and dignified use is the core of the problem," comments Lester Kirkendall. "We stray from the point by concentrating on the individual's state of virginity or nonvirginity."

"It's Likely to Leave You Hurt"

Your children may be unprepared for the emotional vulnerability associated with intercourse, the most intimate of human relationships. M.I.T. psychotherapist Thomas Cottle finds that the new morality, far from being universally liberating, causes some young people "a special sort of insecurity and hurt."

Tell your adolescents that a sexual relationship will engage their emotions in unexpected ways. Teenagers rarely anticipate the feelings that sexual involvement provokes. "Everybody talks about 'recreational sex' and 'sex for kicks,'" says 18-year-old Jonathan. "But going to bed with a girl is *not* like playing a game of tennis with her."

Warn your youngsters that they're likely to be left confused by precipitous sexual activity. Observes Dr. Charles E. Millard of the Brown University School of Medicine: "The so-called liberation is not liberation at all for students, for it obviously is producing severe anxiety in them." Psychiatrist Philip Luloff of Mount Sinai Hospital in New York finds that when young people who are fearful of sex are pressured into early sexual activity "the tragedy is that they cannot handle it—either in terms of the relationships or their own desires."

Caution your youngsters against being used. Teenagers often realize afterward that their partners were interested in them more as sexual utensils than as people. Psychiatrist Warren Gadpaille observes that many adolescents pursue sexual encounters in the interest of self-discovery. "The partner is usually just a handy agent to be exploited for the purposes of proving one's desirability and finding out what it is like to have sex." The other youngster's needs are largely ignored. "Thus the partner, who may acquiesce despite being emotionally unready to cope with sexual intimacy, may be roundly misused, sometimes with resulting significant psychological damage." Dr. Gadpaille also finds that adolescents, even when they espouse sexual freedom, are often unprepared for the disturbing amount of guilt and shame they feel about engaging in intercourse.

Warn your children that when a sexually intimate relationship ends, the hurt can be painful beyond their imagining. It's a myth, says Dr. Richard Lee, that sex on a trial basis is not a commitment and therefore not upsetting when the relationship ends. "Rejection is rejection whether we call it divorce, puppy love or adolescent turmoil. In my opinion, it may hurt the adolescent even more than the adult."

Your daughter is particularly vulnerable in a sexual relationship. Girls are more likely to be hurt because they tend to invest more emotionally. Before becoming involved sexually, your daughter may convince herself she's in love. Then, expecting love in return, she may suffer piercing emotional pain. As medical director of the Planned Parenthood teen clinic in Oakland, California, Dr. Harvey W. Caplan has observed: "Many young women believe that if they engage in sexual intercourse with a man it is a sure sign of 'love' or caring on his part. The end result is usually disillusionment, emptiness, a distrust of men, or lack of sexual fulfillment."

A University of Arizona student named Jane related to investigators Kenneth and Betty Woodward: "I told myself that I was going to stay a virgin until I was married—that only bad girls did those things."

But once in college, Jane found the pressures more than she could resist. Finally, she says, "I met somebody I thought I loved enough to give up my virginity for. But the whole time we made love the TV was on. And when it was over, he just switched to another channel and lit up a joint. God, was I angry! Here I had made the ultimate sacrifice and he didn't even care. I was hoping through the whole thing that he'd say, 'I love you.'"

Writer Helen Pastore expresses vulnerability in an open letter to her 16-year-old daughter:

> Women, more than men, really do need something meaningful, hilltops of companionship as well as pinnacles of climax, affection along with technique. And women more than men can be hurt by the results of impulsive sexual generosity . . . I mean being wounded or rejected, the hurt of which is usually proportionate to the intimacy. I mean the accentuation of loneliness at the end of a precipate affair—especially when the couple is young and inexperienced.

Your daughter may be hurt because of basic differences many boys and girls have over the nature of a sexual relationship. The observations of specialists confirm the truism that a girl is likely to be seeking romance. She can express tenderness and sentiment and expects the same back. She may feel that the closeness of intercourse means a deep if not permanent relationship.

The boy, on the other hand, may be following the adolescent model of a young warrior. He may anticipate the pleasures of intercourse, and seek opportunities for it. Downplaying emotion, he is likely to regard sex as an arena of masculine achievement. He may tell a girl he loves her to increase his chances of sex with her—it's no accident that "screwing" has meanings of both sex and exploitation. She's primed to believe him. When he argues that intercourse will increase his love, this too is easy to believe. Your daughter may thus be devastated when it turns out that she trusted too easily or hoped for too much.

Emphasize to your daughter that she cannot count on a young man's discretion. She may feel betrayed by his boasting to others about their intimacies. Your daughter may give her loyalty to a boy and expect the same from him. His first loyalty, however, may be to his close friends rather than to her. Boys often regard sexual experience as evidence that they have reached manhood, and feel the need to brag to their friends about it. When they break up, the girl may find that their sexual relationship is common knowledge among his buddies. "In fact," says sociologist Lester Kirkendall, "she is likely to find these boys dating her in hopes of obtaining intercourse."

Only if a boy believes himself in love with a girl is he likely to be discreet about their sexual intimacy. A study by sociologist J.

Kenneth Davidson, Sr. of the University of Wisconsin at Eau Claire finds that only 13 percent of the boys who were in love with their first sexual partner immediately told others about the experience. By contrast, when the first intercourse was with a casual date or a pickup, the news of "getting in" was broadcast by 61 percent of the boys.

In all, early sexual intimacy is a hurtful experience for many teenage girls. Sociologist Robert Sorensen found that fully 4 in 10 adolescent girls in his study wished they had waited longer before having sexual intercourse.

But it's not only your daughter who can be hurt in a premature sexual relationship. Your son is likewise vulnerable. Dr. Elizabeth M. Whelan tells of Larry, 16, who was very hesitant about beginning a sexual relationship with Sally. She was the prettiest and most popular girl in his class, and there was no doubt that he was emotionally attached to her. But he did feel guilty about premarital sex.

Sally was pressing for an intimate sexual involvement. She repeatedly spoke of her love for him and told him "not to worry" because she had a supply of birth control pills. Larry still wasn't sure, but not wanting to displease her, or raise questions in her mind about his virility, he gave in. "After all," he thought, "she must be very much in love with me." Concludes Dr. Whelan: "When six weeks later, Sally dropped him suddenly and began dating one of his friends, Larry felt deeply wounded and betrayed."

Tell your children that genuine intimacy can only evolve slowly. If they have the emotional maturity and inner confidence to allow a relationship to progress slowly to sexual intimacy, they are less likely to be hurt and disappointed—and much more likely to choose wisely.

"It May Destroy Your Relationship"

Your teenagers may enter into a sexual relationship believing that intercourse will imbue their relationship with commitment. Actually, it often marks the beginning of the end. "During adolescence," says Dr. Richard Lee, sex "may often destroy the relationship because it places too much pressure on one or both partners." Psychiatrist Sheila Klebanow finds that when teenagers engage in intercourse before they are sufficiently mature, the relationship may be experienced "as overwhelming and . . . may be destined to fail."

If dating escalates into intercourse too quickly, your children may be unprepared for the heavy issues they need to face. Suddenly, they're concerned about venereal disease. They fear pregnancy. They worry about sexual performance. They're subject to jealousy. These extra strains may make the youngsters loathe each other.

Caution your daughter that her disappointment is likely to be especially intense if she expects that intercourse will lead to marriage. Once intercourse begins, some girls become keenly interested in getting engaged or married. They press for expressions of love and try to get the boy to commit himself. They're frequently shocked to find that boys do not share their understanding that sex is the first step of a permanent commitment. A study at a Midwestern school showed that 80 percent of the women who had intercourse hoped to marry their partner. Only 12 percent of the men had the same expectation. Unprepared for a lasting commitment, and in the face of pressure from the girl, many boys simply retreat.

Warn your daughter too that, after pressuring girls to engage in intercourse, some adolescent boys lose interest after two or three acts—and then abandon the girl. Psychiatrist Derek Miller of the University of Michigan School of Medicine explains that for the boys such intercourse "tends to be a masturbatory . . . act, often unrelated to wider loving feelings." After just a few episodes of intercourse, "the experience tends to be felt as insufficiently satisfying." The boy blames this on the girl. "Feeling bored and empty, he is then likely to move on to someone else."

True, psychiatrist Miller finds, boys may be concerned for the girl's enjoyment and may even have a loving relationship with her. Even so, they are often more interested in what the experience of sex is like. If the girl begins to press for permanence, "this is likely to frighten the young man" and he "may rapidly abandon the relationship."

Sexual relationships between teenagers are often short-lived because the boy "loses respect" for the girl. What does it mean to "lose respect?" Sociologist Lester Kirkendall finds that it's a catchall phrase reflecting a variety of feelings boys may have in sexual relationships.

Frequently, a boy has no respect for the girl to begin with, but denies this to himself in his quest for sex. "Boys are likely to feel guilty about having intercourse with girls they don't respect," notes Dr. Kirkendall. Once the novelty of sex with her wears off, the boy can admit the contempt he's felt all along. Elevating himself in his own estimation, he drops the girl.

"Losing respect" may also justify to a boy his terminating a relationship when he has lost interest in the girl, or when he feels pressured by her to make a more permanent commitment. It's never easy to end a relationship in which there has been affection, much less sexual intercourse. Observes Kirkendall: "It is especially hard for young people who lack the courage to face reality, who are unskilled in dealing with tangled emotions and who are unable to speak frankly about sex." Teenagers often end relationships by roundabout methods and face-saving lies. By telling himself a girl is unworthy of respect, a boy can feel less guilty over calling it quits.

A boy may have growing contempt for a girl he's sleeping with because of his own sexual jealousy and feelings of possessiveness. He may be tortured with the thought, "If she had sex with me, what keeps her from doing it with someone else?" His cultural bias makes him think of the girl as a "whore." Dr. Alan S. Berger of the Institute for Juvenile Research in Chicago cites a study showing that nearly half of teenage boys feel that intercourse is permissible for a woman only within marriage. Only about a fifth of the boys feel that intercourse is permissible for a woman in the absence of love.

> In sum [concludes Dr. Berger], unless the individuals involved are married, there is a very good chance that the man will lose respect for the woman who agrees to intercourse. If the couple does not have an established emotional relationship, the chances are even better that he will not respect her. If there is only a relatively casual relationship between the couple, the chances that the female will lose the man's respect if she agrees to intercourse are very good indeed.

The boy may furthermore lose respect for the girl after sex, Lester Kirkendall finds, because that's what he expected to happen: a self-fulfilling prophecy. "Losing respect" may further be how a boy describes his disappointment in the sexual relationship. What the boy may have expected to be the most satisfying of all intimacies instead has produced tensions and hard feelings. Comments Kirkendall: "Inexperienced boys especially often expect more in pleasure, thrill and excitement from sex than is possible."

Sometimes, a boy loses his respect for a girl because of lewd jests made by his friends. Kirkendall says:

> Even though a boy and girl may have respected each other, and behaved in a dignified way, boyfriends are . . . likely to see it as a

salacious, exciting lark. It becomes very difficult for the boy to maintain his feelings of dignity when close friends begin to refer to his relationship with the girl in coarse, vulgar language.

"It's Apt to Be a Bomb"

Your teenagers are likely to be disappointed by the physical aspects of a premature sexual relationship. This is especially true if they undertake intercourse to rid themselves of their "burden of virginity."

"Many young people engage in sexual activity under direct pressure to conform or from the feeling that such activity is evidence of normality," comments psychiatrist Arnold Werner of Michigan State University. "As a result, they may have unenjoyable sexual experiences without meaning, which could have been avoided if they felt freer to choose the terms of their encounter."

If your children are not ready for a mature sexual relationship, they may come away from intercourse feeling it's a hoax. Keen disappointment is possibly the most common negative reaction after first intercourse. Psychiatrist Joel Moskowitz attributes this disappointment to "lack of experience, great anxiety, or unrealistic expectations for the ecstatic moment when rockets are supposed to fire, bells ring, and trumpets blare." Some, he says, become depressed by this failing of sex "to live up to press releases." In a *Seventeen* magazine survey, 1500 girls answered questions about their first intercourse. Half the girls reported feeling worry or shame.

A good many youngsters, conditioned to expect that intercourse is ecstasy, find instead that it's uncomfortable and unsatisfying. "The first sexual experiences of both men and women are usually characterized by high anxiety, poor sexual communication, low skill, and poor contraceptive use," observes psychologist Barry McCarthy of American University. Adds Dr. Sol Gordon: "Usually the first experience of intercourse for a teenager is all wrong. The girls almost never get an orgasm, the boys are very often impotent—the experience is grim."

Dr. Robert J. Collins, who was attending physician at the Syracuse University Health Service, describes the ordeal of a girl we'll call Jan:

> She looked like every other co-ed—long, straight hair, a sweatshirt too big, and dungarees too small. And her story was a familiar one. Her friends teased her about being a virgin so she had tried "it." Now,

tearful and fearful, she described her symptoms. Examination showed only body lice—easily curable. Her reaction spoke volumes: "It sure wasn't worth it—it was no fun at the time, I've been worried ever since—and all it did was give me a dose of crabs."

Tell your children that it's a myth that successful intercourse culminating in orgasm is easy. "I explain to young people that one major difficulty with the view that sex is 'natural,' is that it overlooks the fact that enjoyable love-making usually requires mutual education," says Dr. Richard Lee. "It takes time, effort and patience to learn how to love and make love."

But time and patience are often in short supply in adolescent lovemaking. It frequently takes place between immature strangers in uncomfortable surroundings—and has to be accomplished quickly.

Your daughter is likely to fare poorly when intercourse takes place in such makeshift surroundings. Masters and Johnson found there is "little male concern for the female partner's sexual release." Obstetrician-gynecologist Dolores E. Fiedler of New York Medical College frequently finds that early intercourse for girls is unsatisfactory. For some, the first time is actually "physically traumatic." Recalls 18-year-old Mara: "It was kind of rushed, and when he put his penis in it hurt. Will it always be like that?" In the rush, Mara probably did not have adequate time to become sexually aroused and develop sufficient lubrication and elongation of the vagina to comfortably accommodate the penis. Tension might also have contributed to her failure to lubricate.

Similarly, psychiatrist John Wilms tells of a young woman who was so anxious during her first intercourse "that she could not adequately relax or lubricate to allow penetration." She was especially wounded when her equally inexperienced partner cruelly announced that she was frigid.

From interviews with women in varying age groups, Dr. Leah Cahan Schaefer, a New York psychologist, discovered that today's supposedly liberated young woman often has as much anxiety about her initial intercourse and finds just as little pleasure in it as her purportedly uptight sister of the previous generation. Although a few young women did enjoy their first intercourse and one professed to have had an orgasm, most reported much the same reaction as the older women. "It was painful, and I had been told that sex was pleasurable," one young woman complained. "If I hadn't been told. this, I don't think I ever would have tried it again." Another recalled that "I expected it to be pleasurable, but it was nothing, and I didn't like it. I just didn't *feel* good." Still another said, "It wasn't painful like I expected, but the greatest pleasure I got . . . was from the idea that I had done it."

For your son, a precipitous first intercourse may be a physical disaster. Psychologist Barry McCarthy reports that 1 out of 5 males are unsuccessful in their first intercourse, "generally because they fail to achieve or maintain an erection or because they ejaculate before the penis enters the vagina."

Typically, a young man compounds the problem by keeping it secret, or indeed by lying about his sexual prowess. "Meanwhile," says Dr. McCarthy, "he is deathly afraid of his 'failure' being revealed and even more anxious to 'prove' himself at his next intercourse, which causes a great deal of performance anxiety."

Psychiatrist Robert L. Arnstein of Yale University points out that while your son is extremely sensitive to sexual stimuli and easily aroused, he's also aware that the act of intercourse depends on his maintaining an erection. He may feel, too, that as a male he must take the initiative. This, says Dr. Arnstein, "increases his sense of pressure and perhaps his anxiety." Further, the tension of the girl may well contribute to his difficulty. Her anxiety may result in a failure to lubricate or in vaginal spasms that make penetration difficult, convincing your son that something is wrong with him.

He may be under additional pressure at first intercourse because of a change in the attitudes about female sexuality. The realization that women enjoy sex may increase his anxiety about his ability to perform in a way that also pleases the girl. Thus, it's no wonder that so many boys have difficulty the first time. But if the young man ejaculates prematurely, fails to penetrate, or loses his erection, "whatever anxieties existed initially will be intensified by his feeling of failure," remarks Dr. Arnstein. "The possibility of repeated failure may make another try very difficult."

"It May Worsen Your Problems"

Caution your teenagers that their hurt and disappointment may be keenest if they engage in intercourse in an attempt to solve personal difficulties. "Sex in the early teenager may be an attempt to resolve emotional problems," warns psychiatrist Alfred Auerback of the University of California School of Medicine. But, he warns, "sex in itself rarely resolves . . . problems." Indeed, it can exacerbate them.

Your children may expect not just physical gratification but a sense of self-validation, of security and completeness. Let them know that this is more than the mere act of sexual intercourse can deliver. "Young people are expecting too much too soon from sexual union," observes gynecologist Elaine Pierson of the University of Pennsylvania's student health clinic. Psychotherapist Thomas Cottle notes a "feeling that you can be reborn, if just by being sexually intimate with a person." In Cottle's opinion, there is danger in adolescents' magical notion that sex can solve personal and social problems.

If your youngsters are away from home for the first time, they may imagine that sex can relieve their loneliness and longing for the closeness of family life. Some youngsters seek popularity through sexual activity. "There's a girl in school who says she has sex because she loves it, that with the new sexual revolution that's what you're supposed to do," a high school junior told investigator Alice Lake. "She does it with boys two years older—I think it's just to impress them, to make friends. In a way I feel sorry for her. People use her. They don't really like her."

Using sex to gain companionship often backfires. Sylvia, a college freshman, told a counselor, "Every time a guy starts showing interest in me, I go to bed with him. Then I end up not liking either him or myself." Lacking self-confidence, she had started having intercourse at 15 as a technique to snare and hold a boy. "Now when I want only to be friends, I don't know any other way to relate."

Urge your youngsters to prove their independence from you in ways other than becoming involved sexually. Often angry teenagers seek out rebellious members of the opposite sex. By having intercourse, they punish their parents. The more sexually restrictive you are, the more likely is this maneuver to be used against you.

"Parents who are uneasy, anxious, and threatened when confronted with sexual matters are the most vulnerable to the potent weapon of sexual activity," report pediatrician Michael W. Cohen of the University of Arizona Medical Center and psychiatrist Stanford B. Friedman of the University of Maryland School of Medicine. "In a real sense," they say, "it is the parents' insistence on inhibition of sexual activity which makes the behavior so valuable as a rebellious weapon."

Warn your youngsters that when sexual behavior is motivated by nonsexual needs, it not only fails to resolve their conflicts, but it is "rarely physically gratifying," according to Drs. Cohen and Friedman. Such sexual activity is "more likely to result in social, psychological and medical complications." Further, trying to resolve nonsexual conflicts by means of sexual activity is generally "detrimental to the development of true intimate interpersonal relationships in adolescents and young adults."

Your child's emotional reaction to first intercourse may be severe if the act was performed out of negative feelings like anger or jealousy. Erica, 17, was extremely put out when her boyfriend George decided to spend the weekend fishing with his father and canceled plans with her. To punish George, she called up an old boyfriend and had her first intercourse with him. But Erica was shocked to find that she'd actually punished herself instead. For she was distraught afterward, and required weeks of psychotherapy to help alleviate her shame and guilt.

Let your children know that even when they believe they're fully prepared emotionally for intercourse, they may have unexpected feelings afterward. Even on college campuses where sex is relaxed, says sociologist William Simon, "kids still experience losing their virginity as an identity crisis. A nonvirgin is something they did not expect to be."

Psychiatrist Joel Moskowitz finds that some young people feel confused and bewildered about their first intercourse. Some have feelings of remorse. Notes psychiatrist Arnold Werner: "Following intercourse, a small number of people panic. They are flooded with fears of pregnancy, venereal disease, adequacy of the size or shape of their genitalia or other body parts."

Dr. Warren B. Miller, of the American Institutes for Research in Palo Alto, California, reports that many of the young women in a study he conducted reported changed images of themselves associated with feelings of guilt, shame, and embarrassment. The guilt feelings which often accompany premature sexual relationships may provoke unhealthy attitudes about sexuality, possibly interfering with the enjoyment of sex later in life.

"Early teenage sex creates anxiety, guilt, and performance fears for both girls and boys," remarks psychiatrist Alfred Auerback. "If the girl experiences undue pain, severe coercion or psychological trauma, she may have negative feelings which continue into adult life." Boys often worry about their sexual performance. Their failure may establish a pattern of anticipating failure, with problems that continue into adulthood.

Dr. Auerback finds that the earlier the teenage sex, the more likely it is to give rise to problems. "Particularly disharmonious relationships, pregnancy or venereal disease can result in negative feelings or even distaste for the opposite sex which remains present in the adult."

Your teenagers may suffer a double-barreled problem: they feel bad about having sex, and then worry about their reaction. Psychologist Leah Cahan Schaefer finds this is especially true of teenage girls. They come under new societal pressure to experience and enjoy sex at an early age. While they are no longer *supposed* to feel guilty, they often do—and then feel guilty about feeling guilty.

"It May Stunt Your Emotional Growth"

When 16-year-old Lara became sexually involved with Erik, her life changed dramatically. She dated no one else. Her girl friends soon stopped calling, since Lara no longer had any time to spend with them. Nor did she have any time for her family. All her time—and all her emotions—were spent on Erik.

Like Lara and Erik, most boys and girls entering into a serious sexual relationship lose sight of others around them in their intense involvement. This sense of exclusiveness can have an adverse effect on the emotional and social development of both boy and girl. New York psychiatrist Samuel Kaufman feels that one real tragedy of the sexual revolution is that it robs young people of their opportunity for psychological and social growth. This may be particularly true for your daughter. "A girl who enters into a serious relationship with a boy very early in her life may find out later that her individuality was thwarted. She became part of him, and failed to develop her own interests, her sense of independent identity."

Premature sexual experimentation may also cause your youngsters future problems in forming attachments. "No one knows what effect sex, precociously experienced, will have on the immature mind," says Dr. Mary Calderone, executive director of SIECUS. "Sex experience before confidentiality, empathy, and trust have been established can hinder and may destroy the possibility of a solid permanent relationship."

Dr. Richard Lee agrees that youngsters who have early casual sex may have "major difficulties in establishing intimate relationships. For them, sex is a substitute for intimacy."

This impersonal attitude can pervade your youngsters' relationships in adult life. Dr. Frances K. Harding of the Ohio State University College of Medicine warns that the young person who engages in free sex "cannot expect his eventual marriage to be the best and most enduring of all possible relationships, if previously his relationships . . . have been exclusively physical and transient."

"Here's How to Tell if You're Ready"

Ideally, advises psychiatrist Frederick W. Coons of Indiana University, your children are emotionally ready for a sexual relationship when:

- They can relate to you as one adult to another.
- They are comfortable with their sexual identity.
- They have a system of values.
- They can establish true intimacy with a person outside their family.

How close is your youngster to satisfying all these criteria? Here are some questions and comments you can put to your children to help them sort out their feelings:

"How necessary is sexual intercourse for the relationship?" Sure, it may be desirable. But remind your children that it's possible to express love for another person without engaging in intercourse. "I spend a lot of time helping young people discriminate between desirability and necessity," remarks Dr. Richard Lee. If your youngster is seeking mainly human warmth and friendship, sex may prove a hindrance rather than a help.

"Are you ready to face the consequences?" Ask your children if they can imagine dealing with venereal disease or making a decision about an unwanted pregnancy. Check that they know where to get medical and psychological help.

"Can you jointly decide on birth control?" If your teenager and a potential sex partner aren't open enough to discuss contraception—and mature enough to share responsibility for it—they're not ready for sex.

"Are you afraid of losing the other person?" Ascertain if your teenager is considering intercourse to hold on to the partner. Tell your teenager that if a relationship has begun to deteriorate, sex is not likely to rescue it—in fact, may hasten its demise. Also, if either partner is jealous, sex is likely to aggravate their problems.

"Could you handle a breakup afterward?" Your children may have a fantasy that a sexual relationship will be mutually binding forever. By asking them to anticipate the emotions they might have if the relationship ended, you may help them put it in perspective.

"Is there anything about the other person you mistrust or disrespect?" Such feelings bode ill for long-lasting sexual intimacy. Observes obstetrician-gynecologist Dolores Fiedler: "If partners have established a trusting and open relationship, the reaction will tend to be more meaningful and gratifying than one in which partners know little of each other's emotional or psychological needs."

"Do you feel in any way pressured?" Be sure your youngsters are alert to the danger of being exploited. Are they planning to engage in intercourse because this is what *they* want to do? Or what the other person wants? Young people often aren't aware that they have a right not to be used.

"What do you expect physically?" If your teenagers are anticipating that the earth will move every time they have intercourse, they're investing too much in the bodily aspect of the act and are doomed to disappointment.

"What do you hope to get out of it?" Ask your children if they want intercourse to prove they're hot stuff. Or adults. Or independent. Sex used for such ends usually only worsens their doubts and conflicts.

"Will you feel guilty?" If intercourse is greatly at variance with either partner's moral precepts, the ensuing guilt might poison the relationship.

"Will petting to orgasm suffice?" Petting and all type of mutual masturbation "are perfectly normal modes of behavior that can and will satisfy sexual urges and that at the same time do not carry with them some of the same problems that are found resulting from sexual intercourse," contends psychologist James Leslie McCary of the University of Houston.

Tell your children that many other professionals are coming to the same conclusion: Mutual petting to orgasm should be considered a mature expression of sexuality—not a make-do substitute for the "real thing." "Most adolescents are giving themselves little time for beginning sexual activities and move directly to sexual intercourse," comments psychologist Robert C. Sorensen. "One reason for this may be that in our society sexual intercourse is widely considered the only valid expression of sexual love."

This notion largely derives from Freud's assertion that the only mature form of female sexuality is the so-called vaginal orgasm. Freud was all wet. Says Dr. Richard Hettlinger: "The Freudian idea that masturbation or petting are infantile and that only a penis-induced orgasm is mature deserves to be shown up for the sexist myth that it is."

Those who recommend petting to orgasm point out its numerous advantages over intercourse. Perhaps foremost, it virtually eliminates the two major medical problems of teenage intercourse: venereal disease and pregnancy. Further, concentrating on noncoital forms of lovemaking is likely to improve the quality of the lovemaking. Observes Dr. Eleanor Hamilton, director of the Hamilton School in Sheffield, Maine: "Boys would grow up to be better lovers if they weren't so brainwashed to think that all you have to do 'is put it in.' It is important for young people to realize how fulfilled one can be through using manual stimulation."

Dr. Robert Sorensen, from his survey of adolescents, has come to the conclusion that society should encourage sexual activity short of intercourse for teenagers. A major advantage, he says, is that it "permits one to realize the extent to which one's own sexual satisfaction can be obtained. Passé though it may be, sexual petting is a great initial sexual learning experience compared with intercourse."

Chapter 7

For Enjoyment of Intercourse

Impart these hints for sexual pleasure—and remedies for premature ejaculation, impotence, and orgasmic dysfunction.

NO MATTER HOW parents urge youngsters not to have sex prematurely, some are going to. Moreover, by the time your children are college age, you may feel they have gone through a rite of passage, and are ready for a complete sexual relationship.

But then your children are likely to be disappointed with intercourse. Achingly so, even long after they grow up. Masters and Johnson estimate that 50 percent of all marriages in this country are beset with some form of sexual inadequacy, ranging from serious dysfunctions to lesser complaints such as unequal levels of response.

This sadness over sex seems especially to afflict young people. Whether or not your children have yet had intercourse they may be victims of a fallacy: that sexual pleasure comes automatically. Dr. Richard V. Lee of the Yale University School of Medicine quotes the tenets of a "new ideology" of adolescent sexuality: "Sex is good and good sex means orgasm and anybody can." There is among youngsters a widespread myth of easy sexual prowess. In this mythology, says Dr. Lee, being normal and healthy means being sexy, aroused, and able to have an orgasm. "Sex has become a duty; orgasm a merit badge. Neither are regarded as a pleasure or a luxury to be enjoyed, but rather as a necessity and an obligation."

HINTS FOR SEXUAL HAPPINESS

Young men and women who experience intercourse often feel ashamed and incompetent because they don't really find sex much fun. "A great many young people who come into the office these days are definitely doing it more and enjoying it less," reports Arizona psychiatrist Donald Holmes. Sociologists John Gagnon and William Simon suspect that this is because sexual puritanism has been replaced by sexual utopianism. "The kid who worries that he has debased himself is replaced by the kid who worries that he isn't making sex a spectacular event."

Psychiatrist Philip Luloff of Mount Sinai Hospital has talked with hundreds of teenagers in his capacity as psychiatric supervisor of The Door, an adolescent health care facility in New York City. Many, he reports, "feel inadequate sexually: young women because they think they are not having orgasms; young men because they are not performing as they think they should . . . as if they were machines."

Dr. Luloff believes that many teenagers' feelings of sexual inadequacy stem from their "being pushed into having sex before they are ready for it." Furthermore, he says, while expectations are very great, so is misinformation.

Thus your youngsters may not get nearly as much pleasure out of intercourse as they might. Correct information and advice will be of great value to them. You can offer these hints for enjoying intercourse more:

Communicate. This is the cardinal rule of sexual enjoyment. Lovers are not mindreaders. They need to be told—preferably in words, perhaps in gestures—just what their partners find pleasing: what sort of fondling and stroking they prefer, what sort of pressure and rhythm is best at a particular time. Advises psychiatrist John L. Schimel of New York University-Bellevue Medical Center and the William Alanson White Institute of Psychiatry, Psychoanalysis and Psychology: "If a couple is having difficulties they can help themselves by comparing with each other what actually happens to them in sex, what they prefer, what they appreciate, and what disappoints them."

Psychologist Wardell B. Pomeroy believes that couples should also communicate during the act itself. "If they would just give vent to their feelings and express their pleasure, each partner would realize that the efforts are worthwhile."

It's a myth, says Dr. Pomeroy, that feelings of intimacy are disrupted if partners talk during intercourse. On the contrary, he says, "it seems to me to be difficult to gauge the depth of feelings without discussing them." Dr. Pomeroy deplores that "much of sex in America is performed in a sort of deadly silence."

Encourage your children to ask, "What would you like?"—and then comply. By doing precisely what's wished, they will not only provide greater satisfaction for their partners, but will also derive more pleasure for themselves. Sexual arousal is highly reciprocal. Each partner's body responds to the other's level of stimulation. Masters and Johnson call this the "give to get" cycle. Through a process of giving and getting, both partners intensify their response.

Take your time. Your children are much less likely to experience physical problems if they advance slowly toward intercourse. Comments psychiatrist Arnold Werner of Michigan State University: "Problems occur much less frequently among those who have had prior experience with leisurely sexual experience and have engaged in other sexual acts leading to orgasm."

Likewise, advise your youngsters to try to arrange ample time for leisurely lovemaking. Hasty and surreptitious intercourse is apt to be unrewarding.

Treat it as fun, not a performance. "Since we discuss sex more openly, there is more pressure on individuals to become better sexual performers," says psychologist Hugh Pates of the University of California at San Diego Sex Clinic. "It has become somewhat of a competitive activity, and I think that students are perhaps feeling some of the strain of that competition."

Encourage your children to think of the range of sexual activity as a physical expression of the affection they feel for someone, or at least as the exchange of physical pleasure. It need not be something they should feel obliged to do well, like writing a term paper.

Penetration is but one part of lovemaking. Remind your children that lovemaking is just that: the physical expression of close, intense feeling. It includes all aspects of the shared joyful experience: hugging, kissing, fondling, other sorts of pleasuring—as well as the actual physical insertion of intercourse. Most teenagers concentrate on merely the intromission (genital connection) and the orgasm that is presumed to follow it. This is often self-defeating, for it puts too much emphasis on the supposed goal, and not enough on the process.

Your children are likely to be more relaxed and enjoy sex more if they regard sex as an emotional and whole-body experience, not just a penis in a vagina. Encourage them to consider intercourse the sum total of the pleasure they give and receive.

Urge them to look beyond the widespread misunderstanding of "foreplay." Most teenagers take the term literally. They infer that all the other stages of lovemaking are but preliminaries leading to intromission, supposedly the main event. In fact, for girls especially, sex play is often more productive of orgasm than is penetration. Indeed, the penis in the vagina may be merely one step in helping them become aroused.

Experiment freely. "The concept of sexual 'normality' is utterly meaningless," declares psychologist Wardell Pomeroy. Tell your children that any expression of sexuality that they and their partners willingly share in and enjoy without physical harm is fine.

Experimenting with different techniques and positions also allows them to discover which are preferable in which circumstances. "There is no limit to the number of positions that can be used in intercourse," adds Dr. Pomeroy—it's nonsense that the only "natural" position for intercourse is with the man on top. "Depending on the physical size, age, and needs of the couple, variations on the six basic positions are infinite." These basic positions are: male superior (male on top), female superior, sitting, standing, lateral (side-supported), and penetration from the rear. Permutations on them are unlimited.

While the male on top is probably the most commonly used position, others have many advantages. The female on top allows the woman greater freedom of movement and frees the male's hands for caressing. The lateral position makes it possible for each to move easily. This position may be particularly suitable if there is a great size difference between the partners.

These positions are merely points on a continuum. Encourage your youngsters to move about and experiment. The determinant is what provides most pleasure.

Quality varies. Your youngsters may approach intercourse with unrealistic expectations, and afterward feel like sexual failures. Your daughter may believe that she should have intoxicating orgasms every time. Your son may expect to be in rapture. They are likely to be disappointed and self-doubting if an experience is merely so-so or worse.

Reassure your children that human performance in any area tends to vary from time to time, and nowhere is this more true than in sex. They can expect their sexual experience to vary according to their mood, the time of day, their feelings about their partners, their health, the particular circumstances, and many other factors.

You can also reassure your children that disastrous first experiences do not mean that they are sexually deficient or abnormal. Better sexual experiences will come with practice, and with a partner they especially care for.

Forget simultaneous orgasms. If they happen by accident, wonderful. Far from being a sign of superior sexual achievement, the effort to "come together" can ruin sex.

Striving to coordinate such basically involuntary responses causes the partners to observe themselves mentally, rather than immerse themselves in the pleasures of lovemaking. Masters and Johnson warn against assuming such a "spectator role." They've found it can lead to impotence and orgasmic dysfunction.

Virgin girls may need to stretch their hymens. During first intercourse, a girl may experience pain due to the tearing or stretching of her hymen (maidenhead), a membrane that partially covers the vaginal opening.

Such discomfort may be avoided if a girl uses tampons when she starts menstruating. Reports obstetrician-gynecologist John W. Huffman of Northwestern University Medical school: "Since adolescents have been using vaginal tampons, the cases of 'honeymoon dyspareunia' [painful first intercourse] I have seen have been sharply reduced." By using tampons for a few years, a girl will probably dilate her vaginal opening to a diameter that, says Dr. Huffman, "permits relatively easy intromission of the average-size erect penis."

Your daughter may wish to visit a physician before her first intercourse to have her hymen stretched, especially if she's fearful of the pain and likely to be tense. When obstetrician-gynecologist George F. Melody of the University of California School of Medicine in San Francisco sees a young woman anxious about the possible pain of first intercourse, he often dilates her vaginal opening under local anesthesia until it will accommodate two fingers. Occasionally, he recommends that she do the stretching herself with her fingers. He advises her to pay "special attention to exerting pressure along the [rear] vaginal wall, several times a week, preferably while in the bathtub." Office surgery, a hymenectomy, is generally needed only if the hymen is unusually tough, or if it is so large that it covers too much of the vaginal opening.

By no means is hymenal pain inevitable on first intercourse. Many girls rupture or stretch their hymens without being aware of it, from masturbating, accidents, play. Other girls have small or flexible hymens, posing no barrier to a penis. Obstetrician-gynecologist Albert Altchek of the Mount Sinai School of Medicine sees many children and young girls who have not had intercourse. "Examination shows that many (perhaps 50 percent) would have relatively easy penetration, especially if there were to be adequate local secretion or local use of surgical lubricating jelly."

Suggest to your daughter that if she feels tense or insufficiently aroused, she can ease insertion with a water-soluble lubricant like Ortho-Gynol contraceptive jelly, K-Y, or Lubrifax spread on her partner's penis. If she is particularly anxious during her first inter-course, tension may cause vaginal spasm, making penetration difficult and the attempt painful. Physical abnormalities may make penetration impossible. In such a case, she should consult a doctor.

RELIEVING SEXUAL DYSFUNCTIONS

Some young people suffer from specific sexual difficulties: premature ejaculation, impotence, difficulty in reaching orgasm. "Sexual dysfunctions in all diagnostic categories are common in the early sexual experiences of undergraduates," reports psychiatrist Raymond Babineau of the University of Rochester School of Medicine. This, he says, is not surprising given young people's high expectations and lack of experience. "Sexual functioning with a partner is at least as complicated as playing a musical duet or a fine game of tennis."

Here is what you can advise your children about the main sexual dysfunctions they may experience themselves or encounter in a partner:

Premature Ejaculation: Boys' Major Problem

Among adolescent boys, premature ejaculation is the most common sexual dysfunction. It involves the young man's reaching his climax too soon, either before penetration or within a minute or so thereafter. It is deemed a chronic problem if he cannot maintain control long enough to satisfy his partner at least half the time.

Young women commonly complain they feel used and frustrated. Both partners miss out on the pleasures of slow, leisurely sex. You can tell your youngsters:

It's a conditioned response. Most cases of premature ejaculation arise from the male's being introduced to sex in a way that emphasizes his ejaculation rather than satisfying his partner.

He may thus become conditioned to ejaculating rapidly. This physical response develops outside his conscious control, and he automatically ejaculates very soon after beginning sex play or achieving insertion.

A young man may develop such a habit of "coming quickly" if he starts by having intercourse in situations that call for a hurried response: in the back seats of cars, in living rooms with parents nearby, in dorm rooms fearing the arrival of roommates. Under such pressures he is likely to be concerned with attaining sexual release as soon as he can, with little time to worry about meeting the sexual needs of his partner.

Similar conditioning may result from a form of heavy petting often called "humping." The couple simulates intercourse through their clothes, with no actual penetration. This too is generally a one-sided activity, with the young man's focus on his ejaculation.

Using withdrawal as a birth control technique can make a young man susceptible to premature ejaculation. Both partners may be preoccupied with his pulling out in time. He may withdraw and ejaculate after a few thrusts of the pelvis, and his partner's sexual needs may be left unfulfilled.

Early encounters with prostitutes lie behind many cases of premature ejaculation. If the prostitute wants to turn as many tricks as possible, she may encourage the young man to hurry—rewarding him with smiles and compliments if he finishes in record time. Thereby a habit can be launched.

Some youngsters don't consider ejaculating quickly a problem. Indeed, a teenage boy whose sexual experience consists of masturbation and "circle jerks"—a masturbating competition in which the one to ejaculate first is the winner—may consider fast intercourse a proof of prowess. His inexperienced girl friend may have no greater expectation than that he'll enter her quickly and as quickly ejaculate.

For many young couples, though, the problem dominates—and sometimes defeats—the relationship. One college student, who described himself as a shy person, asked the help of psychiatrist Arnold Werner of Michigan State University in managing a situation that had developed in his first close relationship with a girl. The young man was unable to get an adequate enough erection to achieve penetration, or he ejaculated before entry. His girl friend, understanding at first, was becoming less tolerant, and he felt that the relationship was threatened. A few weeks later, the young man told Dr. Werner that the relationship was over.

If your son, or your daughter's partner, suffers from premature ejaculation, the problem may disappear spontaneously. With greater sexual experience, some young men find themselves learning new patterns of sexual response. Especially if their girl friends encourage delayed ejaculation, they become able to provide greater gratification for their partners and themselves.

For many boys, however, premature ejaculation becomes a chronic problem. The possibility of ejaculating prematurely makes them anxious, which only increases its likelihood. Some young men begin avoiding opportunities for intercourse rather than risk embarrassment.

The squeeze technique can cure it. Premature ejaculation of even many years' duration is often curable. It is almost completely reversible through the "squeeze technique," developed by urologist James H. Semans of the Duke University School of Medicine.

The technique assumes a loving relationship of some depth. It requires a good deal of time, cooperation, and understanding. A critical, exasperated, or impatient partner only aggravates the condition.

Here's how the squeeze technique works: Just before he has an urge to ejaculate, his partner presses his frenulum, the sensitive spot at the bottom edge of the crown of his penis. She firmly applies her thumb for three or four seconds. She holds the opposite side of the crown with her fingers.

The goal of the squeeze technique is to keep him sexually excited at a level short of ejaculation. If he's uncircumcized, his frenulum can usually be located with a little practice. If she worries about how hard she can safely press, he can show her by placing his fingers over hers.

He should expect to lose 10 to 50 percent of his erection after the squeeze is applied, but it's generally soon regained. Over several weeks, he's likely to become more and more able to bring his urge to ejaculate under his own control.

Caution your children to avoid nonprescription drugs like anesthetic creams and jellies, which are supposed to prolong intercourse by reducing penis sensitivity. They are a waste of money, and can trigger a drug allergy.

Masturbating before intercourse rarely delays ejaculation. Nor does wearing two condoms. Nor do attempts at distraction: counting backward from one hundred, thinking about other things. Physical distractions, like pinching or hair pulling, work no better.

Only as a last resort will physicians prescribe tricyclic antidepressants such as Tofranil or Tryptizol. Minute doses can slow down ejaculation without impairing erection.

A small number of teenage boys suffer from rarer ejaculatory problems—such as ejaculatory incompetence—requiring professional help. One 19-year-old told psychiatrist Arnold Werner: "I cannot ejaculate willfully. The only time I ejaculate is during sleep in the form of a wet dream. This bothers me greatly as I am unable to masturbate and cannot come, even when my girlfriend has oral sex with me."

Impotence: Inevitable on Occasion

Mike, 19, was up all Thursday night studying for a difficult exam. On Friday, he took the test, went through the rest of his classes, worked on a paper in the late afternoon, then met his girl friend Elena for dinner. At ten that night, in bed with her, Mike was mortified when he couldn't get an erection.

Tell your children that every man experiences times he's unable to have an erection. If he attempts sexual intercourse on such occasions he's certain to be impotent.

Contrary to the myth of the ever-ready male, such episodes of "transient" or "acute" impotence are normal—nay, virtually inevitable. But if the man becomes anxious about the supposed failure, emotional stress is likely to build up, and the impotence may become chronic.

Much of the anxiety couples suffer in respect to impotence stems from what Masters and Johnson call "phallic fallacies." They observe: "The functioning role of the penis is as well established as that of any other organ of the body. Ironically, there is no organ about which more misinformation has been perpetrated."

When a teenage boy suffers from impotence, it may be devastating. Psychotherapist Thomas J. Cottle of M.I.T. relates this conversation with an anguished 18-year-old we'll call Roger.

"I've met a girl that I guess I love," Roger told Dr. Cottle.

"So, great."

"Not so easy," Roger said. "She's great, I'm great with her, but sex isn't so great. . . . I can't make it. I can't perform."

"You try?"

"I can't do it. . . . I'm just a flop."

"Do you talk about it?"

"You got anything in mind that we should talk about other than that? What do you think we do all night if we can't make it? We talk about it. Seems all I do is talk."

They sat in silence, Dr. Cottle recalls. Roger's eyes moistened with tears.

"It's pitiful," Roger said. "It's all so pitiful. I feel dead inside. Lifeless, burdened, desperate."

You'll help your youngsters if you pass on this information:

Erections are fragile. Erections are extremely fragile, and myriad factors can interfere with one. Tell your children that often the cause of transient impotence suggests its cure. Here are the major reasons a man may not be able to have an erection:

He's too tired. Fatigue such as Mike suffered—from working too long or hard—is one of the commonest causes of impotence. A good night's sleep can produce a "cure."

He's feeling pressured. Pressures of time or place, common in adolescent lovemaking, can result in his failure to achieve an erection. Someone in the next room, a flapping window shade, fear of pregnancy, the need to finish some schoolwork—any such distraction can be fatal to an erection.

He's feeling guilty. A youngster who's uncomfortable about his sexual activity may find that his body betrays his real feelings.

Unconsciously, some teenagers still regard themselves as little boys. Psychiatrist Robert N. Rutherford of the University of Washington believes the typical such male comes from a household dominated by a mother who controlled him by threatening to withdraw her love if he wasn't a "good" boy. Among the evils of life she conveyed to him was sex.

He's trying too hard. Your teenager's culture makes sexual prowess essential to the self-esteem of most young men. The villain in many cases of impotence is a mythic great lover whom psychiatrist Harvey Resnik and his cotherapist-wife Audrey of Chevy Chase, Maryland, call "Super Stud." This fantasy bedroom athlete—with his push-button erection, monumental staying power and *Kama Sutra* know-how—is what many young men and women expect the male to be.

Alas, though he has as little relation to real-life lovemaking as Batman has to crime-fighting, Super Stud sets the standard for much of America's sex life. Psychiatrist John Schimel finds that many young men suffer from self-imposed pressure to be sexual robots, programmed for "getting an erection at a proper time, going through the amount of foreplay, penetrating and being able to perform in that capacity for a certain period of time, having orgasm, promoting his partner's orgasm, and then engaging in lively, loving conversation afterward."

A young man may also be unaware that erections often swell and subside several times during a session of lovemaking. If he wilts, he may panic and become impotent. Or he may hurry his lovemaking so as not to lose his erection, and leave his partner unsatisfied.

Such unrealistic expectations can place tremendous pressure on a young man. "Impotence is very commonly caused by fear of failure and anxiety over performing," notes Dr. Wardell Pomeroy. "Pressures over *having* to achieve an erection need to be eliminated first. The act of 'willing' oneself to get or maintain an erection is the very pressure that must be avoided."

Adds obstetrician-gynecologist Armando DeMoya of Georgetown

University and George Washington University: "No man can will an erection, and the very attempt breeds failure." The young man then may enter a vicious circle, says urologist Sheldon L. Fellman of the University of Michigan Medical School: "Each failure to perform weakens his confidence and makes his next attempt all the more difficult. Finally, he ends up convincing himself that he no longer has his sexual powers."

Psychiatrist John Reckless of Duke University has seen this sequence of events lead to chronic impotence: For one reason or another a man is unable to achieve an erection. His partner may fear, "It's my fault. I'm unattractive." He may worry, "I'm failing her. I'm losing my manhood."

Under such pressures they try again, and the emotional stress renders him impotent. Dr. Reckless has found that two or three such episodes within seventy-two hours can be so traumatic that potency thereafter is defeated by anxiety.

He's drunk too much. Many adolescents try to overcome inhibition by drinking to loosen up. But alcohol can result in impotence.

Even minimal drinkers can be impotent. Dr. Sallie S. Schumacher, program director of the sex clinic at the Long Island (N.Y.) Jewish Medical Center, finds that as little as two drinks can block an erection. That one drink too many explains why many couples, after returning from a party, are disappointed when they try to make love.

He feels inadequate. General feelings of inadequacy at school or work or in personal relationships can leave a young man feeling worthless and unable to perform sexually.

Dr. Daniel L. Araoz of the New York Family Counselors Institute found that men frequently feel threatened by women during intercourse. "The male, identifying symbolically with his penis, can experience the anxiety of being swallowed, assimilated, annihilated by the woman." This great sense of vulnerability can render him impotent.

He's overeaten. After a heavy meal, blood rushes to the stomach, liver, and intestines. The increased volume of blood elsewhere in the body may make it difficult to sustain an erection. Dr. John Reckless points out that overweight and poor physical condition impair sexual performance. "Active sexual intercourse requires a vigorous body."

He's depressed. He may not be aware of an underlying mental depression, but it may account for his loss of interest in sex and his erection problems.

Other signs pointing to mental depression: Impaired energy. Difficulty getting to sleep or getting up. Forgetfulness. Bouts of agitated behavior. "Fortunately," says psychiatrist John Reckless, "the proper antidepressant can usually clear up impotence from this cause."

He's ill. Any debilitating acute illness—influenza, for example—can render the anatomy incapable of intercourse until recovery is complete. Chronic diseases—especially diabetes, Addison's disease, hypothyroidism—may have impotence as a symptom.

He's blocked by drugs. Marijuana has a variable effect on erections, and may cause impotence or difficulty in ejaculating. Many tranquilizers—Librium, Valium, Equanil, Miltown—and antidepressants (Tofranil, Parnate, Marplan) often cause impotence. Amphetamines, used in diet and pep pills, can produce impotence and general loss of interest in sex.

Some drugs for lowering high blood pressure commonly have impotence as a side effect. Merely switching to another medication for the same condition may restore some men's potency.

He harbors resentments. A young man may dislike his partner, but be unwilling or unable to express this verbally. He may find that his distaste is expressed through his body. Impotence may also result from unconscious hostility toward women in general.

Avoid Quackery

Urge your children to beware of quack "cures." The marketplace is full of potency frauds.

All advertised drugs are junk, despite their suggestive brand names. In a fraud order against a product called Stagg Bullets, the Post Office Department commented, "The word sex is not used, but one does not need a magnifying glass to see it." Other supposed medications that have come under attack for mail fraud bear names like Viri-tabs, Instant Erection, Hard-on Powder, and Marvel.

The Vib-Erect Company was found guilty of nine counts of mail fraud for promoting the sale of a device represented as helpful for impotence. It was nothing more than a battery-operated facial massager, selling at drugstores for $1.35. The promoter sold them for $25 each and grossed $30,000 in a few months.

Nor has any food any value as a sexual stimulator. Olives, ginseng, plover's eggs, oysters, radishes, mangoes, and countless other edibles and not-so-edibles have been used as aphrodisiacs. There is no evidence that any have more than a placebo effect: If a man believes something increases his potency, it well may—since his most important sex organ is between his ears.

Recently multivitamin and Vitamin E preparations have been promoted as aids to sexual vigor. Vitamins are of no value in impotence. One supposed impotence pill widely sold at health food stores contained such useless ingredients as papaya leaves, prickly ash bark, ground cockleburrs and radish powder.

Royal jelly, from bees, has been found worthless for restoring potency. Likewise, be wary of products that contain male hormones. Their value in treatment of impotence is limited to specific medical conditions, and they can be dangerous if used without medical supervision.

Also caution them to steer clear of unlicensed "practitioners" and "sex counselors." Dozens of impotent men who've come to Masters and Johnson suffered further psychological damage at the hands of unscrupulous promoters.

Orgasmic Dysfunction: More Girls Are Complaining

"We have been making love for two years and will be getting married in about one year. This is great. The problem is that I am not very interested in sex. . . . I have never come close to an orgasm. Lately, it sort of panics me; here is a man I'll be living with for decades, and I can't even respond to him."

"My fiancé is able to reach a climax even though I cannot. While I love him I do not enjoy intercourse, but I feel I should engage in it for his sake."

These are just two of the many complaints psychiatrist Arnold Werner has received from young women concerned about attaining orgasm. All, he reports, communicate "considerable distress and disruption."

Researchers and therapists are finding that more and more teenage girls are worried about their inability to achieve orgasm during intercourse. "Why don't I experience orgasm?" is a question often put to Dr. James Toolan, psychiatric consultant at Bennington College and Marlboro College in Vermont. "This is a relatively new complaint for adolescent girls," observes Dr. Toolan, "as until recently they were concerned with their virginity."

Such young women—and their partners—may well be victims of ignorance and misunderstanding about female sexuality. With some enlightenment, practice, and encouragement, they'd be likely to achieve orgasm.

Illness may interfere with reaching an orgasm. So may drugs, including oral contraceptives. But difficulty in achieving orgasm is almost always due to psychological stress rather than physical causes. Lack of communication between sex partners can be a major factor in this sexual dysfunction. Often, a young woman's inability to respond sexually is due to feelings of guilt and shame inflicted on her in early life.

She may suffer general anxiety, or hostility toward her sex partner. Masters and Johnson include distractions, fatigue, and preoccupation with other matters as basic barriers to satisfying sexual experience. Failure to have an orgasm is sometimes due to a woman's fear of letting go or losing control.

Many young women fail to achieve orgasm because they are trying too hard. Psychiatrist L. Jerome Oziel of the Sex Therapy and Marital Counseling Clinic of the University of Southern California School of Medicine in Los Angeles finds that orgasm often eludes a woman who concentrates on reaching this goal. Often she tries to force an orgasm because she fears her partner is becoming impatient or that he'll be angry or depressed if she doesn't climax. Or she may feel almost on the point of orgasm, lose the sensation, then labor too hard to reach it again. Or she may be worried about not having orgasms, and so try desperately to reach one every time.

To help clear up the myths and misunderstandings, here's what you can tell your children about female orgasm:

Avoid the word "frigidity." Obstetrician-gynecologist James P. Semmens of the University of California College of Medicine at Irvine states the case against using the word "frigidity." He calls it "one of the most misused, abused, and traumatizing terms in the English language." It's commonly used loosely and pejoratively. If a girl refuses a boy's sexual overtures, he may dub her "frigid" in self-defense. He means cold, unsexy, hard to get. His tossed-off words can have a far-reaching impact.

"Frigidity" is a form of "verbal castration," remarks Dr. Semmens, especially if the word is used by a professional counselor. "The female who is called 'frigid' receives an emotional tattoo that can never be completely erased," he believes. "To her, it means that she is inadequate—a sexual nonentity. . . . She becomes a sexual exile."

Precisely used, "frigidity" has a very narrow definition. It refers to a chronic problem in which the female is unable to respond to *any* form of sexual stimulation. While this is usually accompanied by her inability to reach orgasm, most women who don't achieve orgasm are not in fact frigid. They do respond to various forms of sexual stimulation, and most can become orgasmic. "When given the right circumstances and partner," says Dr. Semmens, "any woman can achieve a satisfactory emotional and physical release." In Dr. Semmens' extensive counseling practice with teenagers, he has never come across a teenage girl who met the criteria of frigidity.

The preferred term for a female who fails to achieve orgasm is "nonorgasmic." Indeed, some therapists have begun using the more upbeat "preorgasmic."

Most women need direct clitoral stimulation. "I am twenty years old. My boyfriend and I have been having intercourse for a year now, but only on weekends since he goes to another school. I have never had an orgasm from intercourse alone. I have had orgasms as a result of clitoral stimulation during masturbation. My boyfriend never touches my clitoris. Is there something wrong with me? Am I undersexed?"

This problem, posed to psychiatrist Arnold Werner, expresses a common experience: Girls are able to reach orgasm during masturbation or petting. But orgasm during intercourse eludes them. Typically, they feel they are somehow deficient.

Actually, it's a male fantasy that women should find their greatest sexual pleasure in penile intromission. Orgasm in the female is usually brought about by stimulation of the clitoris. The lower third of the vagina also has extremely sensitive tissue capable of producing orgasm.

Insertion of the penis generally provides only indirect stimulation of the clitoris. During vaginal intercourse, the thrusting of the penis moves the inner lips (labia minora) at the entrance of the vagina. These lips come together above the vaginal opening and the urethra to form the hood of the clitoris. The rhythmic motion can stimulate the exquisitely sensitive head of the clitoris.

For a minority of women, estimated at as few as 30 percent, this indirect stimulation can bring orgasm. For many more—and this is not widely realized—the action of the penis alone frequently is not enough to lead to an orgasm. To reach sexual climax, most women require more direct stimulation of the clitoris than the penis alone provides.

Ignorance of this fact dooms many young women to frustration and self-doubt. Remarks psychiatrist Jerome Oziel: "A significant percentage of women who receive substantial clitoral stimulation [before insertion] will not have orgasms in intercourse without concurrent clitoral stimulation. . . . Many women, even when aroused, do not find intercourse alone stimulating enough to produce an orgasm."

Most men, Dr. Oziel points out, are much more genitally oriented than women. It is common for a man to spend five to ten minutes in foreplay, devoting no more than a few minutes to clitorial stimulation. Since most men ejaculate several minutes after intromission, "most women receive only a few minutes of direct and indirect clitoral stimulation during an entire sexual encounter." While such brief clitoral stimulation might produce an orgasm when a woman is particularly sexually responsive, "it might be grossly inadequate when the woman is less sexually excitable."

When a woman becomes aroused, her clitoris retracts under its hood, and her partner may have trouble finding it. He may interrupt his lovemaking to go in search of it. The woman is likely to find this distracting and frustrating. Actually, it is rarely necessary for the man to relocate the clitoris. At this stage of arousal, stimulation of the hood or the general area is usually sufficient, indeed preferred.

This is what most women like. Whenever it suits them while making love—before insertion (or instead of it), during intercourse, after the man has ejaculated—many couples stimulate the clitoris. Possibly they do this manually (with hands and fingers) or orally (with lips, mouth, and tongue), or the woman may stimulate her clitoris by manipulating her partner's penis against it. Some young women and their partners regard this as masturbation and have negative feelings about it. Psychiatrist George J. Langmyhr of the University of

Pennsylvania School of Medicine counsels them to "understand and accept that any form of clitoral stimulation is acceptable."

During intercourse, a woman may find that her partner's penis can bring her to orgasm more readily if she is on top of him. In this position she may find the rhythm, angle, and amount of friction that best brings his penis or pubic area in contact with her clitoris.

The female superior position also allows greater freedom of movement for her and permits her or her partner to manually stimulate the clitoris. Rear-entry positions similarly promote clitoral massage. So, too, does the lateral coital position, which permits considerable arm and hand motion.

With clitoral stimulation, there's a very fine line between pleasure and pain. Pressure that's too hard or lasts too long can cause an irritation, ending sexual pleasure. Women differ widely in the stimulation they prefer. Some like it firm and vigorous, or gentle and delicate. Others enjoy a steady rhythm, or stop-start teasing. Some wish a light touch at the outset, with increasing pressure as they approach orgasm. Preferences may vary from minute to minute.

The head of the clitoris (the glans) is especially sensitive, and most women prefer that it be avoided. "The majority of women experience discomfort on direct stimulation of the glans," reports gynecologist Mona Devanesan of the New Jersey College of Medicine and Dentistry. A few women in Dr. Devanesan's practice prefer firm "rolling" of the shaft. Most prefer gentler manual stimulation of the tissues adjoining the clitoris and the labia minora.

Dr. Devanesan finds that many women enjoy a varying in the rhythm and pressure. Gynecologist Mary Jane Grey of the University of Vermont Medical College suggests "initial slow, gentle caressing of the whole vulvar area followed by indirect movement of the clitoris."

Rough hands may be irritating. If that's a problem, the couple should make liberal use of hand lotion. The woman is likely to find manual stimulation of the clitoris pleasurable only when she has adequate lubrication—saliva, vaginal secretions, or moisteners like water-soluble jelly.

There is only one kind of orgasm. In the early 1930s, Sigmund Freud theorized that clitoral orgasm was on an infantile, prepuberty level, but that vaginal orgasm was a mark of "maturity." Wrong as Freud's theory was, it became dogma—and wreaked emotional havoc. A woman would consult a psychiatrist with the complaint, "I'm unable to achieve orgasm during intercourse." She would be told, "You suffer from incomplete psychosexual development." She was usually depressed and anxious to begin with, and on hearing this pronouncement her symptoms would often worsen.

Freud's theory made many women and their partners feel inferior because without direct clitoral stimulation, they could not achieve orgasm, vaginal or otherwise. To preserve their marriages and their husbands' self-esteem, many women were led to pretend they'd achieved orgasm. Often their frustration developed into resentment and bitterness toward the male.

Some psychotherapists challenged Freud's theory from the outset, but to little avail. It took Masters and Johnson's pioneering physiological measurements to prove objectively that an orgasm is an orgasm is an orgasm. There is no such thing as an "immature," "inferior," or "unreal" orgasm.

"Female orgasm . . . is a total body response with marked variation in reaction, intensity, and timing sequence," concluded Masters and Johnson. Clearly, their laboratory work showed, there is not one kind of orgasm involving the vagina, another involving the clitoris. A woman's experience of orgasm may vary according to her mood, her state of health, her feelings about her partner and herself, and where she's stimulated. She may find some orgasms more satisfying, others less. But physiologically an orgasm is the same, no matter how it is produced.

Multiple orgasms are exceptional. Masters and Johnson's discovery that some women experience from five to twenty or more orgasms has created unrealistic expectations in some teenage girls. One wrote to psychiatrist Arnold Werner after taking a course in human sexuality: "During intercourse my boyfriend is able to achieve more than one orgasm whereas I am only able to achieve one. I am very satisfied and fulfilled after having intercourse but can't help but feel that I should be able to have more than just one orgasm. What is wrong with me?"

In fact, multiple orgasms are more apt to occur during masturbation than during intercourse. This is because few men can maintain an erection long enough to help produce multiple orgasms in their partners.

Assure your children that multiple orgasms are the exception rather than the rule. Women who have one orgasm are not in the least deficient. Nor is having a number of orgasms necessarily more satisfying than having one.

Seeking Further Help

Urge your children to seek professional help if they remain concerned about their sexual functioning. Sexual problems are best nipped in the bud, before they become chronic dysfunctions. Often, all that's needed is a word or two of explanation, reassurance, and encouragement.

On many college campuses, your son or daughter can get such help from peer sex counselors. Many work in teams of two—a male and a female student—and are available for consultation daily at certain hours without an appointment. Human sexuality courses, now offered at many colleges, may also provide information and insight that may help your children.

For more serious problems, they should seek professional help: psychotherapy or sex therapy. College mental health services and counseling services frequently offer therapy on an individual basis to students with sexual difficulties.

Recently, some college health services have begun to offer "couple therapy." Being legally married is not usually a requirement in college clinics offering such therapy. "The existence of a personal commitment is the crucial factor," says psychiatrist Raymond Babineau of the University Health Service in New York.

Among the colleges offering individual and couple therapy is Yale University. Obstetrician Philip M. Sarrel of the Yale University School of Medicine and his wife-cotherapist Lorna J. Sarrel, a social worker on the Yale staff, describe their approach to students' sex problems as "eclectic." It involves suggested reading, direct teaching, a noncredit course on sexuality. Often, the Sarrels apply Masters and Johnson techniques although, as they point out, their patients differ from those of Masters and Johnson in one highly signficant way: These young people are seeking help very early, "before their sexual problems multiply and infect other areas of functioning and relating."

Chapter 8

Cohabitation and Promiscuity

If your youngster lives with someone, if your child is sexually indiscriminate—here's what you need to know.

RICK LIVED in a fraternity house, Eileen in a dormitory. Intercourse often took place in Rick's car, sometimes at a motel.

Next semester, Rick took an apartment with a friend, each having his own bedroom. "The arrangement worked well," recounts sociologist Gerald R. Leslie of the University of Florida at Gainesville. Occasionally Eileen spent the night with Rick. She began staying over on weekends. Eventually, she slept in her dorm only one or two nights a week. She kept this arrangement secret from her parents.

COHABITATION: A LIVING ARRANGEMENT

Rick and Eileen are typical of the increasing numbers of college couples who live together. Cohabitation is a growing phenomenon on college campuses, as it is in the nation as a whole. In 1960, a mere 17,000 unmarried people told census takers they were living with a person of the opposite sex. Census figures now show nearly 2 million men and women living together out of wedlock. Some estimates put the number at four times that.

Among colleges, most research shows that cohabitation is the living arrangement for 10 to 40 percent of the student body. The larger the school, the more liberal its tradition, the less restrictive its housing regulations, the more equal its male-female student ratio—the more likely are young men and women on campus to live together. There's more cohabitation at Berkeley than, say, at a seminary.

[131]

"What's meant by "cohabitation"? Cornell University psychologist Eleanor D. Macklin has found such arrangements to be much more stable than the fluid relationships of most adolescent dating. To meet Dr. Macklin's definition of cohabitation, an unmarried couple must have (a) shared a bedroom and/or bed, (b) for four or more nights a week, (c) for three or more consecutive months. Even by these strict criteria, 31 percent of her Cornell sample had cohabited at some time.

So it is on other campuses. At Pennsylvania State University, Dan J. Peterman and his colleagues find that nearly 1 in 3 students have lived with someone ("of the opposite sex" is implied). A study at Arizona State University shows that 3 in 10 sons and 2 in 10 daughters have cohabited at some time.

If your children are going to live with someone, they may do so almost as soon as they hit the campus. Among Penn State freshmen, 1 in 5 young men and 1 in 4 young women cohabit.

If your son lives with one girl in the course of his college years, he's likely to have at least a second partner as well. Penn State's Dan Peterman reports that 62 percent of male cohabitants engage in more than one such arrangement. Only 41 percent of the females do.

Even among students who do not live with someone, there is wide acceptance of the practice. Fully 80 percent of students questioned at a Midwestern University said that they would cohabit if they had the opportunity, although only 20 percent were cohabiting at the time. In the Arizona study, conducted by sociologists Lura F. Henze and John W. Hudson, 57 percent of the young men and 35 percent of the young women who had not lived with anyone said, "I'd like to."

If your children cohabit at college, you may be the last to know. Peterman reports that generally parents are not informed of the arrangement. Only 28 percent of sons and 24 percent of daughters made their parents aware they were living with someone.

Only about a third of youngsters feel any guilt about cohabiting. But concealing this aspect of their lives from you can cause your children great concern. At Cornell, psychologist Eleanor Macklin asked students what difficulties they experienced while living together. Parents were the major source of problems. One-third of the students said their parents definitely did not know about the cohabitation. Nearly 80 percent tried to hide the relationship. Daughters were much more likely than sons to try to keep their parents in the dark.

Nearly half the students feared that their parents would discover and object to the relationship, reports Dr. Macklin. Fully 60 percent expressed some "sorrow at not being able to discuss or share the relationship" with their parents. Among parents who did know about the relationship, about half apparently accepted it, although perhaps grudgingly. About 30 percent, however, strongly disapproved and tried to interfere with the arrangement.

Without necessarily approving, you can open up communication by acknowledging to your youngsters that they may live with someone while away from home. Here are answers to questions you may have about your children's cohabiting:

Will My Child Live with Someone?

Investigators find that youngsters who live together don't differ much from those who don't. Reports psychologist Macklin: "In many respects the two groups were surprisingly similar." Their family and community backgrounds are indistinguishable. Neither group is more likely to come from broken homes. Nor is there any significant difference in their parents' level of education or income.

The youngsters seem not to differ in intellectual or emotional functioning. Researchers find that the major differences between those who live with someone and those who don't are in the areas of:

Religion. In the Arizona State study, cohabitants were less apt to attend church. At Cornell, psychologist Macklin similarly found that those living together were less likely to identify themselves as religious. A low level of religious participation was likewise found by investigators at Virginia Polytechnic Institute and State University.

Liberal Attitudes. In the Arizona study, cohabitants were more likely to identify with a liberal life-style. So, too, psychologist Macklin finds that Cornell students who live together tend to believe that sexual norms on campus are more liberal. More of their friends cohabit. As a group, they tend to have more sexual experience and more liberal sexual attitudes than noncohabitants.

Drug Use. Arizona State researchers find a link between cohabitation on campus and a life-style that includes the use of drugs, primarily marijuana.

Personality. Cohabitants tend to be friendly, outgoing people, according to Penn State investigators. A study at Virginia Polytechnic Institute and State University finds that couples who cohabit seem to have a high energy level. They are "sensitive and alive to the opinions of others." They have "sufficient capacity for organizing work and personal life."

The young men tend to have a combination of "practical and theoretical interests." The young women are "probably energetic and enthusiastic with varied interests," note investigators Nancy Catlin, James W. Croake, and James F. Keller.

Housing Rules. Easing of living regulations mainly accounts for the rise in college cohabitation. Comment the Penn State investigators: "The opportunity to cohabit has increased in recent years, especially as larger numbers of both male and female students move off-campus and into nonrestrictive residential locations (apartments and rented houses, rather than dormitories or fraternities and sororities)." Living in a coed dorm may also increase your children's chances of cohabiting, to the extent of sharing a dorm room with a member of the opposite sex.

Psychologist Macklin attributes the relatively high incidence of cohabitation at Cornell in part to housing rules. The university gives students the option of living off campus, and allows twenty-four-hour visiting privileges for those living on campus.

She reports that the effect of school regulations can be seen in a comparison of two small liberal arts colleges in the Midwest. One allows some off-campus housing and twenty-four-hour visiting. At this school 18 percent of the men and 15 percent of the women have lived with someone. The other school allows no off-campus housing and places restrictions on visitors of the opposite sex. The cohabitation figure is only 9 percent. "And there are probably many schools in sexually conservative regions or with restrictive regulations, at which cohabitation hardly takes place at all."

Is It Only for Sex?

On the contrary. Most couples begin living together because of an emotional attachment. While they're living together, partners often believe they're in love. Or at least they care for each other a great deal. The sexual aspects of their relationship are usually of secondary importance.

In Dr. Dan Peterman's Penn State study, the young men character-ize at least their longest cohabiting arrangements in essentially the same terms as the young women. No fewer than 83 percent of the men and 86 percent of the women describe these as "love" or "intimate" relationships, as opposed to "friendships" or other less intimate relationship forms.

Similarly, psychologist Eleanor Macklin asked cohabitants to check the most important reason they chose to live with someone. About 70 percent picked "emotional attachment to each other." Others checked "security," "companionship," "enjoyment," and "con-venience."

Most of the Cornell cohabitants were involved in a strong affectionate relationship by the time they started living together. The majority of the relationships were exclusive or monogamous. Notes Dr. Macklin: "In the old days we would have said these couples were going steady, but that term is no longer popular."

Macklin asked her entire sample, cohabitants and noncohabitants alike, "What kind of relationship needs to prevail before you could feel comfortable cohabiting?" Half the students felt they would have to have a "strong affectionate relationship" with no dating of others. Some 13 percent believed they would need to be "tentatively engaged." Only 8 percent felt they would have to be either married or formally engaged. Male and female students did not differ signifi-cantly in their responses to this question.

Living together usually evolves slowly over weeks or months. At Cornell, only 1 out of 4 discussed whether to live together before actually starting to do so. Most just drifted into sleeping together more and more often.

Most couples who are living together consider emotional security, mutual affection, and loyalty to each other more important than the intercourse which they may or may not be having. "We should not place undue emphasis on the sexual aspects of these relationships," comments psychologist Macklin. "The pattern which is evolving is primarily concerned with total relationships, and only incidentally with the sexual aspects, which are assumed to grow as the relationship grows."

Indeed, while nearly all the Cornell cohabitations were full sexual relationships, nearly 10 percent of the cohabitants had lived together for three or more months before having intercourse. "While this fact may seem astonishing," remarks Macklin, "studies of cohabitation on other campuses report similar findings."

Macklin goes on to draw an important distinction: "Obviously, spending the night together, even in the same bed, does not necessarily imply full sexual relations, and the terms 'sleeping together' or 'living together' can no longer be used casually as euphemisms for having sexual intercourse."

She finds that cohabitation seems to develop out of a desire to know another as a whole person, and to share with that person as completely as possible. "To focus exclusively on the sexual involvement leads to a very narrow interpretation of the situation," she cautions.

At the same time, 96 percent of the Cornell students rated their relationship as sexually satisfying. For most, sexual problems were common but rarely serious. The problems included differing degrees of sexual interest, fear of pregnancy, and occasional failure to reach orgasm.

How Long Will It Last?

Your children may cohabit for several years, perhaps even marry their mates. But it's much more likely that they'll live with someone for a relatively short time. At Cornell, only 10 percent had future marriage plans at the time they began living together. On the other hand, only 10 percent looked upon the experience as temporary. Many had a "Let's try it out and see" attitude. They felt a deep emotional attachment to each other, but had not reached the point of long-term commitment.

Eleanor Macklin reports that at Cornell and other schools where surveys have been conducted, "most undergraduate couples do not consider themselves married in any sense of the word. In fact, very few even considered marriage as a viable alternative to their present cohabitation. They did not feel ready for that kind of commitment."

Investigators find limited commitment to permanency, particularly among males. At Penn State, for half the men the longest cohabiting experience lasts less than a month. Nearly 1 out of 3 females also have liaisons this brief. For fully 82 percent of the males and 75 percent of the females, the longest relationship lasts less than six months.

Indeed, the relative ease of breaking-up seems to be one of the major attractions cohabitation offers young people. Dr. James L. Morrison of the University of North Carolina at Chapel Hill finds that while married people generally try to work out problems with each other, this effort is much less common among couples living together. They often immediately retreat in the face of any disagreement. Frequently they decide to see other people for a while, and the relationship soon ends. "It's a good thing we didn't get married," they'll say to each other. "See what happened."

Despite the comparative simplicity of a breakup, there are some problems like those of marital separation or divorce. Property must be divided. Each partner must deal with any emotional trauma the parting brings. After being out of circulation, the youngsters must now establish new contacts.

A commitment may become firmer as your youngster gets older. Some researchers note that as the last year of college approaches, the cohabiting relationship may become more durable and may indeed become a trial marriage. In some cases, living together *is* a prelude to marriage. In Dr. James Morrison's sample, one-third married each other.

If cohabiting couples have a child, they usually marry, reports Dr. Conrad Taeuber of the Center for Population Research at Georgetown University's Kennedy Institute for the Study of Human Reproduction and Bioethics. "One reason is to save the child from any social stigmas, but also to save the offspring from suffering legal disadvantages."

Mindful that cohabiting is often a temporary arrangement, encourage your children to keep in their own names any major purchases they pay for—cars, TVs, hi-fis, household appliances. They should also maintain separate checking accounts, and be explicit about the terms of any cash loans or gifts.

Will They Be Damaged?

More likely, the experience will be beneficial. Comments psychologist Eleanor Macklin: "I have been repeatedly impressed by the very strong positive attitudes toward cohabitation held by those who have experienced it. The message one gets from the majority of cohabitants is the number of ways in which the experience apparently fostered their personal growth and maturity."

Dr. Dan Peterman and his colleagues concur: "There are no immediately obvious negative effects of cohabitation." If anything, they find, cohabitation is associated with higher self-esteem and improvements in relating with the opposite sex.

Dr. James Morrison concludes that living together fills a number of interpersonal needs of college students. These include the need for the "security of a relatively stable intimate relationship," and the need for "convenient interaction with the opposite sex."

At Cornell, more than 90 percent of cohabitants evaluate their experience as successful, pleasurable, and maturing. Virtually all recommend the experience to others. Fully 3 out of 4 say, "I'd never marry without living with the person first."

On the other hand, problems are inevitable in intimate living. Cornell cohabitants widely complain of money problems and lack of space. Often there's an absence of privacy, and friction with others sharing the apartment.

The most common emotional problem is a tendency to become overdependent on the relationship. Youngsters often suffer a lack of opportunity to participate in other activities or to be with friends. Many are jealous of their partner's involvement in other relationships or activities. About half occasionally feel "trapped" in the relationship.

Does their schoolwork suffer? You can probably rest assured on this point. At Cornell, parents widely expressed fears that living together leads to neglecting of schoolwork. Eleanor Macklin could find no significant difference in academic performance between those who live with someone and those who don't.

Will They Ever Want to Marry?

Whether or not your children ever choose to marry, cohabitation gives them valuable experience in intimate living. They learn that compromise and consideration are necessary. They glimpse the practical necessities that make up daily life with someone else: taking out the garbage, cleaning the toilets, shopping for groceries, fixing meals, making repairs. They see personal habits in someone else that drive them crazy. Perhaps most valuable, they get a better idea of what they value in a lifelong mate.

Like many parents, you may be concerned that if your children live with someone, they necessarily reject marriage. Investigators conclude this is not the case at all. Young people who cohabit feel the same about marriage as those who do not cohabit. Eleanor Macklin finds that the two groups do not differ significantly in their desire to marry eventually.

What About Sharing a Bedroom at Home?

Even if you know they are living together at college, you may be taken aback by their having sex under your roof. You'd do well to be honest about your feelings, whatever they are.

If you feel strongly against their sharing a bedroom, make that clear. This is delicately handled by Mitch who says, "I tell my daughter and her boyfriend, 'When you're a guest in my home, we try to make you comfortable. I would appreciate it if you would try to make us comfortable by not sleeping together when you're here.'"

On the other hand, you may be perfectly at ease with the situation. Recalls Abigail: "I'd met Brandon and I liked him. When Cari asked if she could bring him home for the Thanksgiving vacation, I just asked, 'How many bedrooms will you need?' She said, 'One.' And that was the end of the conversation."

You may be among the many parents who feel uneasy about their children's lovers sharing their bedroom—but who compromise with reality. "We capitulated," recounts Helene, "because we didn't want the kids running off somewhere. They were bound to spend the night together anyway, so they might as well stay here."

Sarah, mother of two college students, agrees. "I don't accept the new morality, but I live with it. Nowadays well-adjusted parents care most about their child's happiness and the family relationship; they would rather sacrifice some of their own moral values to preserve that relationship."

PROMISCUITY: WHEN TO WORRY

At 18, Miriam has had many lovers, more faces and bodies than she can easily recall. She enters these relationships freely. Her partners are young men she likes a lot. She enjoys sex, and is aware of no guilt or anxiety. She does well at college and at her part-time job waiting tables. She has good friends and a close relationship with her family.

Anthony, 16, is feeling rejected by his parents. They're in the process of divorcing, and are bitter toward each other and sharp with him. He seeks solace in the arms of any girl who will have him—and many girls find his air of suffering attractive. But Anthony never finds the warmth he's desperate for, although he sleeps with one girl after another in his search. While Anthony is the envy of his male friends, only he knows how anxious and unsatisfied his sexual adventures leave him.

Which of these two young people is promiscuous? Many would say Miriam. Anthony is presumably doing what comes naturally to boys. Who ever heard of a "promiscuous" boy? A promiscuous girl, however, is generally marked as "sick" or "bad."

"Promiscuity" is a sexist term, observes pediatrician Adele D. Hofmann, director of the Adolescent Medical Unit of New York University Medical Center. "While the young male who has many sexual partners is often described as merely 'sowing his wild oats,' the adolescent female who behaves in this manner is frequently labeled as being 'promiscuous.'"

Therein lies the rub of discussing "promiscuity," the pattern of frequent, casual sexual intercourse. The term is almost always used disparagingly, and in respect to females. Moreover, the issue of "too much" intercourse is wrapped up in moral values as well as psychopathology. You thus may be too quick to see an emotional problem in a promiscuous daughter, too slow to see one in a promiscuous son.

Of Miriam and Anthony, both are promiscuous if only their sexual activity is considered. But it is Anthony whose promiscuity is more clearly symptomatic of an emotional disorder. Miriam's relationships may be shallower than the monogamous ideal, and she may have intercourse with more partners than most parents would like. But her sexual activity seems to be characterological: part of her personality, not amenable to change. She's untroubled by it, and the rest of her life is apparently in good shape. Anthony, by contrast, is in agony, and engages in indiscriminate intercourse to relieve his pain.

By conventional standards, the promiscuous youngster is missing out on more satisfying relationships. Psychiatrist Frederick Coons of

Indiana University was asked for his opinion about a young woman who, in college, had intercourse with a dozen or more men.

> I think that promiscuous sex is usually a substitute for some other need, such as intimacy. In my value system, it is better to have sex with someone you know well, someone with whom you have an intimate, open relationship, than with someone you don't know well.
>
> For me, getting to know another person well and creating an intimate, trusting relationship requires a good deal of time, energy, and emotional investment. I cannot really imagine being able to form twelve such relationships in a four-year period and still have time and energy left for work, studies, activities, and more casual relationships.

Promiscuity is most likely to be pathological when it is patently compulsive and indiscriminate. Such mindless sexual activity almost invariably reflects underlying emotional problems. Comments pediatrician Adele Hofmann: "The gender of the patient, the number of partners involved, and the frequency of intercourse do not per se define the problem, but rather it is the psychological difficulty of which the specific behavior pattern is a manifestation." Dr. Hofmann lists some reasons adolescents use sexual intercourse "maladaptively":

Joe tries to affirm an uncertain and insecure sexual identity. Beth is seeking a way to relate to others; she fears she can't make meaningful contact on another basis. Lynn wants to become pregnant. Marc wishes to demonstrate his ability to impregnate.

Brooke, unsure of her own self-worth, hopes to bind her partner closer to her. Duane, reflecting an adolescent need for mastery and control, yearns to make conquests. Jan is striving for emancipation from her parents.

Rickie seeks escape from unpleasant realities at home and school. Phil is grasping for status among his friends. Rachel suffers from difficulty in controlling her impulses.

Your adolescents may have few or many sexual partners. They may have intercourse often or rarely. Regardless. Suspect that their sexual behavior represents underlying emotional problems when:

- They experience severe guilt or anxiety about it.
- It interferes with their normal emotional development, schoolwork, social life.
- There is a breakdown in family communication.

Sexual promiscuity rarely exists as the sole indicator of a problem in a troubled youth. Thus, be alert to problems in other areas: school underachievement, the inability to relate well to peers, troubled home relationships.

Family Causes

Psychotherapy may be required if your child engages in promiscuous sexual behavior. But, cautions Dr. Hofmann, results come slowly. "It takes time for new and more constructive patterns to emerge," she says—and the youngster's sexual activity may continue for some time. "Indeed," Dr. Hofmann notes, "sexual continence per se is not the goal, but rather the aim is to assist the youth to make his or her own decisions about all matters in a more mature and healthy manner."

A period of promiscuity will not necessarily warp a child's adult life. "Promiscuity . . . need not have a permanent effect provided the conflicts leading to the promiscuity are resolved," concludes psychiatrist Frederick Coons. Dr. Coons has worked with many young people who were able to identify the need they were seeking to satisfy with sex. These youngsters learned how to "more directly and appropriately satisfy that need." They then became content with sex "only in the context of truly meaningful relationships."

Take the case of Sandy. She became promiscuous at 11½, when she had sexual intercourse with Jeff, a 17-year-old friend of her older brother. She began to walk in the city park and along lonely roads in order to be picked up by men. As she walked at night, she felt the excitement of anticipation, mingled with a fear of rape, as men followed her. She usually refused a number of men before allowing one of them to pick her up, thereby prolonging the sensation of anticipatory pleasure. She did not find the actual sex with these men gratifying.

When she was 13, her parents were only vaguely aware of her sexual activity. They became concerned over an increasing number of phone calls which she received from anonymous men. She repeatedly stayed out late. Her whereabouts on weekends were mysterious. She withdrew from her close relationship with her mother. She was secretive and lied. Her academic performance declined. Her friends fell away. She was frequently irritable or depressed. All this contributed to the parents' decision to take Sandy to psychiatrist William Thomas Moore of the University of Pennsylvania.

Sandy had had no positive experiences with men, Dr. Moore discovered. Her father, a prominent architect, had paid little attention to her. He was openly disappointed with her, considering her unattractive and of only average intelligence. While he was unaffectionate toward her, he was extremely affectionate toward his wife.

"His expression of affection bordered on exhibitionism," reports Dr. Moore. Sandy's parents were commonly nude at home, and touched each other without restraint in the presence of children, relatives, friends—sometimes even in public places. Sandy remarked, "A weekend at home is like living in a nudist camp."

In addition, Sandy's father behaved promiscuously. Apparently his wife fixed him up with other women. "Coming from a family with a way of life characterized by sexual acting out," comments Dr. Moore, "Sandy was bound to react according to the family character."

Besides being cast off by her father, Sandy was scorned by her older brother, who'd picked up her father's attitude. "All her relationships with men were approached with uncertainty, fear of rejection, and bitterness," remarks Dr. Moore. "She had little opportunity to feel accepted, let alone loved, by any of the men in her life."

At 11, Sandy developed the body of a young woman. Much to her confusion, she found herself the object of eager attention from men. She was quick to respond in kind. She reveled in the closeness and warmth of the embrace. She was especially flattered by the attentions of grown men. What she liked was not the genital coupling, but the hugs and kisses and physical warmth that preceded it.

At the same time, Sandy hated men. She was bitterly jealous of her brother, and exulted as she imagined her father's agony if he learned of her promiscuity. "It would serve him right if he only knew what a whore I am."

Sandy's therapy continued for several years. Now, 21 and married, Sandy has moved to another city and is studying for her master's degree. While the problems that gave rise to her promiscuity are largely solved, Dr. Moore observes that some scars remain. "Occasionally some aspects of her relationship with her husband are reminiscent of infantile desires. She looks up to and admires him for his stability and professional capability. Even though she feels loved and valued by him, she is at times unsure of his love and on these occasions becomes unreasonably demanding of his time and attention."

While Sandy's main difficulty was with her father, psychiatrist Daniel T. Gianturco of Duke University Medical Center finds that promiscuous behavior is often connected to disturbed relationships with mothers. At a psychiatric hospital Dr. Gianturco studied twenty girls who had as one of their problems "promiscuous sexual behavior." He found that fifteen of the girls came from homes in which there was marital discord. The fathers were absent, alcoholic, domineering, passive, rejecting.

The mothers were overwhelmed by their responsibilities, and angry at their husbands. They viewed their daughters as burdens and tended to be distant, leaving the girls largely to fend for themselves. "This lack of love and support prevented the daughters from learning to value and cherish themselves as people and as women," reports Dr. Gianturco. "Lacking any sense of self-value or self-respect as persons, they were more ready to sell themselves for the things they desperately needed." They developed a hunger for love and affection, which they sought indiscriminately, not only from boys but from "love substitutes" like drugs, clothes, and cosmetics.

One of the girls—we'll call her Zöe—was 16 and had been expelled from school for stealing from a teacher's purse. She had a severe quarrel with her mother over whether she could date a 21-year-old soldier. She ran away and lived for a while with the man, with whom she had sexual relations and took amphetamines. Zöe explained, "He was giving me drugs and I was paying him back."

She had run away once before, when she was 14, and supported a $40-a-day heroin habit by prostituting. Her father was a cold, remote man, a retired military officer. Her mother was described as verbally seductive with other men.

Kelly, another girl, was a frequent runaway. Her flights from home were usually precipitated by a quarrel with her mother. She would have sex with men indiscriminately. On one occasion she was hidden away by soldiers. Another time she stayed with some truck drivers who had picked her up on the road.

Since early childhood, Kelly had been neglected by her mother. Indeed, relations between mother and daughter were so strained that the mother refused to take her home for Christmas. With time and counseling, Dr. Gianturco reports, her relationship with her mother improved. She had several good home visits. Kelly's father started taking more interest in her. She was discharged from the hospital for continuing therapy at her local mental health center.

Dr. Gianturco found that treatment was most successful in ameliorating promiscuous behavior when the staff established a good relationship with a girl's mother. The mother was then able to vent her rage about her life. "From there, with the help of the staff, she was able to be more genuine and consistent in loving her daughter."

Also, the girl stopped being promiscuous as she acquired a more positive attitude toward herself. Often this resulted from her developing a friendship with a woman staff member, who became a substitute mother. "The [girl's] desire to be like her appeared to be a significant help in developing respect for herself."

Secondary Virginity

A period of promiscuous behavior is often followed by the youngster's deciding to abstain from sex. "When I came to college I was a virgin," recalls 18-year-old Frank, now a sophomore at a large northeastern university.

> I was feeling very uncomfortable about it, and let on that I had sexual experience. Then I started going out with Angie, and we began sleeping together. But we broke up after a few months, and I started going with Sue. After that there was Bobbie, then Carol, then Marsha.
>
> By the time Easter vacation came around, there'd been eight or nine or even more. I'd lost count, and that scared me. I'd also spent a week in a panic when one of the girls thought she was pregnant. I didn't feel sexually free at all. I felt hollow and misled and confused. That's when I decided, 'No more.' I simply stopped having sex. When I start again—and that may not be for a long time—it's going to be different."

Frank is not alone in embracing what psychiatrist Joel Moskowitz calls "secondary virginity." Dr. Moskowitz, director of clinical services at the Resthaven Psychiatric Hospital and Community Center in Los Angeles, has observed that a growing number of young men and women—after a period of sexual experimentation they find hurtful and disillusioning—became scrupulously chaste. Often, they vow to save further sex for marriage, or at the least for an emotionally close and stable relationship.

"A ground swell of sexually experienced students . . . have decided, often in secret, to embrace secondary virginity rather than continue to pay the psychic costs of casual sex," comments Dr. Moskowitz. This decision is closely linked with a wish to have commitment as part of their sexual experience.

Dr. Moskowitz relates the experience of an 18-year-old freshman we'll call Kaye, who came to him for psychiatric help. Her problem? She was convinced she was losing her intelligence. Dr. Moskowitz was perplexed, for he found her an unusually bright and attractive girl, who'd had an excellent high school record. But when she entered college, Kaye told Dr. Moskowitz, her work began to deteriorate. She couldn't concentrate and her memory was failing.

As Dr. Moskowitz gained Kaye's confidence, she was able to talk to him about a more pressing concern. She'd been "promiscuous," she told him, having had intercourse with six different partners during the past year, each for one or two sexual encounters.

Increasingly annoyed with what she saw as self-denigrating behavior, Kaye decided to abstain from sex until she found someone with whom she would be able to have a continuing meaningful relationship. This decision troubled her more than anything else. Was this a normal thing to do? Kaye worried. "Am I losing my sex urge?" she asked Dr. Moskowitz.

He was able to assure her that this was not so, since she continued to have sexual fantasies about men and would from time to time masturbate to orgasm. In the course of the next two months, Dr. Moskowitz gave Kaye reassurance and support, and helped her explore her ambivalent feelings about her decision to return to a virginal state. He helped her understand, too, that "her anxiety about what she interpreted as failing sexual urges was displaced onto a sense of failing intellectually."

Kaye began doing much better in her courses. She became much more cheerful. When Dr. Moskowitz saw her again eighteen months later, she was making plans to live with a young man. "She had abstained from sex during the intervening 18 months," comments Dr. Moskowitz, "but now felt a meaningful commitment had developed and was willing once again to relinquish her 'virginity.'"

Some youngsters have adopted a new chastity by way of religious commitment. The religious movements popular with young people generally stress sexual continence. Psychoanalyst Ira Mintz cites the popularity of the Hare Krishna movement. Before joining the sect, many devotees behaved without sexual restraint. But as members they have found what they apparently need: "under the guise of a religious commitment . . . a strict, ascetic society with a built-in set of controls."

More rules in college living arrangements may also be the wave of the future. Psychiatrist Moskowitz predicts that before long, students who have been living in sexually permissive dormitories may begin to ask for more rules. Indeed, some colleges are already finding that the coed dormitory is becoming less popular.

Dr. Elaine Pierson of the University of Pennsylvania has observed a student movement toward what she calls "nesting"—the tendency of students to live together as a group or as couples. Although such arrangements may look like group or trial marriages, and sometimes are, Dr. Pierson believes that they are more likely attempts by students to "set up limits" to their social vulnerability, to carve out an island of stability amid social flux—even, she feels, to submit to groups that promise to act "much like their absent parents."

Overall, many professional observers have noted, there seems to be a swing back toward more traditional sexual values and activity among some young people. Psychiatrist Nancy A. Durant, of the Union County Psychiatric Clinic in Plainfield, New Jersey, finds this in her clinical work with children, adolescents, and their parents. "Although one can hardly escape the increasingly open portrayals of sex as a purely recreational activity," she comments, "I still feel that we are headed toward more conservative sexual values."

Similarly, Dr. Charles E. Millard, a professor of family and community medicine at the University of Massachusetts Medical School, finds that more and more young people are adopting conservative attitudes toward sex. "Increasing numbers of our youth are . . . recognizing that a lasting and meaningful relationship can be maintained without full sexual commitment until marriage," he has found.

Observers note that the sexual revolution, like all revolutions, has developed its excesses. When this happens, a conservative backlash occurs. "I believe that we are presently witnessing a sexual trend toward conservatism, one that will probably bring the pendulum back from its extreme position," remarks psychiatrist Judd Marmor of the University of Southern California School of Medicine in Los

Angeles. But Dr. Marmor does not believe that the rigid traditional sexual values of the past will once again prevail. "The constructive scientific and social changes that have released people from their former unhealthy fears and guilts about their sexual needs and feelings will, I believe, preclude such an eventuality."

Part III

REDUCE THE HAZARDS

GUARD YOUR YOUNGSTERS against diseases from sex. The VD plague can cause them sterility, cancer, insanity, even death. Also protect them against pregnancy. You won't be encouraging inter-course if you talk up contraception. But expect them to resist the use of birth control methods. What's the best contraceptive to recom-mend to your child? Probably a condom plus foam or diaphragm.

. .

Chapter 9

Diseases from Sex

Insanity, cancer, sterility, death—protect your youngsters from the VD plague.

DICK AND JULIA HARPER were baffled. After a succession of winning seasons, their son Terry and his Los Angeles high school football team had suddenly gone sour. During practice, Terry and the other players barely limped through their wind sprints. Recalls Dick: "The tackling dummy gave them more punishment than it got." Saturday after Saturday, linemen like Terry failed to open holes. "When they did," says Dick, "the backs had trouble finding them. Pass receivers were slow getting downfield and zigged when they should have zagged."

The reason for the squad's deterioration didn't emerge from locker-room chalk talks, but from medical detective work. Terry, complaining of swollen testicles, went to a public-health clinic. He later told his parents, "I had gonorrhea." Investigators found that forty-eight boys and girls at the high school—including nine members of the team—were infected with the disease. All were quickly cured by penicillin. Terry's team came out of its slump and started winning again.

His parents, however, remain a bit shaken. Comments Julia: "I still find it hard to believe that *my* son had VD." Actually, if venereal disease keeps climbing at the present rate, fully 1 in 5 of the city's high schoolers will have contracted gonorrhea or syphilis by the time they graduate. And what's happened to the Harpers and their child might happen to you and yours.

THREAT TO YOUR FAMILY

The nation is in the grip of a VD epidemic of unparalleled proportions—and though you and your children are members of the educated middle class, you are hardly immune. Indeed, "this is by no means a class phenomenon," says Harvard gynecologist John Grover. He has treated VD in the families of clergymen, doctors, bank presidents: "the daughter of the professor as well as the daughter of the milkman."

Nor are you safe because you live in a nice area. VD is widespread in both the city and suburbs. Investigators for the Oakland County, Michigan, Health Department have their hands full tracking down gonorrhea and syphilis in the affluent Detroit suburbs of Bloomfield Hills, Birmingham, and Southfield. In Prince George's County, Maryland, a bedroom suburb of Washington, D.C., the gonorrhea rate has increased fivefold in the last decade.

The statistic that worries officials most is the increase of VD among youngsters around the age of yours. At present one person in five with gonorrhea is under 20. The rate of infection among 15- to 19-year-olds is rising faster than in any other group. More than 55 percent of all reported cases of VD occur in persons under 25. In a typical year, more than five thousand cases are found among youngsters between 10 and 14 and two thousand among children under 9. Estimates Dr. Walter Smartt, of the Los Angeles County Venereal Disease Control Division: "The probability that a person will acquire VD by the time he's 25 is about 50 percent."

The reservoir from which your child might be infected is enormous. As contagious diseases, syphilis and gonorrhea are outranked in incidence only by the common cold. VD is now first among reportable communicable diseases. The number of cases each year exceeds those of strep throat, scarlet fever, measles, mumps, hepatitis, and tuberculosis *combined.*

Each year, over 600,000 new cases of gonorrhea are reported. An estimated four cases occur for every one reported, so the real figure is more than 2 million. In Atlanta, 1 person in 40 has gonorrhea; in San Francisco, 1 in 50.

For syphilis the figures are similarly disturbing. There are half a million Americans with untreated syphilis today. This year their ranks will be joined by 85,000 new cases. At any given time, an estimated 14 million Americans have syphilis or gonorrhea or both.

Most disturbing, the epidemic infects young boys and, especially, girls. Observes epidemiologist Elizabeth Barrett-Connor of the University of California School of Medicine at San Diego: "Gonorrhea is not rare in prepubescent children and probably occurs more frequently than is recognized." Several studies suggest that 30 to 80 percent of infected girls between ages 6 and puberty have been infected by intercourse or sex play.

One team of Public Health Service investigators has found that molestation by relatives accounts for most of the infections in children under 9 years of age. If you come across such a child, you have grounds for calling in the authorities under your state's child-abuse laws. These statutes make you immune from legal action by the parents if it turns out that the child contracted the infection by other means, as from sex play with other youngsters. Above age 10 a child is usually infected through voluntary heterosexual contact.

ALERT YOUR YOUNGSTERS

Your teenager may fall victim to over a dozen venereal diseases besides gonorrhea and syphilis. These include herpes, hepatitis, vaginal infections, lice, and a number of others of growing concern. They're "venereal" in the true sense of the word's derivation—from Venus, the Roman goddess of love (*venereus* is Latin for "sexual desire"). These conditions are also termed STD—sexually transmitted (or transmissible) diseases. You can help your children avoid these hazards by giving them the following information and advice:

Use a condom. Birth control pills have contributed to the VD epidemic. Formerly, condoms were the most popular form of birth control for the young. Since they prevent direct penis-vagina contact, condoms provide a measure of protection against VD, especially gonorrhea. Now, the widespread use of oral contraceptives among young people virtually eliminates condoms as a preventive measure.

Furthermore, the Pill changes the chemical milieu of the vagina from acidic (which tends to kill germs) to alkaline (which does not). If your daughter is on the Pill and has intercourse with a partner with gonorrhea, she's almost 100 percent certain to contract the disease. If she weren't taking birth control pills her chances of infection would be less than 45 percent. With a condom, her chances of contracting the disease are close to zero.

To compound the problem, your teenagers may be under the misapprehension that the Pill *prevents* VD. W. L. Yarber, an assistant professor of health education at Purdue University, sampled teenage girls in the Midwest, most of whom were sexually active. He found that nearly 1 in 4 operate under the misconception that oral contraceptives are "very effective" or "somewhat effective" against VD.

Be extremely selective in your partners. The earlier and more frequent sexual intercourse among the young makes each sexually active teenager more likely to catch the disease—and spread it to a multiplicity of contacts. The analogy of Dr. Joshua Siegel of the Hollywood-Wilshire Clinic: "If you walk across a freeway once, you're less likely to get hit than if you walk across it ten times."

Teenage girls especially are having intercourse younger and more often. Not surprisingly, they are also getting more VD. A British study of people treated at clinics for gonorrhea shows that 25 years ago for every ten male patients there were two females. Now there are four.

A doubling of the number of infected females has a grave epidemiological effect. It is the female who is, as a rule, the carrier of these diseases—unwittingly so, because in women most cases of infection have no symptoms. In spreading VD, the sexually active girl is increasingly a Typhoid Mary.

If a girl is promiscuous, she is that much more of a carrier. Center for Disease Control epidemiologists tell of Truck Stop Annie, a California waitress, who gave syphilis to 311 men.

A promiscuous carrier can infect men indefinitely, each of whom is likely to give the infection to someone else. If she seeks a cure, she is likely to be reinfected by one of her many sexual contacts. Such reinfection is extremely common. Venereologist Arthur S. Wigfield of Britain's Newcastle General Hospital reports that at his VD clinic some 27 percent of men with gonorrhea have had the infection before. Five percent have had it twice, another 5 percent three times. Nine percent have had it twice in one year.

Seek help as soon as possible. Let your teenagers know that if they suspect they have VD, you want them to consult a physician or clinic immediately, even without telling you. In most states, minors can receive treatment without informing or receiving permission from their parents. Indeed, it's possible that your teenager has been treated for VD without your knowledge. If you find out, regard this as an act showing a mature assumption of responsibility, in no way sneaky or duplicitous behavior.

To ward off "Ping Pong" reinfection, ask that a steady sex partner go for treatment at the same time as your youngster. The partner may harbor the disease asymptomatically, and thus may pass it on anew after your child completes treatment.

Urge your teenagers to cooperate in giving VD inspectors the names of any casual sexual contacts. Health officials are combating the VD epidemic by tracking down contacts of known cases. If necessary, your child should give permission to a private physician to report the case. Some doctors withhold such reports out of a misguided wish to spare their patients embarrassment. Reassure your youngster that all VD records are confidential. Neither your teenager nor his contacts will be identified to one another or to anyone else.

In one case, an 18-year-old West Virginian was found to have syphilis during a pre-employment physical examination. In a confidential interview, the young man volunteered the names of 6 recent sexual contacts, 2 of whom were found to have the disease. From interviews with these 2 people, 41 more contacts were examined. Eleven of them were diagnosed as having syphilis. In all, 137 persons were examined, and 18 new cases of syphilis were identified. Both heterosexual and homosexual behavior played a part. One case of a baby born with syphilis is directly related to this outbreak.

Remind your children that VD is nearly always passed from one person to another during sexual contact. The gonorrhea and syphilis bacteria cannot survive long after exposure to air. Thus there is little chance of contracting the disease from public toilets, towels, doorknobs, or other objects that might be contaminated.

Confront VD realistically. Nip in the bud any guilt your youngsters may have about contracting a sexually transmitted disease. From the remarks of teachers or other adults, they may have come to look on VD as justified punishment for a moral transgression, rather than as a category of severe disease. It wasn't very long ago that an infected person could be locked up until cured. These were punitive measures against prostitutes or "lewd" women, who were always assumed to be the sole carriers of these diseases.

Dr. Thomas Parran, a U.S. Surgeon General, blamed moralists for discouraging people from seeking VD treatment by preaching that "all victims of 'VD' are guilty of sexual misconduct, regardless of the facts in the matter." In refutation of such moralizing, Father Francis L. Filas, chairman of the Department of Theology of Loyola University, declared: "To say that the 'venereally' infected get what they deserve is the most raw, uncharitable expression that one can imagine. But even if we were to admit so bigoted an interpretation of Biblical doctrine as to say that 'venereal' disease was punishment for sin, we would still be forgetting that 'VD' can strike the completely innocent."

Your children might not believe that they're in danger because they may have the notion that VD is principally spread by prostitutes. In fact, prostitutes are generally conscientious about avoiding VD and seeking treatment if they contract it. Only 2 percent of the VD patients treated in St. Louis clinics are prostitutes. "Prostitution is not where it's at with VD today," Robert M. Nellis, an investigator with the San Francisco City Clinic, told *Newsweek*. "It's Johnny next door and Susie up the street."

Or your youngsters may not take VD seriously. A cliché among teenagers is: "It's no worse than having a cold. You just lay off balling until it goes away."

Some infected teenagers don't follow their doctors' orders. Youngsters sometimes take only half the antibiotic pills they get at VD clinics, sharing the other half in order to spare friends the trouble of a clinic visit. The result is an inadequate dosage, and no one gets cured.

Adolescent ignorance about VD is nearly universal. Many teenagers fail to realize that they've been exposed, and don't recognize the early symptoms. They don't seek treatment, and remain blind to the hazards to themselves and others. Here's what you need to tell your youngsters about the worst sexually transmitted diseases:

Gonorrhea: No Mild Disease

Disabuse your teenagers of the widespread belief that gonorrhea is a mild disease. This mistaken notion is promoted by the infection's often negligible early symptoms, which soon seem to go away.

Actually, if untreated, gonorrhea can cause your children severe permanent damage and may threaten their lives. Gonorrhea is caused by the gonococcus bacteria, which thrive in the moist, warm mucous membrane that lines body openings such as the penis, vagina, and rectum. After the first symptoms disappear, gonococci usually remain in the genital and urinary tracts. Later they attack the internal reproductive organs.

In your daughter, gonococci may cause pelvic inflammatory disease (PID), often with fever, abdominal pain, and tenderness. The linings of the Fallopian tubes may become mutilated, blocking the passages through which an egg must pass to be fertilized. In this way, your daughter may suffer from infertility. About 25 percent of women with gonorrhea eventually need a hysterectomy to arrest the disease.

In your son, gonorrhea can cause sterility by blocking the tubes through which sperm must pass to fertilize an egg. Gonococci may migrate to his prostate or testicles. Surgical removal of the infected organs may be necessary.

If gonorrhea affects your son's prostate gland, he may suffer from reduced sexual energy, possibly impotence. His ejaculation may be premature, painful, or bloody. Gonorrheal infection has been implicated as a contributor to the development of cancer of the prostate.

Should gonococci attack your son's urethra, the urinary passage from his bladder through his penis, he may suffer a permanent narrowing, called urethral stricture. His urethra will be sealed off by scar tissue, making urination at first difficult and then impossible. Pressure resulting from the buildup of urine in the bladder will cause extreme pain. He'll be able to obtain relief only by frequent visits to a physician to have the urethra stretched, allowing the passage of urine.

Gonorrheal conjunctivitis, a common eye problem of infected infants, can also affect your teenagers. Look for a pus-laden discharge from the eye, with red and puffy eyelids. Have such a condition treated immediately—it can cause permanent eye damage within a single day.

Gonococci may invade your child's bloodstream, causing a systemic infection. Known as disseminated gonorrhea, your youngster may suffer from fever, malaise, and aches and pains in the joints. There may be skin lesions, mostly on arms and legs.

Your teenager can then develop gonococcal arthritis, generally in the knees, wrists, and ankles. After a few days, the pain may localize in one joint, with some swelling. Prompt diagnosis and treatment are necessary, since joints can be rapidly damaged by the gonococci. Symptoms of disseminated gonorrhea usually occur five to seven days after sexual contact, but sometimes not until two or three weeks later. Your child's condition may mimic other diseases, such as allergy, infectious hepatitis, and systemic lupus erythematosus.

Gonorrhea can develop into endocarditis, an inflammation of the inner lining of the heart. Your youngster's heart valves may be affected, and may require surgical replacement. If untreated, endocarditis can lead to congestive heart failure and stroke.

Gonococci can also invade the lining of the brain, leading to meningitis. In the liver, the bacteria can cause hepatitis.

Your warnings to your children are reaching the right ears. Gonorrhea (which they may know as "clap," "dose," "gleet," and "strain") is particularly common among adolescents. At least seventy teenagers acquire the disease every hour.

Tell your children the symptoms to watch for. Your son may see the first signs two to ten days after sexual contact with an infected person. He'll generally have a burning sensation when urinating and a white, pus-laden discharge from his penis. Unless he seeks treatment, he may remain able to spread the disease for as long as two years. He remains infectious even though these early symptoms disappear without treatment.

If your son's infected, he'll usually be uncomfortable enough to go to a doctor. But perhaps 1 in 5 males show no symptoms, thus fail to seek treatment. Indeed asymptomatic gonorrhea in males may be even more common than that. Researchers at the University of Washington have discovered a gonococcal strain that frequently produces asymptomatic infections in white men; it rarely infects nonwhites.

Your daughter, on the other hand, is likely to have no early symptoms. If she has symptoms, she'll probably notice them seven to twenty-one days after exposure. A female with gonorrhea sometimes experiences abnormal menstrual bleeding and frequent urination. She may have a low fever, rectal discomfort, and a light vaginal discharge. If ignored, these mild symptoms usually vanish. Thus, estimates the Public Health Service, 9 out of 10 women with gonorrhea do not realize they are infected. Like asymptomatic men, they can nevertheless transmit the disease.

Your daughter may be alerted to having the disease only when someone with a diagnosed case names her as a sex partner. It may be weeks or months after first contracting the disease that she experiences her first discomfort: pain in the reproductive organs.

The throat, too, may be infected. If your children engage in oral sex with an infected partner, they may acquire pharyngeal gonorrhea:

an infection of the pharynx, the region between the mouth and the esophagus. The disease can be spread from penis to pharynx and from pharynx to penis. It can also spread from infected female genitals to the pharynx. There is no case on record of pharyngeal gonorrhea being spread merely through kissing.

Pharyngeal gonorrhea seldom occurs alone. The victim usually suffers from infected genitals as well. Although some people experience sore throat, pharyngeal gonorrhea is often asymptomatic.

Gonorrhea may also infect the rectum. Indeed, an estimated 15 to 20 percent of gonorrhea cases are rectal. Rectal infections are common in male homosexuals, as they are in women who engage in anal intercourse. Some women acquire rectal gonorrhea when their infectious vaginal discharge soils the mucous membrane around the anus, usually during defecation.

Most often, symptoms of rectal gonorrhea are mild enough to be ignored, especially since there are many types of minor disturbances around the anus. Some victims may experience severe itching, pain, and burning in and around the anus. Sometimes there is a creamy pus-laden discharge, bleeding, and an ineffective urge to produce a bowel movement.

Steer your teenagers to the earliest possible diagnosis and treatment. The disease can almost always be cured, but organs and tissue already damaged cannot be repaired. The infection is detected by taking a smear of the discharge. The gonococci are identified through microscopic examination.

It may be very difficult to detect gonorrhea in your daughter, since there is likely to be no discharge or a discharge may not show the presence of gonococci. Making a culture of smears from several different sites (cervix, vagina, urethra, rectum, pharynx) can result in a more accurate diagnosis for women.

Expect the usual first treatment to be penicillin, taken together with probenecid, a drug that slows body excretion of penicillin. Virulent strains of gonorrhea are becoming resistant to the usual dose of penicillin. Doctors have had to resort to massive doses of penicillin or to such other antibiotics as tetracycline and spectinomycin. Treatment for gonorrhea may need to be continued for several months.

If your child is treated for gonorrhea, suggest a followup check one to two weeks after completion of treatment. For your daughter, the test should include a rectal as well as a cervical culture.

If your daughter is pregnant, she needs to be checked for the infection. An infant born to a mother with gonorrhea may contract the infection in the birth canal. The greatest hazard to babies is gonococcal conjunctivitis. Silver nitrate solution is therefore introduced into the eyes of newborns. In babies, gonococci may also cause meningitis and arthritis. The infection is linked to a higher rate of premature birth.

Syphilis: Insanity, Blindness, Early Death

Warn your teenagers that syphilis is the most severe venereal disease, ranking as a major killer among infectious diseases. Syphilis typically goes through five stages:

The Primary Stage. Usually characterized by a sore called a chancre, which appears from ten to ninety days (average: twenty-one days) after exposure. This primary chancre appears on the penis, in the vaginal area, in or around the mouth or anus—wherever the syphilis germ first entered the body. It may look like a pimple, a blister, or an open sore. It often seems hard and punched out. Rarely does it hurt or itch.

Urge your children to seek treatment for any genital sore. The primary chancre is the most contagious sore of syphilis, containing millions of spirochetes, the syphilis bacteria. These germs can be passed to any person whose mucous membrane tissues come in contact with the sore. An untreated person can remain infectious for as long as two years.

Also warn your teenager not to kiss anyone who seems to have a cold sore. If a syphilis sore is on the mouth, the disease may be transmitted through kissing. On the other hand, the primary chancre may not appear at all, or it may be so small it is overlooked. In your daughter it may be hidden inside the sex organs.

The chancre can easily be ignored or mistaken for something else. Some people, not realizing they have a syphilis sore, attempt self-treatment with salves or ointments. With or without treatment, the chancre will heal spontaneously within a few weeks. This means only that the spirochetes have moved away from the particular site. The disease has gone underground.

A Symptom-free Period. Usually lasts from two to ten weeks. It may last up to six months. Your infected youngster can still spread the disease to others.

The Secondary Stage. By now the syphilis bacteria have multiplied enough to produce symptoms throughout the body. Your child may suffer fever, sore throat, severe headache. Skin reactions are common, ranging from a fine rash to large pox, a measles-type rash or oozing sores. Scalp hair may fall out in patches. Your youngster may suffer from sores around the mouth and lips or on the palms or soles.

Your teenager's secondary symptoms of syphilis may escape notice or be ignored. The rashes don't itch or sting and will always heal spontaneously. The symptoms of the secondary stages are often mistaken for something else, such as prickly heat or an allergy. Because these symptoms mimic those of so many other diseases, syphilis has been called "The Great Imitator." One clue to a syphilitic rash: It's distributed over the body, but not on the face or hands. Another clue: Abnormal patches may appear in the mouth.

Throughout the secondary stage your teenager remains infectious. Anyone in intimate contact may contract the disease. This period lasts from six months to two years.

The Latent Stage. Can last a few years or a lifetime. Your child may feel perfectly healthy, and can no longer transmit syphilis to others—though it persists internally. Only a blood test can now detect the presence of the disease.

The Late Stage. Is characterized by severe damage to body organs. Roughly 23 percent of people with untreated late syphilis develop crippling or fatal forms of the disease. Most common are heart disease, central nervous system damage, syphilitic insanity (paresis), and blindness.

If your daughter is pregnant, she needs to be tested for syphilis as early as possible, for she can infect her unborn child. Many such infants are stillborn. If alive, they often suffer from birth defects. An infant with congenital syphilis may become deaf, blind, or insane if it is not treated immediately after birth.

Have your youngster get a blood test, which detects the antibodies the body produces to fight the spirochetes. These are not always found in the first test. A teenager who has been exposed to syphilis should be retested several times over a 3-month period.

Have your teenager seek early treatment. In later stages, any damage the disease has done to vital organs cannot be repaired. Get penicillin or other antibiotics administered by a physician.

Caution your children against trying to treat syphilis at home, as with leftover penicillin tablets. The large doses of penicillin required in the treatment of syphilis must be taken under a doctor's supervision. Covering chancres or rashes with salves and ointments—especially those containing penicillin—will only disguise the symptoms, making diagnosis more difficult. Some salves, especially those containing steroids, may speed up the production of spirochetes.

Herpes: Incurable, Linked to Cancer

Herpes simplex virus (HSV) can attack the coverings and linings of the sex organs, and can be transmitted through sexual intercourse. Warn your children that genital herpes is a common—and dangerous—venereal disease. It is also painful, and returns over and over again.

HSV type 1 is generally responsible for "cold sores" and "fever blisters," type 2 for genital infections. But caution your children not to engage in oral sex when they or their partner has a cold sore—for it's a myth that herpes simplex can't be spread through oral sex. Type 1 can cause painful genital sores. Conversely, type 2 can infect lips, mouth and tongue.

A genital herpes infection can be particularly serious for your daughter, since it seems to be associated with a greater incidence of cancer of the cervix. The virus has been isolated from cervical cancer cells. In large part because of the link with HSV, cancer of the cervix is considered to be a venereal disease. It is most prevalent in women who engage in intercourse at an early age and with numerous sexual partners. It is practically unheard of in nuns, and in religious sects that forbid intercourse before adulthood.

The virus may also attack the eyes, nose, mouth, throat, lungs, intestines, and the central nervous system, including the brain. If your daughter is pregnant, her baby's life is especially threatened by the disease, principally by spontaneous abortion or by herpes encephalitis—a crippling, often fatal brain infection. She can usually have a baby by normal delivery if she has no active sores in her vagina or on her labia. But if such sores are present, she may require a cesarean so the baby won't be exposed to the herpes virus as it passes through the birth canal.

Herpes sores first appear in the genital area three to six days after sexual contact. They sometimes itch, but are more likely to go unnoticed until they ulcerate and become painful, especially while walking and urinating.

The first attack may last a month or so. Then, at unpredictable intervals, attacks are likely to recur—each lasting from a few days to two weeks. An attack may start with tightness, stinging, tingling, or burning of infected areas. Clusters of small blisters usually follow. These break down in a couple of days, becoming crusty-looking sores. When having an attack of herpes, your teenager may have a fever, swollen glands, and a feeling as though coming down with flu. Attacks may be triggered by fever, sunburn, premenstrual changes.

Caution your youngsters not to have sexual intercourse or other skin contact until such sores, on either themselves or their partners, have healed entirely. The disease can spread easily between sex partners.

Your daughter may be a silent carrier of the disease. She may have no symptoms, yet the virus is in her sex organs and can spread to others. The infection can be detected through a Pap smear.

There's no definitive treatment. Large doses of the amino acid lysine (about 1,000 milligrams per day) appear to promote healing and retard recurrence, according to research reports. Recovery also seems to be speeded by contraceptive creams and foams containing nonoxynol-9, and by exposing the sores to fluorescent light and keeping them dry and aerated.

Vaginal Infections: Extreme Discomfort

Tell your daughter to be on watch for vaginal infections—principally trichomoniasis, candidiasis ("yeast infection," moniliasis), and haemophilus vaginalis. Her partner may have passed the infecting organism on during sexual intercourse. Or she may have picked up the organism elsewhere—and can pass it on herself during sex.

Urge her to see a doctor for any unusual discharge, any itching or soreness, any malodor or burning on urination. If she feels any embarrassment, let her know that vaginal infections are extremely common, and can be acquired in many ways besides sex. The organisms may be normally present in her vagina, but erupt in times of physical sickness or emotional stress. Assure her that all these infections are curable. Treatment usually involves some combination of prescribed tablets and salves, vaginal suppositories, and medicated douches.

Offer her tips for treating the problem. Dr. John F. Connor, a family physician in Redondo Beach, California, advises his patients: Refrain from sexual intercourse for at least two weeks. If you use suppositories, insert them at bedtime with clean fingers, not a plastic gadget that can retain organisms. Finish all the medication prescribed. When drying the infected area, don't rub with a towel. Instead, pat dry. "If you are desperate and feel you must obtain relief from the irritation, pinch the area," says Dr. Connor. "This will overcome the itch-scratch cycle, since pain is a stronger stimulus."

Although vaginal infections are of course diseases of females, if your daughter has a steady sex partner, urge him to be checked for the organism and undergo simultaneous treatment if he proves infected. He may harbor the organisms in his prostate, urethra, and bladder without any symptoms, and thus can reinfect your daughter after she's undergone treatment.

Your daughter's treatment may be complicated by a secondary infection. As one type of organism in her vagina is killed off during treatment, others may overgrow to cause a renewed problem. Thus antibiotics used against haemophilus vaginalis may destroy bacteria that have been keeping candida albicans yeast cells in check—giving rise to a case of candidiasis. Here's what you and your daughter need to know about the major vaginal infections:

Candidiasis. It is most likely to be the cause of your daughter's vulvovaginitis, the term her doctor may use to describe the inflammation of her vagina and vulva (her external genital area). This yeast cell typically causes an intense, agonizing vulvar itching. She may suffer a scalding feeling as urine touches her vulva. In a severe case her labia (vaginal lips) can be beefy red, swollen, dry, and exquisitely tender. Unlike other vaginal infections, there may be no noticeable vaginal discharge.

For treatment, she may first need to reduce the inflammation by means of soda bicarbonate sitz baths and wet compresses, avoiding soap. Her doctor may also prescribe steroids and an antihistamine like

Periactin or Dronactin. This is followed by an attack on the yeast, usually with a month-long regimen of vaginal suppositories such as nystatin (Mycostatin) or candicidin (Candeptin). Gentian violet vaginal cream or jelly or suppositories (Gentia Jel, Gentersal Cream, Genepax Tampons, Hyva Vaginal Suppositories) are effective, but advise your daughter to wear a sanitary napkin—the purple medication will leak out.

Trichomoniasis. Caused by a one-celled animal, the trichomonas protozoan. It is chiefly spread by intercourse. It may appear just after her menstrual period, or several days after intercourse with an infected male.

Your daughter is likely to suddenly suffer a profuse, foul-smelling vaginal discharge that is yellow green, frothy, and irritating. On her vulva she'll usually have itching, burning, and pain.

Therapy is generally oral metronidazole (Flagyl). Have your daughter drink a good amount of water to reduce the small chance of dark urine, aftertaste, or furry tongue. Caution her not to use washcloths or to use a freshly laundered one each time. Trichomonas may survive a day on a damp cloth hanging on the bathtub. If a gray discharge persists after her treatment for trichomoniasis, she probably has a simultaneous haemophilus vaginalis infection.

Haemophilus Vaginalis. A form of rod-shaped bacteria, it is spread primarily by intercourse. It is on the increase mainly because of the rise in adolescent sexual activity.

The organism causes your daughter to produce a gray, malodorous discharge, occasionally with slight frothiness. She may experience mild itching. Treatment usually includes oral ampicillin or tetracycline tablets or suppositories. To avoid an overgrowth of candida yeast organisms, your doctor may prescribe other medications. Nystatin suppositories are advised. Vaginal sulfonamide creams (Sultrin, Vagitrol) and suppositories may be less effective but do not cause candidiasis. Furacin cream may also be used.

Hepatitis: Liver Damage

Your teenager's sexual activities may lead to hepatitis B (genital), a virus inflammation of the liver. It is caused by the same organism as serum hepatitis, the most injurious and lethal form of the disease.

Sexual intercourse appears to be a method of transmission. But oral and anal sex evidently spread far more cases.

Look for yellowing of the whites of your youngster's eyes. This results from bile pigments entering the blood from the diseased liver. The skin may acquire a yellowish "jaundice" color, but many hepatitis victims never develop this sign.

Your child will probably show tiredness, loss of appetite, and upset stomach with or without vomiting. There also may be itching, headache, and pain in the right side of the abdomen. A fever may occur at first but generally stops in a few days. The liver may enlarge and become tender. Urine becomes darker, until it resembles diluted coffee. One curious symptom is that smokers may find the taste of tobacco so nauseating that they give up smoking.

Hepatitis requires a physician's care. The diagnosis is confirmed by a laboratory test of blood serum. Treatment in most cases is bed rest. Getting up too soon or being too active may cause permanent, possibly severe liver damage, especially if your teenager shows jaundice. A neglected case can lead to death.

A diet of at least two thousand calories a day is usually recommended. To counteract poor appetite, serve foods that appeal to your youngster, although foods low in fat are preferable. A daily bowel movement is thought helpful, and may call for a mild laxative.

Your youngster's sex partner may be an asymptomatic carrier of the serum hepatitis virus. Serum hepatitis runs rampant among narcotics users—passed from one friend to another on the tips of contaminated hypodermic needles. It can also be spread by any instrument that punctures the skin. Needles used for ear piercing and tattoos are prime conveyors of the disease. It is sometimes picked up in blood transfusions.

Lice and Scabies: Intense Itching

Remind your teenagers of the possibility of their becoming infested with pubic lice or scabies mites. These vermin are often spread by sexual contact. A case of either calls for a check for other forms of venereal disease, especially gonorrhea.

Pubic Lice ("Crabs," Pediculosis Pubis). A common condition caused by a blood-sucking insect with strongly developed claws and a crablike appearance. As the principal symptom, your youngsters are likely to suffer intense itching. If they scratch, they may develop infections and open sores. Crab lice prefer parts of the body with short hairs. Infestation may be confined to your teenagers' genital area. But the louse can also be at home in other hairy areas of the body: the underarms, eyebrows, eyelashes, beard, mustache.

Crab lice are usually transmitted through sexual intercourse and other close physical contact. It's also possible for your child to become infected through contaminated clothing, bedding, toilet seats.

You'll find the crab louse hard to see. At 1/16 of an inch, it's barely visible to the naked eye. With a strong light and a magnifying lens, the louse looks like a grayish flake of dandruff attached to the thick pubic hairs close to the skin.

Louse eggs (nits) are usually firmly attached to the base of the hairs. They take roughly a week to hatch. To tell a nit from a dandruff flake, try brushing it away. Dandruff comes off easily, nits adhere.

If any of your children may have lice, they need to see a physician. Standard therapy is Kwell (gamma benzine hexachloride), a prescription item. Usually in the form of a shampoo. it is lathered into wet hair for about 5 minutes. Then the hair is combed with a fine comb dipped in vinegar to remove remaining nits. Treatment is usually repeated in twenty-four hours. Shaving the infested part is not necessary. Rid and A200 Pyrinate are over-the-counter products that often work.

Warn your teenagers against trying to treat themselves with home remedies. Turpentine, bug spray, or various ointments can cause rashes worse than the original problem.

Scabies (Sarcoptic Itch). Another type of infestation your teenager may pick up from sexual intercourse or other close physical contact. The condition results when mites, arachnids (close kin of spiders) barely 1/50 of an inch long, burrow under your child's skin. You'll be able to see reddish zigzag furrows. Your youngster will probably suffer maddening itching, often with an allergic reaction. Scratching is to little avail and may lead to impetigo, a skin infection marked by pustules.

Mites picked up during sexual intercourse are likely to infest your youngster's genital area and buttocks. Scabies also commonly occurs in the webbing between the fingers and around the wrists. Skin folds of the elbows, underarms, breast, and feet are often infested.

Merely sleeping in the same bed may spread the infestation. Mites can also travel from person to person through kissing, hugging, handshaking, and contaminated toilets. The mite thrives where people live in crowded conditions and do not bathe.

Scabies often spreads through a family, so you may pick it up from your infested child.

Consult a physician or a hospital clinic when the disease first appears. Treatment usually entails Eurax cream or Kwell lotion or cream (not shampoo). Your teenager applies it from the neck down and leaves it on for a prescribed period before washing it off.

For either scabies or lice, thoroughly clean all clothing and bedding that came in contact with the sufferer. You need not fumigate the mattresses or household.

Of Growing Concern

Inform your teenagers that the increase in sexual activity in their age group has caused formerly rare venereal diseases to become much more common. A half-dozen major ones to warn them about:

Nongonococcal Urethritis (NGU). This presents urinary symptoms like those of gonorrhea but without the gonorrhea bacteria. Your son or daughter may suffer burning, frequent urination, and a whitish discharge. NGU now accounts for over half the male urethritis cases seen at VD clinics.

The most frequent culprits are chlamydia trachomatis organisms, bacterialike parasites that multiply within human cells. Symptoms may appear one to three weeks after contact—which can occur either through sex or in contaminated swimming pools. An inflammation of the eye—"swimming pool conjunctivitis"—also may be picked up in unchlorinated pools.

In adults, the genital infection is apparently not serious. In babies it may cause an eye infection similar to that caused by gonorrhea, but usually less destructive. If untreated, the baby may develop pneumonia. Chlamydia infections are curable with tetracycline and other antibiotics.

Lymphogranuloma Venereum (LGV). Marked by swelling and ulceration of the lymph nodes in the groin. Large masses form, pouring out pus.

The infection, caused by a member of the chlamydia group, may spread to the rectal area, with bleeding, discharge, and scarring. The first swellings appear seven to twenty-eight days after intercourse. Early treatment with tetracycline can prevent permanent damage, which includes scarring, rectal tightening, and abnormal enlargement of the genitals.

Genital Warts (Condylomata Acuminata). Caused by a virus, may appear on the genitals and are especially common around the anus of homosexual males. They are pink, red, or brown. If neglected, the warts may cover the entire area—joining to become a large cauliflowerlike structure.

In your daughter, their growth is likely to be stimulated by pregnancy, oral contraceptives, or irritating vaginal discharge. Treatment is as for other types of warts: with caustic chemicals like podophyllin, surgical excision, electrical burning, or cryotherapy (freezing).

Molluscum contagiosum. Caused by a pox virus. There are multiple tan pimples with a slight depression in the middle of each. From one to six weeks after intercourse, they appear on the abdomen, sex organs, inner thighs, and eyelids. They'll self-heal, or can be removed like warts.

Chancroid. These bacteria attack the genital area, producing painful ragged ulcers with grayish pus and a red border. Lymph glands in the groin swell and may develop abscesses. Symptoms usually appear within a week after intercourse. Chancroid responds well to sulfonamides, but tissues already damaged cannot be restored.

Granuloma Inguinale. Occurs mainly in tropical areas. The bacteria cause beef-red, velvety granulomas—fleshy masses that may eventually cover the genitals. The sores become infected and leave scars. The disease can be easily controlled with streptomycin and tetracycline. If untreated, it can lead to death.

Chapter 10

Protect Them from Pregnancy

You won't be encouraging intercourse if you talk up contraception—but expect resistance.

GIL AND MARY LINDSTROM'S daughter Carrie was a virgin when they sent her off to college. While at the campus, Carrie met Burt. She had sexual intercourse with him once.

From that single sexual contact, Carrie became pregnant. She underwent a relatively complicated late abortion.

Burt was also carrying gonorrhea, which Carrie contracted. The penicillin she took evidently caused her to erupt with candidiasis, another vaginal infection that might have been transmitted from Burt. The drugs she used for the candidiasis apparently led her to develop trichomoniasis, yet another sexually transmissible vaginal infection.

"Needless to say," reports nurse Susan Andrews of New England College in Henniker, New Hampshire, "she required counseling for a long time."

SEXUAL RUSSIAN ROULETTE

Impress upon your teenagers that they're playing sexual Russian roulette if they have intercourse without contraception. All it takes for a girl to get pregnant is one sperm—out of 300 million in the average ejaculation—fertilizing one egg such as she releases every month. This fertilization can take place several days after intercourse. No one knows exactly how long sperm survive or how long an egg remains capable of being fertilized.

[170]

As in Carrie's case, just one encounter is enough. And start driving home your message early. A survey by Chicago Planned Parenthood's Teen Scene Program uncovered 13-year-old Beth, 13-year-old Felice, and 15-year-old Monica. Each of these early teenagers had had intercourse exactly once, and became pregnant.

Without your strong urging toward birth control, your children are not likely to use contraceptives when they begin having intercourse. Some 60 percent of girls begin having sex without any protection whatever, sociologists Melvin Zelnik and John F. Kantner of Johns Hopkins University found in a survey of 2200 young women. Among younger girls, those under 15, only about 25 percent use contraception the first time.

Thereafter, unless you emphasize the need for protection, your teenagers are likely to have intercourse without it. Only 20 percent of the teenagers interviewed by Chicago Planned Parenthood said they always use birth control. An equal number "almost always" has *un*protected intercourse. The rest are hit and miss: They use contraception "often," "occasionally," "seldom," or "just once."

Your youngsters may neglect to use contraceptives even though they profess to want to avoid pregnancy. The Virginia Bureau of Family Planning finds that, before seeking a method of birth control, over 60 percent of teenage girls are sexually active—some for as long as 5 years. Reports the Bureau's social worker Nancy Marvin: "While the adolescents are stating a wish to avoid pregnancy, they are regularly exposing themselves to unwanted pregnancies."

Indeed, you may get an unwanted grandchild from your daughter's not using contraception. Sociologists Zelnik and Kantner found that fully 8 in 10 girls who had unwanted pregnancies were taking no precautions when they became pregnant. Your daughter—and the rest of your family—may thus wind up victims in the current epidemic of teenage pregnancy. Nearly 3 in 10 teenage girls who have premarital intercourse become pregnant. Teenagers account for 1 in 5 births, and more than half of all births that occur out of wedlock.

"WON'T I ENCOURAGE INTERCOURSE?"

"I don't think teenagers under eighteen should have sex," says psychologist Sol Gordon of the Syracuse University Institute for Family Research and Education.

"But," he adds, "nobody has ever asked for my permission, so all I can really say is at least use birth control."

If you're like most parents, you probably take much the same pragmatic point of view. A Gallup survey shows that less than a third of adults feel that premarital sex is "not wrong"—but, even so, over half of adults are willing to provide birth control services for teenage girls. You're likely to be uncomfortable with the thought of your children's having sexual intercourse, but, being realistic, you want to be sure they take precautions against pregnancy. There is, however, likely to be a rub: You know your children require solid information and good judgment. You know you ought to have a detailed, persuasive conversation about birth control. Yet . . .

"I'm afraid to talk about contraception," confesses Gladys, the mother of 17-year-old Ben and 15-year-old Rachel. "If I do, they may consider it permission—maybe even pushing—to have sex."

Chances are you've experienced at least a glimmering of this common fear. You may worry that bringing up the subject of birth control with your teenager will be tantamount to giving your consent to premarital intercourse. Possibly you feel that such a conversation may make your youngster feel pressured into premature intercourse—to meet your supposed expectation.

Most evidence shows that such fears are largely groundless. Comments psychiatrist Warren J. Gadpaille of the Group for the Advancement of Psychiatry's Committee on Adolescence:

> Parents may fear that contraceptive availability and sexual knowledge will promote premarital sexuality—but their fears are probably mistaken. Decisions relating to intercourse evolve from an entire set of value systems and attitudes that have been acquired throughout life. . . . Research has indicated that full contraceptive knowledge is but one more item of information that is incorporated into an adolescent's total value system and does not by itself suddenly change it.

Your daughter may be an exception to this rule. Some girls have decided that premarital sex is acceptable, but refrain only from fear of pregnancy. Psychiatrist Gadpaille considers them the "only group of females for whom such knowledge would result in initiating intercourse." Thus you need to ask yourself: Is your daughter unaware of contraception? Is her fear of pregnancy the only reason she is not having intercourse? Would she be better or worse off being kept in ignorance?

When your children do begin having intercourse, they're more likely to use birth control if you've discussed it with them. Young people who talk about sex with their parents—and who expect positive reactions from them—are much more likely to use contraception than young people whose parents are negative about sex, concludes Dr. Peter Scales of the Institute for Family Research and Education from a review of current literature on adolescent sexuality. Notes sociologist Frank F. Furstenberg, Jr. of the University of Pennsylvania, "The family can and does play a part in transmitting expectations about birth control use." When you give your adolescent specific information about birth control methods, you also impart an attitude that promotes their employment.

If your youngsters feel good about sex, they are more likely to use contraception than those who feel guilty or fearful about expressing themselves sexually. One study reported by Ira I. Reiss of the Family Study Center at the University of Minnesota shows that the key to contraceptive usage is "a general acceptance of one's own sexuality."

If you're a mother, you're especially influential on your daughter, finds Dr. Furstenberg. Your raising the issue of contraception reveals an awareness that your daughter is, or will be, having sexual relations. Observes Furstenberg: "The girl in turn is allowed to define sex less as a spontaneous and uncontrollable act and more as an activity subject to planning and regulation."

As a result, girls who discuss birth control with their mothers are much more likely to use it than are girls whose mothers are closemouthed. Indeed, girls whose mothers strongly disapprove of premarital sexual relations are far more likely to get pregnant than girls from less restrictive families. For one thing, a girl may not buy a contraceptive out of fear her mother will find it. For another, reports Furstenberg, a conspiracy of silence between mother and daughter may lead to the girl's pregnancy.

In such families, the mother fears that advice about contraception will encourage her daughter to become sexually active. She thus maintains a protective silence. Her talks about sex tend to be warnings not to "get mixed up with boys" or do anything "you'll be sorry for later."

To keep from upsetting or disappointing her mother, the girl typically conceals her sexual activity. She tries to maintain her mother's optimistic outlook by confirming her mother's belief that sex instruction isn't necessary. To avoid guilt arising from duplicity, she convinces herself that intercourse results from an irresistable urge, not amenable to her control. Concludes Dr. Furstenberg:

> The interplay ends abruptly when the girl becomes pregnant. It is not hard to understand, then, why so many mothers are genuinely astonished to discover that their daughters have had sexual relations without their knowledge and why, for their part, most adolescents are similarly embarrassed about having let their mothers down.

In sum, it's futile and self-destructive to try to keep your youngsters from sex by keeping them in the dark about birth control. "Lack of knowledge—even lack of good contraceptive methods through most of history—did not keep adolescents out of bed," observes psychiatrist Warren Gadpaille. Likewise, inadequate contraceptive information and availability is not likely to keep your teenagers from engaging in intercourse. Rather, denying them birth control simply increases the chances that they'll engage in unprotected intercourse—and that the girl will become pregnant.

"It's unrealistic to think that access to contraceptives encourages sexual activity or that denial of birth control methods discourages sexual activity," concludes Dr. Ralph I. Lopez, director of the Division of Adolescent Medicine at New York Hospital, Cornell University Medical College. "I personally endorse giving contraceptive advice to teenagers." Obstetrician-gynecologist Diane S. Fordney Settlage of the University of Southern California Medical Center in Los Angeles condemns the belief that to deny teenagers contraception is to keep them from intercourse. She calls the notion "a totally unknown and probably inaccessible premise." Indeed, in view of how pregnancy can ruin the life of an unwed teenager, denial of contraception "seems to be both wishful thinking and punitive."

TALK UP CONTRACEPTION

"Pregnancy would be a disaster in your life. You can prevent unwanted pregnancies. You must use contraceptives."

Strike that theme often in sex talks with your children. Make it part and parcel of their understanding of sex. If they know about intercourse, they need to know about contraception. Chances are they grasp the biological facts about the sperm fertilizing the egg. It's far more important to their lives to understand how to keep that from happening.

Pave the way for detailed discussions about contraception when your children are small, when intercourse is an abstract concept. Even when very young, your children can understand that having children is a choice people can make, and that there are ways to keep from starting a baby. As your youngsters mature, details come easier if you can pick up on earlier conversations, now relating the advice personally to your child.

What if you've waited until your child is an adolescent before having a conversation about birth control? Psychologist Nathaniel N. Wagner of the University of Washington suggests one way for you to approach the subject with your teenager. Pick and choose from Dr. Wagner's ideas. Adapt his sentiments to suit yourself. Repeat and rephrase as you need to. Thus you might present your feelings about sexuality and contraception something like this:

You are now old enough to have a child—that is, you are old enough to be a mother or a father.

We feel very strongly that generally young people under 18 are too young to have a relationship of a sexual nature, including intercourse, and not have it be an overall negative experience.

We think in order to have a meaningful sexual experience it is necessary to have more maturity, more knowledge about life, and more emotional stability than is usually found in teenagers.

So we hope that although you are physiologically capable of entering into a sexual relationship and producing a child, it is something you won't do without a great deal of consideration.

On the other hand, we would like you to know that if for some reason you do become sexually involved, we think you should have contraceptive knowledge and supplies available to you.

Having an unwanted child in the already overcrowded world is a terrible and thoughtless event. The problem of population is enormous—maybe the greatest human problem. The problem to an individual mother and father of bringing a child into this world who is not wanted and not planned for is equally tragic.

Therefore, to prevent the possibility of such an occurrence we want you to know what the pill, the intrauterine device, the condom, the foam, and the rhythm method are and how effective they each are.

We also want you to know that if you need medical assistance, we have talked with Dr. Jones and told him that if you come to him he should help you in any way possible. He won't tell us about it.

You don't need to tell us either, although we are open if you would like to talk and we would welcome it.

"The foregoing . . . seems to me to be in keeping with what we know about the way to develop responsible, moral people," comments psychologist Wagner. "It separates very clearly the question of contraceptive availability from sexual activity."

With this sort of introduction, you place the sexual responsibility on your teenagers. You help them think about what *they* are going to do. You also make it easier for them, notes Dr. Wagner, to withstand "being seduced by all the factors in the society that contribute to early and premature sexual involvement."

In discussing contraception with your teenagers, you may need to overcome their resistance to using it. Adolescents are commonly blinded by their ignorance about pregnancy and birth control. Therefore, hit these points hard:

"Pregnancy Can Happen to You"

Don't be surprised if your teenagers are vastly misinformed about human reproduction. Hariette Surovell, a 16-year-old New York City high school senior, summed up the state of teenage knowledge about pregnancy and contraception in testimony before the National Commission on Population Growth and the American Future:

> How can high school girls be expected to be responsible about using birth control when all knowledge is gotten on the street? Many don't even have a clear picture of how babies are made. 'Oh, I thought you couldn't get pregnant if he only comes one time," a girl once told me. And, "You can only get pregnant right after your period," said another. And then there are others who knew about the Pill so that they took their mother's, sister's and friends' Pills or they took a Pill before they had sex or after they had sex. There are girls who wash themselves out with water or Coca-Cola or vinegar. But most girls just pray.

Your daughter may use no contraception because she believes she is too young to become pregnant. She may be relying on a biological half-truth: Some young girls experience a time when, although menstruating, they are not yet ovulating and thus will not become pregnant. Tell her that counting on this is very unreliable protection. In fact, your daughter can become pregnant before ever having her period.

Disabuse your children of other common notions. Some teenagers don't use contraception because they have intercourse infrequently and believe birth control is thus unnecessary. Others believe girls can become pregnant only if they have orgasms, or only if the boy and the girl have simultaneous orgasms.

Both your son and daughter may be unaware of the times of the month a girl is most likely, and least likely, to become pregnant. They may believe they can go without birth control because they have sex only at the "safe point" in the menstrual cycle. Yet in a Johns Hopkins survey nearly 6 out of 10 girls could not correctly identify the supposedly safe time of the month.

Furthermore, your children might feel magically protected. The young adolescent especially may have a poor grasp of real-life cause and effect. If the magical thinking of childhood lingers in your youngsters, they may be convinced that a girl who truly does not want to have a baby will not become pregnant. They may not use birth control because they don't really believe that intercourse and pregnancy are related, even though they know it intellectually.

In a survey of teenage girls, over 1 in 3 agreed that a girl might not use contraception because "I'd feel like pregnancy would never happen to me."

Teenage girls are in transit between childhood and womanhood, suddenly needing to deal with their sexuality and possible pregnancy. Observes Dr. Sheldon Baroff of Memorial Hospital, San Leandro, California, "Some . . . employ denial as a mechanism for living with these realities. If pregnancy is not thought about, then it won't happen." Each act of unprotected intercourse may confirm a girl's belief that she won't get pregnant. She may thus go for months or years without contraception—and feel double-crossed when pregnancy occurs.

You can encourage your daughter not to gamble with her body by helping her to weigh the risks she's taking. In discussions at high schools, social worker Judy Mage, a Planned Parenthood counselor, has students draw up a list of the now possible *benefits* of taking a chance on pregnancy. Some student responses: "You prove you're fertile." "You prove you're grown up." "You show that you're a 'real' man." "You hold the guy." "You get away from home." "You get attention."

The group also lists the costs of contraception. "I'm embarrassed over getting a contraceptive." "I don't like letting my partner know I want to use one." "I worry about the health effects." "I'm afraid of my parents finding out."

"All of these are real," declares counselor Mage. Following her method, try to get your teenagers to stop underestimating the risks. Discuss the health costs of contraception versus the health costs of giving birth. Compare the messiness of contraception versus the messiness of dealing with 2500 diapers. Concludes Mage: "Teenagers need to understand that in denying the possibility of becoming pregnant, they must be prepared to pay the psychic cost. They need to face the reality that one-third of sexually active teenagers become pregnant by the age of 19."

By pointing up the personal catastrophe that pregnancy would be to your teenagers, you put into perspective seemingly sound arguments against contraception. "There is no ideal contraceptive," your youngsters may tell you. Grant that each method has its disadvantages, and not all contraceptive techniques are psychologically or physically suited to everyone. But remind them, every method provides some protection—and pregnancy's far worse.

"Birth control methods just don't seem natural," you may be told. "The idea of putting on a condom or inserting something chemical or plastic into the body is unnatural." Agree that that may be so. Then add, "Is it more unnatural than an unwanted pregnancy?"

"Plan Ahead for Intercourse"

Remind your youngsters that contraceptives must be used properly and consistently to protect them from pregnancy. Urge them to plan ahead for the possibility that they'll have intercourse on a date.

Even if they're virgins, they need to equip themselves with condoms and foam. Make clear that you have no wish whatever that they have intercourse—and that merely having contraceptives with them is no reason to engage in it. But, make clear, if intercourse should occur—soon or far in the future—you'll feel better knowing they're protected. By so preparing themselves, tell them, they'll be acting like mature adults. If they're shy about buying contraceptives ("Everyone will know!"), offer to make the purchase for them.

"We just got carried away" is one reason your adolescents are likely to give for failing to use birth control. A group of pregnant teenagers described similar impulsiveness. "I didn't plan on sex that night and didn't make any preparations," said Donna. Michelle complained, "Contraceptives are too premeditated!" Toby told a familiar story: "I've been going with this guy for quite a while and I didn't really believe we'd go all the way, but one night it just got away from us and I got pregnant."

Your son may be attracted to the notion of madcap sex. Six out of 10 boys told Madelon and David Finkel that "birth control makes sex seem preplanned." In another survey, nearly 2 in 5 girls agreed, "I'd feel that I shouldn't have intercourse at all, so I wouldn't plan ahead to do it or to use birth control."

Your youngsters' guilt about sex may make them need to feel overcome by sexual urges beyond their control. They therefore tell themselves and each other that sex should be "spontaneous" and that contraception makes it "calculated" and "unromantic." Further, girls often don't want to admit to themselves or their partners that they're sexually active. "If they consider birth control, that would affirm the fact that they have sex—and are bad," says obstetrician-gynecologist Takey Crist, director of the Crist Clinic for Women in Jacksonville, North Carolina.

If your children feel guilty about sex, they may reason that since intercourse in itself is wrong, they should not plan for it—following the logic that a "premeditated crime" is more reprehensible than a "spontaneous" one. Your daughter may believe that using contraception would be proof that she's a whore because "all prostitutes use birth control." "The young . . . are caught in a double bind: sex is 'dirty,' yet it feels good," explains Kathy McCoy, an editor of 'Teen magazine.

Often this double bind prompts irrational, irresponsible, carried-away-by-the-moment sexual activity among teenagers. Unable to admit the fact of their sexuality and the possibility that they may have sex, many teenagers feel that the only "right" sex is accidental sex, that which can be rationalized by blind passion. Planned, premeditated sex is, too often, viewed with horror. Sex is basically "wrong," so planning for it would be wrong. The only right sexual activity is the sex you just couldn't help.

Negative attitudes your teenagers may have about sex are probably not strong enough to stop their sexual behavior. But, concludes psychologist Donn Byrne of Purdue University, guilt and fear about sex are likely to inhibit your youngsters' use of contraceptives. Dr. Byrne showed a sampling of late adolescents films of sexual situations. Youngsters who expressed shock or other negative feelings Byrne categorized as "erotophobes," a term suggesting aversion to sex. Those who were accepting and otherwise positive he called "erotophiles."

The two groups have different backgrounds and sexual attitudes. Typical erotophobes attend church frequently. They don't discuss sex at home, and rate themselves as sexually conservative. They have inadequate sexual knowledge. They live a sex life influenced by guilt, religious belief, and fear of social disapproval. They each have intercourse rarely and with few partners.

By contrast, typical erotophiles attend church infrequently. They discuss sex at home. They feel sexually liberated. They are sexually knowledgeable. They're relatively independent in their sexual attitudes. They have intercourse often, with several partners.

Further, erotophobes disapprove of premarital sex. They feel sex is unimportant, and believe it should always be linked to love. They think that sexually arousing literature is potentially harmful. They dislike oral sex, and disapprove of birth control clinics and abortion. On all these counts, erotophiles hold opposite views.

It's the erotophobes who are least likely to follow four essential steps to successful contraception. These, finds psychologist Donn Byrne, are:

Anticipation. "An individial must know that intercourse is likely to occur." An erotophobe represses that expectation, so sex becomes a spontaneous event.

Acquisition. "Once someone admits that sex is likely to occur, he or she must procure the necessary paraphernalia by going to a doctor and/or drugstore clerk and, in effect, giving public notice of sexual activity." This can be embarrassing for anyone, but it's even more of a trial for an erotophobe.

Communication. "Sexual partners need to communicate about one another's contraceptive plans and practices to make sure somebody has done something." Erotophobes are less likely than erotophiles to talk to each other about sex or contraception.

Action. "The contraceptive must actually be used. Pills require at least one daily thought about sex, and mechanical devices require some direct contact with the genitals." Erotophobes don't like to think about sex or touch their genitals.

If your youngsters are erotophobes, they may seek to justify their seemingly irrational acts of unprotected intercourse. How? Finds Byrne: "By convincing themselves that contraception is sinful, unnatural, dangerous, etc."

Assure your daughter that she won't be thought "promiscuous" if she prepares herself for intercourse. Notes psychiatrist-pediatrician Richard M. Sarles of the University of Maryland School of Medicine: "Some girls feel guilty about planning intercourse. They have a sense of promiscuity about carrying contraceptives around."

Your daughter may be paralyzed by a double standard regarding contraception. Your son will generally be admired if he carries condoms. It's a supposed sign of his virility. But if your daughter uses birth control pills or carries a diaphragm or condom, she is likely to be considered loose, premeditating, and conniving. In fact, reassure your daughter, "There's nothing wrong with your keeping condoms. If a boy's not willing to use them, he's not worth having intercourse with."

"Share the Task"

Urge your youngsters to make contraception the responsibility of both partners. Help them see that preventing pregnancy is a shared task, that the boy as well as the girl has a stake in it. The contraceptives are more likely to be used if both partners agree on it. Their discussing this delicate issue can help their relationship become deeper and more mature. And if each uses a contraceptive—a condom plus, for example, foam or a diaphragm—the effectiveness of birth control markedly improves.

Your teenagers may fail to use contraception because they expect their partners to take responsibility for preventing pregnancy. Observes psychiatrist Carol C. Nadelson of Harvard Medical School: "With the advent of the Pill and IUD, many boys assume that it is the girl's responsibility and they fail to inquire or consider that it is a mutual experience with shared responsibility. On the other hand, many inexperienced girls assume the boy will take responsibility."

Your daughter, especially, may be too embarrassed to discuss contraception with her sex partner. Recalls one pregnant teenager: "I really didn't feel that free to talk about it, and that was probably one of the big hangups." Others told a group of California researchers, "I'd feel embarrassed to ask my boyfriend to pull out or use a rubber."

Yet, even while your daughter may be too shy to discuss her protection, she may look to the boy to provide it. "The adolescent girl, not premeditating intercourse in her early sexual experiences, is not personally prepared to utilize contraception for herself," notes Dr. Louise B. Tyrer of Planned Parenthood. "She may also be woefully ignorant about contraceptive modalities, as she was only recently playing with dolls instead of boys. Obviously, she would expect . . . that the boy would be prepared with condoms and knowledgeable in their use."

If your daughter has intercourse on very rare occasions, she is likely to persist in expecting the boy to provide protection. Help her realize that before her first experience with sexual intercourse she must be fully protected. Encourage her to act from the beginning on knowledge that usually comes only with more frequent intercourse, if it comes at all. It's generally a rare and experienced girl who becomes aware of contraception options for the female. She may then combine, say, foam with condoms.

Your son may seek to evade his share of the responsibility. Many boys believe it's "more masculine" to "go in bareback." Madelon and David Finkel, in their survey of teenage boys, found that more than half believed that "only the female should use birth control."

Nearly half the boys in another study thought that pregnancy is "her fault" when it occurs. "She should have protected herself," they told Darryl Hale and his colleagues at the Chicago Planned Parenthood Association. About the same number of boys told the researchers, "Birth control is for girls only." Some 3 out of 4 rejected the idea that "a guy should use birth control whenever possible."

Indeed, your son may feel punitive toward a partner who gets pregnant. At a recent workshop sponsored by Planned Parenthood of Rochester and Monroe County, New York, one boy declared, "If a girl got pregnant, I would blame her. If she didn't want to get pregnant, she shouldn't have done it." A 15-year-old girl said that she had had sexual relationships with four boys since she turned 14. "Three of the four told me, 'If you get pregnant, it will be because you didn't use birth control or you didn't use it right.'" Even if your son is such a male chauvinist piglet, it may not be difficult to persuade him that there is something in responsible attitudes for him. Observes David E. Cruthis, executive director of the Rochester Planned Parenthood branch, of the many teenage boys he encounters: "They are afraid of becoming fathers or catching venereal diseases. They are becoming more concerned about acting in a sensitive way than about just 'scoring.'"

"Here's Where to Get It"

Getting contraception is much easier—and more effective—for your teenager if it's done with your knowledge, consent, even help. Otherwise, your child is likely to have to cope with feelings of guilt and deceit. To escape those problems, your youngster may take no steps toward obtaining contraception, or even deny the need for it.

Your children can legally buy on their own any nonprescription contraceptive: condoms, or vaginal foam, cream, jelly, or suppositories. In June 1977 the U.S. Supreme Court ruled that minors have a constitutional right to "nonhazardous" contraceptives. The Court held unconstitutional a New York State law that permitted only pharmacies to sell contraceptives. In striking down this statute, the Court made it possible for minors to purchase contraceptives in variety and drugstores, supermarkets, and the like. By making contraceptives widely available, the Court paved the way for widespread sales to minors without parental consent.

In regard to prescription contraceptives—the Pill, diaphragms, and IUDs—the law is less clear. In some states, questions remain whether doctors and clinics can with impunity prescribe contraceptives to minors without notifying or getting consent from their parents. This unresolved legal point has made it harder for many girls to find contraceptive services. Large numbers of hospitals, health agencies, and individual physicians refuse to provide birth control to girls without written parental permission. Many apparently fear being sued for damages, although there is no such case on record in any state.

You can avoid any problems for your daughter by sending her to your family doctor. Presumably, this physician has known your daughter for years, and the youngster is comfortable speaking to an old friend. First check with your physician to be sure your children will be welcomed for sex-related services. Many doctors are heavy-handed in dealing with adolescents who need help regarding contraception or venereal disease. Your daughter will want her birth control to be dispensed nonjudgmentally. She's likely to be extremely sensitive to the attitudes of the people who supply her with contraception. She's bound to be turned off by preaching or silent scorn.

Further, impress on the doctor and your children that anything they discuss is confidential. If your children fear that their secrets will be divulged to you, they may deprive themselves of needed medical attention.

Consider steering your youngsters to a clinic that often provides contraception to unmarried minors. Many such facilities are run by Planned Parenthood and student health services. To find one in your area, look in the yellow pages under "Birth Control."

Seek an organization that will counsel your children about contraception in addition to dispensing contraceptives. Counselors should encourage responsible behavior. Unusually enlightened programs invite boys and girls together for personal discussion, making it clear that contraception is the responsibility of both partners.

Your daughter's counseling should be individualized. Her counselor should let her know that there is no one perfect method, and should consider in her choice of a contraceptive such factors as her frequency of intercourse, and her physical and emotional maturity. The counselor, too, should be sensitive to your daughter's birth control preferences or aversions. If she's uncomfortable touching her genitals, for example, she's not likely to use a diaphragm or foam properly or consistently. If she feels that the pill is dangerous or unnatural, she may simply stop taking it.

Expect the clinic to make the experience as friendly and pleasant as possible. Your child may welcome a program like the Teen Clinic of the Virginia League for Planned Parenthood in Richmond, which uses teenagers as peer counselors, and has walls and furniture painted in bright colors to help give a feeling of informality. The first session the teenage clients attend is a "rap session." Says Connie Berkely, director of women's services, "Among other things, we discuss what is going to happen during their examination, since this is very important to alleviate any fears that the teens may have about what will often be their first pelvic examination."

Especially search for services that are geared to how your adolescents learn. Teenagers often need a great deal of patience and repetition of instruction before they can use birth control effectively. Your youngsters will take time to really absorb information and discover how it applies to them. Dr. Gary Goldsmith of the Adolescent Health Center at The Door in New York City finds that "it takes the average teenager more than one visit to learn what he or she needs to learn in order to use contraception successfully."

Teenagers often come to clinics frightened, explains Dr. Goldsmith. "We find we have to build a relationship with these kids before they really hear the information. . . . This is the reason why these kids are unsuccessful in most family planning clinics where they only visit once or twice."

IS YOUR DAUGHTER PREGNANCY-PRONE?

Merely knowing the facts about birth control may not persuade your children to use it. At the Claremont Colleges in California, over 7 out of 10 pregnant college girls had not used any birth control method, despite their knowledge and the availability of contraceptive services. "The reluctance of intelligent young college women to use safe contraceptive methods was puzzling in view of their acknowledgement that they knew the facts about sex and reproduction," comment Dr. Karem J. Monsour and Barbara Stewart of the Claremont counseling center. "We are forced to conclude that intelligence and information alone were not of much value for assuring rational behavior regarding contraception."

Even if your teenage daughter has not experienced intercourse, you may be able to tell if she's "pregnancy-prone."

Psychosocial factors can make her subject to pregnancy if she becomes sexually active. These warning signs are linked to a higher-than-average risk of pregnancy. Extensive birth control advice—and possibly professional counseling—may be especially appropriate for your daughter if you answer "Yes" to any of these questions:

Does she have a steady boyfriend? Teenage pregnancies generally result from long-term relationships. A couple usually does not start having intercourse until they've dated for a while. Thereafter, they tend to have intercourse frequently enough to put the unprotected girl at significant risk of pregnancy.

Some girls believe that two people truly in love don't use birth control. In other instances, a girl may believe that her pregnancy will be interpreted as a sure sign of love toward her boyfriend. "I've had a few girls 14-15 years old who have asked me why they *can't* get pregnant," reports pediatrician William A. Daniel Jr. of the University of Alabama School of Medicine. "They'll tell me, 'We've been going together now for six months, and we're not using any contraception.'" Dr. Daniel asked one of these girls, "Why do you want to get pregnant?"

She replied, "My boyfriend wants a baby." Recalls Daniel: "I responded by saying, 'Why don't you let *him* have one?' But I don't get very far with such arguments."

A girl who has intercourse with a large number of partners is also likely to become pregnant. Even if she has intercourse fewer times than a girl with a steady boyfriend, her sex partners are less likely to use contraception. In a casual relationship, the boy may be unprepared for intercourse, thus is unequipped with a condom, finds sociologist Frank F. Furstenberg Jr. of the University of Pennsylvania. "The girl is less likely to urge him to use contraceptives," adds Dr. Furstenberg. "Even if she does, he is probably less inclined to respond to her request."

Is she short of money? Regard this as a red flag if you're low on funds or if your daughter is barely making it on her own. There is an association between a lack of money and early pregnancy, in part because the poor have limited access to contraception, sometimes treating it as a luxury item that they're wont to do without.

Thus a vicious circle: Poverty increases the chances of an adolescent pregnancy. Then the pregnancy increases the chances of continuing poverty.

Among some inner-city teenagers, the earlier a girl gets pregnant, the earlier she gets her own welfare check. "Then she's got it made because she's got some money coming in on a regular basis," comments pediatrician William Daniel. "In some areas, pregnancy is very much a status thing: it proves that the girl is grown up and has her own money."

Does she have a poor opinion of herself? Some girls are self-deprecating and do not care what happens to them. They often suffer from feelings of emptiness, helplessness and worthlessness. Typically they have a sense of hopelessness about themselves and their future. When such a girl becomes pregnant, she commonly has a self-punitive feeling that she must have and raise the baby, that there is no choice for her but to accept the consequences.

Researchers who study how pregnant adolescents feel about themselves frequently report they have low self-esteem. This, it is speculated, helps create conditions that invite greater sexual activity and the risk of unwanted pregnancy. A need for approval may motivate the girls to require male attention.

Dr. Calvin E. Zongker of the School of Home Economics at Florida State University in Tallahassee has found that pregnant girls have a much more disturbed self-concept than nonpregnant girls he studied. School-age mothers, notes Dr. Zongker, more often exhibit "feelings of inadequacy and unworthiness." They tend to be more dissatisfied with their family relationships.

They more often dislike their physical selves: their looks, bodies, and performance. In addition. Zongker found "more conflict . . . instability and defensiveness . . . as well as indications of maladjustment and personality disorders." These feelings, he points out, may have been contributing factors to the pregnancy, or results of being pregnant, or both.

In some areas, especially urban ghettos, pregnancy is a culturally acceptable norm, and the girls get a lot of encouragement and approval from friends. "You're not really 'in' until you've had your own baby," notes psychiatrist-pediatrician Richard M. Sarles of the University of Maryland School of Medicine. "These girls speak about their pregnancies with a great deal of pride."

Does she lack goals? A girl may consciously want to become pregnant because she has nothing else to do.

"My life was empty," recalls 19-year-old Maria, mother of 13-month-old Celeste. "I'd graduated from high school. I didn't like my job or any job I'd be likely to get. I was living with a guy I thought I loved. So I decided to have a baby."

Maria loves Celeste, but she's not sure that her decision to have a baby was the proper one. She's finding motherhood unexpectedly confining, and she's not getting along with the baby's father. "Every week, I have a real blowout with Vince, and think of leaving him. I know I never want to marry him." Money is tight. Often they have to manage on one meal a day.

"In the intentional pregnancy the girl is seeking to satisfy some particular need," observes Dr. James P. Semmens, chief of obstetrics and gynecology at the Long Beach, California, Naval Hospital and his associates. For example, pregnancy may help a girl escape from a home. She may unconsciously wish to fulfill her parents' accusations about her sexual behavior. In an extreme case, reports Dr. Semmens, a girl's mother had a hysterectomy and then remarried. The girl became pregnant to give her mother a baby for what otherwise would have been a childless marriage.

Has she a bone to pick with you? A girl's wish to punish her parents often accounts for her inflicting a grave problem on them, even at her own expense. This was true of 17-year-old Andrea, who announced to her parents at the dinner table: "Oh, by the way, I'm two months pregnant." Andrea relished the startled expressions, the upset, the sudden attention she got.

Over the next few weeks, Andrea and her parents had their first serious conversations together in years. They sought a counselor's help in resolving their problem, and decided on abortion. With the counselor's aid, Andrea was able to see how angry she was at her parents' seeming indifference to her—and how great a part this had played in her becoming pregnant. "I guess I just wanted you to really notice me," Andrea told her parents. "I couldn't come up with a better way."

Proving womanhood is another largely unconscious motivation for becoming pregnant. This, too, often has a lot to do with a girl's relationship with her parents. When 16-year-old Laura was told at the clinic that her test was positive for pregnancy, her first reaction was, "Good! I can be a mother. Now my parents can't treat me like a baby anymore."

Is she a lone wolf? If so, she may be predisposed to early pregnancy, suggest researchers at Bowling Green State University in Ohio. Girls who suffer premarital pregnancy score extraordinarily high on a social isolation scale that measures the distance which people perceive between themselves and others. Those high in social isolation feel:

"Relationships are not supportive. Individuals are thrown back on their own resources. Other people are unfriendly and disinterested. Individuals are essentially anonymous and alone."

Pregnant girls are likely to believe that there are few dependable ties between people. They expect most people to be insincere, and not basically considerate or helpful. A common refrain among them: "Real friends are hard to find."

It's not clear whether such feelings precipitate the early pregnancy, or result from it. The researchers note that early motherhood may spring from feelings of alienation, since early motherhood "may be seen as potentially bringing some degree of order and predictability." On the other hand, it seems "just as logical" to assume that premarital pregnancy can enhance feelings of social isolation.

Dr. Virginia Abernethy, of the psychiatry department of Harvard Medical School, finds a constellation of psychological and social factors often characteristic of pregnant teenagers. According to Dr. Abernethy's portrait, a girl likely to become pregnant has low self-esteem. She doesn't like her mother and/or finds her an inadequate role model. The girl's risk of pregnancy is especially high if she has warm memories of early closeness with her mother, followed by feelings of loss or alienation during adolescence. When there is a surrogate mother, such as a grandmother, consistently available to the girl, she is less likely to become pregnant despite her conflicts with her mother.

The pregnancy-prone girl is also unlikely to have satisfying friendships with women. Her parents are unhappily married. She often has an exclusive, intimate relationship with her father, to the exclusion of her mother. This relationship may have a quasi-sexual nature—the girl may feel that she could be a better wife to her father than her mother is. At the same time, comments Dr. Abernethy, such feelings produce anxiety in the girl because of their incestuous overtones. "She may respond by compulsively using sex with other men to place a barrier between herself and her father."

Chapter 11

The Best Contraceptive for Your Child

Probably a condom plus foam or diaphragm, says this buyer's guide.

CHOOSING A CONTRACEPTIVE for your children is loaded with ifs. Among them:

- If it's effective.
- If they'll use it.
- If it has dangerous side effects.

The accompanying table helps you compare the effectiveness of birth control methods. You can see that any choice of contraceptive is a tradeoff between the protection the method affords, the risk of adverse reactions, and the possibility that your youngsters won't comply with it.

Condom with foam appears to balance out as the best method for most teenagers. Protection is extremely high, with the least possibility of side effects. The method is the best one for girls who have intercourse infrequently.

A packet of condoms or a foam kit fits a teenager's pocketbook, in size as well as in price. A girl can thus be spared needless exposure to the IUD or Pill. The method requires little advance preparation by adolescents, whose immaturity makes them short on foresight. The condom with diaphragm, which is even more effective with as few adverse reactions, is suited to older girls who have intercourse more frequently and who can plan ahead reliably. The condom involves the boy in the process—and provides protection against VD.

Birth control: How well does it work?

	Effectiveness if used perfectly all the time	Effectiveness based on surveys of couples who use the method
Pills (combined estrogen and progestogen)	99.66%	90-96%
Mini-pills (progestogen only)	98.5-99%	90-95%
IUD	97-99%	95%
Condom *and* Foam or Diaphragm *	99 + %	95%
Condom	97%	90%
Diaphragm	97%	83%
Foam	97%	78%
Withdrawal	91%	75-80%
Rhythm	87%	79%
Douching	?	60%
No method	10%	10%

These figures are for fertile couples, based on the first year of using a method. "90% effective" means 90 out of 100 couples using the method for one year will not have an unplanned pregnancy.

* Figures are for foam. With diaphragm, effectiveness is greater.

If your daughter cannot comply with the foregoing, suggest an IUD. It provides "passive compliance"—sex can be spontaneous, for your daughter need do almost nothing to be protected. While less effective than the Pill, the IUD also poses less of a present—or potential—problem as to side effects.

The Pill, furthermore, requires perfect daily compliance. On the other hand, the Pill is the most popular form of birth control among adolescent girls. Most girls evidently remember to take it daily, with no apparent severe adverse reactions. Users gain peak protection and maximum sexual spontaneity. The great tradeoff, however, comes with the worrisome question of side effects.

YOUR GUIDE TO CONTRACEPTION

Set before your children the facts about each method of birth control. Be thorough—and objective. "One problem with contraceptive compliance is that every single birth control method has been given a bad rap by the media and lay press," comments Dr. Ralph I. Lopez, director of the New York Hospital-Cornell Medical Center's Division of Adolescent Medicine:

> First of all, the IUD requires that the girl go to a doctor. She's probably heard that it's a painful experience. Her friends have told her that the IUD hurts, that she'll develop cramps, and that "an IUD can rip through the uterus and make you sterile." She's also heard that the pill makes you gain weight, gives you cancer, and causes blood clots. The diaphragm is messy and slips out of place. She's probably read that foam is messy and tastes terrible; it's probably not effective anyway, so why use it?

If your teenagers do have some knowledge, it is likely to be haphazard and incomplete. True, finds a survey by Madelon Lubin Finkel of New York University and anthropologist David J. Finkel of Adelphi University, a large majority of high school boys know that condoms can prevent pregnancy. But few are aware that condoms can also prevent venereal disease, an incentive for their using them. Similarly, 2 out of 3 know that douching is not reliable contraception. But only about 1 out of 3 realize that withdrawal is likewise poor protection. A study by Paul A. Reichelt and Harriet H. Werley of the University of Illinois College of Nursing shows that most teenagers "are either misinformed or uninformed about the various methods of contraception." Some 2 out of 3 teenagers, find Reichelt and Werley, are confused by such dangerous myths as, "The Pill must be stopped every year for three months," and, "The Pill should not be taken by a girl who uses alcohol and/or drugs." Believing either of these falsehoods could lead a daughter on the Pill to deny herself protection.

Almost half don't realize that the IUD remains in the uterus and need not be inserted before each act of intercourse. Not appreciating this fact can make your daughter refuse this effective form of birth control. About 2 out of 3 are unaware of the need to use contraceptive cream or jelly with a diaphragm—a lapse that can considerably cut down on your daughter's protection. Almost half believe that "rubbers break easily." Such a misconception may curtail your youngsters' use of condoms.

Nearly 4 out of 5 think that spermicidal foam "should be washed out with a douche immediately after intercourse." This of course increases your daughter's risk of pregnancy. Perhaps the most unsettling finding reported by Reichelt and Werley: "Teenagers appear to be so convinced of the correctness of their belief that they do not retain the correct information after it is supplied."

Therefore you may need to refer again and again to the following alphabetical guide to contraception and repeat the information over and over until your teenagers comprehend it:

Condom (90–97%): The Basic Contraceptive

Condoms (rubbers, prophylactics, trojans, safes, sheaths, scumbags) offer high protection against both pregnancy and disease. If used correctly with foam or a diaphragm, the condom is practically foolproof. It has virtually no side effects. Moreover, it's inexpensive, widely sold, requires no prescription, and is easily carried in a pocket or purse.

Explain to your children how condoms are properly used—your daughter as well as your son needs to know. Break open a packet and show them the condoms are about eight inches long and generally come prerolled and powdered. Some have a nipple-shaped reservoir at the tip to catch the semen and help prevent the condom from bursting. If it doesn't have a reservoir, the boy should leave half an inch loose at the end when putting it on.

The condom must be fitted over the penis while it is erect. This can be made part of the sex play, the girl helping the boy put it on. With practice, this can be done in the dark in a few seconds, avoiding needless interruption of lovemaking and possible loss of the erection. To add to the sensuousness of condoms, they're manufactured in a variety of designs and colors. Textured condoms, including "French ticklers," can provide a range of sensations.

Warn your youngsters that the condom may slip off inside the vagina as the penis shrinks after ejaculation. The boy should therefore remove his penis before it becomes soft. While doing this, he needs to hold his fingers around the base of the condom so that it does not slip off. He should then move away from the girl while he unrolls the condom, since sperm will now be on his penis. A new condom must be used each time intercourse occurs. If there's any chance that semen has leaked into the vagina, the girl should immediately insert an application of a spermicidal jelly, cream, or foam.

In rare cases, a boy or girl may suffer an allergy to rubber, causing a rash on the genitals. Switching to a condom made from lambskin (a "skin") generally solves the problem.

To avoid breakage, counsel your teenagers not to subject condoms to heat. They may deteriorate quickly if carried in a pocket or wallet, or stored in a glove compartment. Suggest that condoms be bought from a store, not a machine, which may have overage merchandise. Avoid foreign-brand condoms, which are not uniformly subjected to the testing given American condoms and may be defective more often.

Your youngsters should examine, but not test, a condom before using it. It is likely to be damaged by needless stretching or inflating. Condoms that are lubricated in their packages are least likely to break from dryness. For do-it-yourself lubrication, recommend spermicidal jelly or cream. Petroleum jelly or oils should not be used—they can cause the condom to deteriorate and they have no spermicidal properties. If there's any question whatever about the safety of condoms, urge your youngsters to throw them away.

Before your children buy condoms, prepare them for being asked, "What size?" The question refers not to the size of the boy's penis but to the package. Condoms come in packets of three or twelve. Warn them against trying to improvise condoms from plastic sandwich bags or wrappings, an attempt that's uncomfortable and carries a high risk of pregnancy.

Your teenagers may not like condoms without knowing much about them. They may tell you, "You don't shake hands with a rubber glove, and you don't make love with a condom."

Let them know that most men who complain of loss of sensitivity with regular condoms have found those made from lambskin more satisfactory. Indeed, by decreasing penis sensitivity, condoms may delay ejaculation, prolonging intercourse and enhancing pleasure for both partners. Condoms may benefit a boy who has trouble maintaining an erection—the condom exerts a slight touniquet effect on the veins of the penis.

Your youngsters might also believe that condoms break easily, a common teenage myth. Actually, they're thin but tough. Manufacturing defects are extremely rare—condoms are made under the jurisdiction of the Food and Drug Administration and have to meet strict standards. In an unopened box they ordinarily last about a year.

DES: For Emergencies Only

A controversial "morning-after" contraceptive has been approved by the FDA for use in emergency situations such as rape. The pill, a large dose of a synthetic estrogen compound called diethylstilbestrol or DES, is over 90 percent effective in preventing pregnancy. It should be administered within seventy-two hours after intercourse.

The FDA emphasizes that DES should not be considered as a routine means of contraception because of possibly severe side effects. It generally causes violent nausea and vomiting. Other common side effects include extreme breast tenderness, headaches, dizziness, menstrual irregularities. If DES treatment is taken once, it should not be taken a second time. The contraceptive dose is equivalent to about ten months of birth control pills.

A controversy over DES concerns its possible cancer-causing potential. It was banned as a growth hormone for cattle and other food animals after it was found capable of causing cancer in some animals. At one time DES was used to prevent miscarriages. Daughters of women who received DES during pregnancy suffer an unusually high incidence of a rare type of vaginal cancer.

There is no data to show that DES causes cancer in the woman who takes it. The FDA believes that DES, used as a contraceptive, does not pose a "significant threat to the patient."

On the other hand, the cancer-causing potential of DES has not been fully explored. Doctors Roy Hertz and Mort Lipsett, experts in hormonal cancer at the National Institutes of Health, have stated that "DES is such a powerful carcinogen that it is used as a model for producing artificial cancers in animals."

DES should not be taken if there is a family history of cancer of the breast or of the genitals. There may also be a risk if other estrogens have been taken, such as birth control pills.

If DES is ineffective and pregnancy results, the FDA advises considering abortion.

Diaphragm (83–97%): For Mature Young Women

Explain to your daughter that the diaphragm, a soft rubber device with a spring rim, is but one part of a contraceptive *system*. Another essential part is a contraceptive jelly or cream that kills sperm before they can get into her uterus. A condom on her partner raises her protection to the maximum.

To properly use her diaphragm, she spreads on its saucerlike surface a teaspoon of spermicidal cream or jelly—foam doesn't adhere well enough. She then places the diaphragm into her vagina so that it blocks her cervix, the entrance to her uterus. Without the spermicide, she'd be at great risk of sperm getting around the diaphragm rim and making her pregnant.

Obstetrician-gynecologist Phillip Stubblefield of Harvard thinks the diaphragm is the "absolute best" method for teenagers. Properly used, the system is highly effective, and has no side effects. For a while the diaphragm fell out of favor because it seemed less convenient and effective than the Pill or IUD. Now the diaphragm appears to be making a comeback among young women who, fed up with side effects and worried about long-term safety, have abandoned the Pill and IUD.

Moreover, there's no need for your daughter to interrupt sex play so she can insert her diaphragm. In fact, sexual arousal changes the location of the cervix, raising the hazard of an improper fit. A better practice: If your daughter thinks she might possibly have intercourse on a date, she can insert her diaphragm before going out.

The spermicide is certainly effective for up to two hours. If she has intercourse more than two hours after insertion, she'll be safest if she leaves the diaphragm in place, but introduces into her vagina more spermicide (cream, jelly, suppository, or foam). Each application protects her against the sperm in one ejaculation. Before each additional intercourse, she needs another applicator full of spermicide.

After intercourse, she needs to leave the diaphragm in place for at least six hours. She similarly should wait six hours before douching. The diaphragm can remain in place for days without adverse effect. Removing it allows the vagina to cleanse itself. Taking it out also reduces the chance of irritation and infection.

If your daughter properly cares for her diaphragm, it can last for about two years. After removing it, she should wash it with mild soap and warm water, then air dry it and dust it with cornstarch before putting it back in its container. Suggest she check it after every use for weak spots and pinholes by pulling the rubber gently away from the rim as she looks at it in front of a light.

Your daughter is likely to be a good candidate for a diaphragm if she's well-motivated, responsible, and isn't averse to touching her genitals. Observes pediatrician Robert B. Shearin, director of the Division of Adolescent Medicine at Georgetown University School of Medicine:

> Psychologically mature adolescent females who understand the use of the diaphragm and who will adhere to the strict rules governing its use find it an acceptable method of contraception. It has been my experience that the college-age, independent adolescent female who chooses the diaphragm will use it successfully if she has a cooperative sexual partner.

Also, ask where your daughter is having intercourse. If she has a regular place, then a diaphragm might be an especially good contraceptive for her. Couples who have intercourse at a regular spot are at an advantage as far as using contraceptives is concerned. Even if the couple has intercourse in the back of a van, at least it's a fairly predictable place, and the intercourse is generally planned.

The diaphragm is *not* a good choice for an immature girl with a helter-skelter sex life. She'd probably not be able to cope with the equipment involved, the modest skill required for insertion, and the discipline necessary to ensure that the diaphragm actually gets used.

Even though your daughter is as sober as a judge, warn her against the "just this once" syndrome. Dr. Mary E. Lane of the Margaret Sanger Research Bureau believes that virtually every woman experiences such a temptation "against her better judgment, as she tumbles blithely into bed while the diaphragm remains in the medicine cabinet."

Advise her to use her diaphragm throughout her menstrual cycle. No harm results if she starts menstruating with the diaphragm in place. Indeed, some women use it to hold back the blood if they have sex during their periods.

It's essential that your daughter go to a doctor or a birth-control clinic—both to have the diaphragm fitted for her, and also to learn how to insert it properly. She may not realize that the cervix is so far back in her vagina. She can find it beforehand by running her finger along the lower wall of her vagina. A full finger-length in, she'll feel a lump somewhat like the end of a nose. That's her cervix, what her diaphragm must cover. The rim will slip into the recess above the cervix, out of reach. The rubber will feel wrinkled—it will not lie flat over the cervix.

Caution her never to borrow someone else's diaphragm or buy one without a prescription. If the diaphragm is improperly inserted or if it's too small, it can fail to protect her from pregnancy. It might also be displaced during intercourse.

Encourage her to return to the doctor a week or so later to make sure that she's using it correctly and has no problems. If she was a virgin, or had had sex only a few times when the diaphragm was fitted, she's likely to need a new size after a few weeks because her vaginal muscles will expand with sexual experience. Until she returns at the end of that week for a check of the size and her technique, she should use a backup method of contraception, such as a condom or additional vaginal spermicide.

Remind her to return for checkups at least once a year. Even if she uses a diaphragm for years, she may grow careless about her insertion technique. She may need a change in size if she loses or gains more than twenty pounds, or if she has an abortion or a baby. She also needs to go for a check on the size or her technique of insertion if warning signals appear. For example, her partner complains of feeling the rim. Or she develops such discomfort that she must remove the diaphragm prematurely. Or the diaphragm rim no longer remains snug, or she can place a finger easily between the rim of the diaphragm and the recess of her vaginal wall, suggesting that the diaphragm is too small. Or, at a time other than her period, there is blood on the diaphragm when it is removed. This may indicate undue pressure from the rim, improper placement, or an injury or illness.

Should your daughter suffer itching or irritation, she may be allergic to rubber or the spermicide. She may overcome an allergy to the cream by switching brands. Reassure your daughter that a diaphragm can't get lost inside her, as some girls fear. Nor, despite what she may believe, do diaphragms cause cancer.

Douching (60%): As Good As Nothing

Warn your youngsters that douching—flushing out the vagina with a large amount of water after intercourse—is virtually useless for preventing pregnancy. It is essentially the same as no contraceptive at all.

For douching to be in the least effective, it must be done immediately after intercourse. Sperm travel at over an inch per minute and can reach the cervix in less than ninety seconds after ejaculation. Douching should be used only as an emergency measure if a condom breaks. It is a shade better than using no birth control method at all.

Fluids widely used by teenagers for douching, including Coca-Cola and vinegar, are no more effective than water even though they supposedly make the vagina more acidic. Vaginal douches sold for "feminine hygiene" have no contraceptive value. All such chemicals may cause irritation or allergic reactions, marked by redness, itching, and vaginal discharge.

Foam and Other Spermicides: Use with Condom or Diaphragm

Without needing a prescription, your daughter can buy a sperm-killing preparation that she inserts into her vagina before intercourse. Used with a condom, spermicides provide peak protection with no side effects.

Spermicides destroy sperm cells before they pass through the cervix and into the uterus. Some brands contain surface-active agents thought to attach to the sperm, breaking down the cell walls, denying them oxygen and upsetting their metabolism. Bactericidal agents disrupt the metabolism of the sperm. Acid agents are destructive to sperm, which cannot survive in an environment too acid or too alkaline.

One or more of these chemicals are packaged as foams, creams, jellies, foaming tablets, and suppositories. Some come with applicators to ease insertion.

Advise your daughter to insert a vaginal spermicide shortly before intercourse. To make it effective, she spreads the spermicide evenly and thickly high up in her vagina to form a barrier between the cervix and sperm. She must put more in if she has sex again. If she gets off the bed, she needs to apply additional spermicide, since a large quantity may leak out. If she doesn't have intercourse within an hour after inserting the spermicide, she needs another application, for by then most spermicides lose their effectiveness. She can go to the toilet but shouldn't douche or sit in a bathtub for at least 6 hours after intercourse. If she or her partner shows an allergy to a spermicide, relief may be found in a type with different ingredients.

Foam. An aerosol like shaving cream, foam is thought to provide generally the best protection of all types of spermicides. Foams (Because, Delfen, Emko, Koromex) disperse and form a physical barrier to the cervix more rapidly than the others. Foam also has the advantage of being less messy and less easily displaced during intercourse. They may protect somewhat against the transmission of venereal diseases.

Your daughter needs to shake the can of foam at least twenty times before use in order to activate the bubbles and mix the spermicide. Recommend that she insert the foam no more than one-half hour before intercourse because the bubbles go flat. The foam is mostly air, leaving little residue.

Remind her never to inject foam directly into her vagina. Not only can it damage her tissues. If she's pregnant, it can force a lethal air bubble into the enlarged blood vessels of her uterus. To prevent this from happening, she fills the small plastic applicator that comes with it and uses that to deposit about a teaspoonful of foam into her vagina. Prefilled applicators, which are good for one application and can be carried in a purse, are available. Emko Pre-Fil offers a mixture that can be put into an applicator up to a week before use.

Creams and Jellies. These come in a tube with an applicator. Your daughter should apply them not more than fifteen minutes before intercourse. These spermicides are not as effective as foam. But, as with foam, when used with the condom their effectiveness is increased.

Reliable creams include Conceptrol, Delfen, Koromex, Ortho-Creme. Major brands of jellies: Koromex, Ortho-Gynol, Ramses.

Vaginal Foaming Tablets and Suppositories. These are generally least effective. Caution your daughter to use them only when other spermicides are not available. The tablets work only when moist, and are not suitable for some girls with relatively dry vaginas. The tablets lose their fizz within two weeks after exposure to air.

The suppository melts at body temperature and forms a shield. It doesn't spread as well as foam, cream, or jelly—indeed, may not melt at all. For best results, advise your daughter to insert one suppository within fifteen minutes before intercourse, and a second suppository immediately afterward. *The Medical Letter* reports that the Encare Oval, heavily advertised as a "new" type of suppository, "has no established advantage over other typical spermicidal products that have been available for many years."

IUD (95–99%): Automatic, With Possible Problems

An intrauterine device (IUD, loop, coil) may be the best contraceptive for your teenager if she's unable to comply with other forms of birth control. Except for periodic checks, she can forget about an IUD. It's highly effective, and won't interfere with her sexual spontaneity.

The IUD can provide her with automatic protection if she's inconsistent about taking precautions with the condom, foam, or diaphragm. Besides sterilization, the IUD is the only means of contraception that does not require some preparation by the user.

Your daughter's a poor candidate for the IUD if she's loath to touch her genitals, or if she dislikes the thought of a foreign object inside her. An IUD is a small, flexible device that is inserted into the uterus. It is thought to obstruct pregnancy by causing changes in the endometrium (the lining of the uterus), possibly altering the time of month when it is ready to accept implantation. The IUD may also affect the Fallopian tubes so as to prevent fertilization of an egg.

If your daughter opts for an IUD, her doctor is likely to recommend one containing copper (such as the Copper T and the Cu–7). A copper device is smaller than plastic IUDs like the Lippes Loop or Saf-T-Coil. It's suitable for a girl who has never been pregnant and so has a small uterus. Unlike plastic IUDs, which can stay in indefinitely, a copper device must be replaced every two or three years.

Your daughter will find that insertion of an IUD takes perhaps a minute. To avoid discomfort, suggest she ask the doctor to anesthetize her cervix. Alert her to the fact that she's to get a complete gynecological examination, after which the doctor opens her vagina with a speculum, a duck-billed instrument, and inserts the IUD with a tube-shaped introducer. Most doctors prefer to insert IUDs during menstruation when there is no chance of her being pregnant, and when insertion is most comfortable because her cervix is soft.

Expect her doctor to point out that the IUD has a string tail that stays outside her cervix. If the string is reasonably long and silky, rather than short and whiskery, neither she nor her partner should feel it. At least once a week during the first month and after each period, she needs to check the string with her finger to see if it is still in place.

If the string disappears, or if she feels the device in her cervix, she needs to see her doctor. An expulsion generally occurs during menstruation, so advise her to check her sanitary napkins or tampons to make sure the IUD has not been passed out. If she expels one type of IUD, she may be able to retain a different type.

Have her make an appointment to be reexamined within three months, preferably shortly after the first menstrual period following insertion. Annual examinations are usually sufficient after this, unless trouble develops.

As a common reaction, tell her she may experience increased discharge—watery, clear, mucuslike, and odorless—with the IUD. If this bothers her, advise her to use a vinegar douche, two or three times a week, or a pad. If she experiences an unpleasant odor from the discharge, it may be a sign of infection that she should report to her doctor.

Prepare her for some spotting of blood for a week or two after the IUD is inserted. Menstrual-type cramps and backache are also common. Her first few menstrual periods after insertion are likely to be earlier, heavier, and longer. There may be spotting between periods. Reassure her that these discomforts tend to disappear after a few months.

To make her IUD nearly foolproof, recommend that she use a vaginal spermicide for seven to ten days during the high-fertility midpoint between her periods. This is especially important during the first year, when most failures of IUDs occur.

Despite the IUD's advantages, it may cause your daughter side effects. A small percentage of users suffer severe cramps and bleeding from the IUD, and must have it removed. After a while, some users complain of an unpleasant vaginal odor, possibly due to bacteria encrusting the IUD tail. This usually clears up quickly with a vaginal antibiotic.

It is estimated that IUD users are four times more susceptible to pelvic inflammatory disease (PID) than nonusers. Some physicians feel that a young woman who's never been pregnant should not use an IUD if she has more than one partner, thereby increasing the possibility of PID or VD infection that might lead to infertility or even the necessity for hysterectomy. Some doctors prefer not to recommend IUDs at all until after the woman has had at least one successful pregnancy.

Such infections tend to occur during menstruation. If your daughter experiences unusual pain during her period, she needs a prompt examination for pelvic inflammation. Often this is a relapse of a previous infection. Most such infections can be treated with antibiotics. Removal of the IUD is generally advisable.

An extremely rare complication of the IUD, occurring about once in every 2500 insertions, is perforation of the uterus—the device penetrates the uterine wall. In most instances there is no pain or any other symptom. Perforation of the uterus may be the result of faulty insertion. An IUD that has entered the abdominal cavity should be removed.

If your daughter has an abnormally small or irregularly shaped uterus, she may not be able to wear the device. IUDs are generally not recommended for women who have had recent pelvic inflammatory disease, venereal disease, or other gynecological infections. The IUD is also ruled out for women who have severe anemia, heavy menstrual bleeding or abnormal uterine bleeding, cancer of the uterus, or fibroid tumors in the uterus.

Dispel any myths your daughter may have about IUDs. There are no known cases of uterine or cervical cancer resulting from the device. The IUD has no effect on fertility after it is removed.

Pill (90–99%): Beware of the Side Effects

If your daughter is having frequent intercourse, then an oral contraceptive is probably the easiest solution—if she can be relied on to take it, and if she is untroubled by side effects.

The Pill's major advantage for your daughter is its high degree of effectiveness in preventing pregnancy. It is more effective than the IUD, although it presents many more potential problems. The Pill is a method appropriate for mature women with established sex lives and regular daily habits. It may not be suited to a teenager whose daily routines and sexual activities are apt to be unpredictable. A number of investigators have found that adolescents, especially unmarried girls having infrequent sexual activity, are often unable or unwilling to use oral medication regularly for long periods of time.

Your daughter is a candidate for the Pill only if her menstrual cycle is established and reasonably regular. Most oral contraceptives combine the two kinds of female sex hormones: estrogens and progestogens. They prevent ovulation, the production of the egg cell. They also thicken the liquid in the neck of the uterus, obstructing sperm. Further, they change the lining of the uterus so that it cannot receive a fertilized egg. The combined pill is effective because, if one of the reactions fails to occur, another will do the trick. Combination brands include: Brevicon, Demulen, Enovid, Loestrin, Lo/Ovral, Modicon, Morinyl, Norlestrin, Ortho-Novum, Ovral, Ovulen, Zorane. A "mini-pill" contains progestogen only. It does not stop ovulation, but works by thickening the liquid in the cervical canal so that it is more difficult for sperm to reach the egg. Major mini-pill brands: Micronor, Nor-Q.D., Ovrette.

Before getting a prescription for the Pill, your daughter needs an internal examination. Be sure her doctor takes a careful medical history to find out whether she has a tendency toward any condition that would make it best for her not to take the Pill. He also should take her blood pressure, examine her breasts for lumps, and take a Pap smear to check for cervical cancer.

Your daughter starts her first course of pills on the fifth day after her period begins. Remind her to use another method of contraception as well for the first two weeks. Until then, she is not fully protected by the pill alone.

Caution her that if she misses even one pill, she risks becoming pregnant until her next period. After such a lapse, she should take the pill or pills missed, then continue taking pills daily for the rest of the month—but also use another contraceptive method, such as condoms, spermicidal preparations, or a diaphragm. Contrary to popular belief, there's no medical reason to give her body "a rest" by periodically discontinuing the pills for a month or two. Warn her against using someone else's prescription—or believing she's protected if she takes a single pill before (or after) having intercourse.

Expect the doctor to use this examination to decide which oral contraceptive to prescribe. For example, if your daughter tends to be hairy, he's likely to prescribe a pill with a low progestogen content. If she develops complications such as vaginal bleeding, he may switch her to a pill with a higher estrogen content. Many brands of the Pill are available in 21- or 28-day packets. It's a good idea for the doctor to prescribe the 28-day packet, the last seven pills of which are blanks. That way, your daughter gets used to taking a pill every day. If she goes off the Pill, she needs to start another method of contraception right away. Even if she wants to conceive, miscarriage is more frequent in the first two to three months following stoppage of the Pill. Advise her to use another method of contraception for at least three months.

Before thinking about taking the Pill, your daughter needs to face whether its benefits offset its risks. Certainly, she should not consider the Pill if she has intercourse only at great intervals. Its risks are too great for her to take it "just in case." *The Medical Letter* recommends that "the risks in the use of oral contraceptives should be weighed against the psychological effects of fear of pregnancy and the possible physical consequences of pregnancy or abortion." The editors of the publication advise women to use other effective methods of birth control if they can do so.

If your daughter is like about 1 in 5 users, she'll experience reactions to the Pill. Many of these side effects are similar to the symptoms of early pregnancy, and may disappear after a few months. They may include nausea and vomiting, a bloated feeling, tender breasts. Many users complain of being perpetually damp, from excessive vaginal secretions. Chloasm is darkening of the skin—the "mask of pregnancy," especially common among brunettes and worsened by exposure to the sun. Headache, dizziness, acne, and emotional depression are less common complaints associated with the Pill. Loss of scalp hair is an uncommon side effect.

At unexpected times of the month, your daughter may experience some breakthrough vaginal bleeding, marked by staining of her underpants. There is often a tendency to gain weight, probably caused by an increase in appetite and water retention. A change of hormone combination may eliminate or reduce specific side effects. So may a change in dosage or the taking of concurrent drugs, like diuretics to reduce the bloating.

If your daughter has a chronic health problem, it may be made worse by an oral contraceptive. Migraine, depression, and asthma are often aggravated by the Pill. Among other contraindications: High blood pressure, diabetes, fibroid tumors in the uterus, and heart, liver, or kidney disease. The Pill may also interfere with the absorption of vitamins and minerals.

Teenagers seem at much less risk than adults of getting thromphlebitis—blood clots in the veins possibly leading to loss of limb, paralysis, loss of sight, or death. Nonetheless, contact her doctor immediately if she ever experiences severe headaches, shortness of breath, blurred vision, or pain in the leg or chest. Also, while she is taking the Pill, report any unusual swelling and any color changes, such as brownish spotting or yellowish discoloration of the skin or eyes.

Increased risk of stroke, heart attack, and birth defects have also been linked to the Pill. After using the pill for more than four years, she'll face almost twice the normal risk of developing malignant melanoma, an often fatal skin cancer—and three to five times the normal risk of getting cancer of the cervix.

Rhythm (79–87%): Too Much Trouble?

Rhythm (natural family planning, periodic abstinence) almost certainly is a poor choice for your teenage daughter. The method requires her to abstain from sexual intercourse on the days of her menstrual cycle when she is most likely to conceive. It is the only contraceptive method sanctioned by the Roman Catholic Church, so it may appeal to some teenagers on religious grounds.

Your daughter, however, is likely to find that rhythm methods require too many calculations and too much time and attention. The methods are based on three assumptions: 1) that ovulation occurs some 12 to 16 days before the beginning of menstruation; 2) that the egg survives for 24 hours; and 3) that sperm are capable of fertilizing an egg for a period of 48 to 72 hours.

The Temperature Method. It calls for your daughter to record her basal (lowest) body temperature on awakening. She uses a special thermometer to chart these small fluctuations. A slight raise in temperature indicates that she has started to ovulate, release an egg. She must not have intercourse from the end of her period to three days after this temperature rise, requiring abstinence for two weeks or more.

The Vaginal Mucus Method. Requires your daughter to examine her cervical mucus for changes. Clear, slippery mucus that looks like egg white and can be stretched between the fingers indicates the peak period in which she can conceive. About the fourth day after ovulation, the mucus becomes cloudy and sticky, and reduces in volume or dries up entirely. This shows her safe period for inter-course, which lasts until her next menstrual period. Your daughter would need individualized training and practice to learn the method properly.

The Sympto-Thermal Method. Has your daughter observing changes in her basal body temperature in combination with other signs of ovulation. These include: changes in her cervical mucus; pain or bleeding, breast tenderness, abdominal heaviness around the time of ovulation, and changes in the position of the cervix and cervical opening. The method is complex to learn. You can get information about rhythm methods and instruction from the Human Life and Natural Family Planning Foundation, 1511 K Street, NW, Washington, D.C. 20005.

Failure of the rhythm methods can occur if your daughter misreads or misunderstands the various changes. They may be complicated by factors such as illness or nervous tension. Moreover, the long period of abstinence is often beyond the endurance of sexually active teenagers.

Warn your daughter against improvising her own rhythm method. It's likely to be based on the now-obsolete "calendar method," which supposedly predicts her safe days by averaging the middle of her menstrual cycle. This method is especially unsuited to teenagers, since adolescent menstrual cycles tend to be irregular.

Nonetheless, Johns Hopkins University researchers Melvin Zelnik and John Kantner find that 40 percent of girls who have intercourse without contraception do so because it is the "time of the month" they would not get pregnant. Zelnik and Kantner have also found that only half of sexually active girls know when the theoretically safe period occurs.

Withdrawal (75–91%): Leakage Can Cause Pregnancy

Caution your children that withdrawal (coitus interruptus, pulling out) is better than no method but is woefully subject to failure. It requires the boy to pull his penis out of the girl's vagina just before he ejaculates, so that his semen is deposited away from where it can cause pregnancy.

In theory this common method among teenagers costs nothing and is always available. But it can make the girl pregnant if the boy is slow in withdrawing and deposits even a drop of semen in her vagina. His sperm may also leak into her vagina long before he ejaculates. If he ejaculates near her vagina, some sperm may get inside and swim up into her uterus.

Withdrawal makes great demands on the boy's self-control. The split-second timing required can interfere with a couple's enjoyment of sex. The stress connected with the frequent use of withdrawal may lead to sexual and psychological problems. The girl is often anxious over whether the boy got out in time. The boy may not know if he did, and so may be plagued by worry and guilt.

Also warn your teenagers against relying on frequent ejaculations, through intercourse or masturbation, as a form of birth control. Frequent ejaculation tends to decrease the boy's semen volume and sperm concentration, possibly reducing the chances of pregnancy. But pregnancies occur even with very low sperm concentrations and poor semen quality. Furthermore, as soon as the boy cuts down on the frequency of his ejaculations, his sperm count and semen quality quickly return to high enough levels to greatly increase the chances of pregnancy.

Part IV

"MY WORST FEARS ARE REALIZED!"

IF PREGNANCY DISRUPTS the life of your teenage daughter or son, do these first things first to help decide what to do. Should your daughter opt for abortion, expect misgivings—but here's how to find emotional comfort and physical safety. On the other hand, if she's carrying to term, secure a safe delivery by reducing the abnormally high risks faced by her and your grandchild. Then help her decide if she should keep the baby or release it for adoption, and advise her how best to fulfill either choice. And, with or without a pregnancy, your teenage son or daughter may be considering marriage. Here are questions you can ask to head off a precipitous wedding.

• •
•

Chapter 12

"I Think I'm Pregnant"

When that news involves your daughter or son, do these first things first.

ENID'S 16-YEAR-OLD-DAUGHTER Cindy had been morose for days. She spent most of her time in her room, playing the same blues record over and over. When Enid asked her what was wrong, she would snap, "Nothing!" Then she'd quickly leave the room.

Now Enid was on the porch, where Cindy was irritably flipping pages in a magazine. "Cindy, I don't want to press you," Enid said. "But I want you to know that if you need any help, I'm available."

Cindy took a deep breath. "Well, if you must know, my period is late and I think I'm pregnant."

If a similar scene is played out in your family, you are hardly alone. The so-called sex revolution is of neither the size nor type most parents imagine. Nonetheless, teenage pregnancy is a problem for parents of every race and religion, of every income bracket and section of the country. Each year, about 1 in 10 teenage girls becomes pregnant. To envision the human beings behind that number, imagine your daughter's high school gym class of about fifty girls. The equivalent of five of those girls will be pregnant this year.

Further, erase from your mind all stereotypes about "the kind of girl who gets pregnant." A pregnant teenager can be anybody's daughter. Your dauther's gym class provides as good a sample as any. Honor students and dropouts alike become pregnant. So do athletes, cheerleaders, musicians, editors, members of the student council, and other all-around good citizens. So, too, do girls who defy any sort of glib description.

Every year, crises caused by pregnancy affect the mothers and fathers of about 670,000 girls ages 15–19, plus the parents of about 30,000 girls under 15. In addition to those parents are the mothers and fathers of the 700,000 boys involved, who are also generally school-age and dependent.

As soon as your children reach puberty, drive home their need to use contraception, and let them know that, if pregnancy occurs, you stand ready to help them. The odds that you'll need to confront teenage pregnancy are statistically worsening. The rate of teenage pregnancies is on the rise, jumping by one-third over a mere five years. Sociologists Melvin Zelnik and John F. Kantner of Johns Hopkins University attribute the increase almost entirely to a greater incidence of adolescent sexual intercourse, which has also increased by one-third. Drs. Zelnik and Kantner conclude that this higher frequency of intercourse has more than offset any gains made by teenagers' easier access to contraceptives, resulting in more pregnancies.

AFTER THE SHOCK

If your teenager becomes pregnant, your first reaction is most likely to be shock ("This couldn't be happening to us") and self-doubt ("What did I do wrong? What didn't I do that I should have done?"). Anger—at yourself, your child, or both—may follow.

Be mindful of your feelings in this crisis. They may paralyze your decision-making powers. They especially may render you unhelpful during the brief remainder of the first trimester, the initial three-month period when abortion would be least complicated if that were your daughter's option. Your daughter will also need your advice and support in weighing her other choices: having the child and keeping it, putting it up for adoption, perhaps marrying the child's father.

Your daughter's pregnancy may be the greatest challenge you've faced as an adult. Few parents are emotionally prepared to deal with such a contingency. Most people tend to view it as something that happens to someone else's child, not one's own.

How do you respond when your dreams for your daughter shatter? What do you do when your child's future seems to have stopped before it ever started?

The mother of 16-year-old Liz, a bright student from a family of professionals, had to answer those questions after the girl became pregnant. Liz reversed her decision for an abortion, and decided to marry Ricky, an 18-year-old dropout from a different religion and socioeconomic class. After two years of marriage, Liz has seen romance replaced by reality—tight finances, job hunting, male versus female rights.

All this was sadly foreseen by Liz's mother. Based on her painful experience, she offers this counsel to other parents: "To you who may someday face your own trial, remember that the mind will accept before the heart. The sooner you can face this fact, the sooner will come a deeper acceptance and peace." Some guidelines that may help you through your ordeal:

- Recognize that it's the girl's decision. However strongly you may feel about what's best for her, it's her body—and her baby, if she chooses to have it. Under most state laws, even though she's a minor who can't marry without her parent's consent, she has the absolute say-so about her child.
- Be the best parent you can be. But bear in mind that you're human, thus can't help being fallible in an arduous situation.
- Resist self-recrimination. The pregnancy was not your fault.
- Be there when your youngster needs you, and provide love and care. Yet don't expect to fully understand the complex problems facing your teenager.
- Remember the rest of your family: your spouse, your other children and yourself. You can't live your life through your children, or suffer away your years in their behalf. Realize your own dreams and potential.

CONFIRM THE PREGNANCY

As your first response, make certain your daughter is actually pregnant.

The first hint of pregnancy is usually a skipped period. But a missed menstruation can also result from other causes. Teenagers often have irregular periods. Also, a girl's anxiety about the possibility of getting pregnant can affect her hormones, delaying her menstrual cycle. She may then conclude she's "pregnant."

Other common first signs of pregnancy include enlarged, tender breasts, sometimes with a sensation of tingling and fullness. Your daughter may often be sleepy. She's likely to urinate frequently.

To confirm pregnancy, a urine test—on the first urine of the day—is 95 to 98 percent accurate. You can have this test done through your family doctor, at a hospital clinic, or through organizations such as Planned Parenthood.

Don't rely on do-it-yourself pregnancy kits. Even if you follow the kit's instructions correctly, you'll get dubious results. In about 1 out of 5 instances when it shows you're not pregnant, the kit is wrong—you are pregnant. Also, warns *The Medical Letter*, the kit may falsely give a negative result in some hazardous abnormal pregnancies. You need a physician's internal examination for an accurate diagnosis of pregnancy.

ASSIST IN HER DECISION

"Should I tell Mom? What if she tells Dad? Will he kick me out? Should I tell him myself? Not tell them at all? Have an abortion? Then tell them? Not tell them? Go to Planned Parenthood? Ask Claudia for help? Sally? Joanie? Aunt Phyllis? Mrs. Cleary? Will they tell Mom? Will she tell Dad? Should I tell Ivan? What if he wants to marry me? Do I want to marry him? What if he doesn't want to marry me? Should I have the baby? How'll I bring it up? Should I give it up? Will that kill me more than anything? Should I run away? Where'll I go? What'll I do? What about school? Should I tell Mom? What if she tells . . ."

And on and on and on her questions swirl, roaring through her mind, endlessly turning back onto themselves, invading her dreams, keeping her wakeful while asleep, and in a nightmare while awake. . . .

Consider yourself fortunate if your daughter confides in you that she's pregnant. It may well bespeak her confidence in your acceptance of her, your ability to help her in a crisis, the strength of your relationship. She almost certainly needs your considered opinion now. The typical pregnant adolescent is not mature enough to make unaided a decision that may affect all of you for all your lives.

Your pregnant teenager may try to go through the crisis alone. Indeed, many have abortions—and a few have babies—without their parents ever finding out.

Expect your daughter to be unable to confront the reality of her pregnancy and her need to decide what to do about it. She may deny the possibility of pregnancy as long as she can. At work in her unconscious may be the magical feeling that the pregnancy will go away if she doesn't think or talk about it.

A very young adolescent girl cannot realistically perceive a pregnancy. She has little concept of the fetus or the future child as a real being. She is not realistic in her perception of the actual consequences of a childbirth to herself or anyone else.

Your pregnant daughter may put off telling you for months. Giving birth may seem less real, thus less difficult to a frightened teenager than the pain of approaching her mother and father. This delay may reduce her options for abortion.

Social workers and counselors call this denial stage the "wishing-the-baby-away syndrome." As one therapist put it, "Teenagers say, 'But I don't want my parents to find out!' There they are, fourteen to sixteen weeks pregnant, their parents will know in a few weeks just by looking at them, and they're too late for the much easier first trimester abortions."

Even after she tells you, your pregnant adolescent may be paralyzed by indecision—apathetic, listless, unable to concentrate. You may find her seeking to escape from the problem by frantic activity. She may be unable to sleep, or she may sleep half the day away. She may lose her appetite, or else be in a frenzy of compulsive overeating.

Resist any urge to reproach your pregnant daughter. Her ability to cope is almost certainly strained to the utmost. Any additional defensiveness is likely to make her resist your advice. What's more, it's probable that no scolding can make her feel worse about herself than she does already. A teenager's pregnancy generally sets her back severely in her adolescent strivings for emancipation. When she becomes pregnant, she's likely to become more dependent on her parents. She may now be even more ambivalent about leaving the material support and emotional security you offer.

This conflict often evokes great anxiety and anger. In addition, she is likely to bear heavy burdens of shame over her condition and guilt over hurting you with it.

Also refrain from taking over the decision about what to do regarding the pregnancy. A pregnant teenager's immaturity often makes her seek to escape responsibility for deciding. She may see herself as a child, incapable of making so grown-up a choice. Even if she's begun to lead an independent life, as at college, she may not yet have developed her own value system or an ability to exercise mature judgment in a period of extreme stress.

Unless she makes the decision herself, she may be permanently remorseful, and resent you, and the world at large, for "pushing me into it." Social workers Betty Russell and Sylvia Schild of the California State University at Sacramento tell of Connie, an 18-year-old freshman who was dating a boy her parents found unacceptable. When Connie became pregnant, her mother told her, "You got what you deserved."

Connie was unable to accept responsibility either for creating the problem or for resolving it. She tried to get others to deal with it for her. Her mother chose abortion as the solution, and proceeded to implement the plan. Connie's feelings of shame and helplessness intensified. She began to fail three out of five subjects. She refused to discuss her problem with her boyfriend, and got into endless quarrels with her roommate and friends.

To assist a pregnant teenager in reaching a decision, Professors Russell and Schild advise developing a relationship of "co-equal partners working together to resolve a problem in living." Connie was thus helped to see that she was responsible for getting herself into the situation, and also responsible for getting herself out of it. For many girls, coming to grips with an unwanted pregnancy is their first experience in mature problem-solving. Through long, supportive talks, Connie came to realize what she actually wanted out of life, what her strengths and weaknesses were, what help from others she might count on.

"The problem-solving needs to be articulated in the context of a growth experience," note Russell and Schild. "The focus is on the life situation as the problem rather than the unwanted pregnancy." In this way, they report, Connie accepted her abortion as her own decision—with no undue emotional reaction. Moreover, she grew from the experience. The competence she gained from resolving her pregnancy she now uses for dealing with other areas of her life.

GET THE BEST ADVICE

The following chapters offer information and advice that can aid you and your daughter in making a decision about what to do about her pregnancy: seek an abortion, bring up the baby on her own or with your help, get married, or give the child up for adoption or foster care.

Even so, the decision may present such difficulties—or conflicts between you—that you need professional help to resolve it. Group or individual counseling is part of many programs for the pregnant teenager. Most such programs also offer early prenatal care and classroom education.

Comprehensive programs are generally administered under the auspices of the school system or the health department, so that's where your inquiries can start. All pregnancy counselors should help clarify for your daughter how she feels about her pregnancy, and how the various alternatives may affect her future and the lives of those close to her. Stress to your daughter that a counselor's job is to help, not to judge. If the person chosen makes her feel uncomfortable or is difficult to talk with, help her find another counselor. Remind her, too, that everything she says to a counselor is confidential.

Look for a program like those at Teen Scene, a division of Planned Parenthood that conducts rap sessions, VD tests, and medical examinations. Counselor Kay Levin talks with pregnant teenagers:

> We try to get them to look at all the options. Having the child and raising it alone or with a parent or putting it up for adoption. We let them know where to get help if that's their decision—a hard one for teens to stick with if they don't have parental support. And if they decide on abortion, Teen Scene refers them to Planned Parenthood's problem pregnancy department.

Consider joint mother-daughter counseling. Because mothers play such an influential role in the lives of their pregnant teenagers, social service agencies are increasingly including them in counseling services. Look for a program like the one at the Adolescent Guidance Clinic of the Mount Sinai Medical Center in New York City. There the mother's counseling sessions with her pregnant teenager aid "planning for the baby's welfare," and help the mother "adjust to her daughter's new role of motherhood."

For other counseling alternatives, consider your county mental health center, or private therapy with a psychologist or psychiatrist. A specialist in family therapy may also be a good bet.

Search out counselors who have worked with pregnant teenagers and their parents. Social workers may be attached to hospitals, voluntary organizations, and departments of social services. They're trained in giving practical help. Church welfare groups may also offer pregnancy counseling and day-to-day assistance. College health services usually make pregnancy counseling a part of the student health program.

Planned Parenthood clinics offer pregnancy counseling and referrals. Some offer special services for teenagers. Counseling is often free, or based on ability to pay. The telephone directory lists local chapters.

Women's centers, community counseling organizations, crisis centers, hot lines—all have proliferated throughout the country and usually offer free, nonjudgmental counseling. Look in the yellow pages under "Abortion," "Birth Control," "Counseling," and "Pregnancy."

Keep your own counsel until the decision is final. You may be tempted, when the problem first hits you, to unburden yourself to friends, to get many opinions on what should be done. If you resist this temptation, you avoid unnecessarily embarrassing your daughter and compounding your own confusion.

What's more, your neighbor's recommendations are likely to have little bearing on what your daughter finally decides. *Good Housekeeping* has asked one thousand readers, "What should an unmarried pregnant teenager do?" Adoption is the preferred solution of 41 percent of this sampling of Americans. Abortion is favored by 27 percent. About the same number believe, "The girl should marry the boy and have the child."

Less than 10 percent think the girl should have the child without marrying and raise it herself. This is actually the most frequent preference of pregnant teenagers, with abortion ranking second. Under 10 percent surrender their babies for adoption or foster care.

"MY PARENTS STUCK BY ME"

If your daughter decides to have the baby, either to keep the child or put it up for adoption, you may need extra patience during her pregnancy. Try not to take personally her turbulent moods. You may be a party to irrational outbursts of anger. You may see her experience inexplicable highs of wild euphoria. Then she may crash into feelings of helplessness and self-pity, of anxiety and depression.

Such wild mood swings are typical of pregnancy in general. But your daughter is not only pregnant. She is also an adolescent.

Under any circumstances, the adolescent's search for indepencence may be accompanied by emotional stress. But if her uncertainty is suddenly intensified by the discovery that she is pregnant, she is likely to display symptoms of depression, anxiety, and withdrawal. She may resent your failure to give her adequate advice on how to avoid pregnancy.

This won't surprise you when you consider that an adolescent awaiting childbirth must face three life crises at once: She's in the difficult transition from adolescence to adulthood. She must deal with the physical and emotional upheaval accompanying pregnancy. And she has to accept her new role as a mother (or perhaps as a wife and mother).

These are among the most difficult adjustments any woman must make in a lifetime. Ordinarily, they are spread out over several years. Trying to adjust to all three at once can be staggering to your teenager—she has little idea of what to expect, indeed of whom she's turned into. On top of these life crises, a pregnant teenager often has to deal with embarrassment and community disapproval as her pregnancy becomes more obvious. All at once, she may tell you, "I hate my life."

Especially for an unwed adolescent, pregnancy can be fraught with anxiety. Pregnant girls commonly suffer from fears about the child: Will it be deformed? Stillborn? Will I be a bad mother? It's common for a girl to feel that she's awkward and unattractive. Anxiety about death during childbirth is not unusual.

Most women experience pregnancy as a psychological crisis. "Throughout a normal pregnancy, a woman may experience . . . real and irrational fears, bodily discomforts and shifts in body image," says social worker Judith Weatherford Shouse, formerly of the Adolescent Maternity Center at Children's Hospital in San Francisco. This emotional upheaval is likely to be exacerbated by adolescence. In rare cases, anxiety and depression can be so extreme that a pregnant teenager may try suicide.

Your daughter's state of mind depends to a great extent on your reaction. Observes social worker Shouse: "There seems to be a correlation between a girl's health and well-being during pregnancy and the amount of acceptance and emotional support she receives from her mother." The responses of other members of the family are also important. In the girl's vulnerable state, she can be brought up or down by the reactions of not only her parents but also her brothers and sisters, even her aunts and uncles and cousins.

To illustrate the effect on pregnant girls of the family's attitude, Judith Shouse presents the contrasting cases of Doris and Mary. Doris's mother got wind of her daughter's pregnancy when she took Doris to a doctor who'd been treating the girl for a bladder condition. "I heard her crying in her room," recalls Doris. "That really made me feel bad. But what really helped me the most is that she didn't argue and deny me."

Doris's mother was upset that her daughter now could not be a debutante at a church ball. "But my father thought of me as an individual, what would the baby need, what he had to do for the house in order to prepare for the baby . . . and didn't really think about what people might say. So my father really took it the best."

Even though Doris's parents acted with compassion, she moved away from home for a while. "I couldn't stay in the house with my mother and father because I had let them down." Her conscience evidently plagued her. "Every time they looked at me or said something, I felt that it was all against me, which it really wasn't. It was just a change I was going through."

Doris's brothers and sisters were totally accepting. They bought maternity gifts. One brother offered to quit college and go to work to help pay the hospital bill. "Before the baby was coming they were picking out names and we really had a good time." Her aunts, however, were contemptuous. "I said, 'I don't care. I don't need them.' Then I realized that I need all my people." She made a special trip to see her aunts. "They all just looked at me, did real bad things and spit on me." Doris persisted. "I told them all I was sorry and that I know I had hurt all of them by becoming pregnant." They forgave her, except for one aunt who constantly says Doris will become pregnant again.

When Doris went into labor, her father and mother drove her to the hospital. Her father visited her every day, having dinner with her and advising her about taking care of the baby. "It was really nice, I had no problem at all," she remembers with warmth. "My parents stuck by me."

In cold contrast is the experience of Mary with her mother. Mary was in late pregnancy when she spoke to Judith Shouse. Her mother learned of the pregnancy when she came across Mary's bill for the lab test. She told Mary, "Well, we will just have to work it out." This cheered Mary. "I felt relieved that she knew because it was so good." Then, reasons Mary, her mother realized she was divorced, had to work, and was bringing up four other children. "She told me she wasn't going to do anything. And she hasn't helped me do anything since."

Mary left home, planning to marry her boyfriend Bob. "I don't have any relationship with my mom at all, and now more than ever I need her. I mean every day I need her and I can't even phone up and say, 'Hi.' And it is just horrible." On Easter Sunday, Mary had a yearning to spend the holiday with her family. She popped into the kitchen and said, "Hi, Mom, Happy Easter." Recalls Mary: "She just looked at me and didn't say anything. She just turned around. So I stayed about ten minutes and left."

Her mother's rejection is hard on her and Bob. "My mom could be making it so much easier on everybody. It is like the first time you feel the baby kick: You want to say, 'Mom, it is kicking!' But you can't."

Mary is grateful to her father for his emotional and financial support. "We talked about the whole thing. . . . He has really helped a lot, but I think my mother feels more like I did it against her, where my father just sees it as, 'Well, you are pregnant and we have to do something about it.'"

Mary sees a "big strong wall" between her and her mother. "She will always feel that she ran out—and even ten years from now when the kid is ten years old she will still know that when I was pregnant she wasn't there. . . . I still can't forgive her. . . . It is just getting worse, and neither of us can fix it."

HELP HER STAY IN SCHOOL

Pregnancy is the most common reason girls drop out of school. Leaving school would almost certainly be harmful to your daughter. Her hopes and plans are likely to be frustrated. Her earning power will be limited, particularly if she keeps her baby. She may become locked into a life of welfare and poverty.

Thus do what you can to help your daughter at least finish high school, optimally go on through college. Your local school systems may provide innovative education programs for pregnant teenagers and school-age mothers. These often include courses in child care, day-care facilities, and special counseling.

You may have to do battle with your local system, though, merely to enable your daughter to continue attending classes. If administrators try to prevent her from attending because of her pregnancy, you can take legal action. Enlightened government policy protects her right to remain in her own school. Title IX of the Educational Amendments of 1972 bans sex discrimination by all educational institutions receiving federal aid, virtually all schools in the country. Regulations drafted in 1975 for enforcing Title IX deal specifically with pregnancy. The law provides that:

> A recipient shall not discriminate against any student or exclude any student from its education program or activity, including any class or extra-curricular activity, on the basis of such student's pregnancy, childbirth, false pregnancy, miscarriage, abortion or recovery therefrom, unless:
>
> (1) the student requests voluntarily to participate in a different program or activity; or
>
> (2) the student's physician certifies to the recipient that such different participation is necessary for her physical, mental or emotional well-being.

Despite the law, many systems urge a pregnant adolescent to leave school as soon as her pregnancy becomes obvious. If she wants to continue her education, they may offer her at-home instruction.

Don't do it. Your daughter would almost certainly feel like an outcast. She'd be deprived of the intellectual and social stimulation of her friends at school. She'd be isolated and lonely, cut off from her usual contacts just when she needs them most. At-home instruction is likely to be inferior, and she'd be unlikely ever to return to school. A school policy that would force out your daughter merely punishes her for being pregnant.

Furthermore, don't be snowed by any of the reasons school administrators may give you for taking your daughter out of school. Common rationales for withdrawing pregnant girls from classrooms were debunked in a study by the Atlanta Adolescent Pregnancy Program, a research project involving the Atlanta public schools, the Department of Gynecology and Obstetrics of Emory University School of Medicine, and several community agencies. The researchers concluded that all the reasons pregnant girls are asked to leave school are "illogical."

Supposedly, your daughter should be kept out of school "for her own protection" because other students will be "cruel and unkind" to her. On the contrary, determined the research group: Peers are generally supportive of pregnant girls—and the "cruel and unkind" thing to do would be to deny the girls this support.

It's also contended that your daughter should be taken out of school "for medical reasons." The Atlanta researchers point out that no one claims that a pregnant housewife is "too delicate" to take care of her children or do her housework. Thus it's illogical to be concerned about pregnant schoolgirls carrying books and walking up and down stairs.

Indeed, a policy of enforced withdrawal is also detrimental to a girl's health. It can prompt her to conceal her pregnancy for as long as possible, perhaps going on crash diets and putting off prenatal care.

"In general," continues the Atlanta report, "the underlying belief which dictates expulsion from school is that the pregnant schoolgirl is a 'bad girl'"—her pregnancy being a clear indication that she has had intercourse at least once. More illogic, note the researchers. If it is fair to remove a pregnant girl from school because she's experienced intercourse, "then authorities should also expel her . . . partner."—or, in fact, any student who's had intercourse.

IF IT'S YOUR SON

Suppose your teenage son gets a call from a girl he's had intercourse with. "I'm pregnant and I've decided to keep the baby," she tells him. "It's your baby and you're going to have to pay child support."

If he's typical of boys who get such news, his first reaction is disbelief. "Me—a father?" exclaimed one 17-year-old. "You've got to be kidding. Impossible. No way!"

Then, typically, he fears his life is collapsing. Can he go to college? What will his parents say? Does he really have to pay for this child? He doesn't know what to do or where to turn for help.

Some boys deny the problem. Your son may not comprehend what having a baby will mean. He may feel pride in proving his masculinity and creating a new life. At the same time, the responsibilities involved may so stagger him that he tries to put them out of his mind.

He's likely to need your help in getting a grasp on reality. The pregnancy, and its aftermath, is likely to be full of turmoil and anxiety for him. His schoolwork may go to pot. He may withdraw, feeling guilty yet helpless. The gravity of the situation he's brought about can leave him frightened and confused, and uncertain about his responsibilities.

He can be profoundly affected by the decisions of the girl carrying his child. Yet his needs and plans are often overlooked by the girl and her parents. Social service agencies do not routinely involve the boy in decision-making about the pregnancy. And parents may fail to realize the effect of potential fatherhood on a teenage son.

As his parents, talk to him about his anxieties and concerns about the pregnancy. Determine how he feels about the girl. Let him know what you can and cannot do to help—how much support you can provide, to what extent you'll help with the medical expenses.

"Parents have a responsibility and a right to assert themselves in these respects," advises Reuben Pannor of the Vista Del Mar Child Care Service in Los Angeles, an authority on unwed fatherhood. "A clarification of this kind . . . helps the parents take a definite position without excess feeling of guilt. It helps the teenagers to learn what their parents are feeling and what they are prepared to give."

Encourage your son to take part in the decision about the outcome of the pregnancy. Even though the girl controls the resolution, it is almost certain to have considerable impact on him. If she has an abortion, he may feel guilty and regretful. Placing the baby for adoption can give rise to similar feelings—but his consent may be required before the adoption can go through. He may want you to consider raising the child rather than have it adopted by strangers.

It's the girl's decision to keep the baby that can most drastically alter your son's life. You may need to act as your son's emissary to the girl and her family. They may assume he has little interest in his child. He may have to overcome a stereotype they have about the unwed father.

"Unwed fathers are not so-called delinquents, irresponsibly taking advantage of innocent girls," observes Reuben Pannor. "The relationships between our unwed mothers and fathers are not the result of hit-and-miss affairs, but meaningful to both." When teenage boys realize a new life has come into the world as a result of their actions, "they do want to act in a responsible way . . . they are concerned for the well-being of the child."

Urge your son to join the girl's maternity program. It may help him through his own crisis related to the pregnancy. His involvement will also generally benefit the mother. At Reuben Pannor's pioneering Vista Del Mar Child Care Service, boys are actively encouraged to share in the decision-making. "Whenever the unmarried father was willing to stand by the unmarried mother and to share responsibility for her predicament, this proved to be of considerable psychological help to her."

The boy's involvement often dispels her fear of hostile desertion. "She could see the father as a person who was not running away, but who was concerned, perhaps even frightened—at any rate, willing to help."

When the father is involved in the decision regarding the pregnancy, the girl is usually more confident that the final decision is the right one.

The extra encouragement you offer may be needed for your son to join a maternity program. "One of the problems we've had in getting the boys more involved in the program is their fear that we are seeking them out for punitive reasons," reports nurse Susan Panzarine of the Adolescent Program at the University of Rochester Medical Center. Out of respect for confidentiality, a program may be reluctant to contact your son directly, fearing that he may not have told you of the pregnancy.

You may also need to assure your son of the emotional benefits of discussing problems arising from the pregnancy. An obstacle that keeps boys from taking advantage of nurse Panzarine's program: "There is no *medical* reason for them to come to the clinic, and the notion of 'just talking' about issues is not a familiar one to many."

Such talks, however, can clarify issues for your son and the girl. "It is not unusual to find that these couples are really not communicating with one another about their expectations for each other during the pregnancy, labor and delivery, and after the birth of the baby. Joint sessions can then be helpful to facilitate more effective communications."

Legal Counsel

What Are the Unwed Father's Legal Responsibilities? Under the law, he can be required to help support his child, regardless of his age or whether he is married to the child's mother. He is responsible until the child is 18 or is legally adopted by someone else.

If he and the girl fail to agree on the amount of child support, she may seek a court order. If he fails to pay, he may be fined by the court. In some states, his earnings can be attached—his employer may be required to deduct the child support from his paycheck. But some fathers cannot or will not pay, and the courts are usually reluctant to impose the full penalty of the law: jailing them for nonpayment. Similarly, it is generally difficult to extract payment from a teenage boy with no income.

Fathers as young as 14 have been successfully sued for child support. Even though a 14-year-old is unlikely to have any income for years to come, the judgment may stand—and may considerably affect his future. When he reaches legal age, and if the court decision is prosecuted, he may find himself with a heavy financial burden.

What's more, recent legislation makes it easier to track down negligent fathers. The federal government is empowered to collect child support from any parent who is not contributing an appropriate amount. Each state may develop a parent locator service for finding the absent parent, establishing paternity, and obtaining child support payments. Since Social Security and Internal Revenue Service records can be used to locate the missing parent, even fathers who have gone abroad might be sought out.

What if There's a Question of Paternity? If an unmarried teenage mother claims a boy is the father of her child and he denies it, she has to file suit to establish his paternity before she can petition for him to pay child support. Also, unmarried mothers who wish AFDC (Aid to Families with Dependent Children) must file paternity suits as a condition for receiving welfare payments.

The blood tests that the mother and the alleged father will need to take are about 95 percent accurate. They include the human leukocyte group A (HLA) antigen test, an advanced form of tissue-typing using an analysis of genes.

A young man who may have some doubt about his paternity may become convinced after these blood tests that he actually is the father, and may accept paternity.

An older type of blood test can prove that a man could *not* be the father. Parents with certain combinations of blood groups cannot possibly have children belonging to other blood groups. For example, a man with the blood-type AB cannot have a child with blood-type O.

Chapter 13

Opt for Abortion?

If so, expect to have qualms. Here's how to find comfort and safety.

"KILLING UNBORN BABIES is no different from Hitler's gassing Jews," declares an Illinois family physician. "Both procedures are or were legal, court- and legislature-approved. Legality and morality don't always coincide."

"Abortion is taking a life," contends a pediatrician in California. "It is a serious matter and should not be done as a privilege of the mother." Asserts an Ohio obstetrician-gynecologist: "Life begins when the sperm fertilizes the egg and is a continuum. The interference with or distortion of this continuum is killing. Thou shalt not kill."

Concludes a Pennsylvania cardiologist: "One can scarcely conceive of a practice more utterly degenerate, more selfish and narcissistic, than the deliberate destruction of one's own progeny, an act that strikes at the very core of society."

These doctors, polled by the journal *Medical World News,* sum up most of the arguments against abortion. Your pregnant teenage daughter may share their views that life begins at conception, that the fetus is a person with a soul or other right to life, and that destroying it is tantamount to murder.

If she's persuaded by the moral arguments against abortion, you and she may do well to consider it no further. Instead, prepare for the probability that she'll have the baby. Help her plan her courses of action after delivery. If she's keeping the baby, how will she arrange for its care? Is marriage with the father in prospect? Will she put the baby up for adoption?

The moral arguments against abortion can be totally persuasive to your daughter. If she proceeds with one against her conscience, she may be plagued with lifelong guilt. Ruth Sue, now 28, had an abortion when she was 18 and in college. She told writer Judith Wax: "For several years after I would have said it was fine, great—you have to justify—but I felt like dirt and for a while afterward, I slept with just anybody.

"Over the years I began to realize that I had ended a life just as valuable as mine and I had to deal with that. Now I work with the pro-life people. I can't bring the baby back, but I can help other girls."

OF TWO MINDS

Abortion is the choice of nearly 1 in 3 pregnant teenagers, about 300,000 a year. The younger your daughter, the more likely she is to opt for abortion. Among pregnant girls 14 and under, there are more abortions than deliveries.

Your daughter is likely to need your help in reaching a prompt decision about whether or not to have an abortion. Pregnant teenagers often try to tune out. Frightened and ashamed, your daughter may regress to a stage of helplessness not experienced since her early childhood. Lacking your experience, she may be incapable of dealing with a situation that calls for action. Paralyzed by indecision, she may do nothing. Thinking like a child, she may hope that her pregnancy will somehow go away. She may thus become a mother by default.

She'll also need your help in going through the abortion. Girls who do not have the aid of their parents often report missing it. After Katy had an abortion, she told Dr. Karem J. Monsour and Barbara Stewart of the Counseling Center at the Claremont Colleges in California: "The strain of being secretive was a big personal burden—and the fear of public knowledge. It would be nice if one could have support of parents but I couldn't tell them." Andrea told Monsour and Stewart that worry over her parents' possible reaction worsened her stress. "There's a big fear built up around it, a religious fear for some people that I think is probably very real and there is a social fear—like what if anyone found out, what would my family think of what I've done?"

If your daughter is contemplating an abortion, expect her, and yourself, to feel considerable ambivalence over it. The U.S. Supreme

Court itself is undecided over the critical question of when life begins. In its 1973 ruling liberalizing abortion, the Court declared that the issue could not be resolved by law. "When those trained in the respective disciplines of medicine, philosophy and theology are unable to arrive at any consensus, the judiciary, at this point in the development of man's knowledge, is not in a position to speculate as to the answer."

Even women who are intellectually committed to liberalized abortion often feel emotional qualms when confronted with one. For two weeks Lindsy Van Gelder, a contributor to the feminist magazine *Ms.*, thought she was pregnant. She recalls finding herself "genuinely distraught" at the prospect of an abortion. "Given my life situation at the time, I'm reasonably sure that had the pregnancy been confirmed, I would have had an abortion and been grateful for the option. Nevertheless, I did feel I was about to destroy something living."

Van Gelder decries what she calls the "Women's Movement protection game," which has possibly contributed to self-doubt you may feel about your normal misgivings over abortion. "It is . . . near-heresy in some feminist circles to acknowledge that abortion might be any more complicated than having a wisdom tooth removed. . . . A public examination of why some women feel a sense of loss after an abortion and others don't at all would be viewed as 'helping the other side.'"

During her own close call with abortion, Van Gelder desperately wanted sympathy and understanding for her feelings of ambivalence. "Instead, people kept telling me I was misguided, brainwashed by the patriarchy. They patiently explained that the fetus was just a bunch of cells. . . . Movement women who would probably have taken in stride an announcement that I had fallen in love with a cucumber were clearly baffled by my abandonment of the 'correct line.'" Van Gelder articulates the frustration she felt: "I wanted to *deal* with the moral balance sheet of abortion—not to have to deny that one existed for me."

In drawing up your own moral balance sheet, you may find it complicated by the reality of your daughter's pregnancy. In the abstract, abortion may have once seemed to you an unthinkable destruction of a human life. Now, in light of how childbirth would affect your daughter, you may accept abortion as a necessity. Conversely, you may have formerly regarded the fetus as little more than undeveloped cells. The imminence of an abortion may give you pause, causing you to envision an unborn grandchild whom you would mourn.

Suppose your daughter proceeds with an abortion despite your misgivings. You may find comfort in adopting the laissez-faire attitude suggested by the Committee on Psychiatry and Law of the Group for the Advancement of Psychiatry. The committee submitted that the moral issue of abortion as murder is "insoluble—a matter of religion and religious principle and not a matter of fact." Therefore, resolved the committee: "We suggest that those who believe abortion is murder need not avail themselves of it. On the other hand, we do not believe that the existence of this belief should limit the freedom of those not bound by identical religious conviction."

Even if you hold to this attitude, your daughter's decision in favor of abortion may cause you pain. On one hand, she may be caused so much grief by it that you want to weep for her. Sixteen-year-old Adrienne told writer Judith Wax: "I used to rub my stomach and cry and say, 'I'm really sorry this has to happen, baby,' because I felt it was a human being we gave life to. I love my boyfriend and want to marry him someday, but we still want to run around and act like idiots and play tennis. How could I with a stomach out to here? Still it hurts to think about it, so you try to deaden your mind."

On the other hand, you may be upset by your daughter's seeming lack of sensitivity. "It's my body, my life," Jean told Judith Wax. "A child depends on you for nine months . . . maybe for twenty years! I'm not ruining my life for something that has to depend on me, so I never felt like I was destroying anything or anybody. All I kept saying was, 'Thank God I have the right to choose.' Without it, I probably would have killed myself."

Fathers especially seem likely to resist a daughter's having an abortion. To comfort his daughter, a father may say, "Have the baby. We can manage." A reply, frequently given by mothers and daughters alike, reveals deep reservations many women have about the traditional concept of motherhood: "You're a man, and you don't know what it's like to have a baby."

Far from thinking of the fetus as a living child, such women regard it as an unwanted growth, a tumor that takes over the body during pregnancy and then gives rise to an unwelcome, intrusive responsibility. "Men seldom realize that pregnancy, as uncomfortable as it is, is only the beginning," comments Frances, who encouraged her 18-year-old daughter Tracy to have an abortion.

> A father rarely appreciates that a young child absolutely dominates its mother's day. Until the baby sleeps through the night, the mother's usually exhausted from lack of sleep. Yet she has to be on call to meet its needs—and they can be bottomless. For years, she's a prisoner to the child, hardly having a moment to herself. If you want the child, you love it and put up with the ordeal—as I did with Tracy. In fact, I love Tracy so much that I wouldn't have her go through that torture for a child she didn't want.

Frances's position in favor of abortion is shared by about 60 percent of the physicians in the *Medical World News* poll. "About 25 abortions are done in this hospital a week," says a California psychiatrist. "They are among the most humane, decent, civilized things we do here. Taking away a woman's right to her body is dictatorship of the worst kind." A Texas gynecologist adds: "About 99 percent are grateful and thankful that they could have it done, even those who were strongly against abortion before their need for one arose. I saw too many girls whose lives were drastically changed or ruined before abortions were legal."

In sum, physicians favoring abortion tend to agree with Dr. Alan F. Guttmacher, a pioneer of the Planned Parenthood Federation:

> I can think of nothing more immoral than forcing an unwilling mother to bear an unwanted, unloved child. A great deal of emotional and unscientific literature has been written about the mental anguish of women who undergo abortion. I suggest that the suffering endured by both mother and child as a result of compulsory childbirth is far better documented.

YOUR LEGAL RIGHTS

While the moral debate over abortion rages, some of the legal problems are being resolved. Under the U.S. Supreme Court decision of January 1973, your daughter is legally entitled to an abortion during the first three months of pregnancy. The Supreme Court held that the Fourteenth Amendment right of privacy "is broad enough to encompass a woman's decision whether or not to terminate her pregnancy." In the second trimester (the middle three months of pregnancy), abortion procedures may be regulated by the state in ways "related to maternal health," but the decision for abortion services remains solely between your daughter and her physician. Requiring approval by a panel of doctors is not constitutional.

During the third trimester (the last three months of pregnancy), the state may regulate or forbid abortion, except in cases where it is necessary to save the mother's life or her health. Constitutional rights legally apply only to what is classified as "persons." Thus abortion opponents urge passage of amendments to confer "person" status on the unborn from the moment of conception. In June 1975 the Court ruled that the First Amendment of the Constitution, which protects freedom of the press, cannot restrict the advertisement of abortion services.

Your daughter may have an abortion without your knowledge. In July 1976, the Supreme Court ruled 5 to 4 that states may not issue "blanket" restrictions requiring all single minor women to have parental consent for an abortion. But the court clearly left the door to parental influence ajar by intimating that some limited restrictions might be imposed.

A physician asked for an abortion by a minor may find himself in a quandary. Many doctors believe they have a moral obligation to inform parents that their daughter is pregnant if she is below the age of 18. However, betrayal of her confidence is contrary to the Hippocratic oath. A physician may encourage your daughter to have you share in her decision on abortion. But if she is unwilling to do this, the doctor has no legal or ethical right to act against her wishes.

Guidelines for the physician are set down in the report of the Committee on Education in Family Life of the American College of Obstetricians and Gynecologists:

> When she (a minor) is unwilling to tell her parents that she is sexually involved, or that she is pregnant, the physician may not be free to do what he believes is in the best interest of the patient, because the law is either restrictive or unclear. In such situations, the physician has three choices: He may refuse to help the girl unless she agrees to inform her parents. He may himself inform them, thus betraying her confidence. Or he may agree to give her advice and help without the parents'

knowledge. The third choice probably represents a less serious violation of the physician's duty than either of the other two.

What if the physician judges that your daughter is incapable of making a rational decision on her own? The committee recommends that he select a medical colleague or a member of another helping profession, such as a clergyman or psychologist, as a consultant—and share the decision and responsibility with that colleague and your daughter. If your daughter so chose, you would remain out of the picture.

While such a legal situation may offend you as a parent, it is unlikely to be changed. Granted that performing an abortion on a minor without at least the knowledge of the people who care most about her deprives her of counsel and support she needs at a time of crisis. Granted, too, that the parent who will reject the pregnant teenager is rare.

But, as a practical matter, most teenagers are shortsighted. If parental notification were required, pregnant teenagers would avoid medical facilities altogether until it was too late for the simple suction procedure. Then if they elected to abort, they would be subject to the more complicated and riskier second-trimester methods. Or they would carry the pregnancy to term and give birth to unwanted infants. Or they would seek out illegal abortion, with great risk to health and life.

HEAD OFF GUILT

If your daughter is like most girls who willingly have an abortion, her predominant reaction to it will be relief. Observes pediatrician Adele D. Hofmann, director of the Adolescent Medical Unit at the New York University Medical Center: "The emotionally intact girl who has made a free choice in electing this procedure and has been well prepared for it handles it reasonably well without serious short- or long-term difficulties. For most there is an inevitable period of depression and mourning, but this is usually worked through quite well."

At California's Claremont Colleges, Dr. Karem Monsour and Barbara Stewart interviewed twenty who'd had abortions. Eighteen said they'd experienced no adverse psychological symptoms. Typical of their reactions:

Lotte: "Knowing you're pregnant and you don't want to have a baby is worse than any abortion could be. . . . An abortion is an operation and people go through operations every day."

Connie: "Unwed mothers have a hard time. An unwanted child is a bad thing. When I was pregnant, the idea of having a baby was just impossible. I didn't feel I was destroying life."

Stephanie: "Girls who have the baby seem to me to feel they are expiating their sins and bearing the burden of the baby. I think that's an awful attitude and is the result of social attitudes that are bad. The main reason for having children is whether you can raise them properly, really want them and give them a good home."

One young woman expressed guilt about destroying life. These feelings gradually waned, and disappeared after about five months. The remaining girl said: "I felt miserable for eight or nine months, especially if I saw a baby. Then I went to see a counselor and that helped me a lot. Now I feel much better."

If pregnant again under the same circumstances, nine of the young women said they'd again elect abortion. Ten said their choice would depend on the quality of the relationship with the man and the possibility of marriage. If marriage were not possible, they'd choose abortion again. One said that, if pregnant again, she'd have the baby regardless of the circumstances.

The earlier your daughter has her abortion, the less likely she is to suffer emotional trauma. "At fifteen weeks, a woman knows she is dealing with 'otherness,'" cautions the Reverend E. Spenser Parsons, a leader in the National Clergy Consultation Service on Abortion, a counseling group. "How she interprets that otherness is terribly important. . . . When a woman believes that that otherness is a baby and she aborts it, the aftermath can be very serious, because she now sees herself as a baby-killer, and that can yield serious psychological consequences."

An early abortion may also help your daughter feel better in the face of antiabortion presentations that may be given in her school. The speaker may refer to the "child," "infant," "baby," "son or daughter"—words that suggest an independent living being rather than a potential one. Through the second month of development, the more exact term is "embryo"; from the third month until delivery, physicians prefer the word "fetus." Those medical terms have a precise intent: they express the distinction between stages of pregnancy and actual birth.

After seeing antiabortion slides, girls who've had abortions some-times run out of the room hysterical. These slides show "murdered babies," with limbs and faces. Reassure your daughter that the photographs are greatly blown up. Even at twelve weeks, after a period of rapid growth, the fetus is under four inches long, however like a fully formed baby it may seem. "It is a biological error to consider a fetus only a few weeks old as a human being," observes geneticist Jacques Monod. "An embryo cannot have consciousness, for it has no central nervous system—up to five months."

Possibly the best way to head off post-abortion guilt and depression is through preabortion counseling, offered by many hospitals and abortion clinics. Your daughter may resist such assistance. Some girls have a strong urge to rush headlong into an abortion. "Many young people want to treat it like a nightmare and want to have a general anesthesia so that when they wake up, it is all over," notes Dr. Gary Goldsmith, clinical director of a New York adolescent health center. "We try to get them to understand what will happen so that they can somehow come to terms with it."

If your daughter's an early teenager, it's especially important that a sensitive counselor explore the meaning that abortion has for her. Otherwise, unexpected feelings may erupt later. "There are usually more psychological problems surrounding an abortion than are recognized," observes Dr. Goldsmith. "This is particularly so with the younger adolescents. Guilt, depression, and repeat abortions are common symptoms of unresolved feelings about an abortion."

A pre-existing emotional problem may signal that your daughter is in danger of major post-abortion distress. "There does appear to be a significantly higher incidence of such problems among the early and mid-adolescent," finds pediatrician Adele Hofmann. For younger girls, "sexual encounters and pregnancy itself are more frequently (although not invariably) a form of rebellion."

Psychiatric nurse-therapist Sharon Gedan counsels many pregnant teenagers at health agencies in Honolulu. "Emotional counseling is an essential part of care for the woman who elects to terminate her pregnancy," she says. "I am convinced that helping a woman express her feelings about abortion can make it a more comfortable event and, in some cases, can help the woman grow emotionally."

Nurse Gedan suggests traits to look for in your daughter's counselor. She finds in working with teenagers that a counselor needs to be particularly accepting and open with them to enable them to express their emotions, for they are often frightened and embarrassed by their feelings. During adolescence, the changes that occur lead to extremely strong reactions. "Teenage love is felt deeply and is a highly sensitive area of the teenager's life. Feelings about children, although often romantic and unrealistic, are strong. Anger, jealousy, and sadness are often new experiences." Because your daughter is unused to these feelings she may be scared or ashamed of them and attempt to deny them.

Your daughter may feel she is being interrogated and she may resent the intrusion of an authority figure into sensitive areas. But, says Gedan, if the counselor takes some initiative in exposing her own thoughts and feelings, particularly in the beginning of the interview, your daughter is likely to follow her example. "Openness on the part of the counselor makes the tone of the interview a conversation between equals."

Skilled abortion counselors, notes Gedan, can help your daughter sort out how she may be influenced by peers and idols. Young adolescent girls often choose to emulate movie actresses.

In the past few years a number of single actresses have kept out-of-wedlock babies and expressed joy in raising them, without having a stable relationship with a man. The adolescent girl who has identified with these actresses may be unable to see any alternative to her pregnancy except raising her baby alone. Adolescents do not realize that their attitudes may change drastically in years to come and that teenage idols are temporary gods. This subject must be handled with great sensitivity because the teenager's loyalty is usually strong and emotionally charged.

Further, recommends Gedan, your daughter's counselor should involve you in their discussions. Your participation can help you as well as your daughter. You can be aided in exploring and expressing your feelings about the abortion. And you can discuss with the counselor what support your daughter needs.

Also expect your daughter's abortion counselor to talk turkey with her about contraception. Perhaps 10 percent of girls who've had abortions think of the procedure as a form of birth control. The rest seem to respond well to advice on contraceptive methods. Refrain from trying to extract from your daughter a promise that she'll stop being sexually active. In the throes of her pregnancy and abortion, she may think, "I never *will* again." That resolve is almost certain to weaken as she recovers. Unless she's been prepared with birth control, she may soon be pregnant again.

Also consider *post*-abortion counseling, a feature of many clinics. A New Paltz, New York, Planned Parenthood leaflet illustrates what post-abortion groups offer:

> You decided you were *not* going to bring an unwanted child into the world. You've made your decision:
>
> —But it may have been very hard for you. . . .
> —You may have felt confused. . . .
> —Perhaps you couldn't talk about your innermost feelings to anyone important to you. . . .
> —Or you tried . . . and they couldn't really understand. . . .
> —Perhaps your abortion was some months ago. . . .
> —But you still feel a lot of hurt. . . .
> We help each other with the feelings and conflicts brought up by our shared experience.
> We help each other build confidence in ourselves.

Post-abortion counseling may go by another name. "We found that when a group was set up specifically for post-abortion counseling, the girls were not so interested," reports Dr. Gary Goldsmith. "However, in therapy groups where kids were coming for other reasons, abortion would come up and kids would share unresolved feelings about it."

Teenagers who are interested in group experience are generally those who are more open about their feelings, more in touch with their experience, and more able to use it to learn. If your daughter tends to be more isolated, she may be better off with individual counseling.

You may help your daughter adjust to her abortion by acknowledging it if the subject comes up with people she feels close to. Abortions are had by about a million women a year, largely married members of the middle class. Your daughter may find herself in a substantial subculture of women who have been through the experience—and can sympathize with her. Recalls 15-year-old Jill: "I was so ashamed of my abortion that I finally broke down and told my guidance counselor at school. It turned out that she'd had an abortion, too."

At the same time, advise your daughter to be discreet. Antiabortion zealots may cause pain. Some groups pay nurses for lists of women who have had abortions, the same way diaper companies used to pay nurses for lists of women who had given birth. Your daughter is then likely to get a phone call from a woman who will ask, "How are you?"

After your daughter drops her guard, the caller may say, "Well, we know that yesterday morning you murdered a six-week-old baby girl, and we'd like to offer you some guidance."

Alert your daughter to the possibility that such things can happen, that some adults in their strong beliefs can be extremely cruel. Advise her to hang up immediately, as she should to an obscene phone call.

WHERE TO GO

You won't find an abortion for your daughter with equal ease in all parts of the country. In some sections, physicians who do abortions are scarce and facilities are lacking. Planned Parenthood reports that Indiana, Mississippi, and Utah are notable for the difficulty teenagers have in getting abortions.

If you live near a big city, your daughter will probably be able to get her abortion close to home. Otherwise expect to travel. Only about 5 percent of abortions are performed in nonmetropolitan areas, although the estimated need is about five times that number.

You're also likely to find an abortion convenient if you live on the East or the West Coast. About a third of all abortions are done there. Such unequal distribution of abortion services makes it impossible for some teenagers to get abortions when they want them, particularly if they don't enlist their parents' help. Planned Parenthood estimates that at least 125,000 teenagers a year cannot obtain needed abortion services. Most of them deliver unwanted, and often out-of-wedlock, births. Some resort to self-induced or illegal abortions.

Several agencies can help your daughter obtain a safe, low-cost abortion. Planned Parenthood and the National Clergy Consultation Service on Abortion have affiliates in most states. Both are non-profit agencies and charge no fee for referrals. If there is no local listing for these organizations, call their national offices in New York City to get the location of the facility nearest you. Planned Parenthood's phone number is 212–541–7800. That of the Clergy Consultation Service is 212–254–6230.

Stay away from private abortion referral services. Such commercial enterprises have sprung up in the first states with legal abortion, like New York, and have victimized mainly out-of-state women seeking abortions. These referral services have charged women over $150 merely for abortion referral—the same information the non-profit organizations offer free of charge.

Check out any private health insurance plan your family may have. Some policies pay some or all of abortion costs. Also look into what Medicaid provides.

Abortions may be done at hospitals, doctors' offices, or clinics. Since the legalization of abortion, there has been a proliferation of free-standing abortion clinics. In 1973, hospitals accounted for 57 percent of abortions and clinics 40 percent. By 1976, that trend had been completely reversed; clinics accounted for 60 percent and hospitals only 37 percent.

Abortion clinics are usually your best bet for safe, low-cost abortions. But they're often run as businesses. They range from pleasant, competently operated facilities to the dregs of the medical world, with substandard equipment and rude personnel.

To secure an abortion at lowest cost, look for a non-profit clinic. The cost of abortion may depend on when in your daughter's pregnancy it is performed. The average cost of a first-trimester abortion in the U.S. done on an outpatient basis in an abortion clinic is about $175, and ranges from $125 to $225. For a first-trimester abortion done in a hospital, the cost runs about $300, including the doctor's fee. For a second-trimester abortion, which necessitates a two- or three-night hospital stay, total cost can be anywhere from $350 to $700.

You can avoid nasty shocks by getting an idea beforehand of what you'll need to pay. Expect prices to vary with the type of anesthesia that is used. You may also encounter extra charges for routine tests or for any complications.

Personally inspect any abortion clinic you're considering for your daughter. Planned Parenthood has listed the physical facilities which an abortion clinic must have if it is to be considered acceptable. Subject any one to this checklist:

☐ Adequate, private space specifically designated for interviewing, counseling, and pregnancy evaluation

☐ Conventional gynecologic examining or operating accessories, drapes, and linen

☐ Approved and electrically safe vacuum aspiration equipment, and conventional instruments for cervical dilation and uterine curettage (in adequate supply to permit individual sterilization for each patient)

☐ Adequate lighting and ventilation for surgical procedures

☐ Facilities for sterilization of instruments and linen, and for surgical scrub for all personnel

☐ Laboratory equipment and personnel (or immediate access to laboratory facilities) for preoperative and emergency determinations and for tissue diagnosis of uterine contents

☐ Postoperative recovery room, properly supervised, staffed, and equipped

☐ Adequate supplies of drugs, intravenous solutions, syringes, and needles, including four to six units of plasma volume-expander liquids for emergency use (until blood is available)

☐ Dressing rooms for staff and patients, and appropriate lavatory facilities

☐ Ancillary equipment and supplies, including stethoscopes, sphygmomanometers (for taking blood pressure), anesthesia equipment—including oxygen and equipment for artificial ventilation and administration of anesthetic gases—and resuscitation equipment and drugs

☐ Ability to transfer a patient without delay to a conventional operating theater and a written letter of agreement from a full-service hospital regarding transfer of emergency patients

☐ Special arrangements for patient emergency contact (on a 24-hour basis) for evaluation and treatment of complications, for postoperative followup and examination, and for family planning services

Also look for human touches, signs of a staff that cares. At Choices, an abortion clinic in Queens, New York, the initial interview takes place in one of six private rooms furnished in plush chairs, soft lights and warm tones, with perhaps a Miro poster on one wall or a woman's lib poster depicting Ms. Liberty with a tear in her eye in sympathy with the abortion struggle. There is no desk, by design of psychologist Merle Hoffman, director of the clinic. That's to reduce the sense of authority figure and patient vulnerability.

"The important thing is to make the woman feel powerful, not walking out with their heads down, their system screwed up," Ms. Hoffman says. Instead of the usual gaping hospital gown, a patient wears a smart slipover of Navy blue. And gynecologists use a preheated speculum in their examinations to counter any sense of shock and invasion. Ms. Hoffman's idea is to give a clearer sense of control to the patient, including an extensive description of the process of abortion.

WHAT TO EXPECT

Remind your daughter that no one should ever try to abort herself. Abortion is safe only in competent medical hands. Attempting to dislodge a fetus with knitting needles or coat hangers can be fatal.

So can an attempt at do-it-yourself suction with a vacuum cleaner. This could perforate the uterus and suck out part of the intestine. Other home remedies for abortion—drugs, herbal drinks, laxatives, violent exercise—range from useless to dangerous.

Before the abortion, your daughter's medical history should be taken. Routine tests include blood typing, blood pressure, temperature, urinalysis, sometimes gonorrhea and Pap smears. If she and the fetus have an Rh incompatibility—with opposing positive and negative blood types—she'll need an injection to keep her from miscarrying future pregnancies. To confirm her stage of pregnancy, she should be given a pelvic examination by the doctor who is about to perform the abortion.

Advise her not to eat or drink for at least eight hours before her abortion. An emergency may require the use of general anesthesia, which puts her at risk of throwing up, then choking on her vomit.

The method of abortion is determined by her length of pregnancy. This is measured from the first day of her last menstrual period.

You may find a physician or clinic that does menstrual extraction, a simplified approach to early abortion that is becoming more widespread. This technique is generally used before the sixth week of pregnancy. This is usually before a definite diagnosis of pregnancy can be established.

Based on the suction principle, the method involves a plastic cannula (tube) and a suction device. The abortion can be completed in a couple of minutes, practically without pain or loss of blood. With proper counseling beforehand, it is usually done without any anesthesia, and with little or no dilation of the cervix. The cannula is designed with a blunt tip that bends on contact, reducing the possibility of perforation of the uterus.

Menstrual extraction can be performed in a doctor's office or outpatient clinic, usually for under $100. Thus, this method has distinct advantages for the woman whose period is just one or two weeks late. After six weeks of pregnancy, however, the technique is not recommended. There is a high percentage of continuing pregnancies or retained fetal tissue when the method is used between the sixth and twelfth week.

Avoid a controversial aspect of this technique. Some women's self-help groups use it not only to end pregnancy but also monthly to avoid menstruation, and as a form of contraception. Medical authorities are concerned over possible injuries. Dr. Evelyn Gendel, director of Maternal and Child Health of the Kansas Department of Health and president of SIECUS warns that "young and enthusiastic girls purchase the extraction devices and, by using them with no training and perhaps just a friend to help, may do themselves harm." There are risks both of perforating the lower uterus and of introducing infection.

Up to twelve weeks, the most commonly used abortion procedure is suction, or vacuum aspiration, usually done under local anesthesia. The cervix (the opening of the uterus) is usually anesthetized, then dilated. A vacuum pump attached to a thin tube is inserted into the uterus. Gentle suction dislodges the fetus. Your daughter may feel some cramps during the dilating, but the suction is usually quick (five or ten minutes) and painless.

The procedure might involve an overnight stay in a hospital. More commonly it takes a half-day at an abortion clinic.

Dilation and curettage (D & C) was formerly the most common abortion procedure in the U.S. It is now used in only a small percentage of abortions. For D & C the cervix is dilated more than for suction and the uterus is scraped with a curette, a surgical scraper.

To dilate the cervix in first-trimester abortions, some clinics use laminaria, a species of seaweed. The material is water-absorbing, expanding its diameter 3 to 5 times when wet. A clinic that uses this method inserts laminaria the day before the abortion. Laminaria decreases the possibility of cervical injury, but the incidence of infection may be slightly higher. Report any fever, severe cramps, or bleeding to the doctor.

Beyond the twelfth week, your daughter's risks increase. This is a significant problem for teenagers, since many teenagers go through a long stage of denial or have irregular periods and don't know they're pregnant. A New York City study finds that nearly half the girls 15 and younger who sought abortions are pregnant thirteen weeks or more. This contrasts sharply with the more mature population of total women seeking abortion, only 1 in 5 of whom are that far along.

After sixteen weeks, saline is used for most abortions. In this procedure, the physician applies a local anesthetic and inserts a hollow needle through the abdominal wall into the amniotic sac surrounding the fetus. He draws out some amniotic fluid and replaces it with a concentrated salt water solution. The salt injection induces an abbreviated form of labor within three days.

Complications of the saline method include infection and retained placental tissue, often with bleeding and fever. Infection can generally be treated with the proper antibiotics. Retained placenta is usually treated by performing a D & C.

Hormonelike chemicals called prostaglandins have been approved by the FDA for use in inducing labor between the third and sixth months. Like saline, the prostaglandin technique involves an injection into the amniotic sac, but of a much smaller amount of fluid. Most women experience some degree of nausea and vomiting.

Your daughter may have a problem in obtaining an abortion in the last part of her second trimester. Many doctors are reluctant to do abortions much beyond twenty weeks because of the small possibility of delivering a live child. Their concern stems in part from the 1975 conviction for manslaughter of Boston gynecologist Dr. Kenneth Edelin. The abortion that Dr. Edelin performed on a 17-year-old in her twentieth to twenty-fourth week of pregnancy was itself legal. The jury convicted him because it decided he had purposely allowed to die a fetus that was viable, able to sustain life outside its mother's body. The conviction was reversed in appeal, but was nonetheless frightening to Dr. Edelin and other physicians. The Edelin case stiffened mounting resistance by doctors and nurses to performing second-trimester abortions, with their increased risk of viable fetuses. Their concern is heightened by the fact that fetuses are becoming viable earlier in pregnancy thanks to improved intensive-care techniques.

After her abortion, your daughter may be given about six ergotrate tablets to be taken every four hours for the first twenty-four hours. The drug helps keep the uterus contracted and diminishes the amount of bleeding. She'll experience cramps after taking each tablet.

Your daughter would be wise to take it easy for a few days. A menstrual-like flow of blood is normal after abortion. It may stop completely for a few days, then resume. Your daughter should wear sanitary pads, not tampons. She needs to report to her doctor any bleeding heavier than the heaviest menstrual flow she's experienced, and any passage of large clots.

She should also report severe cramps which begin later than a day after the abortion. Other danger signs: fever, a greenish foul-smelling vaginal discharge, and burning or frequent urination. She should have a followup examination about two weeks after the abortion.

At twelve to sixteen weeks, many doctors are reluctant to do abortions. There is thought to be a greater risk of hemmorhage with suction or D & C. Yet, it is widely felt, the uterus is still too small for late abortion methods. Since the uterine lining becomes soft and spongy during this period, physicians often reason that their chances of perforating it are also high.

This reluctance may not be medically justified. A study by the Joint Program for the Study of Abortion under the auspices of the Center for Disease Control found that dilation and evacuation (D & E, similar to D & C) done during the thirteenth to sixteenth weeks of gestation is safer, more effective, less taxing emotionally, and cheaper than instillation procedures done two to four weeks later. "It's been traditional for women who ask for an abortion during this time to wait out this 'gray zone' until instillation can be done safely," says Dr. Willard Cates, Jr., chief of CDC's abortion surveillance branch. "But we can find no study documenting the factual basis for setting a 12-week threshold on curettage or instrument procedures. There seems to be no scientific basis for it."

QUESTIONS OF SAFETY

Just how safe are abortions? Should you be concerned about your daughter having one?

Early abortion is one of the safest of all surgical procedures. The more advanced your daughter's pregnancy is, the more dangerous her abortion becomes. But in the hands of a competent physician, abortion at any stage is no riskier than her delivering a full-term baby.

The vast majority of women having legal abortions develop no complications of any kind. A study of 73,000 abortions by the Joint Program for the Study of Abortion shows that, during the first twelve weeks of pregnancy, your daughter's chances of having abortion complications are a mere 5 percent. After twelve weeks, this percentage increases to 22 percent. Most complications are minor—such as a day of vomiting and fever. Other possible risks of abortion include damage to the cervix or to the uterus. There also may be infection, hemorrhage, and adverse reaction to anesthesia.

Death from abortion is extremely rare. In some years, the Center for Disease Control has reported only one death for every 100,000 legal abortions. The death rate increases as the pregnancy progresses. Out of 100,000 abortions done before the ninth week of pregnancy, there are 0.7 deaths; at twenty-one weeks or later, there are 22.9 deaths.

Does abortion affect future pregnancies? The answer to this question largely depends on the safety of D & Cs, which may weaken the cervix and uterus. A World Health Organization study—done at institutions in eight countries where abortion is legal—indicates an increased risk of spontaneous abortion in subsequent pregnancies. But this risk is related to D & Cs—not to suction procedures, which are now standard in the U.S. for early abortions. The rate of spontaneous abortion was more than twice as high for women who had had an abortion by D & C (8.2 percent) as for women who had had an abortion by suction (3.3 percent).

The preliminary findings of a study funded by the National Institutes of Health (NIH) similarly show that women who had abortions—usually by D & C—tended to have more miscarriages and other problems in subsequent pregnancies. The study compared the experiences of more than 65,000 women in New York and Hawaii. Women who had had abortions had 35 percent more miscarriages, plus other pregnancy problems, such as low birth weight and premature births (25 to 50 percent higher than in the nonabortion group).

On the other hand, studies of abortions done with current medical techniques find no correlation between abortion and any later pregnancy problems. An investigation of the pregnancy records of some 32,000 women at the Kaiser-Permanente Medical Center in Walnut Creek, California, detected a higher rate of miscarriages among women who had abortions before 1973, when D & Cs were common. Since 1974, the researchers found, suction removal of the fetus has been the norm. Now women who have abortions face "little or no risk" of suffering unusual numbers of miscarriages thereafter. Dr. Janet R. Daling, an epidemiologist with the Washington State Department of Social and Health Services in Olympia, studied 590 women who had had an abortion, usually by suction. Dr. Daling found that abortions were in no way related to low birth-weight, premature delivery, stillbirth, infant death, miscarriage, or congenital malformations in subsequent pregnancies. Moreover, the abortion procedure itself and the length of pregnancy were not related to any occurrence of low-birthweight babies or premature delivery.

Dr. Stephen C. Schoenbaum, director of medical services at the Boston Hospital for Women, studied five thousand deliveries over a nine-month period. He compared three groups of women: those who had had no prior pregnancies, those who had had a pregnancy resulting in a live baby, and women who had had a previous pregnancy that was aborted. Dr. Schoenbaum found "few differences among the three groups." There was no excess of low-birthweight babies among the women who had had previous abortions. Nor did those women experience a higher incidence of birth defects or infant deaths.

Chapter 14

Secure a Safe Delivery

Reduce abnormally high risks faced by your daughter and grandchild.

IF YOUR TEENAGE DAUGHTER decides to go on with her pregnancy, she and her infant face significant medical risks.

In general, the younger your daughter is, the greater is the chance she'll suffer complications. Medical problems are especially common in the pregnancy of an adolescent under 16.

Also at greater risk are adolescents, regardless of age, who are nonwhite, or from low-income families. Complications are exceptionally frequent if a girl has a poor health history or receives inadequate prenatal care.

In addition, there are hazards to your daughter's infant, your grandchild. The younger your daughter is at conception and delivery, the greater is the likelihood that your grandchild will die before its first birthday. A baby born to a mother under 16 is three times more likely to die in the first year of life than the child of a mother aged 20–24.

Young mothers are more likely to start labor prematurely. Delivery may be prolonged and difficult, multiplying the hazards to your daughter and grandchild. There is also a higher incidence of abnormal positioning of the fetus, requiring a forceps or cesarean delivery.

Premature birth is a major risk to your grandchild. A baby born to a mother under 16 is more than twice as likely to be born early, and to have a birthweight less than five and a half pounds. Such a baby has a greater chance of having health and developmental problems than full-term babies of normal weight.

Very small babies are more likely to suffer from infections and from birth defects such as cerebral palsy, epilepsy, visual and hearing defects. Babies born to women under 15 have three times the number of brain and nervous system disorders of children born to mothers older than 15.

FIND THE RIGHT HELP

Your primary need is for a good doctor. Help your daughter find a board-certified obstetrician-gynecologist (OBG), a surgeon who specializes in childbirth and female medical problems. His (or her) certification by the American Board of Obstetrics and Gynecology indicates a high degree of competence in the specialty.

In addition, you want him to be sympathetic, and experienced in dealing with teenage pregnancy and its special problems. If he bungles your daughter's case psychologically, she'll be needlessly unhappy. She also is likely to disregard his advice. She may fail to keep appointments or mention serious problems. She may suffer painful physical complaints of emotional origin.

Your family doctor may be able to recommend the right OBG for your daughter. Friends who've been in the same boat may also come up with names. If you're starting your search from scratch, begin with the best hospital in your area, generally one affiliated with a medical school. Phone the physician-referral service. You may thus learn of OBGs who have privileges at an institution where your daughter will get good care, and who are convenient to your home.

Encourage your daughter to check an OBG out personally. For the price of an office visit, she can find out if she likes the doctor, finds him easy to talk with, and feels confidence in his ability. If not, have her visit another one—until she finds an OBG she'd like to stick with through her delivery. Sensitive OBGs are used to being interviewed, indeed welcome this trial visit as a sign of the patient's involvement. Suggest that your daughter raise any questions that may bother her, as for example: "How do you feel about my being pregnant before I'm married?" "Do you think I'm bad?" "Are you going to treat me any different from someone who's older or married?"

Discuss fees with the doctor right off. OBGs typically have pay-as-you-go plans, so you may be able to budget for his charges. If money's a problem, your daughter's care may be covered under Medicaid. The doctor may reduce his fee, or refer your daughter to a clinic where he can see her free.

By having early diagnosis of pregnancy and good prenatal care, your daughter can prevent many of the complications of teenage pregnancy and reduce the risk of having a child with birth defects. An early prenatal examination can spot potential problems that may interfere with normal pregnancy. Some girls, for example, have ectopic pregnancies—those occurring outside the uterus, usually in the Fallopian tube. These need to be detected early and surgically removed.

Many pregnant adolescents delay prenatal care, or go without it entirely. Planned Parenthood estimates that seven out of 10 girls under age 15 do not get any prenatal care through the first trimester of pregnancy. This is nearly three times the proportion of pregnant women ages 20–24. Nearly 1 in 4 pregnant girls under 15 get no prenatal care at all or delay it until near the end of the pregnancy, four times the proportion of those 20–24. Teenagers generally are twice as likely as those in their early twenties to go without prenatal care through the first six months.

Government policies contribute to this problem. Many states do not consider a low-income pregnant woman eligible for public assistance until after she has delivered her baby, so pregnant adolescents are unable to get Medicaid for prenatal care. Nor can they get cash assistance to buy food during pregnancy. The requirement that the young applicant must name and help locate the father of the baby also deters many adolescent mothers from seeking public aid.

During the first six months of your daughter's pregnancy, her doctor will probably want to see her about once a month. At each visit, he'll check her weight, blood pressure and urine, and the growth of the fetus. After a few months, he'll be able to listen to its heartbeat. From about the sixteenth week, he'll be able to feel the unborn baby in the uterus. Between the eighteenth and twenty-fourth weeks, your daughter will begin feeling the baby's movements.

In her seventh and eighth months, she'll probably see her doctor every second week; and in her last month, every week. A baby born after the twenty-eighth week can often survive with proper medical care. Full-term delivery occurs at about thirty-six weeks, or 280 days.

Urge your daughter to take childbirth-preparation classes. They're invaluable for providing nuts-and-bolts information about pregnancy, delivery, and care of the newborn. Most include basic physiological information. Many offer instruction on methods for relaxing and breathing during labor to reduce pain.

Consider programs for the Lamaze method of so-called natural childbirth—delivery that relies not on anesthesia for the control of pain during labor, but on relaxed muscles and proper breathing. Most Lamaze classes call for your daughter to have someone with her to share the preparation and act as her coach during labor. This is usually a woman's husband, but it can as easily be the girl's mother, father, or friend.

Other instruction in childbirth preparation usually includes general fitness exercises, and child care. Such classes are held in every major city and many smaller communities. For information on classes in your area, consult the phone directory or write the International Childbirth Education Association, Box 20852, Milwaukee, Wisconsin 53220, or (for the Lamaze method) Society for Psychoprophylaxis in Obstetrics, 1523 L Street NW, Washington, D.C. 20005.

RULE OUT VD

Have your pregnant daughter's doctor rule out venereal disease, which runs rampant among sexually active teenagers. During pregnancy VD is harmful not only to the pregnant teenager, but can also injure her infant.

Gonorrhea may cause difficult pregnancies. At University Hospital in Seattle, a study of pregnant women with gonorrhea suggests that they are likely to experience early membrane rupture and premature labor. There is also likely to be bacterial infection of the fetal membranes.

The babies of such women often have gonorrhea bacteria contaminating their upper gastrointestinal and respiratory tracts. The Seattle researchers found that many infants were suffering from fever, jaundice, poor appetite, and weakness. A number had pneumonia. Some died.

As early as possible, have your daughter also tested for syphilis. The disease can be passed to the unborn infant, causing congenital syphilis. Many such babies are stillborn. Others may become deaf, blind, or mentally defective unless they receive immediate treatment.

Yet another common venereal disease—herpes simplex virus infection—can cause grave damage to the fetus as it passes down the birth canal. The infection may start as a skin disease. It usually rapidly involves the liver, adrenal glands, and brain. Between 75 and 90 percent of the babies die. Of those who survive, an estimated 60 to 80 percent will be left with neurologic damage.

To prevent such a tragedy, warn your daughter to be on the alert for any suspicious genital lesions. If herpes is caught early in her pregnancy, she can usually be cured before damage to the baby occurs, and she can deliver her baby normally. But if the infection is discovered only near the end of term, her doctor may deliver the baby by cesarean in order to bypass the infected genital tract. The doctor may also advise keeping the baby isolated from your daughter until she is free of infection.

ALERT HER DOCTOR

Report to your daughter's doctor any vaginal bleeding. That's typically the first sign of an impending miscarriage (spontaneous abortion), suffered in about 1 in 10 pregnancies. Other symptoms include cramps, backache and nausea. Most miscarriages occur during the first twelve weeks of pregnancy.

Little can be done to avert a threatened miscarriage, especially if there is heavy bleeding and severe cramps. If the bleeding is slight, with little or no abdominal cramps, the doctor will most likely advise bed rest until twenty-four hours after the bleeding has stopped. Strenuous physical activity and sexual intercourse are usually forbidden until the bleeding has completely stopped for 24–48 hours. These measures may save the infant.

After a miscarriage, your daughter needs an examination to be sure all the fetal and placental tissue has been discharged. If she experiences an incomplete spontaneous abortion, in which some of the material remains in the uterus, she must have the remaining material removed. This is done either by a D & C (dilatation and curettage: stretching the cervix and scraping the uterus), or by the use of a drug that stimulates the uterus to contract and expel the remaining material.

The pregnancy that ends in miscarriage usually has an abnormal fetus—to this extent it may be a blessing in disguise. In other cases, the miscarriage may be due to the mother's malnutrition, or to a medical condition such as genital infection, anemia, diabetes, hepatitis, or heart disease.

Also, if your daughter experiences swelling of her hands or feet, tell her doctor right away. Edema, the accumulation of fluid in the tissues, is an early sign of toxemia, a severe metabolic disorder marked by the excretion of protein in the urine. Pregnant teenagers are evidently at greater risk than older women of developing toxemia.

Heavy vomiting and sudden weight gain are other frequent signs of toxemia. In the course of the disease, a victim may experience blurred vision and severe headache. Her blood pressure generally rises abnormally.

If unchecked, toxemia (also called pre-eclampsia) can progress to eclampsia, a condition of convulsions and coma. Eclampsia is fatal in about half the cases, and often results in the death of the fetus.

Nutritional deficiencies, especially lack of protein, may be a cause. Toxemia occurs most often in first pregnancies. It generally appears after the twentieth week of pregnancy. It is most likely to affect girls who have diabetes and girls carrying more than one fetus.

While it's prudent to bring any swelling to the attention of your daughter's physician, most cases of edema have nothing to do with toxemia. Some swelling due to increased water retention is normal during pregnancy. Your daughter's fingers may be somewhat puffy and stiff, especially in the morning.

Good prenatal care can detect toxemia in its early stages, and generally get it under control. If your daughter suffers any of the symptoms associated with toxemia, she'll generally be put on a high-protein diet with supplements of folic acid, iron, and vitamin D.

In cases of severe hypertension, drugs may be prescribed. Bed rest alone, at home or in the hospital, can often control mild or moderate hypertension. If symptoms of toxemia persist after treatment, the physician may recommend inducing labor. Toxemia disappears within a few days after delivery.

In addition, be watchful for signs of anemia, a deficiency of the oxygen-carrying red blood cells. Teenagers seem more likely than older mothers to suffer from anemia during pregnancy. Let your daughter's doctor know if she's weak, easily tired, or sleepy—symptoms resulting from the inadequate oxygen received by her tissues. She also may suffer from dizziness, headaches, irritability, spots before her eyes.

To correct anemia, the doctor may prescribe iron tablets. Adding to her diet iron-rich foods like meat, fish, poultry, and green vegetables (spinach, kale, broccoli) may be helpful. Organ meats—

liver, kidneys, brains—are unusually high in iron and also inexpensive. Raisins and dried apricots are good for snacks. Whole-grain breads are generally higher in iron than enriched white breads.

Expect Minor Discomforts

Your daughter is likely to suffer from a variety of minor physical discomforts during pregnancy. Reassure her that the following are normal. Some may be easily alleviated:

Morning Sickness.   Nausea and vomiting in early pregnancy can often be relieved by eating five or six small meals a day instead of three large ones. Very hot or very cold liquids may help, as may sucking a lollipop.

If your daughter feels especially nauseated in the morning, she can keep a few dry crackers next to her bed for munching before she gets up. Starting the day with a carbonated beverage may also help. She should avoid overtiring herself.

Indigestion. Can usually be prevented by avoiding fried foods. Small sips of water or milk may be helpful. She needs to consult her doctor before taking any antacids.

Constipation. Can often be relieved by eating plenty of fruits and vegetables, and drinking lots of water. Raisins, prunes, or prune juice help.

Leg Cramps. Can often be relieved by massage, or the application of hot compresses like a hot-water bottle. If she gets leg cramps frequently, tell her doctor about it. These cramps may be due to an excessive accumulation of phosphorous caused by drinking too much milk.

Fatigue. Can be avoided by resting frequently, perhaps taking a nap every afternoon.

Dizziness and Fainting. Affect some pregnant women. If your daughter feels a spell coming on, she should sit down or lie on her side and wait for the feeling to pass.

Shortness of Breath. May bother her, especially if she's overweight. If it interferes with sleep, propping up her head and shoulders with several pillows may bring relief. Inform the doctor if the problem is persistent and troublesome.

Low Backache. May affect her late in pregnancy. Low-heeled shoes may improve her balance, relieving back strain. Standing with buttocks tucked under may also help.

Increased Urination. Is common during pregnancy. If it is especially troublesome, have her doctor check to see if she's suffering from a urinary tract infection.

Excessive Sweating. May be bothersome during pregnancy, causing perspiration odor and calling for more frequent bathing.

Skin Discoloration. May appear in the form of brownish spots and patches on her forehead, cheeks, abdomen. This "mask of pregnancy" is most common in brunettes and girls with dark skin. Dark moles, freckles, birthmarks, and circles under the eyes tend to become darker during pregnancy.

These are temporary and almost always disappear after delivery. Since these pigmentations are intensified by exposure to sun, she can block out the sun with a sunscreen preparation. A regular suntan lotion won't do. Enlarged blood vessels may show up as red spots or spiderlike tracings anywhere on her body, and are normal.

Stretch Marks (Striae). These are thin white scars on the abdomen that may occur as the skin stretches with the growth of the baby. They may disappear eventually, but more often are permanent. An emollient cream can keep the skin of the abdomen soft, help relieve the taut feeling, and minimize itching. It is questionable if such creams or lotions can keep stretch marks from forming.

TAKE THESE PRECAUTIONS

To help lower the risks of her pregnancy, your daughter should:

Take no drug unless there is a strong medical need for it. Virtually all drugs pass through the placenta, entering the unborn child's circulation and possibly harming it. *The Medical Letter* recommends that physicians give pregnant women as few drugs as possible. It cautions that "except for urgent indications, all drugs should be withheld during the first trimester [three months]."

Since 1962, when the drug thalidomide was found to cause severe physical abnormalities in the fetus, many other drugs—including some antidepressants, antibiotics, and antihistamines—have been implicated in potential birth defects. Iodides, contained in many cough medicines, can cause large goiters and respiratory distress in newborn infants. Progestogen, estrogen, and androgenic hormones can cause masculinized external genitals in the female fetus. Antibiotics containing tetracyclines may inhibit fetal bone growth or produce teeth discoloration.

Other drugs that are suspected of causing fetal damage include antinauseants, anticoagulants, and anticonvulsants.

If her doctor prescribes a drug, your daughter should take it only in the doses and at the times indicated. She should never take a drug that has been prescribed for someone else.

Cut out all nonprescription drugs. Except on her doctor's advice, she shouldn't take aspirin, vitamins, remedies for colds, laxatives, or medicated nose drops. Lotions or ointments containing hormones or other drugs should be avoided.

Avoid illicit drugs. The effect of LSD and marijuana on the fetus is unknown. Heroin, morphine, or methadone addiction in the mother can cause severe physiological problems or death in the newborn.

Cut out cigarettes. Girls who smoke during pregnancy have a greater than average risk of stillbirths or early infant deaths. The Public Health Service's report to Congress on cigarette smoking estimates that 4600 stillbirths a year can almost certainly be attributed to the smoking habits of the mothers.

The infant of a smoking mother is more likely to die within its first month. Smoking during pregnancy also tends to reduce the size of the infant, compounding one major risk of teenage pregnancy.

If your daughter gives up smoking by her fourth month of pregnancy, she is likely to eliminate the risk to her baby. The danger to the fetus seems to come from the cumulated toxic effects of the nicotine.

Refrain from vaginal douching. Douche only if prescribed by the doctor for a medical condition.

Stay physically active. Exercise helps control weight and keep muscles strong. Most doctors urge healthy pregnant girls to continue with the kind of exercise they are used to until it becomes uncomfortable to do so. Walking is particularly good.

Your daughter should do what is comfortable for her, but avoid overtiring herself. Pregnancy is no time for her to learn a new sport. If she is accustomed to tennis or water-skiing, she need not give it up until her growing abdomen compels her to.

Delay most immunization. Live virus vaccines (for smallpox, mumps, measles, polio, rubella) may be harmful to the fetus. If your daughter is exposed to these or other communicable diseases, she needs to consult her physician about possible preventives.

On the other hand, tetanus toxoid is generally recommended if her immunization has lapsed. The shot will also protect her baby through his first month.

Steer clear of X rays. They can be dangerous to the fetus, particularly during the first three months. All nonessential abdominal X rays should be postponed until after delivery, or at least until the fourth month or later. If your daughter must have an X ray elsewhere on her body—such as a dental X ray—make sure her reproductive organs are protected with a lead apron.

Be careful with oral sex. Throughout the pregnancy, it's imperative that no air be blown into her vagina. Deaths to mothers-to-be have resulted when the forced air passed into the blood vessels of the placenta, causing bubbles that blocked circulation to the heart.

If your daughter experiences vaginal or abdominal pain or bleeding during intercourse, or at any other time, she should abstain from sex until she has talked with her doctor. Otherwise, sexual intercourse can ordinarily continue throughout a normal pregnancy. Some doctors caution against intercourse during the last weeks of pregnancy. A study by the U.S. Collaborative Perinatal Project suggests that infants of women who engage in intercourse during the last weeks of pregnancy are more likely to suffer infections.

Wear a seat belt low. It's not necessary to stop wearing a seat belt during pregnancy. Contrary to misbelief, there is no evidence that seat belts pose any threat to the fetus, and in accidents they could save the lives of both the mother and fetus.

But your daughter should wear the belt low, snugly fastened across the pelvic bones and upper thighs, not across the uterus. For added protection, she should wear a shoulder harness too. She can continue to drive as long as she can fit behind the wheel.

Air travel in a pressurized cabin poses no special hazards. But it's wise for her to avoid long airplane trips during the last weeks of pregnancy because of the possibility of labor or delivery during the flight. She should arm herself with a note from her physician before going to the airport. Some airlines require a doctor's note to the effect that childbirth en route is unlikely before they'll permit an obviously pregnant woman to board.

WHAT SHOULD SHE EAT?

"I know when you're pregnant you're supposed to eat for two," said 15-year-old Andrea, "so I had an extra hot dog, a large coke instead of a small, and a big chocolate bar for dessert."

Andrea is on her way to compounding an already risky pregnancy with nutritional problems. Eating properly is of paramount importance in maintaining a teenager's good health during pregnancy and in assuring a healthy baby.

While your daughter should resist putting on excess weight, she should also not gain too little. If she has stopped growing and is of normal weight, she needs to gain between twenty and twenty-five pounds during pregnancy. If she's still growing, her goal should be about a thirty-pound gain.

She may hate the idea of gaining weight. Explain to her where the pounds go. In addition to the weight of the infant (five to ten pounds), the placenta and amniotic fluid weigh over three pounds. The larger uterus weighs two pounds. Her enlarged breasts weigh nearly another pound, her increased blood volume several ounces.

An additional few pounds of unaccounted-for weight appears to be in the form of fat around the hips and thighs. It is evidently a built-in safety factor for energy storage. If she's overweight, she'll generally lose it easily after the delivery.

Your daughter's eating habits during her pregnancy may depend on her developmental stage. An early adolescent (about 12 to 14 years) may not be able to understand why she should eat well for her baby's welfare, notes pediatrician Elizabeth R. McAnarney of the University of Rochester School of Medicine. "She may not have developed the ability to think about cause in the present and effect in the future: the effect of her present nutritional intake on her child. She may be more interested in what tastes pleasant in the present."

By middle adolescence (15 or 16 year old), a girl may realize that her eating has an effect on her baby's health. Even so, she may have trouble following the diet her doctor has given her. Observes Dr. McAnarney: "She may feel pressured by peers to eat what they enjoy: candy, soft drinks, and hot dogs."

By late adolescence (17 through 19), a young woman generally knows why she should eat well for her baby's health, and she'll usually do so if the proper food is available.

Teenagers are notorious for their bizarre eating habits—they have the worst diets of all age groups. Frequently, adolescent girls have even poorer diets than adolescent boys. The fashion for slimness provokes many teenage girls into following unnecessary diets. In Berkeley, California, 43 percent of surveyed girls in the ninth grade and 51 percent of girls in the tenth grade wanted to lose weight. But objective measurements showed that less than half of them were even mildly overweight. Another study found that teenage girls were taking in from 200 to 400 fewer calories per day than their growth and health required.

Encourage your pregnant teenager to have regular, adequate meals. Many teenagers habitually skip breakfast. Snacks on the go may replace other meals if social events interfere with lunch and dinner times. Many teenagers insist they simply don't have time for proper sit-down meals. Some teenagers may snack intelligently (fruit, cheese and crackers, yogurt). Others seem to subsist on empty calories: soft drinks, potato chips, french fries, ice cream, candy. Teenagers' diets are often low in calcium, vitamin C, and iron.

During adolescence, your daughter needs increased amounts of nutritious food merely for her own growth and development. If her diet is already poor, her body is ill prepared for pregnancy. The additional nutrient demands of pregnancy can compromise her own growth and worsen the health risks to her and her baby.

Start reforming your daughter's diet by encouraging her to eat breakfast, considered by many nutritionists to be the most important meal of the day. The body needs fuel after being without food for about 12 hours. Teenagers who skip breakfast take longer to make decisions, have greater neuromuscular tremors, and reduced energy output.

Be creative with breakfast. It doesn't have to run to the standard cereal or eggs and toast. There's no reason why breakfast can't be a leftover casserole, creamed soup, tuna salad, or any other nutritious food.

Tailor your daughter's diet to her food preferences. Meals are likely to become a running battle unless your daughter gets to eat food she likes. If for a vegetable you serve boiled kale, it's likely to be met with profanity. But kale blended with other vegetables into a creamed soup, spiced with herbs and decorated with parsley, may be welcomed as a gourmet dish.

Other sleight-of-hand: Slip a layer of spinach into a lasagna. Make an eggnog of raw egg, skim milk, and chocolate or vanilla extract. Slide a fish and vegetable concoction into pocket bread.

Involve your daughter in planning the meals she'll be having with the family. Some of teenagers' favorite dishes can make valuable contributions to her pregnancy diet. These include pizza, spaghetti and meatballs, hamburger with bun and salad, peanut butter and jelly sandwiches, chicken or beef pot pie, tamales, tacos, and enchiladas.

Also help her work her pregnancy diet into her snacks. Nutritious snacks can include cheese, fruit, smoked oysters on crackers, raw vegetables, nuts, and seeds.

A pregnant teenager needs more food. But not much more—she certainly needn't eat double for two. Pregnant girls between 14 to 18 require about 2500 calories a day if they're of average height and weight, about two hundred calories more than usual. They also need increased amounts of protein, calcium, iron, and many vitamins. Your daughter can follow a healthy pregnancy diet by selecting foods from the following categories:

Milk or Milk Products—4 Servings a Day. Dairy foods provide calcium essential for the baby's bones and teeth. They include yogurt, buttermilk, cream soup made with milk, pudding made with milk, cottage cheese and other cheese.

Meat, Fish, or Poultry—3 Servings a Day. Also in this category are other such high-protein foods as eggs, nuts, beans, black-eyed or split peas, seafood. These foods are excellent sources of iron, particularly important to avoid anemia in pregnancy. During adolescence, considerable iron is necessary for growth, to replace loss during menstruation, and to maintain iron stores. The iron intake of adolescent girls is often not sufficient for pregnancy. Doctors usually prescribe supplemental iron tablets, organ meats such as liver and kidneys, oysters and clams, whole-grain breads.

Vegetables and Fruits—6 Servings a Day. These foods provide many vitamins and minerals, and dietary bulk to help prevent constipation.

Dark green or yellow vegetables provide vitamin A. These include broccoli, spinach, kale, carrots, winter squash, chard, pumpkin, sweet potatoes, tomatoes, collard, mustard and turnip greens.

Some fruits—oranges, grapefruit, cantaloupe, strawberries, lemon—provide vitamin C, important in the formation of the baby's gums, blood, and bones.

Important vitamins and minerals are provided by lima beans, navy or pinto beans, rice, noodles, spaghetti or macaroni.

In general, the more fruits and vegetables your daughter eats, the better her pregnancy diet is likely to be. Other nutritious fruits and vegetables include celery, green pepper, peas, corn, asparagus, squash, brussels sprouts, melons, berries, bananas, peaches, plums.

Breads and Cereals—4 Servings a Day. They supply vitamins, iron, and energy. Whole-wheat grains, especially bran breads, help in preventing constipation. This group also includes muffins, rolls, pancakes, french toast, waffles, crackers.

BABY SHOCK

When 16-year-old Nikki was presented with her newborn baby on the delivery table, she became hysterical. The infant was covered with a cheesy, greenish-gray fluid. "I'm being punished!" Nikki cried. "I'm cursed with a monster!"

Like Nikki, your daughter may be alarmed by the appearance of a perfectly normal newborn. A teenager may have an idealized expectation of what her baby will look like, influenced by ads for baby powder and disposable diapers, that show round, robust babies at least a month old. Warn your daughter that besides being covered with the cheesy fluid, her newborn is likely to be puffy, with thin, dry red skin that mottles when it cries. Her baby may have whiteheads on its nose and chin. Many babies are born with rashes, hives, or welts.

Her baby's veins may throb and swell. Its lips and nails are bluish. There may be a temporary growth of hair on its face, arms, and shoulders.

A baby boy's genitals are enlarged. So are his breasts. Small amounts of fluid may come from the baby's breasts during the first few weeks of life. Tell your daughter that she should not massage the breasts or squeeze out the fluid.

After a day or two, her baby will most likely have a slightly yellow jaundiced look. This will disappear after a few days.

Your daughter's newborn will have a temporarily elongated head from its passage through the narrow birth canal. Its arms are longer than its legs. Its nose is likely to be broad and flat, and its jaw is undersized. Its trunk and neck are stubby. Its skull is soft.

It will look cross-eyed until seven or eight months. A newborn baby's eyes are always blue at first. They may change color within a few months.

Inform your daughter that a newborn's breathing is normally rapid and irregular, seeming to stop at intervals. Its abdomen bounces when it breathes. Its chest seems to cave in when it has hiccups.

The stump of its umbilical cord protrudes from its abdomen, and should be washed several times a day. Your daughter should keep it uncovered—it will fall off by itself. The baby should not have a tub bath until a week after the umbilical stump falls off.

The hair on the baby's head will fall out. The hair that replaces it may be of an entirely different color.

Before the baby leaves the hospital, it will lose several ounces of its original birth weight. Reassure your daughter that this is perfectly normal.

AFTER-BABY BLUES

Like all new mothers, your daughter may experience mood swings or mild depression. She may be irritable and hypersensitive, crying for no apparent reason.

She may experience the feeling of having lost control of her life. She'll likely get little sleep, and all her time may seem taken up with catering to the baby's needs. She may feel exhausted and overwhelmed, and it may seem to her as if life will always be this way.

Postpartum depression, also called after-baby blues, is normal. It usually disappears by itself within a few weeks. Postpartum depression is thought to result from a combination of psychological stress and hormonal changes following delivery.

Help her get over the blues by helping her arrange for time away from the baby at frequent intervals. Just a couple of hours of freedom a day may make her feel refreshed and renewed.

If her depression is severe or prolonged, get professional psychiatric help. For a few women postpartum depression develops into a serious emotional disturbance.

Her own physical discomfort may come as a shock to your daughter. If she's been delivered with anesthesia she may be suffering the aftereffects of drugs.

A common problem is discomfort in the vaginal area around the stitches. Her doctor may prescribe a soothing cream. Hot sitz baths several times a day may help. She's also likely to be more comfortable sitting on a pillow than on a hard chair. Sweating, especially at night, is common. She may have some loss of appetite.

If she is breast-feeding, her breasts may feel overfull and sore as the milk comes in. Constipation may be a problem—walking soon after the baby is born is thought to prevent a severe case. If any of these problems are more than a little troubling, she should tell her doctor.

She'll bleed from the vagina for several weeks after the baby is born. She should wear sanitary napkins, not internal tampons. In the first weeks after delivery, she needs to get as much rest as she can.

PREEMIE PROBLEMS

Your teenage daughter may have a premature or low-birthweight baby, a special hazard for very young mothers. All babies who weigh less than five pounds are treated as premature. Having a premature baby is an emotional strain for a teenager. Reassure her that it's not her fault.

A very small premature baby may weigh little more than two pounds. A premature baby's chances of survival increase with its birthweight and how close it is to full-term. If the child is only a little below five pounds, its chances for survival and normal development are excellent.

A premature infant will be put into an incubator. This see-through box simulates conditions inside the uterus. It is controlled for heat, moisture, and oxygen, and provides portholes so that nurses and doctors can care for the child without removing it from its special environment. Monitoring equipment keeps track of the baby's breathing and body temperature.

If the baby has breathing problems, a respirator may be used. The baby may need to be fed intravenously, through a tube passed through its nostril into its stomach, or through an eyedropper. Some premature babies need blood transfusions because their immature livers are not functioning properly in removing waste products from the blood.

A premature infant usually remains in the incubator or in the hospital until it is five to five and a half pounds. This may be six or more weeks from birth.

When your daughter takes her preemie home, it will need extra care. Since a preemie is more susceptible to body temperature changes, it should be neither too hot nor too cold. For the first few weeks, it should be kept out of public places and away from strangers because of the increased danger of infections. A premature baby may need to be fed more often during the first few weeks at home, and may be slow in starting to gain weight.

Calculate a preemie's development not from one's birth date, but from the probable date of conception. Thus, if the baby was born two months early, its development eight months after delivery will be roughly on a par with a full-term baby of six months. The smaller a premature baby is, the longer it takes to catch up. Within two or three years it's likely to be of average size.

A few preemies will always be small. Their reading ability, emotional maturation, and muscular development may lag somewhat behind those of their age peers. It is often advisable to start a preemie in kindergarten at six, instead of five, so the child will be more on a par with classmates.

Chapter 15

Keeping the Baby

Getting a "toy" may push your daughter toward poverty and child abuse.

"WHEN RONNIE SAID she would have the baby and keep it, I remember feeling a sudden profound sorrow for her," said 38-year-old Sarah. "After all, sixteen can be such a happy, irresponsible time. Suddenly, her youth seems gone forever. She has to become an instant adult. And no matter what I say, I know she really doesn't know what she's getting into.

"But," Sarah went on, "I must admit that my real concern was for myself. I've been a mother for so many years. Now, with my last child in junior high and a degree in economics, I've looked forward to really starting a career, not just having jobs.

"But I'm afraid I'll somehow get trapped into bringing up this child. Ronnie says the baby will be her responsibility. But I can't see how she'll manage it. I know I'll feel guilty if I don't come through for Ronnie, but resentful if I do. I'd looked forward to being a grandmother, but not like this. Maybe my attitude will change when the baby is born, but right now I'm angry at the whole thing."

If your pregnant teenager decides to have her baby, you may be in the same boat as Sarah. The odds are overwhelming that your daughter will keep her baby rather than give it up for adoption. Of the 200,000 out-of-wedlock babies born to teenagers each year, 94 percent are kept by the mothers, according to the National Center for Health Statistics.

Immature mothers like your daughter constitute a sizable, but generally unnoted, population group. It is by no means uncommon for a child to have a child. One out of every five births is to a teenager. Nor is childbirth an extremely unusual event among adolescents. One out of every 10 girls in the United States becomes a mother before the age of 18. Indeed, child-mothers are becoming more prevalent. The birthrate in the country has significantly declined in all other age groups. But it has remained constant among girls aged 14 to 17—and actually gone up among those who are 14 and younger. These young mothers come from all types of backgrounds: Sixty percent of school-age mothers are white.

Like your daughter, few of these girls wanted to become pregnant. Most have had an extended relationship with only one boy and have just begun to have sexual intercourse. By the time the child is born, about half of the girls are married. Thus there is an even chance that your daughter will have to deal with a new husband as well as a newborn baby.

FACING REALITY

"When I found out I was pregnant I was happy. Abortion crossed my mind but I never really thought about it seriously. Adoption never crossed my mind. I figured if I am going to carry a baby for nine months I might as well keep him."

So recalls Marcia, a member of a YWCA Teen Moms group in Kingston, New York. "When people found out about me being pregnant it was something else for them to talk about. I heard a lot of things said about me and other girls who were pregnant. People on the street stared and it made me feel kind of ashamed. You seemed to be known as an 'easy piece.'

"My mother went nuts at first. She cried and thought it was her fault—that she brought me up wrong. She wanted me to get an abortion but I said no. After a while though I found out she was a better friend than I had thought. She stuck by me through it all.

"My boyfriend wanted a baby so when I told him he was happy. He stayed home with me a lot and was a big help throughout my pregnancy. When the baby was born he was overjoyed. It was fantastic. He loves his son very much."

Like many teenagers, Marcia is undeveloped in her grasp of reality. She tends to romanticize her situation. Her expectations of the baby's father seem painfully limited. She appears grateful for his interest—and evidently entertains no hope that he'll marry her or take permanent responsibility for their child.

If your daughter decides to keep her child, she may be as unrealistic as Marcia, and be taking on a greater burden than she can imagine. The outlook for teenage mothers and their babies is bleak. The teenage mother loses her childhood. She's prematurely thrust into the role of a parent. Her teen years, which could be a time of freedom for her to explore life's opportunities, will be dominated by her child. A good part of her future is ordained. Among problems you may need to help her resolve:

Adjustment Problems

Your daughter is likely to have trouble adapting to her new role. Most teenage mothers live with their own families. But is your daughter still a child in your household? Or is she an adult mother with the same status as you?

The members of your family are likely to have trouble adjusting to their new roles and finding new ways of relating to each other. Quarrels and jealousies may erupt over who is to do what for your grandchild. As an adolescent, your daughter is in the midst of struggling with her conflicts over emotional independence. If you have mixed feelings about her growing up, caring for your grandchild can become the primary battleground for dealing with her moves toward emancipation. Reports nurse Susan Panzarine of The Rochester Maternity Project at the University of Rochester Medical Center:

> We often see disagreements occuring in the areas of feeding and discipline, and the new mother and grandmother have difficulty deciding who will be making the important decisions about the child. The shifting of roles which must occur within the family system as a result of the introduction of the adolescent's infant is often problematic, especially if the family's flexibility and coping mechanisms are limited.

Those questions are almost certain to bother her. You may give her an idea of what to expect by telling her what's proved to be the experience of girls in her position. For two years after having their babies, 550 unwed mothers, nearly all of them white, were followed by Lutheran Social Service of Minnesota, a private nondenominational agency.

Over 85 percent of the school-age girls dated since becoming mothers, shows a report by Carol A. Nettleton and by psychiatrist David W. Cline of the University of Minnesota Medical School. About 60 percent were dating someone "steadily" at the time of the questionnaire. More than half were having intercourse. About half were still dating the child's father.

Some teenage mothers find themselves competing with their babies for their parents' attention. The new baby can be much like a sibling in your daughter's eyes, in rivalry with her for your love.

Your daughter will also have to negotiate her new role with respect to the rest of the world. How will she reply to questions about the baby's father? What about dating? What are her chances of a satisfactory relationship with a man?

Inadequate Education. Your daughter is likely to have an uphill battle to complete her schooling. A study made by Planned Parenthood shows that 8 out of 10 women who give birth at ages 15 to 17 never complete high school. Among 15-year-old and younger mothers, 9 out of 10 don't finish high school, and 4 in 10 drop out before finishing eighth grade.

Thus your daughter may lack key skills to compete in the job market. The younger your daughter when pregnant, the less likely she is to be employable. One New York City study cited by Planned Parenthood finds that 79 percent of 15- to 17-year-old mothers have no job experience at the time of their baby's birth. This is six times the proportion among women who do not have their first child until ages 20 to 24.

Poverty. Unemployment is likely to remain a severe problem for your daughter, even after she passes out of her teens. Over 90 percent of the mothers who gave birth between ages 15 and 17 were unemployed and 72 percent of them were receiving welfare. Forty-one percent of the 18- and 19-year-old mothers were also receiving welfare—2.6 times the proportion of mothers who began childbearing in their early twenties.

U.S. Bureau of the Census statistics also show that the younger a woman is when she first gives birth, the more likely her family will be living in poverty. Fully one out of three mothers who had their first child between the ages of 13 and 15 are below the federal poverty line, an incidence 2.6 times greater than among women who postponed childbearing until age 20 or later. Those who first gave birth at ages 16 and 17 are two times more likely to be poor. Even those who gave birth at ages 18 and 19 are 1.4 times more likely to be poor.

When unmarried mothers do work, they often can't manage on their earnings. Once they've paid work-related expenses such as carfare, clothes, child care, they often have less money than they had while on welfare. The median earnings of women who head families is less than half that of male family heads.

Child Abuse. Because of the severe economic and social pressures to which teenage mothers are subjected, they are more likely than older parents to abuse their children. According to Dr. Vincent J. Fontana, medical director of the New York Foundling Hospital and a widely recognized expert in the field of child abuse, "Troubled parents, particularly single adolescent mothers, become saturated with a sense of desperation, alienation and anger that during stressful situations leads them to lose control and strike out at what is closest to them—their child."

Your daughter may stop short of actual physical violence. But she is likely to bring considerable ambivalence to her relationship with your grandchild.

She may be wildly inconsistent toward the child. On one hand, your grandchild may suffer from smothering overprotection. Your daughter may value the youngster disproportionately because of the lack of other sources of emotional satisfaction in her life. She may lavish too much affection on the child, affection which would normally be shared by a husband.

Or, your daughter may be crushingly rejecting. She may resent your grandchild as an obstacle to her freedom, but refuse to surrender her right to raise the child. In addition, your grandchild may be a constant although unconscious reminder to your daughter of her rejection by the child's father and her consequent disillusionment.

Adolescent mothers like your daughter often give their children inadequate amounts of love and attention. Your grandchild is thus likely to have physical, social, and psychological problems.

Investigations at the Johns Hopkins School of Hygiene and Public Health compared 86 mothers under 18 with mothers 18 and older, starting with the birth of their first child and proceeding over twelve years. If your daughter is typical of mothers under 18, compared with older mothers she will spend less time with her child. She is less likely to rear your grandchild in a family situation rated by social workers as healthy. She will have relatively more children during a six- to eight-year period.

Your grandchild is more likely to be dependent and easily distracted. He (or she) is apt to show strong inappropriate reactions or infantile behavior. He is likely to be underweight and shorter than his peers. He'll tend to be deficient in reading-grade level. He'll have a lower IQ.

For mothers who abuse their children either physically or mentally or feel that they may, many areas have chapters of an organization called Parents Anonymous. For more information, write them at 2810 Artesia, Redondo Beach, California 90287.

Inadequate Child-care Services. Most adolescent mothers cannot complete their educations or get jobs without access to day care for their babies.

Your daughter may learn firsthand that such facilities are in extremely short supply. According to studies by the Child Welfare League of America, subsidized day care services are needed for at least 7 million children under 6, but there are facilities for only 4 million children of all ages. Only about 750,000 children of all ages are being cared for in licensed or approved facilities that meet minimum standards of acceptability.

The overwhelming majority of children are being taken care of by sitters or relatives in the child's home or in other unlicensed private homes. Many such arrangements "are at best custodial and at worst destructive," according to the National Council of Organizations of Children and Youth.

Your daughter's greatest need is for infant care, since, if she must wait until her baby is three—or even two—to place the child, the likelihood of completing her own interrupted education becomes remote. Yet some states have laws prohibiting licensed day care centers from accepting infants. Even without such prohibitions, few day care centers will enroll children under two. Licensed nonprofit centers, where available, are usually low in cost and geared to the mother's ability to pay. Public programs are likely to admit infants and to offer flexible hours. Some provide preschool education. But waiting lists are long, places few, and most such programs accommo-date mainly children from poor areas.

Profit-making day care centers may be run by private schools or may be part of a franchise operation. Cost may run to fifty dollars a week or more. Hours may not be flexible, and most such centers will not care for infants. These may provide the only type of day care in middle-class areas.

Family day care involves paying a woman to look after your child in her home, usually with a group of other children. This arrangement can be low-cost and flexible, and some women can be loving substitutes for the mother. But others are unstable, uncreative, and neglectful of the children in their care.

Another alternative is privately hired care, in which someone comes into the home to care for the child. This can be a most satisfactory situation if the person is loving and trustworthy. But it's also the most expensive.

"I WANT MY BABY"

In view of the hardships your daughter is likely to endure, why would she want to keep her baby? A group of adolescent mothers explained why they chose to raise their babies themselves:

"My baby is what I need to make my life complete." "I got pregnant because I was lonely." "I needed someone to take care of and love." "It makes me feel good about myself." "My man wanted a child."

Among your daughter's peers, unwed motherhood may be socially acceptable. When asked why she is keeping her baby, your teenager might counter, "Why not?"

"For the most part, society no longer disapproves and seldom punishes," observes social worker Helen L. Friedman, formerly of Crittenton Hastings House in Boston. "It is possible to explain the new trend of keeping babies with three old clichés—changing societal values, changing life-styles, and youth asserting itself."

Among nonwhites and in many lower middle-class communities the expectation has traditionally been that a baby born out of wedlock would be cared for at home by its mother or by relatives. "The baby is its natural mother's flesh and blood. To abandon it is wrong." Helen Friedman notes that this sentiment blends two attitudes: admiration for the courage it takes for the unwed mother to face the world—and punishment; she created the child and she should care for it.

Formerly, reasons social worker Friedman, the middle class could not accept the baby born out of wedlock. Today social class appears to be irrelevant. Middle-class as well as lower-class girls are bringing their babies home.

The attitude of many teenagers is shown by their response to a pair of movies made by the Children's Home Society of California. The first version was called, "I'm 17, I'm Pregnant . . . And I Don't Know What To Do." The film portrays the true story of a teenager who tried to keep her baby, but finally gave it up for adoption. Students' reactions to the film were overwhelmingly negative about the girl's putting the baby up for adoption. The girl "really took a copout," was a common reaction, as was the sentiment, "I'd really put down a girl who gave up her baby."

A new film made by the same organization, "Growing Up Together," depicts the real-life stories of four teenage mothers who are keeping their babies. Adults and adolescents tend to have opposite views on the content of the film. Adults tend to see the young mothers as frighteningly unresponsive or ambivalent toward their children. On the other hand, many high school students see nothing wrong with the situations in which the four girls find themselves.

Typical reactions: "Now Annie's got someone of her very own to love. . . . The baby might fill Criss's life. She's lonely . . . she's a cool mother, like I want to be."

Further, your daughter may believe a baby will solve all her problems. Your daughter may see the baby as a cure-all. It will solve all loneliness; all emptiness will vanish. The baby may represent relief from boredom or depression. The baby may slow her down, help her correct her ways, control her impulses, purify and assuage her personal guilt.

The baby may seem to promise freedom—to leave, to have an apartment of her own, to choose her own friends and her own life without interfering adults. The actuality, of course, is more often the opposite: worsened confinement and increased restrictions. But to an immature teenager, the baby is symbolic of adulthood, which, despite harsh realities, carries the fantasy of freedom.

Your daughter may also fancy that a baby will prove her worth. It will need her, she will be important to it. Bringing up the baby is a means of finding herself and having someone who will not go away or desert her.

The child can give your daughter a sense of accomplishment. She sees her child and thinks, "At last I have done something good. I can't be bad and the world can't be such a bad place after all."

Having a baby can provide your daughter with a reason for being, a sense of fulfillment. The baby—tiny, alive, warm, helpless, and dependent—is something to protect from an uncertain world.

"Some teenagers feel helpless and hopeless," comments pediatrician Adele D. Hofmann, director of the adolescent care unit at New York University-Bellevue Medical Center. "They have no real sense of community or home. They have no sense of their role in life, and they suspect nobody really cares about them. In their floundering they turn to a baby as a source of identity. That translates into instant adulthood, an instant role and instant femininity."

Moreover, your daughter may see childbirth as a way to have her own person. To some teenagers, having a baby is like owning a very special toy. "She's all mine, my very own," 14-year-old Nadja said about her baby daughter. "My mother has my little brother. He belongs to her. But my baby is all my own."

Your daughter may entertain a myth about the perfect baby and the perfect mother. She may see her baby's total dependence on her as total love. Many a girl who's had an unhappy childhood wishes to relive it. Having a child provides a second chance. Says 16-year-old Linda: "I'm going to bring my baby up right, and have for him what I didn't have myself."

For some girls this impulse is complicated by the desire to show their mothers up. A girl may keep her child to prove to her mother, "I will be a better mother than you were."

Conversely, a girl may want to please her mother. Some girls respond to their mother's unspoken needs. Indeed, the mother may be verbally urging her daughter to have an abortion. But she may be sending out more subtle messages to the contrary. She may be confused about her own identity now that her daughter is growing up.

"The mother sees her own youth and fertility disappearing," Dr. Adele Hofmann has said, "and if her daughter does have a baby, this is a way for her to hold on to her child-rearing role. It offers her a way not to resolve her own conflict."

HERE'S HELP

Where can your daughter get help caring for her baby? First of all, from you. She's likely to look to her parents for emotional and financial support.

Let her know in concrete terms what she can expect from you. Avoid generalities like, "I'll help you all I can." Such vague assurances can lead to bitter misunderstandings. Instead, reach specific answers to practical questions like these: How much money can she count on? Where will she be living? What hours can you help with the baby? Who will look after the baby if she goes to school, works, sees friends, dates? What help, if any, will be provided by the baby's father or his family?

If you demand instant adulthood with motherhood, you may run into trouble. At the same time, your daughter is likely to resent your treating her like a child. You're best off having frank discussions about what you expect of each other. What roles will you each have in caring for the baby? How much responsibility do you expect her to assume?

Be as flexible as you can. If one baby-care or work arrangement seems not to be working after a time, negotiate another one.

Don't expect miracles of your daughter or yourself. Regard the first years of the baby's life as a period of transition, bound to be stressful for your family. Allow yourselves time to absorb the new situation. While your daughter is adjusting to her new role as mother, you are adjusting to being the child's grandparents.

You're also learning to handle the reactions of friends and neighbors to the birth of your daughter's out-of-wedlock child. While this no longer carries the stigma it once did, you may be subjected to raised eyebrows and thoughtless remarks. Explain your daughter's marital status in the same tone you might use if she were widowed or divorced. Practice saying, without embarrassment, "She's a single mother," or, "She's not married." Other sources of help include:

School Programs. Your daughter will have a better chance for a satisfactory life—free from poverty and welfare dependency—if she completes her education and trains for an occupation. Remaining in school will also give her an opportunity to meet people at just the time she's likely to feel most isolated.

Schools in your area may have a program as far-reaching as the one at Citrus High in Azusa, California, where mothers are allowed to bring their babies right into the classroom. The school is equipped with playpens, cribs, and toys. The mothers come to school for morning child-care courses, but may study their standard academic subjects at home in the afternoon.

The girls work at their own pace, but many of them graduate early. Some win college scholarships. A young mother summed up her response to the program: "I'm not an outcast anymore. I feel like a human being again."

Your daughter may also be able to be trained for skilled occupations in adult education or home-study courses, through on-the-job training, apprenticeships, or government-aided programs.

Your local social services agency, or the Women's Bureau (U.S. Department of Labor, Washington, D.C. 20210) may provide more information.

Welfare. Your daughter may be eligible for welfare payments under welfare's largest program—AFDC (Aid to Families with Dependent Children). The payments barely keep a mother and child fed and housed, but 3 million single mothers depend on welfare for survival.

Your daughter can claim AFDC if:

1. She has one or more dependent children under 18 (or under 21 if in school full-time) living with her; *or*, in those states which grant aid to unborn children, she is pregnant; *and*
2. Her assets and income from all sources (including child support) fall below the limit set by state law; *and*
3. The father of her child is dead, disabled, or not living with her; *and*
4. She is willing to cooperate in seeking support from the father, and to assign her support rights to the state.

To apply, your daughter should call the nearest welfare office and make an appointment for an interview. She should bring all documents that will help establish her eligibility and need: the baby's birth certificate or a doctor's statement that she's pregnant, medical bills, rent receipts, utility bills.

She'll fill out an application form, and the welfare department may check out the facts given in the application—for example, visiting to check the address and to make sure the child's father doesn't live there. Welfare regulations allow a mother to earn up to a certain amount (after work-related expenses are deducted) before the AFDC benefit is reduced.

Psychological and Social Services. Direct your daughter to programs specifically geared toward helping unwed teenage mothers. Among these are group meetings with other unmarried mothers.

"These groups don't offer solutions," says Marie Mendicino of the Schoolage Parents Program at Rochester, New York's YWCA. "What they offer is an outlet, a support by their peers, someone to say, 'You're normal. We all feel that way sometimes too.'" Another important aspect of such a group is its potential as a preventive of child abuse. The group's meetings can serve as a place for your daughter to learn ways to cope with her frustration and anger, her child's behavior and problems.

Your daughter may benefit from the kind of group that has met through the auspices of the Catholic Charitable Bureau of Cambridge, Massachusetts. It's made up of perhaps eight teenage mothers. Over many weeks, the girls discuss such shared problems as parental disapproval and financial difficulties. Topics shift from discussion of being an AFDC mother and the public criticism of welfare recipients, to what men think of them, to concern that they might turn out like their own mothers, to recreation, to masturbation, to hints on child care. Members generally visit each other between meetings.

Contacts like these can keep your daughter in the mainstream of life. They provide opportunities that may otherwise be lacking for friendship and gossip. From other girls in her situation, your daughter can get ideas and information on home management and child-rearing.

Young women who are fearful, isolated, and concerned about their worth often receive support through a teen-mothers group. They retain ties to the larger society's perspective on their attempts to cope with the tasks of motherhood. Their capacity to meet the demands of the mothering role are strengthened.

As an alternative, seek out a hospital program that helps adolescents become better mothers. Cincinnati General Hospital invited teenagers who delivered babies at the hospital to attend groups with their babies and receive instruction on infant care. Mothers ask questions about their babies' development, become more attentive to their babies' needs.

During later sessions, mothers play with their infants with toys and interesting objects in an adult-sized playpen on the floor. The informality of these sessions produces lively discussions. The mothers receive a great deal of encouragement and friendly advice from each other. They learn to enjoy their babies, play with them, talk to them. In turn, their babies are responsive, sociable, and well-developed.

Hot Lines. These community switchboards can literally be a lifesaver for a teenage mother in a panic and contemplating suicide. Suicide prevention services in nearly all areas provide twenty-four-hour phone service. Sympathetic volunteers—many of whom have been in similar trouble—will listen, encourage, and put the desperate teenager in touch with professional help.

At least one crisis center has been set up especially for teenage mothers. Houston's Jefferson Davis Hospital has a 24-hour, 7-day-a-week hot line as part of a program for teenagers who delivered at the Joyce Goldfarb Adult Development Clinic. On discharge, each patient receives phone numbers for the coordinating nurse and an assistant.

Many of the calls deal with contraceptive use and misunderstanding. These teenage mothers often rely on poorly informed family members, peers, neighbors, or lay reading material for vital information.

Other questions deal with health problems of the mother and infant. The hot line not only alleviates the mothers' concerns and anxieties; In some cases, it saves the infant. Several babies have been rushed to the hospital emergency room after the nurse recognized emergency symptoms described by phone.

Chapter 16

Arranging an Adoption

Ease the trauma of separation for your daughter and grandchild.

"I COULDN'T BRING MYSELF to have an abortion, but I was only sixteen and there wasn't any way to keep the baby," recalls Laura, now a 19-year-old college student. "I decided on adoption."

"When I came home from the hospital I felt empty. I cried my eyes out and wondered if I'd done the right thing. I nearly died the day the adoption became final. I think I gave my little girl the best start I could. But I often wonder: What's she like? What color are her eyes? Does she talk a lot? Is she musical? Does she make up stories with dolls?"

If your pregnant teenager is considering adoption, encourage her to take several months to make up her mind. Your daughter's peers may exert a powerful influence on her to keep the baby. She'll need your help in resisting this pressure and coming to an independent decision. Inertia, denial, an inability to reach a decision may further keep her from coming to grips with the question.

At the same time, refrain from pressuring her into having the child adopted. Unless she's satisfied that the decision is entirely her own, she's likely to have regrets, and feel lifelong resentment toward you. It will do neither of you much good if you keep at her with obvious arguments like: "A child should have a stable family situation and a secure future." "You have no means of providing a home for a child." "You have your whole life ahead of you." "You can't cope emotionally with a child at this point in your life." "It is fairer to the child to have it brought up by people who really want children."

All of which may be true, of course, and worth judicious mention. But imagine what your reaction would have been if, while you were awaiting the birth of your first child, someone told you, "It'll get a better start in life if you give it up for adoption." In addition, your daughter is a frightened, confused adolescent. In her present distress, her reasoning powers may have regressed to an earlier stage of childhood. Now her decision cuts to the core of her emotions, and may be inaccessible to your logic.

Here, then, is a strategy to help your daughter make the determination that's best for her—and come out of the experience as whole as possible:

CONSULT AN ADOPTION AGENCY

As soon as adoption is a possibility, put your daughter in touch with a good adoption agency in your area. Most adoption agencies are run by voluntary or religious groups. Some are state or city departments.

Locate a reliable agency through recommendations of your physician or friends. Or write to the North American Center on Adoption, 67 Irving Place, New York, New York 10003. Ask any agency right off:

"Do you offer prenatal counseling?" The best agencies provide disinterested professionals whose goal is to help your daughter explore her feelings and realize the ramifications of any decisions she makes. If an agency sounds suitable, visit it to see if the atmosphere is pleasant and if the staff—especially your daughter's counselor—seems knowledgeable and sensitive.

"Is my daughter committed to adoption?" Have it established in front of your daughter that the agency provides services for pregnant girls, and unwed mothers, even if no adoption results. See that it's clear to her that, in taking counseling, she is not promising to give up her baby. Even if she is now inclined toward adoption, she should understand that she can change her mind. In her counseling sessions, her caseworker should discuss alternatives besides adoption.

If an agency requires her to sign a release prematurely, or puts any other pressure on her, find another agency. Indeed, most responsible agencies would not allow your daughter to formally consent to adoption until after her child is born and she's had time to reconsider. Agency workers know that girls like your daughter may change their minds many times during pregnancy.

"Do you provide financial assistance?" You may be able to secure payment for medical expenses, plus living expenses if the child can't live at home. Some agencies offer your daughter room and board until the baby arrives.

(Again: Even if your daughter accepts such help, she should feel under no obligation to release the baby.)

A few agencies, like the Louise Wise Services in New York, offer a postnatal residential program in which the new mother can continue in school while exploring her options in regard to the baby. Agencies that don't provide direct financial help may assist your daughter in finding other sources of financial aid.

AGENCY VERSUS PRIVATE ADOPTIONS

If your daughter decides to go through with an adoption, in all but a handful of states she can arrange it privately as well as through an agency.

In one type of "independent" adoption, you may know a couple who's been wanting a child, and your daughter may let them adopt her baby. Often in such private adoptions the child is placed with a cousin, aunt, or other relative.

Alternatively, a private adoption can be arranged by a go-between such as a lawyer, obstetrician, nurse, or clergyman. Your daughter may tell her doctor, "I'd like to have my baby adopted." The doctor is likely to contact a lawyer who handles private adoptions. The lawyer in turn gets in touch with a couple who's interested in adopting. They agree to pay your daughter's living and medical expenses, all legal fees, and their own travel expenses to pick up the child.

Which type of adoption is best for your daughter and your grandchild? By going through an agency, your daughter has a better chance of maintaining a link with her child than if she dealt with a private go-between. Ten, twenty, thirty years from now she may need to inform the child of essential medical information—or the child, now grown, may have a vital query of her. The agency, with its records, will probably still be in existence and may be able to serve as a clearinghouse. By contrast, a lawyer who arranged an adoption may have long since retired.

Also, with an adoption agency, you can count on a rigorous—some feel too rigorous—screening of would-be adoptive parents. A couple seeking a baby is subjected to a good deal of scrutiny. Agency caseworkers visit the home, sometimes several times, and try to assess the couple's emotional maturity, their motives for adopting, the strength of their marriage, their attitudes toward children. Most agencies ask couples to provide from three to six personal references—friends or neighbors or colleagues who can verify their potential for being good parents.

Agencies also check into their financial status. Insurance policies, tax forms, bank statements will be required to determine whether the couple is able to support a child. Other documents such as marriage and birth certificates may also be required. If prospective adopters pass this inspection and are accepted by the agency, you and your daughter can have some degree of confidence that the child will go into a good home.

As a further service, some agencies help adoptive parents with their new roles. Look for an agency that gives prospective adopters a chance to meet with adoption workers and experienced adoptive parents. Some agencies counsel new adoptive parents through a transition period.

In an independent adoption, the investigation of adoptive parents is not likely to be as thorough. Most states require that the couple be checked by a state agency for suitability. Although the couple may prove to be fine parents, such checks are not nearly as exhaustive as investigations by a licensed adoption agency.

An independent adoption is especially likely to appeal to your daughter if she's allergic to bureaucracies and regulations. Some girls find agency caseworkers impersonal. Your daughter may prefer a go-between who treats her with warmth and individualized consideration.

In addition, an independent adoption gives your daughter a say as to who receives her child. Indeed, through private contacts, you and your daughter may arrange an "open" adoption. In contrast with the conventional "closed" adoption, in which all records are sealed, an open adoption is one in which your daughter would meet the adoptive parents, and participate in the placement process. She would relinquish all legal, moral, and nurturing rights to the child. But she would retain the right to visit the child. If the adoptive parents agree, such rights could be extended to you as a grandparent.

Los Angeles social workers Annette Baran and Reuben Pannor and

University of California psychiatrist Arthur De Sorosky suggest your daughter consider an open adoption if she can neither raise her own child nor face the finality of the traditional relinquishment. Note these specialists: "The young single mothers who have an emotional attachment . . . to their children desperately need a new kind of adoptive placement in which they can actively participate. They want the security of knowing they have helped provide their children with a loving, secure existence and yet have not denied themselves the possibility of knowing them in the future."

In an independent adoption, your daughter is virtually assured of adequate financial assistance. This brings up a seamier side of independent adoptions: If the baby is white, healthy, and available for adoption, it's worth its weight in gold.

These youngsters are particularly attractive to typical adoptive parents: white middle-class couples who long for a child such as they believe they might have had themselves. Adoptive couples sometimes wish to fulfill their fantasies of parenthood. Rarely does the fantasy include a child who's out of infancy, disabled, or of another race.

At the same time most white unwed mothers keep their babies. Thus, compared to the demand of would-be adopters, there is a great shortage of healthy white infants. One couple, unable to conceive because of the wife's infertility, learned they'd have to wait three to seven years to adopt a baby through an agency. They advertised in the San Francisco *Chronicle* for a "babymaker"—offering $10,000 to a woman who'd submit to artificial insemination with the husband's sperm in order to bear a child for the couple.

Many people who want babies are willing to pay an unethical go-between an additional under-the-table sum for the child. In this "gray market," a supposed friend may then put powerful pressure on your daughter to go through with the adoption. Both the couple and the middleman have a vested interest in her consent.

To keep your daughter from being so compromised, urge her to accept no more money than she needs for reasonable living expenses. Some lawyers are willing to sprinkle girls with money if they will surrender their children for adoption. Lynne McTaggart, a reporter for the Chicago Tribune-New York News Syndicate, described what happened when she posed as an unwed mother. "When I went to adoption agencies, they said I could not qualify for welfare. I was not indigent; I was just an upper-middle-class girl who was knocked up in

New York." By contrast, when she went to see a private attorney, "he said all my expenses would be taken care of and not to worry about it. He gave me money for tuition. He gave me rent money. He gave me money for food and a promise of money for clothing and hospital expenses. And when we totaled it up, being very frugal on the clothing expenses and some of the others, it came to over $4,000." In addition, the lawyer himself charges his clients $2,500.

Several shades murkier than the gray market is the "black market." Avoid it. It's nothing less than the illegal selling of babies. In these independent adoptions, all legal formalities are bypassed or fudged. The middleman may sell babies to couples for as much as $25,000.

Your daughter may be tempted by the money. Some pregnant unmarried white teenagers have been offered up to $15,000 cash for their babies. Young women visiting abortion clinics may be approached with a cash offer to carry her baby to term, then hand it over to the purchaser. Some middlemen approach doctors, lawyers, and social workers with money for leads to healthy white babies. They then sell these babies at a profit.

In such illicit adoptions, the interests of the child are not at all protected. No one checks on the suitability of the adopting parents. Indeed, they may very well have been rejected by reputable agencies for compelling reasons—such as alcoholism, child abuse, or mental instability.

PLAN TO GET THE FATHER'S CONSENT

Don't be surprised if the adoption agency or the court asks for the written consent of the child's father to the adoption.

Adoption proceedings increasingly recognize the rights of unwed fathers. Until recently, the unmarried father was a complete nonparticipant with no rights at all. The unmarried mother could exclude him by refusing to name him, even if he wished to claim paternity.

Now decisions of the U.S. Supreme Court have begun to change the situation. The case of Stanley versus Illinois involved a man denied custody of his biological children when his common-law wife died, even though he had materially and psychologically acted as their parent. The Supreme Court decided that alleged biological fathers must have the right to a court hearing on custody of contested children. The court further ruled that all children have two legal parents, regardless of the marital status of those parents.

In another case, Rothstein versus Lutheran Social Services, an unwed mother surrendered her child without telling the child's father. He was denied a hearing on his parental rights. The Supreme Court remanded this case back to the Wisconsin Supreme Court with orders to reconsider its decision in view of the Stanley case recommendations. The Supreme Court also suggested that the length of time a child had been in the adoptive home should be a consideration in the final decision.

These cases prompted the U.S. Department of Health, Education, and Welfare to set these guidelines:

• A natural father, known or unknown, has rights to the custody of the child. These rights must be dealt with before the child may be securely placed for adoption.

• The father must be given an opportunity to show his fitness as a custodian.

• If he is known, he should be personally served in any litigation which would affect his rights.

• If he is unknown, or if his whereabouts are unknown, service by publication (such as legal advertisements) would be necessary.

States have responded in various ways to court decisions involving unwed fathers. In some states, both biological parents must release the child for adoption. In others, the mother's consent is not legally sufficient unless the biological father is notified before the child is released for adoption and given notice of an opportunity to challenge it. If, however, he does not show up at a custody hearing, his consent is implied and the adoption can proceed.

What else does the law provide? Even though your daughter is a minor, she has full authority to decide for or against adoption. Although you are her parent, your consent is not required. Nor does your withholding permission have any legal effect. However, if you wish to adopt your grandchild you will probably have little trouble. The courts tend to smile on adoptions within families.

State laws may require health reports on the physical conditions of the child and the parents. In all states, adoptive parents must be adults—but, depending on the particular state, this can be either 18 or 21. In many states, adoptive parents must be at least 10 years older than the child. The adoptive parents often must have lived in the state for a specified time, usually six months to a year. While adoption procedures vary in detail from state to state, the basic steps are similar:

The natural parents give their written consent for the child to be placed for adoption. A release for adoption is legal only if it is written on a specified legal form that usually has to be notarized and filed in court in the presence of an authorized official.

The couple seeking a child makes the proper application. The suitability of these would-be adoptive parents is investigated by a licensed adoption agency. In the case of independent adoptions, the law may require inspection by a state agency.

Eligible parents are brought together with a child. A court hearing is held to make sure that all forms are in order and that the adoptive parents' investigation has been satisfactory. The court then issues an "interlocutory decree." This allows the child to be placed with the adoptive parents.

The child lives with the adoptive parents during a waiting period before the adoption becomes final. This is usually six months to a year, and is a probationary period. The agency caseworker may visit the home and see how things are going. During this period, the natural mother may still have rights over the child. Generally she must apply to the court if she wants the child back.

The court issues a final adoption decree. The child is now the legal responsibility of the adoptive parents. Agency and court records are sealed, and a new birth certificate is issued. The natural mother has no rights to the child and cannot get him back.

RELEASE THE BABY AT BIRTH

It's likely to be psychologically much better for the child if your daughter gives it up at birth. Your grandchild faces severe emotional risks if your daughter tries to cope with an impossible situation for two or three years, and then has to relinquish the child for adoption. By that age, it's likely to be traumatic for the child to be separated from its mother. Many child-care specialists urge that child placement be treated as an emergency.

Moreover, if your daughter excessively delays releasing the child, she can gravely impair its prospects of ever being adopted. For adoption purposes, a child is nearly superannuated once it's old enough for nursery school. Agencies often find teenage mothers bringing their children in for adoption once they find out they can't live on welfare allowances. By then many of the children are losers.

"A mother now is much more apt to take her baby home and take care of it as long as it's still a toy," says Elton Klibanoff of the Massachusetts Commission on Adoption and Foster Care. "Once the child has reached the age where he can do things for himself and may get in the mother's way, the mother will put the child into foster care. This is a very cruel thing. The older child's chances for an upbringing in a healthy home have been greatly diminished."

If your daughter surrenders her baby for adoption, she may not want to see it after it's born. Be sure that the baby gets cuddled and held despite your daughter's withdrawal. Infants urgently need animal warmth and attention. Without that, they can fall prey to "institutionitis," a failure to physically thrive because of emotional deprivation.

Also see that the adoptive parents take the child promptly. Ordinarily a mother and infant start learning each other's physical and emotional responses from the first day of the baby's life. A mother who is separated from a baby for the first few days of life often has difficulty responding to its signals later on. The rapport between mother and child has suffered a setback. Their disturbed relationship may show itself in increased crying by the baby and nervous tension in the mother. Adoptive mothers often need to overcome the effects of a similar setback. The longer their delay in assuming care of the baby, the greater will be the adjustment that both mother and child will have to make.

Once your daughter releases the baby, she'd best regard her consent as irrevocable, unless she can prove fraud or duress. Some states have tightened their laws on adoption releases in the wake of New York's "Baby Lenore" case. An unwed mother released an infant girl to the Spence-Chapin agency, which placed the child for adoption with Nick and Joan De Martino. Shortly afterward, the mother reversed her decision. The agency refused to return the child. To get the girl back, the mother sued.

The De Martinos did not know of any of this until eighteen months later—when the court directed them to return the little girl, whom they'd named Lenore. The decision against them was upheld by the higher courts. The De Martinos fled to Florida. There a more sympathetic court, operating under different laws, awarded the couple custody of Lenore and granted them a legal adoption. The case led many states to make a mother's consent irrevocable after thirty days. The New York legislation was known as the "Baby Lenore Bill."

For the entire period during which your daughter might legally withdraw her consent, the adoptive parents will probably be holding their breath. Wrote one adoptive father who was sweating out such a legal revocation period: "Our new daughter is six months old, her name is Anna Grace, and I'd love to show some baby pictures here but don't dare. At this point I don't even dare say where we got her, from what agency, state or country, for fear of attracting the natural mother's attention. Fear is endemic to adoption where we live. Under the laws . . . a natural mother can reclaim her child from its adoptive parents any time until the adoption becomes final, which takes a minimum of six months and sometimes much longer."

EXPECT GRIEVING

If your daughter decides on adoption, she's likely to go through a period of grief over the loss of the baby, much as if it had died. Even girls who are sure of adoption from the start almost always have some ambivalence, marked by crying, anger, remorse. Some girls compare relinquishment with an amputation—"It's like having part of my body cut off."

Your daughter may also feel guilt over the problems she's caused her family and the baby. She may be convinced she's worthless—inadequate, unable to help herself—because she could not provide for the child adequately. For most girls such feelings usually pass after a few weeks. If your daughter doesn't soon resume her normal activities, she may benefit from professional counseling.

Will she later regret her decision? Especially if prepared by prenatal counseling, teenagers can be so resilient that many who give up babies for adoption are bothered by no afterthoughts. They may wonder what the child is like and how it's faring. But they don't regret the decision.

Conversely, others become bitter about having given the baby away, particularly when their circumstances change, or they feel they might have managed after all. Regret is most likely to plague your daughter if she feels she was coerced into having the child adopted. This was true of Linda Shipley who, as a shy, inexperienced 16-year-old, dated an older man and became pregnant. Linda's parents told her, "Don't bring the baby home." They told her brothers and sisters, "Linda went to the hospital to have her appendix removed."

In the hospital the social worker told Linda: "You're not fit to raise this child. You have nothing to give this child. The only chance she has for a normal life is if she is put up for adoption."

Now, eleven years later, Linda confesses to a desperate need to find out what happened to the child. Here is the heart's cry of a girl who was forced to give up her baby:

> My greatest hope is that my daughter will seek me when she is grown, not because her adoptive parents have not filled her needs, but because they have raised her to be such a fulfilled, open, compassionate person, that her love and forgiveness extend even to me. I hope that she will accept me as a friend, but I have no fantasy that I can ever replace the 20 years of nurturing, memories and family love that I hope her adoptive parents will give her.
>
> If I could have a few crumbs of my child's life, I would be grateful, but I have no intention of pushing myself on her adoptive family. . . . I'm hoping some day the time will come when I can explain to her that I didn't abandon her.

TAKE COMFORT IN THE CHILD'S PROSPECTS

Adoption may cause your daughter's child some emotional problems apparently distinctive to adopted children. But the selection process adoptive parents go through—and their deliberate desire for children—evidently more than offset any stress your grandchild may have as a result of being adopted.

By any criteria, it appears that adoptive families compare well to ordinary ones. Perhaps the most comprehensive investigation to date is the National Child Development Study, in England, which followed the progress of all children born in one week of 1958. At the age of 7, the adopted children were doing at least as well as the other children in all areas of ability and attainment that were examined. Overall, the adopted did markedly better than the other children in general knowledge and oral ability. The adopted did as well as others in their level of creativity.

Adoption is likely to succeed for your daughter's child because the parent-child relationship is not only a matter of blood. It also entails caring, nurturing, and the day-to-day business of growing up and living in a family. In this respect, adoption gives your grandchild a good chance for a happy, loving childhood.

Moreover, adopted children know they are wanted. Authorities agree that they should be told of their adoption, usually couched in plaudits like "We picked you out special." Adoptees generally are surrounded by so much anxious care that your grandchild's personality is likely to resemble that of the only child: responsible, cautious, a high achiever.

Your grandchild's good start in life may come at a price, however small it is to pay. Adopted children, no matter how secure, are likely to suffer from "genealogical bewilderment," a lingering sense of rejection stemming from their separation from biological parents. Adoptees often confirm this. Declares Elsa, now in her twenties, with her own children:

> I still feel a sense of rejection, regardless of my natural mother's reasons, and she did have ample reasons. No set of parents could have loved a child more than my adopted parents, yet this sense of rejection persists. Now that I have my own children, I have reinforced my belief that, except in very rare cases, no one can love a child as its natural parents can.

Psychologists speak of the "Achilles heel" of the adopted child— the fear of another traumatic separation and the consequent un-willingness to make deep emotional commitments. Adopted children, even if adopted at an early age, seem more prone to emotional disturbances and personality disorders than nonadopted children. This has been found to be the case even when they did not experience psychological trauma before adoption. Some researchers explain these findings in terms of the adoptive parents' unconscious aversion toward parenthood. Presumably on a conscious level, some adoptive parents want the child, but beneath their level of awareness they may resent their loss of freedom, the burdens of parenthood, the sense of bringing up a child not biologically one's own. To the extent these hidden attitudes shape their treatment of the child, the child will have problems.

WILL THE CHILD TURN UP?

Even though your daughter releases her baby for adoption, she may see the child again. After it's grown up, it may seek her out.

Indeed, cautions The North American Center on Adoption, don't believe an adoption agency if it promises you confidentiality. Courts increasingly are unsealing adoption records, often for medical reasons. In one recent case (Chattman vs. Bennett, 393 N.Y.S.2d 768), a New York appeals court ruled in favor of a woman who'd been denied permission to see her adoption file. She testified, "I'm reluctant to have children. I'm afraid they'll inherit a possible genetic disease in my family background." This constituted good cause to allow her access to any medical reports or related matter in her adoption records, ruled the court. "Medical information of this or any other nature concerning the adoptee should be freely disclosed."

Your grandchild is likely to be curious about who its family is. One study, reported by Mary Kathleen Benet in her book *The Politics of Adoption,* suggests that most adopted people desire more information about their origins. Adoptees between the ages of 21 and 30, and their adoptive parents, were interviewed. Both groups asserted that adoption had been a success, that parents and children were very close in their families. But many more adoptees than parents saw adoption as causing youngsters psychological limitations or handicaps. The parents seemed more committed to seeing adoption in a favorable light, and less willing to admit that there had been any problems.

Further, your grandchild may be dissatisfied with how much is told about your family. Evidently adopted children have far more interest in their origins than adoptive parents perceive. A quarter of the adoptive parents in the study said they had been given full information about the natural parents. But only one-tenth of the adoptees believed this to be the case.

Moreover, either adoptive parents block out the child's questions, or the child asks only in fantasy. More than half the adoptees said they had pressed for additional information about their biological parents. Only one-fifth of the parents recalled such questions. Almost three times as many parents as adoptees asserted that the children had never voluntarily raised the subject.

Your grandchild's adoptive parents may discourage any inquiry about you. When the British Parliament was considering a bill that would ease restrictions on adoption records, most letters opposing the legislation came from adoptive parents. They mainly feared that the adopted child might reject them. Adopters also reason that your daughter, who has started another life without her child, would not want it to appear on the doorstep, perhaps to the surprise of her new family. Adopted children retort that a successful search not only eases their own identity crises but can be deeply relieving to the natural mothers as well.

Your grandchild, then, may have a yearning toward your daughter. This impulse is expressed by Joan, now in her forties and the mother of three: "When you are adopted, you grow up with loving parents and you love them, but you know they are not the blood of your blood and somewhere else there are two people who created you and whom you look like, whose genes and heredity you share. But they are cut off from you."

Your grandchild's wondering about your daughter may develop into an overwhelming need to find her. People who embark on such a search are likely to find that it involves years of laborious digging. Florence Fisher spent years finding out the truth and tracing her natural parents. She succeeded in the end, and wrote *The Search for Anna Fisher* about her efforts to challenge hospital administrators, lawyers, and relatives whom she saw in a conspiracy of silence against her. She says, "Fear and the unknown are inextricably linked," and that adoptive children fear the worst until they know the truth. Many adoptees suspect that their mothers were prostitutes, which is almost never the truth.

To locate your daughter, your grandchild may seek the help of the organization founded by Florence Fisher, the Adoptees' Liberty Movement Association (157 West 57th Street, New York, New York 10019). ALMA aids adopted people who wish to seek out their roots through mutual sharing of experiences. Another organization with a similar purpose is Orphan Voyage (R.D. 1, Box 153A, Cedaredge, Colorado 81413), which puts out a newsletter and serves as a clearinghouse for parents and children in search of each other.

By the time your grandchild is old enough to seek you out, the laws of many states may well be changed to facilitate the search. Adoptee organizations argue that it is a denial of civil liberties to keep adoptees from learning of their origins. A legislative movement for adoptees to gain access to their birth records is gaining momentum.

What would a reunion between your daughter and her long-lost child be like? At one extreme, it may be a bitter disappointment. Her child may harbor resentment over a supposed abandonment. Their different experiences and their unresolved feelings may make them permanent strangers to each other.

During a discussion at the Lutheran Social Service of Minnesota, the majority of a group of adults who'd been adopted as children said that they would not want to locate their natural parents. Two members of the group had done so and regretted it. "There are doors that should never be opened," one woman said, "and once they are, they are so difficult to shut."

But sometimes persistent searchers will find their natural parents, and the reunion will be as joyous and fulfilling as described in this letter to the *Log* of Orphan Voyage:

I found them—both my father and mother in the same day. They had not seen or heard from each other since I was conceived and my father left for World War II in June of 1942. My mother has carried the burden of giving me up and I have relieved her of this burden at long last. She had tried to keep me for seven months, but being unmarried and only seventeen years old, and the times being what they were, she just found she could not provide for me. . . .

My father has nine daughters and my mother has seven sons and one daughter, so I am blessed with seventeen brothers and sisters. I have met all of my mother's family except one brother, but he has written. I was welcomed into the family with open arms, and a real sense of belonging. I look a great deal like my mother, much more so than her other children. She is very happy and so am I. . . .

I seem to be on the same wave link as my natural family, we are so much alike, a feeling I never had with my adoptive family. I am sure I had a lot of advantages with my adoptive family I never would have had, and they were never what you would call mean to me, but my adoptive mother always let me know in some way that I was not the same.

AVOID FOSTER CARE

At first glance, foster care may seem the ideal solution if your daughter can't decide whether to keep the baby or have it adopted. In foster care, children remain under the legal control of their parents. Foster families are paid by the state to give children a temporary home, until they are either reclaimed by their natural parents or adopted. Thus foster care appears to provide a breathing space in which your daughter can consider adoption or find ways of providing for the child.

But foster care also has serious drawbacks that should make your daughter reluctant to choose it. She should consider foster care a real alternative only if she has a strong impulse to keep the baby, but her immediate circumstances make this impossible. If there is a good likelihood that her circumstances will change for the better in the near future—for example, she finishes school and gets a job—foster care is a logical solution for the interim.

Otherwise, your grandchild is likely to become an orphan of the living. However well-intentioned, the natural parents of most foster children neither keep them in their own homes nor let them go entirely free for permanent adoption. Thus, estimates the Child Welfare League of America, for over 300,000 foster children, presumably temporary care stretches into years. Meanwhile, the children become harder and harder to place for adoption. Permanently in foster homes, they grow out of childhood and into adolescence and adulthood.

Dr. David Fanschel of Columbia University reports that "temporary" foster care is temporary for only one-third of the children in foster homes. In the first year of foster care, only 3 of 10 children leave foster homes to return to their biological families or to join adoptive families. After that, only 1 child in 10 leaves foster care.

Your grandchild is likely to be lost in the limbo of foster care, too often shuttled from home to home without any sense of continuity, permanence, or security. Even families who agree to undertake the long-term foster care of a child are seldom as permanent as a real family should be. For example foster families may have to give up a foster child if they move out of the county where the child was originally placed. Or the foster family may become unable to care for the child because of illness, death, or divorce. "I've had kids come in here who have been in as many as seven foster homes," said Kay Donley of Michigan's Spaulding for Children. "I've even heard judges talk about a permanent temporary foster home."

The effect of these tenuous relationships on your grandchild can be emotionally devastating. The youngster may have no opportunity to form an attachment to a mother-figure during its first three years. As a result, it is likely to develop the typical symptoms of maternal deprivation. For the child's entire life, it may be capable of only superficial relationships. It may have no real feelings, no capacity to care for people or make true friends. Your grandchild may be unreachable to others, exasperating those who try to help. Even as an adult, it may demonstrate an abnormal shallowness of emotional response, a lack of concern. Its character may be flawed by pointless deceit, evasion, and stealing. It may have reading and other school problems, the result of an inability to concentrate.

It is likely to be equally traumatic for your grandchild if it is largely ignored by your daughter for several years, and then suddenly reclaimed by her. The emotional scars from such shifting of mother-figures may be permanent.

Major conflicts are likely to erupt between your daughter and your grandchild's foster mother. Your daughter may resent the foster mother's caring for her child, and resent the circumstances that make it possible. She is likely to find fault with how the foster mother is bringing up the child. She may be intensely jealous of the foster family.

The foster mother, on the other hand, may think of the child as her own. She may resent the interference, and may scorn your daughter for not taking care of her own child. The two may come to engage in a tug-of war for your grandchild's affections—with the child in the middle, being torn apart. If the fostering continues for a number of years, the child may come to love the foster mother better than the visitor, your daughter. The relationship may be further complicated by the child's sense of rejection and rage, and your daughter's guilt and frustration.

A single mother we'll call Paula summarized the hazards she encountered in foster care:

> The foster parents, though lavishing affection upon my daughter, became very possessive and succeeded to some extent in alienating her

from me by preventing my visiting her on friendly pretexts, and by teaching her to regard me as an aunt rather than her mother.

After a bitter struggle and argument I was able to secure her release at the age of two years. During this time I received very little sympathy from the social worker who seemed to feel that I had been an inadequate mother and unwilling to seek a home for my daughter and myself. I felt bitter and heartbroken as I had really tried hard to find a home for us both, with no success.

On reflection, I feel now that such a long-term fostering was bad for both my daughter and myself. . . . In my view, fostering must be minimal if the child is to remain well-balanced.

Finally, your daughter may not be able to reclaim her child. To get children out of long-term foster care, there's a movement in child-welfare circles to free them for adoption. The law generally protects the rights of natural parents to their own children. Increasingly, though, it is believed that more legal rights should be given to the children and foster parents, and that the courts should act in the interests of a fostered child.

About half the states provide for the involuntary termination of the natural parent's rights. For example, New York altered the traditional foster care system to provide that a homeless child's case must be judicially reviewed within twenty-four months. Unless there are unusual circumstances warranting an extension of foster care for a certain period, the child may be released for adoption. Parents are especially likely to lose their child if they leave it in foster care for several years without regular contacts or interest in the child's welfare, and with no plan to reinstate parental responsibility. In these states, the courts are seeking to end "Hallmark parenthood"—in which the child is technically not abandoned if its parent sends it a birthday or Christmas card once a year.

Even in states where foster children are not periodically considered for release for adoption, the courts might rule that your grandchild should stay with the foster family instead of being returned to your daughter. A court in Washington, D.C. ruled that a 9-year-old girl should remain in the foster home where she'd spent all her life, rather than go with her natural mother.

In the opinion of the court, the child's best interests were the essential consideration, not the rights or desires of any adults, be they biological, foster, or adoptive parents. In this particular case it was felt that the child's best interests were met by the continuation of established family ties with the foster parents. Ruled the court: "The best interests of this child would not be served by removing her from this warm and happy home she has known all her life . . . to place her in an environment where she feels uncomfortable and anxious, to live in a place she does not want to live and with a woman more an acquaintance than a mother."

Chapter 17

Questions of Marriage

You may avert a disaster by asking about feelings, money, sexual expectations.

IF YOUR TEENAGE SON OR DAUGHTER wants to get married, use as much influence as you can to delay the wedding. Urge the couple to wait at least a year. Accept their having sexual intercourse, with contraception. Acquiesce to their living and traveling together. Your goal is to give them time to reconsider.

The alternative—their getting married—may well prove to be a disaster. A significant number of teenage boys and girls, immature in their judgment, enter marriage for childish reasons. Their marital knot often turns out to be a noose. To untie it, many couples soon spend a painful period going through divorce. Their premature (literally pre-mature) marriage may blight their early years, stunt their intellectual and emotional growing, and leave them scarred for life.

Remind your youngster that marriage in general is increasingly risky. The divorce rate has doubled in the past ten years. In a given year, for every two marriages there is one divorce. Among these 1 million divorces each year, teenagers are greatly overrepresented.

It's estimated that between 25 and 50 percent of all teenage marriages end in separation or divorce. According to a study at Washington's Urban Institute, if your daughter marries between 14 and 17, she is over two and a half times more likely to break up with her husband than if she weds at the more mature age of 20 to 24. If she marries at 18 or 19, she's at a 60 percent higher risk than if she holds off until her early twenties. Statistically, your son fares a little better: If he marries between 14 and 17, he's twice as likely to split up with his wife than if he marries between 22 and 24. Should he marry between 18 and 21, his chances of divorce or separation are still 50 percent higher than if he waits those few years, to achieve greater maturity.

What if your daughter is pregnant? She may want to rush into marriage—between 30 and 50 percent of teenage marriages are spurred by a premarital pregnancy. A wedding may provide a measure of social sanction, "legitimating" the pregnancy. But the marriage is not likely to last, for pregnancy puts a teenage marriage on even thinner ice.

A Baltimore study finds that, in some age groups, 3 out of 5 marriages involving pregnant teenage brides break up within six years. One-fifth of the marriages dissolve within a year, concludes sociologist Frank F. Furstenberg Jr. of the University of Pennsylvania. That's two and a half times the rate of broken marriages among comparable teenage brides who were not pregnant.

Almost half (49 percent) of all divorces involve women who married before the age of 20, according to the National Center for Health Statistics. Most divorces—three times the overall rate—occur in the below-25 age group, which is largely made up of couples who married as teenagers.

The scars from an early catastrophic marriage may be deeper and longer-lasting than your child imagines. "While divorce is always a bad experience, a marital breakup in the emotionally vulnerable teen years can be most traumatic of all," cautions Keith Daugherty, executive director of the Family Service Association of America. "Young people caught up in these human tragedies—and there is no softer word—may feel that it is all just an incident in their lives that will soon be forgotten. They are deluding themselves. A divorce is almost certain to leave wounds that can hurt for a long time."

Even if your child stays married, the arrangement may be a grudging nondivorce rather than a happy marriage. Teenagers typically lack perspective, thus have little idea of what to expect from a complex relationship with another person. All their lives they've generally been treated like children: cushioned from the outside world, held to few responsibilities. When they thrust themselves into marriage, they often act like children playing house. Compared with older couples, youthful brides and grooms soon suffer greater disillusionment, disappointment, and despair.

Dr. Rachel M. Inselberg of Carnegie-Mellon University, a specialist in family sociology and developmental psychology, investigated the problem areas of high school marriages and the degree of marital satisfaction expressed by the couple. Dr. Inselberg then compared the teenagers' responses with those of couples who married between ages 21 and 26. Her findings suggest a dismal picture for your adolescent contemplating marriage. In the areas of economic, social and personal adjustment, the younger couples revealed more and much worse problems than did their older counterparts.

For a comprehensive survey of "Trends and Prospects for Young Marriages in the United States," sociologist Lee G. Burchinal of the U.S. Office of Education analyzed virtually every study of teenage marriage. Dr. Burchinal summed up these studies in three words: "Uniform negative assessments."

SILVER LININGS

If your teenager remains determined to marry, take heart. Dr. Lee Burchinal concludes his study of young marriages with the warning not to overgeneralize the negative findings. For many young couples, marriage does work out. However bleak the prospects, however grim the outlook, your child may overcome the obstacles and make a go of it.

Indeed, you can't predict an individual outcome for certain, cautions Dr. Vladimir de Lissovoy of Pennsylvania State University's College of Human Development. Dr. de Lissovoy followed forty-eight couples who married in high school. The brides ranged in age from 15 to 18, the grooms from 14 to 19. All but two of the girls were pregnant before marriage. The great majority of both husbands and wives left school without graduating.

De Lissovoy began his research with great pessimism—previous studies indicated such kids were marital losers. But, over three years of visiting young couples, he found that the feelings of their day-to-day lives could not be gauged by conventional scientific techniques. "Many subjective elements in their relationships . . . are difficult to represent as empirical data. The gamut of emotions when reduced to descriptive terms such as hostility, devotion, ambivalence, understanding, sympathy, or anger do not permit a clear evaluation of an ongoing relationship between husband and wife."

From the scientific literature on teenage couples, de Lissovoy expected to witness a mass breakdown of marriages. Indeed, he drew up a forecast of which couples would split when. Heading the list was an extremely unpromising pair. When married, the boy was 14, the girl 15 and pregnant. "As it turned out this was a very happy marriage." Despite the experts' gloomy prediction, out of de Lissovoy's total sampling, only two couples called it quits.

Should your teenager go through with the marriage, you can help it succeed by acting positively. Any difficulties you pose are likely to subject your child to painful conflicts—and damage relations between husband and wife. Your abandoning the young couple would similarly cause emotional strains that could contribute to the breakup of the marriage.

Your teenager, even when married, needs you. In the extended family of tradition, husband and wife could look to a wide range of accessible relatives to find companionship, comfort and assistance with children and household chores. The young couple were given a great deal of time to find themselves in their new life. The wife would go back and forth between her parents' home and her own. When her first baby came she would be in the center of a group of mothering women while she gained her own experience of mothering. The young husband too could count on help and companionship.

In contrast, today's nuclear family—composed of only husband, wife, 2 children—imposes tremendous burdens on the married couple. The husband and wife, often in dull and frightening isolation, are required to fulfill all each other's needs.

Married teenagers may feel the trials of this way of life most keenly. Observes anthropologist Margaret Mead: "With our insistence that marriage, as an adult relationship, means living in and fending for one's own home, the high price of early marriage too often is unprotected isolation and extreme loneliness." Contributing to this isolation is the fact that young marrieds exist in limbo. "They are treated neither as full adults nor as children. They are accorded neither the full rights that go with adult responsibilities nor the protections that go with childhood dependence."

Any pessimism you retain about the marriage may be caught by the young couple. Anthropologist Mead warns against making their divorce a self-fulfilling prophecy. "The greatest enemy of young marriages, I believe, is the fact that from the beginning we anticipate their failure. Almost no one—neither the friends of the young couple nor their parents, teachers, and employers—expects a very young marriage to grow in stability and happy mutuality."

Conversely, in his study of high school marriages, Dr. Vladimir de Lissovoy found a "kin network" providing psychological support. He credits this positive parental attitude as a major "marriage sustaining" force that kept these seemingly doomed young couples together. At first, most of the parents were in a state of shock. They opposed the marriage. Their attitude changed to resignation and finally support.

All but three of the couples were given substantial weddings by their families, with the ceremony in church, a rectory, or the bride's home. Afterward, most of the parents frequently exchanged visits with the youngsters and gave cash and other assistance. Recalls de Lissovoy from his interviews: "There were a considerable number of spontaneous expressions of gratitude by husbands for help received."

The girl's father often would become very close to his young son-in-law, sharing many activities. Contrary to popular notions, the husbands tended to like their in-laws when first married—and like them even more three years later. Wives, however, had a harder time with their in-laws. The girls saw their mothers-in-law as helpful and well-meaning, but intruding—especially after the birth of the baby. Two couples said they were "controlled" by the in-laws with whom they lived. Two other couples suffered outright rejection from their parents, and had no contact with them.

Both sets of parents did not always help a couple equally. Eight couples reported a definite "coolness" on the part of the boy's parents; four couples found the girl's parents distant and unhelpful. After the baby was born, aid from parents tended to increase. Thus all but four of the couples said they became "closer" to their families.

TAKE A POSITIVE TACK

A parent's blind opposition to a marriage may only propel a teenager into it, especially if the youngster is marrying chiefly as a show of independence. As a last resort, of course, you can withhold parental consent, which most states require before allowing a minor to marry. But before you do that, be satisfied that falling back on the law to win an argument won't be self-defeating.

It's prudent to be careful about how you use your veto power. Your strenuous, arbitrary objection to your child's marriage may set an angry tone to your relations with your child for years to come. A really determined youngster may go to another state, or seek permission of a court, or simply run off. To get an idea of what you're up against, ask your youngster, "What will you do if I don't give my permission?"

Urge premarital counseling. A qualified counselor can help acquaint young people with the social, economic, and personal responsibilities of marriage. If this prospective marriage is a cause of a great deal of family conflict, join the couple in counseling. Or take joint counseling with your child alone, without the prospective spouse.

Your taking a positive tack before the wedding may prompt your child to willingly call it off. How to help your teenager evaluate the prospects of marriage realistically? Adopt an attitude that says in essence: I'd like to be sure that you know what you'd be getting into if you marry; please consider these questions:

"How Long Have You Gone Steady?"

Dr. Evelyn Millis Duvall, an editor of the journal *Marriage and Family Living*, suggests that, before marrying, a couple should know each other well enough to be able to "predict each other, empathize with each other, know where their likes and dislikes concur and differ."

For your child to know a possible spouse that well will take time. Indeed, time is the most important test of all your youngster's relationships. Unless the young couple has been going steady for at least a year, they enter marriage at their peril. The briefer their courtship, the greater their marital instability is likely to be.

Serious long-term dating can be an invaluable screening process for your youngster. It subjects the relationship to a variety of stresses. It gives the couple an increasingly better idea of how they'd interact if they married. It permits them to see if they're growing in the same direction.

By contrast, whirlwind romances tend to soon fly apart. Remind your child that adolescent love affairs are notably unstable because the partners are going through rapid changes, possibly in opposing ways. Not only are their personalities in flux. Teenagers also are extremely vulnerable to shifts in family, friends, school, work. Unaware of their own volatility, a teenage couple may feel eternally devoted to each other. Then a school term may end. Or one of them may develop a different interest, or acquire a new friend, or get on a revised schedule. Suddenly the relationship will be obsolete.

Normally, a young couple breaks up, and each goes on to someone who fits the changed conditions. Abnormally, they're married—and the disintegration of the relationship is as painful as the marriage is legally binding.

If your youngster wants to get married because of a pregnancy, special hazards are in the offing. Reports sociologist Frank Furstenberg: "Premarital pregnancy disrupts the courtship process and cuts short a necessary stage in preparation for marriage." Couples who marry because of pregnancy may not be ready to settle down. They may have reservations about the suitability of their mates. They may be unable or unwilling to assume the responsibilities of married life. Sociologist Harold T. Christiansen of Purdue University speculates that such marriages often occur "in the absence of love, or in the face of ill-matched personalities."

Your pregnant daughter's marriage has the strongest chance of surviving if she marries the child's father soon after conception, suggests Frank Furstenberg. But her marriage is likely to survive only if she and the boy had a long-lasting and exclusive relationship for at least a year prior to the pregnancy. Her marriage is twice as likely to go on the rocks if she went steady with the boy for less than a year. Also, she has less of a chance of achieving a stable marriage if she'd had sexual relations with more than one partner just prior to becoming pregnant.

After the baby is born, your daughter may be tempted to marry not the father of the child but another man. Such hastily developed "extemporaneous" marriages are twice as likely to break up as marriages with the child's father. "Having a child takes on a very different meaning in these two types of unions," comments Furstenberg. "Among couples with a developed relationship, the child reinforces the conjugal bond, serving as a common interest and focus of attention. The effect of the child could be just the opposite within the extemporaneous union, where he serves as a divisive intrusion." Furstenberg warns that in an extemporaneous marriage the couple is really a triangle: consisting of husband, wife, and father of the child.

"Are You in Harmony?"

Opposites may attract, but likes stay together. "Attraction between opposites is usually based upon friction," cautions psychiatrist Phillip Polatin of Columbia University's College of Physicians and Surgeons.

"Friction may lend excitement to courtship, but in everyday living can degenerate into two people rubbing each other the wrong way. Compatibility between extremely different personality types is rare."

Explore your child's life goals and those of the intended spouse. If your daughter has no interest in intellectual pursuits and has dreams of living in a palace, she's not likely to be happily wed to a boy who's a big reader and is little concerned with material things. Each will probably feel thwarted and bored. Likewise, if your son is physically active, he'll be restless with a girl who hates to perspire. Up to a point, such opposites can reach satisfactory compromises, ideally accepting in each other what they cannot change. But, warns psychiatrist Polatin: "At least some personality traits in common are essential to insure harmony."

For your child's marriage to work, the couple must be "in tune" with each other, suggests marriage counselor David R. Mace of the Bowman Gray School of Medicine. "This means something much more than being 'in love' in the popular sense," observes Dr. Mace. "It is based on compatibility in the truest sense—a state of affinity and harmony between two personalities which is felt intuitively by both."

To warn of opposite personality types that can be sources of constant irritation, ask your youngster: Do your general dispositions suit one another? By the other's standards, is either of you too aggressive or too shy? Too depressed or too manic? Too aloof, too social? Too brainy, too lowbrow? One reason pregnancy often leads to unstable marriages is that a forced wedding frequently unites people who are different in personality and cultural values.

A prerequisite for your child's marital harmony is the ability of both partners to communicate. In order to grow together, they need to talk about their thoughts, feelings, problems. They also need to share the same ambitions. If they're absorbed in their own aims and needs, each is likely to regard the other as an appendage.

How to spot inconsiderateness in a potential partner? New York psychologist and marriage counselor Salvatore V. Didato has passed on to writer Lester David questions you might pose to your daughter about a boy (or your son about a girl): "When you're with him, does he constantly steer the conversation to *himself* and *his* plans and problems? When you go out do you always end up where *he* wants to go? If you talk to him about an incident that involves you and your feelings, does he respond with empathy or appear to listen with one ear without showing you that he really knows how you feel or wants to know?"

Another requirement for your youngster's marital success is the willingness on the part of both partners to gracefully change their attitudes and behavior. Both young people can expect to try out many new ideas and life patterns in the early years of marriage. This requires tolerance and flexibility, and a readiness to listen calmly to logical arguments.

Warn your youngster against a potential mate with a quick temper, which can be expressed by sulky silence as well as by screaming rages. Observes Dr. Didato: "Such a person had temper tantrums as a child and will continue to erupt like a volcano as an adult. Emotionally immature, he has poor impulse control. He demands instant gratification. When he doesn't get his own way, look out!"

A common religion seems especially important if your youngster is marrying because of pregnancy. Dr. Vladimir de Lissovoy found that religious activities were a major marriage-sustaining force for the high school couples he followed. "The church became an important center in the lives of these couples," notes Dr. de Lissovoy. The youngsters regarded the church as the nearest thing to "community." It was to the local church that most couples turned for advice and help. Indeed, the church was the only community institution with which the couples had a continuing relationship.

Wives, especially, felt that church activities enabled them to see "other people." The activities not only provided companionship but also were free or inexpensive, a boon to financially strapped couples. Some investigators have observed that couples with a premarital pregnancy often developed a "crisis religion," possibly turning to the church to remove guilt feelings. Concludes de Lissovoy: "While it is not possible to differentiate the relative contributions of the 'sacred' or 'secular' church activities, it is feasible to assume that a positive orientation to a stable community institution could have contributed to the maintenance of the marriages."

"How Sure Are You It's Love?"

Help your child examine whatever motives are making marriage seem desirable. Warn that adolescents commonly interpret as "love" a number of strong feelings that are actually products of immaturity.

Some insecure young people think they're in love when in fact they have a need to dominate another person. They often show their desire to possess through bursts of extreme jealousy—which they may defend by saying, "It proves I love you." Some jealousy is normal, especially among young people who feel their emotions deeply. Observes psychiatrist Ralph R. Greenson of the University of California in Los Angeles: "People who never feel the normal pangs of jealousy are people who do not feel any loss—and people who do not feel any loss of love are people who do not give enough love to lose."

But your teenager can be put on the rack by a partner's excessive jealousy. Unjustified jealousy is a persecuting emotion, which may constantly throw your child on the defensive. With a jealous mate, your youngster can expect probing questions, unwarranted accusations, and embarrassing public rages.

Also caution your child against rebellion as a motivation for marriage. While some rebellion is a trait of adolescence, some young people go off the deep end. They head for the altar to get a rise out of their parents. Although they may call it love, what they may actually feel is the need for an ally in their wars against the system. Excessively rebellious couples may live as if on a battlefield as they engage in a constant struggle against the world. Unable to tolerate restrictions, allergic to authority, such couples are in constant, stressful conflict. Their marriage is on shaky ground. The angry partners may turn on each other. Or one may make a truce with the world, bringing the alliance to an end.

How to spot the pathological rebel? The youngster may frequently have trouble in school because of defying teachers and rules. Warn your teenager against the job-hopper who quits or is fired because of disagreements with bosses and co-workers. Watch out for the young person who collects traffic tickets, which may forewarn a more serious disregard for the law.

Ill treatment of parents can likewise signal a bad marriage risk. Visit the other parents and watch how their child gets along with them. Does the youngster treat them with consideration and respect? Show affection? Share in household tasks? If not, once the romantic glow wears off, your teenager is likely to be trapped in a marriage with a surly, unaffectionate, irresponsible spouse.

Beware, too, of a youngster who's overdependent—and may seek marriage as a way of being "grown up." The late Dr. Abraham Stone, dean of America's marriage counselors, once wrote that a newly married couple "should be emotionally free from parental domination, and they should be able to strike a balance between their loyalty to their parents and their relation to each other."

Steer your teenager clear of anyone who's dominated by a parent, usually by the mother. After a lifetime of making few if any independent decisions, an immature youngster will generally consult with Mama even after marriage. Your child will play second fiddle—except when it's time to be on the receiving end of carping and bullying, an infantile way of releasing frustration and self-hatred.

"Can You Handle the Commitment?"

For at least a month, immerse your teenager in your household nitty-gritty: the shopping and cleaning and straightening, the myriad chores, the unending dull details. Point out how often you need to do something for someone else. Make sure your youngster understands how many hours married people put in on making and conserving money.

"Teenagers do not understand the marital commitment," notes obstetrician-gynecologist James P. Semmens of the Medical University of South Carolina. "They believe that it would be pure bliss rather than sacrifice coupled with joy. There must be understanding that marriage is husband plus wife—a full-time arrangement, not a sometime thing—not mother's little girl escaping to the comfort of the parental home, or back to the old gang when the going gets tough for the boy."

The romantic fantasy of love makes many adolescents believe that together they can overcome all obstacles. Disappointment may be swift, for very often they have no real notion of what marriage may entail. "I hate doing dishes, ironing clothes and cooking," 16-year-old Brooke, married a month, confided to writer Evan McLeod Wylie. "My husband lied to me. He said marriage would be fun. I'm not looking for advice. I just want you to know that I thought I was an exception and I was wrong. Getting married at my age is rotten and I know what I'm going to do. I'm getting out!"

Marriage can be especially difficult if your youngster is trying to combine it with high school. Time pressures alone can be crushing. "I have lots of schoolwork, and so does Melissa," complains her 18-year-old husband Jed. "Now that we're married, we both have jobs. We hardly have a minute for each other."

Ask explicitly if your child is strongly committed to a permanent union. When teenagers hedge their bets with, "I can always get a divorce," their marriage is not likely to survive. Rather than solve their marital problems, an immature couple often dissolves the marriage.

Your teenager may find it difficult to make such a commitment. Until age 25, your child is likely to be going through what psychologist Erik Erikson termed an "identity crisis": the difficult stage in which young people find out who they are and what they want. Until adolescents resolve their identity crisis, they're not ready to enter into a relationship with another. If they cannot know themselves, how can they hope to understand another person?

During the identity crisis, your adolescent's values can go through fundamental changes. What—or who—seems important at 17 may be irrelevant at 18, even more so at 25. Teenagers often sense this, thus are rarely surprised when they go through rapid cycles of friendships, activities, and surroundings. Indeed, one characteristic of the identity crisis is a strong desire for freedom and travel—to get out and see the world, to take one last fling before facing the responsibilities of a family.

Youngsters who wish to tie themselves down permanently are often lacking in self-awareness. Suggested Dr. Lester A. Kirkendall while at Oregon State University:

> Young people about to marry should ask themselves, "Are we really ready to give up our freedom and social life for marriage?" Some young people forget that the demands of marriage will require them to forgo some of the things they prize. They may want to marry because all of their friends are doing it or to satisfy their sexual desires, but they may be unready to settle down to the everyday routine of married life.

"What About Money?"

Urge your child to hold off marrying until the couple can be fully self-supporting. Financial independence gives a marriage better prospects than one that remains dependent on parents. In the same practical vein, warn your youngster against a partner who can't handle money. No matter how bright and seemingly compatible a couple may be, their marriage rests on quicksand if one of them has never learned the basic principles of personal money management. Declares Lawrence I. Brown, a New York lawyer who has handled many hundreds of divorce cases: "One major cause that recurs is living beyond one's means. This brings all the inevitable consequences—debts, hiding from creditors, more borrowing to cover other debts. Resentments, accusations, lacerating quarrels follow, and the marriage collapses."

If people are unable to live within their means as teenagers, the chances are high that they won't be able to when they're married adults. Watch out for teenagers who are always broke, or who borrow from friends. Those are bad signs. See if the youngster maintains a savings account—a good sign.

At best, your teenager can expect money problems after marriage. Teenagers who work nearly invariably have to start with low-paying jobs, often at the minimum wage. Such pay is hardly enough to set up comfortable independent housekeeping.

Married teenagers, accustomed to being supported by their parents, are often shocked to discover the number of items that they now have to pay for—and their cost! "I couldn't believe how expensive toilet paper is," recalls Mary, a bride at 17. "I'd never thought about the price of toothpaste before, or floor wax, or light bulbs. I never realized that meat costs so much. I thought we'd eat steak, but we can't even afford hamburger."

Adds 18-year-old Daryl: "I thought I knew how to manage money. But I now realize that the only choices I had to make were whether to spend babysitting money on a new record or a new sweater. I never had to choose between dinner and a new pair of shoes."

After marriage your teenager is unlikely to be able to afford many of the things older couples consider necessities. A car may be out of the question. Housing is likely to be inadequate. Health and life insurance may be unaffordable luxuries. Dinner out and a movie may be reserved for only the grandest of celebrations.

Teenagers are typically overly optimistic as they enter a marriage, particularly in regard to finances. The high expectations and the typically low financial resources of most young couples lead to disappointment that may well carry to other areas of marital adjustment. "We have many quarrels about money," sociologist

Vladimir de Lissovoy was told by nearly all the high school couples in his study. On closer look, de Lissovoy discovered that spending the youngsters' income was "not the real problem; it was the lack of adequate income."

Many of the couples were on welfare or food programs. Even this early in their marriage, young couples were heavily in debt. One-third of the couples had debts requiring regular payments. Over half had borrowed from finance companies at exorbitant interest rates.

When de Lissovoy revisited the couples nearly three years later, he found their financial problems even more troubling to them. The problem of enough financial resources to live on was a very real one to these couples. ". . . It was a . . . point of many irritations and undoubtedly had an . . . effect upon other areas."

Money worries might have sunk these marriages were it not for the generosity of parents. Contributions to the couples came in the form of goods, money, and miscellaneous services. Gifts included such items as canned goods, clothing, appliances, even shelter. Three years into the marriage, parents continued to assist, especially with food items and clothing for the children.

Your married teenager's economic disadvantages may prove permanent unless the couple finishes school. Money problems that beset the young married couple are primarily due to their dropping out. A study of married high school students by the North Central Association of Colleges and Secondary Schools shows that 2 out of 3 girls and 1 out of 2 boys drop out. In some states, 4 out of 5 married students leave school.

The study also suggests that the younger your teenager is at the time of marriage, the more likely the child is to leave school. Freshman students are twice as likely as seniors to drop out.

Remind your child that the freedom gained by leaving home and school becomes the obligation to work—to be self-supporting. But lack of education means that a very large proportion of the very young married live at the poverty level. They have no reserves to fall back on, and little hope of getting out of poverty and debt by getting better-paying jobs that require greater skills. What's more, married teenagers who leave school are at a greater disadvantage than ever before. To compete effectively for jobs in an increasingly complex society, workers need more training than in the past.

Conceivably, your teenager may be forced out by school policies that bar married students. You might think that schools would try to meet the needs of married teenagers and help them prepare for work. Instead, some school systems expel married students—merely because they are married.

Other school policies are equally bizarre. Some districts allow married students to attend school, but will not allow them to participate in extracurricular activities. In others, they cannot hold school office. Some school policies require that if both married students are enrolled in the same school at the same time they're married, one of them must withdraw.

Challenge such policies. In virtually every case where parents have fought for their children's educational rights, the unjustified policies have been defeated. They rarely stand up to court scrutiny.

Also, to help your child remain in school, look into work/study programs. Enlist the support of guidance counselors in designing a program that might keep your child attending school while training for a career. Sometimes local businesses are amenable to apprenticing students part-time at little or no pay, perhaps with the offer of a job after graduation.

How can you best help with finances? Doing so can call for a good deal of tact. While you want to assist, you also want the couple to feel independent and learn to manage money on their own.

Whenever you hand over money, let them know in no uncertain terms if it is a gift or a loan. If it's a gift, you're likely to avoid resentment if you let them spend it as they wish, rather than for a particular item you think they ought to have. Edie thought her daughter Jane should have a dishwasher. A battle ensued when Jane used the money for winter coats for herself and her husband.

If you prefer to lend the money, consider making the loan formal. Get an I.O.U. containing a repayment schedule. Expect the interest you'd get if you kept the money in a bank. Have your child's in-laws cosign for at least half the loan, so you're not stuck for the full amount if the marriage dissolves.

Should you support them completely, do so for a specified period— two years, for example, or until a certain event takes place: graduation, landing a job, completing a particular course of training. Warns anthropologist Margaret Mead: "Mere financial support can mean a prolongation of parental control and childhood dependence and lead to resentment that invades all the family relationships."

Your family relationships are likely to be strained if the young couple has to live with you. Lack of privacy often results in friction between the older and younger couples, a sexual tension all around. Have frequent scheduled meetings to vent grievances. Give the house over to each other as much as possible.

In the long run, the best financial aid you can render is to further the education of your married children so that they can better make their own way.

"How Will a Baby Fit In?"

As a grandparent, you may need to go to the rescue of children produced by your teenager's marriage. Having a baby too soon can gravely injure the couple's relationship. Until they've been wed for two or three years, they may not have enough solidarity between themselves to withstand the stresses introduced by a baby.

Your grandchild may bear the brunt of its parents' ambivalence and frustration. It's not unusual for young couples to reject the child who trapped them into marriage or who makes it difficult for them to get out of it. Some immature parents smother the child with excessive attention—born of guilt about their feelings about their marriage's not working out, sometimes (when the child was conceived pre-maritally) about their sexual behavior.

Let your child know what to expect from life with a baby. Initially, the high school couples interviewed by sociologist Vladimir de Lissovoy had an "ideal notion" of parenthood. They had little discussion of the realities of caring for a child. Thus they were sent into a tailspin when the infant actually arrived.

Draw on your experience with your own children to point up the stages at which children normally develop. Otherwise, the inexperienced parents are likely to worry unnecessarily—or take it out on the child—when their unrealistic expectations are not met. Of de Lissovoy's group of young marrieds he found: "They were ignorant in regard to the most fundamental knowledge and principles of child development."

On the average, these adolescent parents expected their infant to smile at 3 weeks. Actually, the first smile rarely occurs before 8 weeks. They expected the baby to sit up by itself by 2 months, rather than the normal 7 or 8 months. They looked for the first steps at 10 months, some 2 to 5 months too early. They expected to hear the baby's first real word at 7 months. Few children begin to talk before a year.

The young parents wanted to start toilet training before 6 months. Bladder and bowel control are physiologically impossible until 1 to 3 years. They started obedience training—forcefully saying "No!"—at 7 months, and expected the child to know right from wrong at about a year. Pediatricians warn that children can't consistently obey before 2 years, or reason before 3 years.

You may find you need to intervene to prevent child abuse. Younger mothers tend to be severe in their treatment of young children. Often they're irritable and quick to punish. In his sampling, de Lissovoy observed: "These young mothers with a few notable exceptions were impatient and intolerant with their children." The sociologist found it difficult to maintain his scientific objectivity as a neutral onlooker. On four occasions he witnessed physical punishment of children under two years of age. Twice he felt obliged to step in and advise the parents on how to better treat the child.

Your grandchild is thus likely to become beset with problems. Anxieties and recriminations, often accompanied by sexual disturbances, may disrupt the young marriage, emotionally injuring your grandchild. Dr. Sol Nichtern, Assistant Clinical Professor of Psychiatry at New York Medical College in New York City, tells of a young couple we'll call Sally and Peter, who came to him because of problems with their son, Andrew. The boy had sleep disturbances, was hyperactive and demanding. He had trouble making friends and adjusting to school.

Sally and Peter had gotten married because of Andrew, who was born out of wedlock. Both parents were in their late teens at the time the child was conceived. Peter was a college student. Sally was one of the local girls in the small college town. Sally was determined to have her baby, and Peter felt obligated to marry her. He was fond of Sally. Her pregnancy made him feel he was in love with her.

The marriage was stormy from the beginning. Neither youngster was prepared for the responsibilities of child-rearing or their relationship to each other. They became dependent on their parents for support and care of Andrew. They alternately lived with each set of parents and shared with them the responsibilities of raising the boy.

After several years, they got their own home but found it harder and harder to care for Andrew or live with each other. The frequency of their sexual contacts began to decrease. Peter was occasionally impotent. Sally became frigid. Peter threw himself into work, seemingly under the pressure of supporting the family. Sally began to work. As Andrew became more and more troubled, Sally had various other people take care of him. This was her way of freeing herself from the tensions she experienced in contacts with her child.

Any time off you can give the young couple is likely to benefit not only them but also the baby. The birth of your grandchild is almost sure to accentuate any resentments your child has about marriage. Pamela, married at 18, feels trapped at home with four-month-old Tim. She's exhausted by the baby's care and hates her narrowed life. She resents her husband Ron's greater freedom, his job, his time out, the money in his pockets. Ron, who had been an outstanding student, has other resentments. He feels Pamela planned the pregnancy to hold onto him when she sensed their marriage was on the rocks. His work on an automobile assembly line is no measure of his potential—he learned all there is to know about his job in mere hours. "I'm bored out of my mind," he complains. "But the job pays better than I can get elsewhere unless I go back to school, which I can't do because of the baby."

Each blames the other for this sorry state of affairs. They are not seasoned enough to deal with such adult problems. Each is locked in anger and self-pity, but has no appreciation of the concerns and frustrations of the other. Baby Tim is in the middle. Pamela handles him with impatience. Ron ignores him.

You're likely to see your teenager's money problems considerably worsen if the young couple has a baby. In addition to normal bills, they'll have the expenses of the child: food, doctor bills, baby clothes. As a new mother, the young wife will be in no position to provide much of an income, if any. Many young couples find it hard to make ends meet, even including the wife's pay. If she stops working after the baby is born, it may be impossible.

The consequences for the young father can be grievous. If there were no baby, he might be able to finish high school even while married. With a baby coming, he must usually get a full-time job as soon as possible, and thereby interrupt the schooling that would have helped prepare him for a career. Men who marry in their teens are more likely to have unskilled, low-paying work, with less job security and chance for advancement. It's a rare young father who has the time or energy to support a family and continue his education.

Your youngster's money problems are likely to be compounded by more births. The younger a wife is when she has a baby, the more children she is likely to have. Married women who begin child-rearing before they are 18 average four children. Those who wait for their first baby until they are 20 to 24 generally have fewer than three children. "Relations may be further complicated by a rapid succession of additional pregnancies," concludes sociologist Frank Furstenberg. "The husband, particularly, may begin to feel trapped by the accumulating economic and emotional responsibilities. On her part, the wife may resent the heavy burdens of caring for several young children and have little emotional energy to invest in the marriage relationship."

"Are You Prepared to Be Lonely?"

"I never expected to feel so isolated," says 17-year-old Betty, married just three months. "I don't have much in common with my girlfriends anymore. They're in school and giggle all the time about which boys they're dating. I'm working, but the people in my office are all older than I am and not very interesting."

Alert your child to the prospect of long hours of loneliness. Married teenage couples are relatively rare. They have no natural peers except for perhaps the few other married teenagers of their acquaintance. They have little place among their unmarried friends. Nor do they have much in common with older married people. So they are left without much social support and are almost totally dependent on each other.

The presence of a baby usually increases this sense of isolation. The baby may become just one more obstacle to freedom. The mother is permanently stuck at home. The father is almost equally confined— or goes out alone. There is often no money now for pleasure and almost nowhere the young couple can go for amusement with the baby.

It is generally the young wife who bears the greater burden of isolation. Young married wives commonly complain that their husbands have not "settled down" and are "running around too much." In his study of high school marriages, Dr. Vladimir de

Lissovoy found that the husbands remained "boys" in a number of ways. They went "out" with their "buddies," stayed after school, played basketball and other sports. If they worked part-time, they socialized after working hours. Comments Dr. de Lissovoy: "The realization that a married status required a different orientation to life came slowly."

The wives, on the other hand, felt "dropped" by their friends and led rather lonely lives. While husbands' friends and classmates dropped in often, very few of the wives reported callers. The wives did not welcome the husbands' friends. Many of the girls told de Lissovoy that they felt they were "taken for granted" or "left out." Only seven couples of the forty-eight reported regular activities with other couples.

Nearly three years later, de Lissovoy found that the husbands continued to see their friends even after the coming of a child. The reaction of the wives was marked more by resignation than the irritation which was prevalent at the beginning of the marriage. The wives made references to "being too busy with the baby to do much." They were consistently dissatisfied with their marriages in the areas of social activities and mutual friends.

If your teenager insists on getting married, what can the couple do to counteract social isolation? Suggest that some kind of shared household may provide needed companionship. Derek and Carole, both 18, felt the burdens of domestic chores and loneliness. After they became friends with 19-year-old Ben and 17-year-old Emily, they decided to experiment with living under the same roof, splitting household expenses and chores. They rented a house that had been remodeled to accommodate the owner's in-laws. It has two separate bedroom and kitchen areas, with a living room connecting them. This gives each couple privacy, and also the opportunity for spending time together. They can choose to cook together and share a meal, or eat apart. Their expenses are considerably reduced, and the chores divided four ways are much less of a burden.

Also advise your child to join groups of other teenage married couples. Churches, Y's, and community centers widely sponsor small groups in which married teenagers talk things out. They can dispel their isolation, and learn that other young marrieds also have trouble adjusting to one another and their new role.

"Could You Deal with Sexual Problems?"

Let your youngster know that disappointment is a common feeling teenagers have about married sex. Difficulties often arise because of idealized expectations. The vast majority of teenagers depend upon romantic fiction and information from their peers regarding sex. Both partners have possibly heard that sex in marriage was more beautiful and uninhibited. Thus they're likely to be plagued by the question: What went wrong?

Dr. Vladimir de Lissovoy asked his sampling of high school couples to rate their sexual relationship. Early in marriage, the young husbands were mildly dissatisfied, largely because they wanted to have intercourse more often. The wives were more sexually satisfied than their husbands. Indeed, they wanted to have sex *less* often.

Close to three years later, de Lissovoy found that the couples' sexual adjustment had gotten worse. Husbands were far more dissatisfied with their infrequency of intercourse. Their wives wished to have sex even less often than before.

Problems often result from the young husband's ignorance about normal female sexual response. Observes obstetrician-gynecologist James Semmens: "Because many adolescent boys read sensational treatments of sex in pulp magazines and books they think that the female orgasmic response should be a violent eruption, throwing her into ecstasy with every muscle in spasm, and leaving her spent and exhausted." Boys often expect to live out this fantasy with every act of intercourse. "When it fails to happen, they feel cheated and accuse the wife of being 'frigid.'" The teenage wife rarely knows more than her husband, even about her own response, and so is unable to guide him.

Some young married men suffer from what Dr. Semmens calls the "loving giant syndrome." Nineteen-year-old Eric lifted weights. He was proud of his physique—and his large penis. He had a compulsive drive to impress his 17-year-old wife with his virility.

Before intercourse Eric would do a number of handstands and pushups while Mindy watched from the bed. He'd flex his muscles and pose, a way of showing her he was the envy of all the guys he knew. This excited him and he'd come to bed with an erection. But he also expected Mindy to become sexually aroused by his performance. He'd begin intercourse with little or no foreplay. With a poorly lubricated vagina, Mindy found sex uncomfortable. Full penetration by Eric's penis painfully stretched ligaments connecting her uterus and lower back. Comments Dr. Semmens: "He achieves a climax and his wife gets a backache!"

Like many teenage boys, Eric had the mistaken notion that rippling muscles and a big penis necessarily make for proficiency as a lover. He also thought that the female sex role is essentially one of service to the male, and that full penetration was required for Mindy to have an orgasm.

Roger, 18, is another type of sexual athlete who feels that sex is a service. He expects intercourse morning, noon, and night, irrespective of how his 16-year-old wife Maria feels. He puts more stress on sex than on anything else in their relationship. Maria found soon after their marriage that Roger was almost insatiable in his demands for sex. "It's free and it's legal," he'd say. "And it's my right."

He'd often grab Maria for quick sex at inopportune moments— when she wanted to read, after she'd gotten dressed up to go out, just before they were expecting company. Maria would be left sore and unsatisfied. She also felt used. "The only time he is willing to treat me as a human being is when he is interested in going to bed with me," Maria confided in Dr. Semmens. She began avoiding Roger more and more—because just to be near him was to invite a sexual assault.

Worse yet, she suffered from bladder and vaginal irritations. In all such instances, the young wife is unlikely to be sufficiently stimulated to experience orgasm. Increasingly, she tends to reject her husband for physical as well as psychological reasons. She, like her husband, may think she's "frigid." Both are likely to be resentful and frustrated.

If your child is married, you may detect early indications that the couple's sex life is for the birds. The young husband may seek out old friends to spend evenings with. The young wife may develop vague gynecological complaints or headaches. They may both complain publicly of being overworked and exhausted. In private they'll be "too tired" for sex.

As a parent, you can head off sexual problems in your child's marriage by starting early with sex education. Most sexual problems in a teenage marriage result from ignorance and from lack of experience in talking about sexual matters. Embarrassment may account for a young couple's inability to tell each other what feels good. Both may need reassurance that what they like to do is "normal." Your youngster is likely to be free of such hang-ups if you've provided authoritative information and advice.

If your child is preparing for marriage, take the suggestion of obstetrician-gynecologist Charles E. Flowers, Jr. of the University of Alabama Medical Center. Dr. Flowers once said that the best wedding present parents could give their children is a complete premarital physical examination and counseling session. This can help avoid the anxieties that young people face in spite of their facade of sexual knowledge. It would alleviate the problem of the marriage that cannot be consummated because of physical reasons, such as abnormalities of the vagina or hymen. If your daughter is a virgin, the simple fact that she has regular periods or uses tampons does not mean that intercourse will be free of trauma.

Premarital counseling also helps to clarify misconceptions and dispel fear. It may be an ideal time for the couple to discuss family planning and sexual physiology, even if merely a review. The physical examination offers assurance that a normal physical relationship can be expected. If a minor problem is found, it can usually be corrected before the wedding.

Bibliography

Abernethy, V. "Illegitimate Conception among Teenagers." *American Journal of Public Health* 64 (July 1974): 662–64.

Abernethy, V., and Abernethy, G. L. "Risk for Unwanted Pregnancy among Mentally Ill Adolescent Girls." *American Journal of Orthopsychiatry* 44 (9 April 1974): 442–49.

"Abortion Rate Is Rising for Girls under Age 15, 1974 Data Show." *The New York Times*, 26 October 1977.

Abortion Research Notes 6, Nos. 3 and 4 (December 1977) and 7, Nos. 1 and 2 (August 1978). International Reference Center for Abortion Research.

"Abortion Surveillance: United States 1975." Center for Disease Control. *Morbidity and Mortality Weekly Report* 26 (29 July 1977).

"Abortion Surveillance: United States 1976." Center for Disease Control *Morbidity and Mortality Weekly Report* 27 (26 May 1978).

"Adolescent Attitudes Toward Abortion: Effects on Contraceptive Practice." *American Journal of Public Health* (April 1971).

"Adolescent Fertility: Risks and Consequences." *Population Reports*, Series J, No. 10 (July 1976).

"Adolescent Pregnancy Bill Passed." *Focus* (January 1979).

"Adolescent Pregnancy and Childbearing: Growing Concerns for Americans." *Population Reference Bureau Bulletin* 31 (May 1977).

"Adolescent Sexuality." *Journal of Clinical Child Psychology* 3 (Fall-Winter 1974).

"Adolescents: Sexually Active, but Unhappy." *Sexuality Today* 1 (26 June 1978):1.

"Adolescents: They Seek Care Outside the System." *Medical World News* (2 April 1979).

"Adopting a Child: The Wait Is Long, the Babies Few." *Business Week* (4 May 1974):89–90.

"Adoption Enters the New Age." *New Age Review* (May 1977).

Allen, N., and Mondschain, B. "Medical Role in the Adolescent Crisis Intervention Center." *Adolescence* 11 (Summer 1976):157–65.

Ambrose, Linda. "Misinforming Pregnant Teenagers." *Family Planning Perspectives* 10 (January-February 1978).

Amstey, Marvin S. "Herpes V.D.—A Serious Problem in Pregnancy." *Medical Aspects of Human Sexuality* (August 1974).

Andrews, S. W. "College Contraceptive Clinic." *American Journal of Nursing* 76 (3 April 1976):592–93.

"Are We Headed Toward More Conservative Sexual Values?" *Medical Aspects of Human Sexuality* (December 1978).

Arnold, Charles B. "Proper Use of the Condom. *Medical Aspects of Human Sexuality* (September 1975).

Arnold, C. B., and Cogswell, Betty E. "A Condom Distribution Program for Adolescents: The Findings of a Feasibility Study." *American Journal of Public Health* (April 1971).

Arnold, S., and Hoffman, A. "Chicago Planned Parenthood's Teen Scene: A Sociological Study for Participants." *Adolescence* 9 (Fall 1974):371–90.

Arnstein, Robert L. "Virgin Men." *Medical Aspects of Human Sexuality* (January 1974).

Ashdown-Sharp, Patricia. *A Guide to Pregnancy and Parenthood for Women on Their Own*. New York: Vintage Books, 1977.

"At Long Last, Rational Adoption Legislation?" *Contributions to Obstetrics and Gynecology* 10 (November 1977).

[320]

Babineau, R. "Coed Dorms and Premarital Sex." *Medical Aspects of Human Sexuality* 12 (October 1978): 163.

Babu, D. S., et al. "Social and Behavioral Aspects of Venereal Disease among Resident Male University Students. *International Journal of Epidemiology* 5 (June 1976):121–24.

Bacon, L. "Early Motherhood, Accelerated Role Transition and Social Pathologies." *Social Forces* 52 (March 1974):333–41.

Badger, E., et al. "Education for Adolescent Mothers in a Hospital Setting" (Cincinnati General Hospital). *American Journal of Public Health* 66 (May 1976):469–72.

Baldwin, B. A., et al. "A Campus Peer Counseling Program in Human Sexuality." *Journal of the American College Health Association* 22 (June 1974):399–404.

Ballard, Walter M., and Gold, Edwin H. "Medical and Health Aspects of Reproduction in the Adolescent." *Clinical Obstetrics and Gynecology* (June 1971):338.

Baran, A., et al. "Open Adoption." *Social Work* 21 (March 1976):97–100.

Barnard, C., and Calderone, M. S., eds. "How Parents Should Teach Their Children about Sex." *Today's Health* 51 (December 1973):68–70.

Barrett-Connor, Elizabeth. "Personal Prophylaxis for Venereal Disease." *Medical Aspects of Human Sexuality* (May 1978).

Bauman, K. E., et al. "Premarital Sexual Attitudes of Unmarried University Students: 1968 vs. 1972." *Archives of Sexual Behavior* 5 (January 1976):29–37.

Bean, F. D., and Aiken, L. H. "Intermarriage and Unwanted Fertility in the United States." *Journal of Marriage and the Family* 38 (February 1976):61–72.

Beiser, Helen F. "Sexual Factors in Antagonism Between Mothers and Adolescent Daughters." *Medical Aspects of Human Sexuality* (April 1977).

Belanger, K., et al. "Two Groups of University Student Women: Sexual Activity and the Use of Contraception." *Journal of the American College Health Association* 19 (June 1971):307–312.

Bell, L. N. "Alternative to Abortion." *Christianity Today* 15 (18 June 1971):17–18.

Bender, S. J. "Sex and the College Student." *Journal of School Health* 43 (May 1973):278–80.

Benet, Mary Kathleen. *The Politics of Adoption.* New York: Free Press, 1976.

Benjamin, R. R., and Fink, R. "Screening and Counseling: A Unique Approach to Adolescent Health." *Adolescence* 11 (Summer 1976):181–93.

Berg, D. H. "Sexual Subcultures and Contemporary Heterosexual Interaction Patterns among Adolescents." *Adolescence* 10 (Winter 1975):543–48.

Berger, D. G., and Wenger M. G. "Ideology of Virginity." *Journal of Marriage and the Family* 35 (November 1973):666–76.

Berger, M. M. "Fathers' Discomfort at Daughters' Sexual Maturation." *Medical Aspects of Human Sexuality* (September 1978).

Berman, J. and Osborn D. "Specific Self-esteem and Sexual Permissiveness." *Psychological Reports* 36 (February 1975): 323–36.

"A Bill of Sexual Rights: Student Committee on Sexuality of Syracuse University." *Journal of Clinical Child Psychology* (Fall-Winter 1974).

Blake, J. "Teenage Birth Control Dilemma and Public Opinion." *Science* 180 (18 May 1973):708–712.

Blouin, William Robert. "Sexual and Contraceptive Knowledge, Attitudes and Practices of Adolescent Males." Master's Thesis, Yale University School of Nursing, May 1978.

Bogue, D. J. "Long-term Solution to the AFDC Problem: Prevention of Unwanted Pregnancy." *Social Service Review* 49 (December 1975):539–52.

Boydston, Donald N. "College Students' Sex Questions." In *Sex in the Adolescent Years.* Edited by Isadore Rubin and Lester A. Kirkendall. New York: Association Press, 1968.

Bradt, Jack O. "Types of Immature Nonmarital Sexual Relationship." *Medical Aspects of Human Sexuality* (August 1976).

Brill, Rabbi Mordecai. "Everyone Is a Sex Educator." *Journal of Clinical Child Psychology* (Fall-Winter 1974).

Brown, B. B. "Public School Policies on Married Students." *Education Digest* 38 (December 1972):48–49.

Brown, Fred. "Sexual Problems of the Adolescent Girl." *Pediatric Clinics of North America* (August 1972):759.

Brunswick, A. F. "Adolescent Health, Sex and Fertility." *American Journal of Public Health* 61 (April 1971):711–29.

Bryan, Shirley K. "Venereal Disease and the Teenager." *Journal of Clinical Child Psychology* (Fall-Winter 1974).

Bryt, Albert. "Adolescent Sex Crises." *Medical Aspects of Human Sexuality* (October 1976).

Burchinal, Lee G. "Trends and Prospects for Young Marriages in the United States." *Journal of Marriage and the Family* 27 (1965):243–54.

Burkart, J., et al. "The Unwed Mother: Implications for Family Life Educators." *Journal of School Health* 43 (September 1973):451–54.

Canfield, Elizabeth K. "Dealing with Reality: Birth Control and Pregnancy Counseling in a Student Health Center." *California School Health* (October 1971).

———. "Toward a Manifesto of Rights and Responsibilities for the Sexual Adolescent." *Journal of Clinical Child Psychology* (Fall-Winter 1974).

Carns, D. E. "Talking about Sex: Notes on First Coitus and the Double Sexual Standard." *Journal of Marriage and the Family* 35 (November 1973):677–88.

Carrera, Michael A., and Welbourne, Ann. "Answering Questions over the Phone: A Community Based Service." *Journal of Clinical Child Psychology* (Fall-Winter 1974).

Cassill, R. V. "Up the Down Co-ed." *Esquire* 80 (December 1973):190–92.

Castadot, R. G. "Need for, Difficulties and Experience with, Sexual Behavior Questionnaires among Teenagers." *Maryland State Medical Journal* 24 (April 1975):40–42.

Catlin, N., et al. MMPI Profiles of Cohabiting College Students. *Psychology Reports* 38 (April 1976):407–410.

Chapel, Thomas A. "Subtle Signs of Venereal Disease in Women." *Medical Aspects of Human Sexuality* (October 1977).

Chess, S., et al. "Sexual Attitudes and Behavior Patterns in a Middle-class Adolescent Population." *American Journal of Orthopsychiatry* 46 (October 1976):689–701.

Chez, Ronald M. "Taking Some Risk out of the Pill." *Emergency Medicine*, October 1977.

Chiappa, Joseph A., and Forish, Joseph J. *The VD Book.* New York: Holt, Rinehart, and Winston, 1976.

"Children and Sex: Answers to the 10 Questions Parents Most Often Ask." *Good Housekeeping* 181 (October 1975):166.

Christiansen, Harold T., and Rubinstein, Bette B. "Premarital Pregnancy and Divorce: A Follow-up Study by the Interview Method." *Marriage and Family Living* 18 (1956):114–23.

Clayton, R. R. "Premarital Sexual Intercourse: A Substantive Test of the Contingent Consistency Model." *Journal of Marriage and the Family* 34 (May 1972):273–81. Reply with rejoinder by D. W. Grimes and R. W. Libby. *Ibid.* 35 (February 1973):9–14.

Cohen, Michael W., and Friedman, Stanford B. "Nonsexual Motivation of Adolescent Sexual Behavior." *Medical Aspects of Human Sexuality* (December 1975).

Cohen, R., and Rudin, C. "How Schools Can Fight the VD Menace." *Education Digest* 34 (November 1973):27–29.

Collins, R. J. "A Physician's View of College Sex." *Journal of the American Medical Association* 232 (April 1975):392.

"Community Sex Information: Fulfilling a Major Need." *Sexuality Today* 1 (24 April 1978):4.

"Concerns of Parents about Sex Education." *SIECUS Study Guide*, No. 13 (1971).

Conley, J. A., et al. "Attitudes of College Students Toward Selected Issues in Human Sexuality." *Journal of School Health* 43 (May 1973):286–92.

Conley, J. A., et al. "The Generation Gap in Sex Education: Is There One?" *Journal of School Health* 44 (October 1974):428–37.

Conley, J. A., et al. "On Improving Instruction in Sex Education." *Journal of School Health* 43 (November 1973):591–93.

Connell, Elizabeth B. "Various Types of Intrauterine Devices." *Medical Aspects of Human Sexuality* (October 1977).

Connor, John F. "Instruction Sheet Helps Women with Vaginitis." *Patient Care*, 30 June 1972.

"Contraception." U.S. Department of Health, Education and Welfare. *Publication No. (HSH) 76–16024*, 1976.

"Contraception—When Avoiding Pregnancy Is the Issue." *Patient Care*, 15 September 1978.

"Contraceptive Sponge Fights VD, Too." *Medical World News*, 17 October 1977.

Cook, P. W. "A Great Experiment in Sex Education: The Anaheim Story." *Journal of School Health* 42 (January 1972):7–9.

Coons, Frederick W. "Sex on Campus: Informing and Advising a New Student." *Medical Aspects of Human Sexuality* (September 1974).

Cottle, Thomas J. "Adolescent Voices." *Psychology Today*, February 1979.

———. "Sexual Revolution and the Young: Four Studies." *The New York Times Magazine*, 26 November 1972, pp. 36–37 + .

Crist, Takey. "Assistance for the Sexually Active Female." *Journal of Gynecology and Neonatal Nursing* 2 (1973).

Cunningham, Ann. "Sex on Campus: Intellectual Exercise?" *Mademoiselle* 77 (August 1973):294–95.

Curran, D. "Sexeducation: A 12-letter Word for Parents." *New Catholic World* 218 (July 1975):165–69.

Curtis, F. L. S. "Observations of Unwed Pregnant Adolescents." *American Journal of Nursing* 74 (January 1974):100–102.

Cutright, H. "Timing the First Birth: Does It Matter?" *Journal of Marriage and the Family* 35 (November 1973):585–95.

Cutright, P. "The Teenage Sexual Revolution and the Myth of an Abstinent Past." *Family Planning Perspectives* 4 (January 1972):24–31.

Daniel, G. "Single, Pregnant, Sweet Sixteen." *PTA Magazine* 68 (December 1973):28–29.

D'Augelli, J. F., et al. "Relationship of Sex Guilt and Moral Reasoning to Premarital Sex in College Women and in Couples." *Journal of Consulting and Clinical Psychology* 43 (February 1975):40–47.

Davenport, Charles W. "How to Talk with Boys about Sex at Puberty." *Medical Aspects of Human Sexuality* (October 1974).

———. "How to Talk with Girls about Sex at Puberty." *Medical Aspects of Human Sexuality* (August, 1978).

David, L. "Case of Teen Divorce." *Seventeen* 35 (August 1976):256–57.

———. "Marriage: The Kind of Men to Avoid." *Seventeen* 34 (April 1975):75–76.

Davis, P. "Contextual Sex-saliency and Sexual Activity: The Relative Effects of Family and Peer Group in the Sexual Socialization Process." *Journal of Marriage and the Family* 36 (February 1974):196–202.

Dearth, P. B. "Viable Sex Education in the Schools; Expectations of Students, Parents, and Experts." *Journal of School Health* 44 (April 1974):190–93.

de Lissovoy, V. "High School Marriages: A Longitudinal Study." *Journal of Marriage and the Family* 35 (May 1973):245–55.

Diamond, Milton. "Contraceptive Counseling for Sexually Active Adolescents." *Medical Aspects of Human Sexuality* (November 1977).

"Dr. Carrera: 'Young People Can Be Sexually Responsible.'" *Sexuality Today* 2 (11 December 1978):2.

Dukelle, R., and Stevenson, N. "Legal Rights of Unmarried Fathers: The Impact of Recent Court Decisions." *Social Service Review* 47 (March 1973):1–15.

Eastman, W. F., et al. "Sexual Problems and Personality Adjustment of College Women." *Journal of the American College Health Association* 18 (December 1969):144–47.

Ehrman, M. L. "Sex Education for the Young." *Nursing Outlook* 23 (September 1975):583–85.

11 Million Teenagers. New York: Alan Guttmacher Institute, 1976.

"Embarrassed Virgins: Women and Sexual Pressures." *Time* 102 (9 July 1973):64.

Englebardt, S. "Now: Health Care Teenagers Can Believe in; Work of R. J. Hobbie at Adolescent Medical Clinic of Bridgeport Hospital." *Today's Health* 51 (June 1973): 16–19+.

"The E.P.T. Do-it yourself Early Pregnancy Test." *The Medical Letter* 20 (21 April 1978).

Esman, Aaron H., ed. *The Psychology of Adolescence.* New York: International Universities Press, 1975.

"Estimating the Need for Family Planning Services among Unwed Teenagers." *Family Planning Perspectives* 6 (Spring 1974).

Evanston, Reuben D. "Solving Teenagers' Sex Problems." *Today's Health* 50 (May 1972):26.

Fair, E. "The Sexually Active Female Adolescent." *Journal of the Oklahoma State Medical Association* 66 (May 1973):198–202.

"Family Impact Perspectives on Policy Towards Teenage Pregnancy." *Sexuality Today* 2 (15 January 1979):1.

Family Planning Digest. vols. 2 and 3 (March 1973, January 1975). U.S. Department of Health, Education and Welfare.

"'Family Theater' and Teenage Sex." *Sexuality Today* 1 (29 May 1978):2.

"Female Physical Examination for Contraception." U.S. Department of Health, Education and Welfare. *Publication No. (HSA) 76–16023, 1976.*

Ferm, D. W. "Teenage Sex before Marriage." *Parents' Magazine and Better Homemaking* 48 (December 1973):36–37+.

"15 Facts You Should Know about Abortion." *Zero Population Growth*, September 1976.

Finkel, M. L., et al. "Sexual and Contraceptive Knowledge, Attitudes and Behavior of Male Adolescents." *Family Planning Perspectives* 7 (November-December 1975):256–60.

Fisher, Alexander A. "Allergic Reactions to Contraceptives and Douches." *Medical Aspects of Human Sexuality* (January 1975).

Fisher, E. "Sex on Campus: Unhappy Androgyny." *Mademoiselle* 77 (August 1973):296–97.

Flatter, J., and Pietrofesa, J. J. "Human Sexuality: What Is the School's Role?" *Education Digest* 38 (February 1973):42–44.

Folland, David S. "Treatment and Epidemiologic Procedures for Children with VD." *Medical Aspects of Human Sexuality* (May 1978).

Forthmann, S. "Sex Education: How Effective Are the High School Programs?" *Clearing House* 48 (February 1974):369–71.

Fosburgh, Lacy. "The Make-believe World of Teen-age Maternity." *The New York Times Magazine,* 7 August 1977.

Freeman, E. W. "Abortion: Beyond Rhetoric to Access." *Social Work* 21 (November 1976):483–87.

Friedman, H. L. "Why Are They Keeping Their Babies?" *Social Work* 20 (July 1975):322–23.

Frye, B. A., and Barham, B. "Reaching Out to Pregnant Adolescents." *American Journal of Nursing* 75 (September 1975):1502–1504.

Furstenberg, F. F., Jr. "Birth Control Experience among Pregnant Adolescents: The Process of Unplanned Parenthood." *Social Problems* 19 (Fall 1971):192–203.

————. "Premarital Pregnancy and Marital Instability." *Journal of Social Issues* 32 (1976):67–86.

Gadpaille, W.J. "A Teenager Contemplating First Coitus." *Medical Aspects of Human Sexuality* (March 1975).

Galbraith, G. G., and Crow, C. "Retrospective Parental Ratings and Free Associative Sexual Responsivity in Male and Female College Students." *Psychological Reports* 38 (June 1976):759–65.

Gallagher, Ursula M. *Changing Focus on Services to Teenagers.* U.S. Department of Health, Education and Welfare. Office of Child Development, September-October, 1973.

Gardner, Richard A. "Exposing Children to Parental Nudity." *Medical Aspects of Human Sexuality* (June 1975).

Garfield, M. G., and Morgenthau, J. E. "Sex Talks Between Mothers and Daughters." *Medical Aspects of Human Sexuality* 10 (November 1976):6.

Gedan, S. "Abortion Counseling with Adolescents." *American Journal of Nursing* 74 (October 1974):1856–58.

Gerson, A. "Promiscuity as a Function of the Father-Daughter Relationship." *Psychological Reports* 34 (June 1974):1013–14.

"GH Poll: What Should an Unmarried Pregnant Teen-ager Do?" *Good Housekeeping* 177 (November 1973):54+.

Gianturco, D. T. "The Promiscuous Teenager." *Southern Medical Journal* 67 (April 1974):415–18.

Gilbert, G. C. "Counseling Black Adolescent Parents." *Social Work* 19 (January 1974):88–95.

Godenne, G. D. "Sex and Today's Youth." *Adolescence* 9 (Spring 1974):67–72.

Goldfarb, Alvin F. "Adolescent Gynecologic Problems." *Obstetrics and Gynecology,* September 1978.

Goldsmith, S., et al. "Teenagers, Sex and Contraception." *Family Planning Perspectives* 4 (January 1972):32–38.

Goldson, Mary Funnyé. "Matching Adoptable Children with Adoptable Parents." *Contemporary Obstetrics and Gynecology* 10 (November 1977).

Goodall, K. "Students of the 70s—Moving from Drugs to Sex: Peer Counseling Program at the University of North Carolina." *Psychology Today* 8 (February 1975):32.

Goodman, J. D. "Behavior of Hypersexual Delinquent Girls." *American Journal of Psychiatry* 133 (June 1976):662–68.

Gordon, Sol. "The Sexual Adolescent: Communicating with Teenagers about Sex." North Scituate, MA: Duxbury Press, 1973.

————. "What Place Does Sex Education Have in the Schools?" *Journal of School Health* 44 (April 1974):186–89.

————. "Why Sex Education Belongs in the Home." *PTA Magazine* 68 (February 1974):15.

Gordon, Sol, and Dickman, Irving R. "Sex Education: The Parents' Role." *Public Affairs Pamphlet No. 549,* 1978.

Grady, B. H. "A Family Living Course for Young Adolescents." *Child Today* 2 (July-August 1973):18–19 passim.

Graves, W. L., and Bradshaw, B. R. "Early Reconception and Contraceptive Use among Black Teenage Girls after an Illegitimate Birth." *American Journal of Public Health* 65 (July 1975):38–40.

Grimble, A. S. "Venereal Disease and the Young Patient: A Perspective." *Guys Hospital Report* 120 (1971):323–36.

Grimes, D. A., and Romm, F. J. "Fertility and Family Planning among White Teenagers in Metropolitan Atlanta." *American Journal of Public Health* 65 (July 1975):700–707.

Groat, H. T., et al. "Social Isolation and Premarital Pregnancy." *Sociology & Social Research* 60 (January 1976):188–98.

Grover, J. W. "Problems of Emerging Sexuality and Their Management." *RI Med* 58 (July 1973):274–79 passim.

Guttmacher, A. F., et al. "Sex on the Campus and the College Health Services." *Journal of the American College Health Association* 21 (December 1972):145–48.

Hale, Darryl, et al. "Attitudes of Adolescent Males Towards Abortion, Contraception, and Sexuality." Study by Planned Parenthood Association/Chicago Area, Inc.

Hamelstein, Helaine. "Youth and Their Sexual Problems." *Journal of Clinical Child Psychology* (Fall-Winter 1974).

Hampe, G. D., and Ruppel, H. J., Jr. "Measurement of Premarital Sexual Permissiveness: A Comparison of Two Guttman Scales" (with reply by H. T. Christensen and rejoinder). *Journal of Marriage and the Family* 36 (August 1974):451–68.

Harper, Robert A. "Pro's and Con's of Petting." In *Sex in the Adolescent Years*. Edited by Isadore Rubin and Lester A. Kirkendall. New York: Association Press, 1968.

Harvey, A. L. "Risky and Safe Contraceptors: Some Personality Factors." *Journal of Psychology* 92 (January 1976):109–112.

"The Hassles of Becoming a Teenage Parent." U.S. Department of Health, Education and Welfare. *Publication No. (HSA) 77–5624.*

Haughton, R. "Sex Education and Religion." *New Catholic World* 215 (January 1972):12–13 +.

Hausknecht, Richard U. "Termination of Pregnancy in Adolescent Women." *Pediatric Clinics of North America*, August 1972, p. 803.

Hein, Karen. "Need for Pap Smears Among Sexually Active Adolescents." *Medical Aspects of Human Sexuality*, March 1977.

Heit, P. "A High School Peer Sex Information and Referral Program." *Journal of School Health* 44 (December 1974):572–75.

Heller, J. R., and Kivaly, J., Jr. "Educational Program for Pregnant School Age Girls." *Clearing House* 47 (April 1973):476–82.

Hempel, W. V. "Sexual Freedom in Adolescents: A Reaction Formation?" *American Journal of Psychiatry* 130 (June 1973):722.

Hendin, Herbert. "Fallacies of 'Sexual Freedom' in Young Adults." *Medical Aspects of Human Sexuality*, October 1978.

Henze, L. F., and Hudson, J. W. "Personal and Family Characteristics of Cohabiting and Non-Cohabiting College Students." *Journal of Marriage and the Family* 36 (November 1974):72–77.

Hilldrup, R. P., and Gordon, S. "Why Sex Education Belongs in the Schools; Why Sex Education Belongs in the Home." *PTA Magazine* 68 (February 1974):12–17.

Hinman, A. R., et al. "Medical Consequences of Teenage Sexuality." *New York State Journal of Medicine* 75 (August 1975):1439–42.

Hodgman, C. H. "Talks Between Fathers and Sons." *Medical Aspects of Human Sexuality* 9 (1975):9.

Hofmann, Adele D. "Adolescent Promiscuity." *Medical Aspects of Human Sexuality*, May 1974.

———. "A Guide to Medical Care for the Sexually Active Adolescent." *Journal of Clinical Child Psychology*, Fall-Winter, 1974.

———. "Identifying and Counseling the Sexually Active Adolescent Is Every Physician's Responsibility." *Clinical Pediatrics* 11 (November 1972):625–29.

Hofmann, Adele D., and Pilpel, Harriet F. "The Legal Rights of Minors." *Journal of Clinical Child Psychology*, Fall-Winter, 1974.

Horn, J. M., and Turner, R. G. "Minnesota Multiphasic Personality Inventory Profiles among Subgroups of Unwed Mothers." *Journal of Consulting and Clinical Psychology* 44 (February 1976):25–33.

Howard, Marion. "Comprehensive Community Programs for the Pregnant Teen-ager." *Clinics in Obstetrics and Gynecology*, 14 June 1971, p. 473.

———. "Teen-age Parents." *Today's Education* 62 (February 1973):39–40 +.

"How Do Young People Usually React to Their First Intercourse?" *Medical Aspects of Human Sexuality*, January 1976.

"How to Gain Consent for Sex Ed in the Schools." *Sexuality Today* 2 (16 April 1979):1.

Huber, J. "Married Students vs. Married Dropouts." *Education Digest* 36 (January 1971):42–43.

Huffman, John W. "Management of Difficult Defloration." *Medical Aspects of Human Sexuality*, July 1976.

Hyams, Lyon. "Areas of Sexuality Producing Anxiety in College Women." *Medical Aspects of Human Sexuality*, May 1976.

"'I Can't be Pregnant': Three M.D.'s Talk about Helping Teens." *Youth and Student Affairs*. Planned Parenthood Federation of America, Inc.

Inman, M. "What Teen-agers Want in Sex Education." *American Journal of Nursing* 74 (October 1974):1866–67.

Inselberg, Rachel M. "Marital Problems and Satisfaction in High School Marriages." *Marriage and Family Living* 24 (1962):74–77.

———. "Social and Psychological Factors Associated with High School Marriages." *Journal of Home Economics* 53 (1961):766–72.

"Interfaith Statement on Sex Education." *Journal of Clinical Child Psychology*, Fall-Winter 1974.

Isay, R. A. "The Influence of the Primal Scene on the Sexual Behavior of an Early Adolescent." *Journal of the American Psychoanalytic Association* 23 (1975):535–53.

Jarvis, D. L. "Preventing Illegitimate Teenage Pregnancy Through Systems Interaction." *Child Welfare* 51 (June 1972):396–400.

Jensen, Gordon D., and Robbins, Mina. "Ten Reasons Why 'Sex Talks' with Adolescents Go Wrong." *Medical Aspects of Human Sexuality*, July 1975.

Jermann, T. C. "Can the Young Make Good Marriages?" *America* 128 (14 April 1973):329–30.

Jessor, S. L., and Jessor, R. "Transition from Virginity to Nonvirginity among Youth: A Social-psychological Study over Time." *Developmental Psychology* 11 (July 1975):473–84.

Joe, V. C., et al. "Social Attitudes and Sexual Behaviors of College Students." *Journal of Consulting and Clinical Psychology* 43 (June 1975):430.

Johnson, C. L. "Adolescent Pregnancy: Intervention into the Poverty Cycle." *Adolescence* 9 (Fall 1974):391–406.

———. "Attitudes Toward Premarital Sex and Family Planning for Single-never-pregnant Teenage Girls." *Adolescence* 9 (Summer 1974):255–62.

Johnson, S. K. "Business in Babies." *The New York Times Magazine*, 17 August 1975, pp. 10–11 +.

Johnson, W. T., and Delamater, J. D. "Response Effects in Sex Surveys." *Public Opinion Quarterly* 40 (Summer 1976):165–81.

Josselyn, Irene M. *Adolescence.* New York: Harper and Row, 1971.

Juhasz, A. M. "Changing Patterns of Premarital Sexual Behavior." *Intellect* 104 (April 1976):511–14.

———. "Understanding Adolescent Sexual Behavior in a Changing Society." *Journal of School Health* 42 (March 1972):149–54.

Kantner, J. F., et al. "Sexual Experience of Young Unmarried Women in the United States." *Family Planning Perspectives* 4 (October 1972):9–18.

Kaplan, H. S. "Can You Ruin Your Daughter's Sex Life?" *Harper's Bazaar* 109 (October 1976):119 + .

Katchadourian, Herant A. *The Biology of Adolescence.* San Francisco: W.H. Freeman & Co., 1977.

Katchadourian, Herant A., and Lunde, Donald T. *Fundamentals of Human Sexuality.* New York: Holt, Rinehart and Winston, 1972.

Keen, Sam. "Some Ludicrous Theses about Sexuality." *Journal of Clinical Child Psychology,* Fall-Winter 1974.

Kennedy, Father Eugene M. "The New Sexuality: Here Comes Everybody." *Journal of Clinical Child Psychology.* Fall-Winter 1974.

Kestenbaum, Clarice J. "Adolescent Homosexual Experiences." *Medical Aspects of Human Sexuality,* January 1975.

———. "Sex among Very Young Middle-class Adolescents." *Medical Aspects of Human Sexuality,* February 1978.

"Kids, Sex and Doctors: Medical Rights of Those under 18." *Time* 104 (25 November 1974):91 + .

"Kids Today are Pretty Level-headed on TV . . . Sex . . . Drugs . . . Family." *U.S. News* 81 (6 September 1976):48–49.

King, Janet, C., and Jacobsen, Howard N. "Nutrition and Pregnancy in Adolescence." In *The Pregnant Teenage Girl.* Edited by Jack Zackler and Wayne Brandstadt. Springfield, IL:Charles C. Thomas, 1975.

Kirk, R. "On Being Sexually Educated." *National Review* 26 (15 February 1974):209.

Kirkendall, Lester A. "How Premarital Sex May Hurt Girls." In *Sex in the Adolescent Years.* Edited by Isadore Rubin and Lester A. Kirkendall. New York: Association Press, 1968.

———. "The Relationship Between Sex and Love." *Ibid.*

———. "Understanding the Male Sex Drive." *Ibid.*

———. "What Males Lose by the Double Standard." *Ibid.*

———. "Why Boys 'Lose Respect.'" *Ibid.*

Kolodny, R. L., and Reilly, W. V. "Group Work with Today's Unmarried Mother." *Social Casework* 53 (December 1972):613–22.

Komarovsky, M. "Is There a New Morality?" Analysis of Daniel Yankelovich, Inc. study. *Parents' Magazine & Better Homemaking* 50 (December 1975):33–35 + .

Kowinski, W. "So What's Left? The Free-love Blah." *Esquire* 78 (September 1972):84–85 + .

Kramer, R. "Revolution in Our Adoption Laws." *Parents' Magazine & Better Homemaking* 46 (December 1971):37–39 + .

Krishnan, P., and Kayani, A. K. "Estimates of Age Specific Divorce Rates for Females in the United States, 1960–1969." *Journal of Marriage and the Family* 36 (February 1974):72–75.

Kutner, N. G., and Brogan, D. "Investigation of Sex-related Slang Vocabulary and Sex-role Orientation among Male and Female University Students." *Journal of Marriage and the Family* 36 (August 1974):474–84.

Kuvlesky, W. P., and Obordo, A. S. "Racial Comparison of Teen-age Girls' Projections for Marriage and Procreation." *Journal of Marriage and the Family* 34 (February 1972):75–84.

Lake, A. "For Teenagers Only: Confidential Birth Control Clinics." *Good Housekeeping* 182 (June 1976):132–33 +.

———. "Right to Say No." *Seventeen* 33 (June 1974):110–111 +. Same abridged with title: "Girls' Right to Say No." *Reader's Digest* 105 (September 1974):91–94.

Lance, L. M. "Sex-integrated and Sex-segregated University Dormitory Living: A Trend Analysis of College Student Sexual Permissiveness." *Human Relations* 29 (February 1976):115–23.

Lane, Mary E. "Common Errors Patients Make with Diaphragms and Foams." *Medical Aspects of Human Sexuality*, March 1974.

Langston, R. D. "Sex Guilt and Sex Behavior in College Students." *Journal of Personality Assessment* 37 (October 1973):467–72.

Lee, Richard V. "Adolescent Sexuality: Fact and Fantasy about the 'New Morality.'" *Medical Aspects of Human Sexuality*, December 1977.

———. "What about the Right to Say No?" *The New York Times Magazine*, 16 September 1973, pp. 90–92.

Leese, S. M. "Sexual Urges in Adolescents." *Nursing Times* 70 (19 September 1974):1475.

"Legalized Abortion." *Medical World News*, 23 January 1978.

Leiblum, Sandra Risa. "Common Male Errors in Lovemaking." *Medical Aspects of Human Sexuality*, December 1978.

Leslie, Gerald, R. "Sexual Behavior of College Men: Today vs. 30 Years Ago." *Medical Aspects of Human Sexuality*, July 1978.

Lewis, R. A., et al. "Premarital Coitus and Commitment among College Students." *Archives of Sexual Behavior* 4 (January 1975):73–79.

Libby, Roger W. "Adolescent Sexual Attitudes and Behavior." *Journal of Clinical Child Psychology*, Fall-Winter 1974.

———. "Configurations of Parental Preferences Concerning Sources of Sex Education for Adolescents." *Adolescence* 9 (Spring 1974):73–80.

———. "Parental Attitudes Toward High School Sex Education Programs." *The Family Coordinator*, July 1970.

List, S. S. "When Our Daughters Discover Love and Sex." *McCall's* 100 (September 1973):65 +.

Lobsenz, D. H. "What You Wish Your Teenager Never Told You about Sex." *Ms.* 3 (May 1975):16–18.

"The Log" of Orphan Voyage. October 1976.

London, H. "Lovemaking in School: Controversy over a Film on Sex Education at New York's Monroe High School." *Commonweal* 102 (10 October 1975):460–63.

Lorenzi, M. E.; Klerman, L. V.; and Jekel, J. F. "School-age Parents: How Permanent a Relationship?" *Adolescence* 12 (Spring 1977):13–22.

"Loss of Virginity in the College Woman." *Sexuality Today* 2 (25 December 1978):2.

Louko, Kenneth, R., and Wagner, Paul E. "Signs of Sexual Difficulties in Adolescents." *Medical Aspects of Human Sexuality*, July 1976.

Macklin, E. D. "Cohabitation in College: Going Very Steady." Study at Cornell University. *Psychology Today* 8 (November 1974):53–59.

"'Magic bullet' Japanese Abortion Drug Stirs Hopes and Questions." *Time*, 17 April 1978.

Marinoff, Stanley C. "Contraception in Adolescents." *Pediatric Clinics of North America*, August 1972, p. 811.

Marinoff, Stanley C., and Schonholz, David H. "Adolescent Pregnancy." *Pediatric Clinics of North America*, August 1972, p. 795.

Markham, M., and Jacobson, H. "Unwed Teenage Mothers." *Parents' Magazine & Better Homemaking* 51 (June 1976):36 +.

Marks, Judi. "Sex Education: Does It Make the Grade?" *'Teen*, March 1978.

"Marriage Declines among U.S. Youth." *Futurist* 10 (June 1976):165.

Martin, J. W. "School-age Mothers Go to Classes." *Education Digest* 36 (January 1971):44–45.

Masters, W. H., and Johnson, V. E. "Teaching Your Children about Sex: Questions and Answers." *Redbook* 145 (September 1975):68 +.

Mathis, J. L. "Adolescent Sexuality and Societal Change." *American Journal of Psychotherapy* 30 (July 1976):433–40.

Matteson, R. "Adolescent Self-esteem, Family Communication, and Marital Satisfaction." *Journal of Psychology* 86 (January 1974):35–47.

Maykovich, K. "Attitudes versus Behavior in Extramarital Sexual Relations." *Journal of Marriage and the Family* 38 (November 1976):693–99.

Maynard, J. "Embarrassment of Virginity." *Mademoiselle* 75 (August 1972):258–59 +.

McAnarney, Elizabeth R. "The Precious Dyad: Special Requirements of the Pregnant Adolescent and Her Fetus." The Infant and Early Childhood Feeding Symposium, 16–18 October 1978, Michigan State University, East Lansing, Michigan.

McCary, James Leslie. *Human Sexuality*. Princeton: D. Van Nostrand Company, Inc., 1967.

———. "What I Would Tell My Daughter about Premarital Sex." In *Sex in the Adolescent Years*. Edited by Isadore Rubin and Lester A. Kirkendall. New York: Association Press, 1968.

McCoy, Kathy. "Adolescent Sexuality: A National Concern." *Journal of Clinical Child Psychology*, Fall-Winter 1974.

———. "What *'Teen* readers Are Asking about Sex . . . and What We Are Telling Them." *Journal of Clinical Child Psychology*, Fall-Winter 1974.

McDermott, Robert J. "A College Student Talks about Sex." In *Sex in the Adolescent Years*. Edited by Isadore Rubin and Lester A. Kirkendall. New York: Association Press, 1968.

McNamara, Joan. *The Adoption Adviser*. New York: Hawthorn Books, 1975.

"The Man Who Cares." U.S. Department of Health, Education and Welfare. *Publication No. (HSA) 75–16010*.

Mead, M. "Birth Control in the High Schools." *McCall's* 99 (January 1972):59.

———. "Too Many Divorces, Too Soon." *Redbook* 142 (February 1974):72 +.

Medical Aspects of Human Sexuality: 750 Questions Answered by 500 Authorities. Compiled by Harold I. Lief. Baltimore: Williams & Wilkins, 1975.

Merritt, C. G., et al. "Age at First Coitus and Choice of Contraceptive Method: Preliminary Report on a Study of Factors Related to Cervical Neoplasia." *Social Biology* 22 (Fall 1975):255–60.

Miller, P. Y., and Simon, W. "Adolescent Sexual Behavior: Context and Change." *Social Problems* 22 (October 1974):58–76.

Miller, W. B. "Sexual and Contraceptive Behavior in Young Unmarried Women." *Primary Care* 3 (September 1976):427–53.

———. "Sexuality, Contraception and Pregnancy in a High-school Population." *California Medical* 119 (August 1973):14–21.

Mintz, I. L. "Today's Adolescent." *The New York Times Magazine*, 29 April 1973, p. 88 +. Reply by P. I. Nardi, 3 June 1973, p. 57.

Miranda, A. M., and Hammer, E. L. "Premarital Sexual Permissiveness: A Research Note." *Journal of Marriage and the Family* 36 (May 1974):356–58. Reply by I. L. Reiss, vol. 36 (August 1974):445–46.

Monsour, K. J. "On Abortion and the College Woman." *Mademoiselle* 78 (November 1973):64+.

Monsour, K. J., et al. "Abortion and Sexual Behavior in College Women." *American Journal of Orthopsychiatry* 43 (October 1973):804–814.

Montgomery, T. L. "Adolescent Sexuality and Paramarriage." *American Journal of Obstetrics and Gynecology* 124 (15 April 1976):818–24.

Moore, K. A., et al. "The Effect of Government Policies on Out-of-wedlock Sex and Pregnancy." *Family Planning Perspectives* 9 (July-August 1977):164–69.

Moore, W. T. "Promiscuity in a 13-year-old Girl." *Psychoanalytic Study of the Child* 29 (1974):301–318.

Morgan, Elaine. "In Defense of Virgins." *Medical Aspects of Human Sexuality*, June 1978.

Morgenstern, J. "New Face of Adoption." *Newsweek* 78 (13 September 1971):66–68+.

Morgenthau, Joan E., and Sokoloff, Natalie J. "Sexual Revolution: Myth or Fact?" *Pediatric Clinics of North America*, August 1972, p. 779.

Morrison, J. L., and Anderson, S. "College Student Cohabitation." *Education Digest* 39 (May 1974):57–59.

Moskowitz, Joel A. and Arlene S. "Secondary Virginity." *Medical Aspects of Human Sexuality*, December 1975.

"Mother as Sex Educator of Her Daughter." *Sexuality Today* 6 (27 November 1978):2.

Nadelson, Carol C. "Inadequate Contraceptive Use among Sexually Active Adolescents." *Medical Aspects of Human Sexuality*, January 1976.

Nelson, Jack L., and Carlson, Kenneth. "Neglected Dimensions of Sex Education." *Intellect* 101 (January 1973).

Nelson, S. E. "All About Sex Education for Students." *American Journal of Nursing* 77 (April 1977):611–12.

Nettleton, C. A., et al. "Dating Patterns, Sexual Relationships and Use of Contraceptives of 700 Unwed Mothers During a Two-year Period Following Delivery." *Adolescence* 10 (Spring 1975):45–57.

Neubeck, G. Sexual Semantics. In *The Adolescent Experience*. Edited by James R. Semmens and Kermit E. Krantz. New York: Collier-Macmillan, 1970.

"New Approach to Adolescent Sexuality." *Sexuality Today* 12 (15 May 1978):3.

"New Study Finds Lamaze Births Lead to Fewer Complications." *Medical World News*, 24 July 1978.

Nicholas, Leslie. "Venereal Diseases in Pediatrics." *Medical Aspects of Human Sexuality*, February 1978.

Nichtern, S. "Effects of Sexual Disturbances on Family Life." *Medical Aspects of Human Sexuality* 11 (1977):116.

Nilson, D. R., et al. "Parental Consent and a Teenage Sex Survey." *Hastings Center Report* 7 (June 1977):13–15.

"Nutrition in Pregnancy." *The Medical Letter* 20 (28 June 1978).

Nye, Ivan F. "School-age Parenthood: Consequences for Babies, Mothers, Fathers, Grandparents, and Others." *Extension Bulletin* 667. Cooperative Extension Service, Washington State University, 1977.

Okada, Louise M., and Gillespie, Duff G. "The Impact of Family Planning Programs on Unplanned Pregnancies." *Family Planning Perspectives* 9 (July-August 1977).

"Oldest Secondary School in U.S. Introduces Baby-care Class for Boys." *Sexuality Today* 2 (1 January 1979):3.

"On Stage: Teen Sex Counseling." *Getting It Together* 8 (October 1977).

"One-quarter of Young Brides Either Pregnant or Already Mothers When They Marry." *Sexuality Today* 2 (30 October 1978):4.

"Oral Contraceptives: Another Look at the Risks of the Pill." *Patient Care*, 15 January 1976.

Osofsky, Howard, J. "Adolescent Out-of-wedlock Pregnancy: An Overview." *Clinical Obstetrics and Gynecology*, 14 June 1971, p. 442.

————. "Adolescent Sexual Behavior: Current Status and Anticipated Trends for the Future." *Clinical Obstetrics and Gynecology* 14 (June 1971):393–408.

Oswalt, R. M. "Sexual and Contraceptive Behavior of College Females." *Journal of the American College Health Association* 22 (June 1974):392–94.

Our Story: Teen Mothers Talk. Y.W.C.A., Kingston NY, 1978.

"Outmoded Virginity." *Time* 99 (22 May 1972):69–70.

Oziel, L. Jerome. "Inconsistency of Coital Orgasm in Women." *Medical Aspects of Human Sexuality*, September 1978.

Page, R., et al. "Sexual Activity and Contraception Use in Young Adults." *New Zealand Medical Journal* 82 (22 October 1975):261–64.

Pannor, Reuben. "Teen-age Unwed Father." *Clinical Obstetrics and Gynecology*, 14 June 1971, p. 466.

Pannor, Reuben; Massarik, Fred; and Evans, Byron. *The Unmarried Father.* New York: Springer Publishing Co., 1971.

Panzarine, Susan. "Problems of Teen Parents." Seminar at Y.W.C.A. of Rochester and Monroe County, New York, Fall 1978.

"The Parent as Sex Education Teacher." *Sexuality Today* 2 (2 April 1979):1.

"Parents' Role in the Sexual Learning of their Children." *Sexuality Today* 2 (5 February 1979):1.

Parlee, Mary Brown. "The Sexes under Scrutiny: From Old Biases to New Theories." *Psychology Today*, November 1978.

Pastore, H. "My Beautiful Stranger: A Mother's Look at Her Teenage Daughter." *Ladies' Home Journal* 90 (August 1973):92–93 +.

Patrikios, T. "Marriage Age 16, Civil Majority 18, Voting Age 21: Why?" *UNESCO Courier* 26 (October 1973):24–31.

Perkins, Barbara B. *Adolescent Birth Planning and Sexuality: Abstracts of the Literature.* Consortium on Early Childbearing and Childrearing, 1974.

Perlman, D. "Self-esteem and Sexual Permissiveness." *Journal of Marriage and the Family* 36 (August 1974):470–73.

Peterman, D. J. "Comparison of Cohabiting and Noncohabiting College Students." *Journal of Marriage and the Family* 36 (May 1974):344–54.

Petras, J. "Needed: A Different Focus in Teaching Children about Sex." *Sexuality Today* 1 (1978):1.

Pietrofesa, John J. "The School Counselor in Sex Education." *Personnel and Guidance Journal*, March 1976.

Planned Births, the Future of the Family and the Quality of American Life. Report of the Ad Hoc Committee for a Position Paper on the Status of Family Planning in the United States Today, June 1977.

Plionis, B. M. "Adolescent Pregnancy: Review of the Literature." *Social Work* 20 (July 1975):302–307.

Pomeroy, Richard, and Lardman, Lynn C. "Public Opinion Trends: Elective Abortion and Birth Control Services to Teenagers." *Family Planning Perspectives* 4 (October 1972).

————. "Sex Questions You'll Have Trouble Answering Correctly." *Today's Health* 51 (August 1973):34–37 +.

"Poor Sex Ed: Teenage VD Epidemic." *Sexuality Today* 2 (22 January 1979):1.

"Position Paper: Human Sexuality Programs on the College Campus." *Journal of School Health* 44 (March 1974):126–29.

Positive Policy Handbook: Organization Statements Supporting Sexual Health and Education Services for Youth. Planned Parenthood Federation of America, Inc., June 1975.

Post, P. "Not Enough Sex Ed.?" *Seventeen* 34 (December 1975):46.

Potter, S. J., and Smith, H. L. "Sex Education as Viewed by Teenage Unwed Mothers." *Intellect* 104 (April 1976):515–16.

"Power Strategies in Sexual Encounters." *Sexuality Today* 2 (18 December 1978):1.

"Pregnant Teenagers; With Teacher Opinion Poll." *Today's Education* 59 (October 1970):26–29 + .

Rauh, Joseph L., and Burket, Robert L. "Adolescent Sexual Activity and Resulting Gynecologic Problems." *Medical Aspects of Human Sexuality,* April 1979.

Ravenholt, R. T. "Demographic Implications of Adolescent Reproduction." Presented at First Inter-Hemispheric Conference on Adolescent Fertility. Airlie, Warrenton, Virginia, 1 September 1976.

Reed, C. E. "An Analysis of the Perceptions of High School Principals in Public and Catholic Schools Relative to the Importance of Sex Education in the Curriculum." *Journal of School Health* 43 (March 1973):198–200.

Rees, B., et al. "The Effects of Formal Sex Education on the Sexual Behaviors and Attitudes of College Students." *Journal of the American College Health Association* 22 (June 1974):370–71.

Reichelt, P. A. "The Desirability of Involving Adolescents in Sex Education Planning." *Journal of School Health* 47 (February 1977):99–103.

Reichelt, P. A., et al. "Contraception, Abortion and Venereal Disease: Teenagers' Knowledge and the Effect of Education." *Family Planning Perspectives* 7 (March-April 1975):83–88.

Reichelt, P. A., et al. "A Sex Information Program for Sexually Active Teenagers." *Journal of School Health* 45 (February 1975):100–107.

Reid, E. A. "Effects of Coresidential Living on the Attitudes, Self-image and Role Expectations of College Women." *American Journal of Psychology* 131 (May 1974):551–54.

Reiss, Ira L. "Premarital Contraceptive Usage: A Study and some Theoretical Explorations." *Journal of Marriage and the Family* 37 (August 1975):619–30.

———. "Premarital Sexual Standards." *SIECUS Study Guide No. 5,* 1976.

"Relation of Nutrition to Pregnancy in Adolescence." *Clinical Obstetrics and Gynecology,* 14 June 1971, p. 367.

Remsberg, C., and Remsberg, B. "Do Teens Make Good Sex Counselors?" *Seventeen* 34 (September 1975):134–35.

Reuben, D. R. "Everything You Always Wanted to Tell Your Teenager about Sex but Were Afraid to Bring Up." *Ladies' Home Journal* 92 (November 1975):88 + .

———. "Solving Teenagers' Sex Problems." *Today's Health* 50 (May 1972):26–29.

"The Right to Choose: Facts on Abortion." *Zero Population Growth,* August 1977.

Robbins, Mina B., and Jensen, Gordon D. "Lying about Sex." *Medical Aspects of Human Sexuality,* November 1977.

Roberts, Elizabeth J. *Aspects of Sexual Learning.* Presented at the workshop on sexual learning, 2–4 December 1977, Dellroy, Ohio.

Rockwell, W. J., et al. "Sex on Campus: Changing Attitudes Towards the Double Standard." *Journal of the American College Health Association* 25 (June 1977):314–16.

Roiphe, A. "Teen-age Affairs." *The New York Times Magazine,* 5 October 1975, pp. 22–23 + . Discussion, *ibid.,* 2 November 1975, pp. 90–93 + .

Rondell, Florence, and Murray, Anne-Marie. *New Dimensions in Adoption.* New York: Crown, 1974.

Rosenberg, P., and Chilgren, R. A. "Focus on Feelings, the Heart of the Matter in Sex Education." *PTA Magazine* 69 (September 1974):14–17.

Rosenfeld, Alvin. "Parents' Fears about Their Children's Sexuality." *Medical Aspects of Human Sexuality,* December 1978.

Rosenthal, M. B. "Sexual Counseling and Interviewing of Adolescents." *Primary Care* 4 (June 1977):291–300.

Rosner, A. C. "An Exemplary Awareness Program for Parents." *Journal of School Health* 43 (June 1973):396–97.

Roznoy, M. S. "Taking a Sexual History." *American Journal of Nursing* 76 (August 1976):1279–82.

Rubenstein, J. S.; Watson, F. G.; and Rubenstein, H. S. "An Analysis of Sex Education Books for Adolescents by Means of Adolescents' Sexual Interests." *Adolescence* 12 (Fall 1977):293–311.

Rubin, Isadore. "The Importance of Moral Codes." In *Sex in the Adolescent Years.* Edited by Isadore Rubin and Lester A. Kirkendall. New York: Association Press, 1968.

Rubin, Isadore, and Kirkendall, Lester A., eds. *Sex in the Adolescent Years.* New York: Association Press, 1968.

Russell, B., and Schild, S. "Pregnancy Counseling with College Women." *Social Casework* 57 (May 1976):324–29.

Sarrel, Philip M. and Lorna J. "Birth Control Services and Sex Counseling at Yale." *Family Planning Perspectives* 3 (July 1971).

Satterfield, S. "Common Sexual Problems of Children and Adolescents." *Pediatric Clinics of North America* 22 (August 1975):643–52.

"Save Us from Teen-agers: Views on How the Future Will Cope with the Overpopulation Problem." *Science Digest* 80 (December 1976):27.

Scales, Peter. "How We Guarantee the Ineffectiveness of Sex Education." *SIECUS Report* 6 (March 1978):1.

———. "Males and Morals: Teenage Contraceptive Behavior Amid the Double Standard." *The Family Coordinator,* July 1977.

———. "Questions College Students Ask about Sex." *Journal of Clinical Child Psychology,* Fall-Winter 1974.

Scarlett, J. A. "Undergraduate Attitudes Towards Birth Control: New Perspectives." *Journal of Marriage and the Family* 34 (May 1972):312–14.

Schalmo, G. B., et al. "Presence of the Double Standard in a College Population." *Psychological Reports* 34 (February 1974):227–30.

Schenkel, S., et al. "Attitudes Toward Premarital Intercourse in Determining Ego Identity Status in College Women." *Journal of Personality* 40 (September 1972):472–82.

Schiller, Patricia. *Creative Approach to Sex Education and Counseling.* Chicago: Follett Publishing Co., 1977.

———. "A Sex Attitude Modification Process for Adolescents." *Journal of Clinical Child Psychology,* Fall-Winter 1974.

Schimel, John L. "Do We Overestimate Sex?" *Medical Aspects of Human Sexuality,* January 1974.

Schmidt, G., et al. "Changes in Sexual Behavior Among Young Males and Females Between 1960–1970." *Archives of Sexual Behavior* 2 (June 1972):27–45.

Schoof-Tams, K., et al. "Differentiation of Sexual Morality Between 11 and 16 Years." *Archives of Sexual Behavior* 5 (September 1976):353–70.

Schulte, E. L. "Teenagers and Pre-teens, Too!" *Parents' Magazine & Better Homemaking* 51 (February 1976):16+.

Semmens, James P. "Marital-sexual Problems of Teen-agers." In *The Adolescent Experience.* Edited by James P. Semmens and Kermit E. Krantz. New York: Collier-Macmillan, 1970.

Semmens, James P., and Krantz, Kermit E. *The Adolescent Experience.* New York: Collier-Macmillan, 1970.

Semmens, James P., Lamers, William M., Jr., and Semmens, F. Jane. "Teen-age Pregnancy." *Ibid.*

Semmens, James P., et al. "Sex Education of the Adolescent Female." *Pediatric Clinics of North America* 19 (August 1972):765–78.

"Sensuous Teen-ager." *Scientific American* 226 (May 1972):50 + .

"Sex and the Teen-age Girl." *Newsweek* 79 (22 May 1972):65.

Sex Counseling for Adolescents and Youth. American Association of Sex Educators, Counselors and Therapists. Washington DC, 1977.

"Sex Education." *SIECUS Study Guide No. 1,* 1965.

"Sex Education as an Aid to Therapy." *Sexuality Today* 2 (19 March 1979):1.

Sex Education for Adolescents and Youth. American Association of Sex Educators, Counselors and Therapists. Washington DC, 1977.

"Sex Education in Nation's Largest Suburban School System." *Sexuality Today* 2 (18 December 1979):2.

"Sex Education Returns to the School Curriculum." *Sexuality Today* 1 (19 June 1978):2.

"Sex Education via the Student Newspaper." *Sexuality Today* 2 (23 October 1978):1.

"Sex on Campus." *Journal of the American College Health Association* 22 (June 1974):355.

"Sexual Survey #17: Current Thinking on Adolescent Sexuality." *Medical Aspects of Human Sexuality,* December 1978.

Shanas, B. "Help for Girls in Trouble: Special High Schools in New York City." *Parents' Magazine & Better Homemaking* 46 (June 1971):42–43 + .

Shapiro, Howard I. *The Birth Control Book.* New York: St. Martin's Press, 1977.

Sheppard, S. "A Survey of College-based Courses in Human Sexuality." *Journal of the American College Health Association* 23 (October 1974):14–18.

Shouse, Judith Weatherford. "Psychological and Emotional Problems of Pregnancy in Adolescence." In *The Pregnant Teenage Girl.* Edited by Jack Zackler and Wayne Brandstadt. Springfield, IL. Charles C. Thomas, 1975.

"Sixteen and Pregnant? Yes, and Scared." *Patient Care,* 30 September 1978.

Smith, F. "Unmarried Father" (Great Britain). *Contemporary Review* 220 (January 1972):22–27.

Smith, P. B., et al. "Hotline for Teen-age Mothers." *American Journal of Nursing* 75 (September 1975):1504.

Sonne, J. C. "Family Therapy of Sexually Acting-out Girls." *International Psychiatry Clinics* 8 (1971):95–118.

Sorensen, A. A., et al. "Premarital Sexual Behavior and Sociocultural Factors of College Students: A Comparison of Two Eastern Universities." *Journal of the American College Health Association* 24 (February 1976):169–74.

Sorensen, Robert C. "Adolescent Sexuality: Crucible for Generational Conflict." *Journal of Clinical Child Psychology,* Fall-Winter 1974.

———. *Adolescent Sexuality in Contemporary America.* New York: World, 1973.

Spanier, G. B. "Formal and Informal Sex Education as Determinants of Premarital Sexual Behavior." *Archives of Sexual Behavior* 5 (January 1976):39–67.

Stepto, Robert C., Keith, Louis, and Keith, Donald. "Obstetrical and Medical Problems of Teenage Pregnancy." In *The Pregnant Teenage Girl.* Edited by Jack Zackler and Wayne Brandstadt. Springfield, IL. Charles C. Thomas, 1975.

"Study Shows: Future Life of a Teenage Parent Is Grim and Problematic." *Sexuality Today* 1 (17 July 1978).

Sturrock, John B. "Sexual Problems of College Students." *Medical Aspects of Human Sexuality*, January 1978.

Sugarman, D. A., and Hochstein, R. "Is Virginity Obsolete?" *Reader's Digest* 100 (June 1972):103–105.

Sussman, Alan. *The Rights of Young People.* New York: Avon Books, 1977.

Swartz, Stephen L., et al. "Diagnosis and Etiology of Nongonococcal Urethritis." *Journal of Infectious Diseases* 138 (October 1978).

Szasz, G. "Adolescent Sexual Activity." *Canadian Nurse* 67 (October 1971):39–43.

"Teachers' Pets: Questionnaires Exploring Faculty-student Sexual Involvement." *Newsweek* 82 (26 November 1973):75.

Tebbel, J. "Sex Education: Yesterday. Today and Tomorrow." *Today's Education* 65 (January 1976):70–72.

"Teen-age Births: Some Social, Psychological and Physical Sequelae." *American Journal of Public Health*, April 1971.

"The Teenage Pregnancy Epidemic." *McCall's*, July 1978.

Teenage Pregnancy: Everybody's Problem. U.S. Government Printing Office. Washington DC, 1977.

"Teenage Pregnancy: A Major Problem for Minors." *Zero Population Growth*, August 1977.

"Teenage Pregnancy: Prevention and Treatment." *SIECUS Study Guide No. 14*, 1971.

"Teen-age Sex: Letting the Pendulum Swing." *Time* 100 (21 August 1972):34–38.

"Teenagers' Access to Contraceptives." *Children's Rights Report* 2 (April 1978).

"Teenagers and the Hush-hush Epidemic." *Senior Scholastic* 100 (28 February 1972):13–16 + .

Teenagers: Marriages, Divorces, Parenthood, and Mortality. Vital and Health Statistics: Data from the National Vital Statistics System, Series 21, No. 23. U.S. Department of Health, Education and Welfare, 1973.

"Teens Don't Use Contraceptives Because of Guilt and Non-availability." *Sexuality Today* 2 (1 January 1979):2.

"Teensex: How Far Do They Really Go?" *Ladies' Home Journal*, February 1973.

"Teensex? It's Okay to Say No Way." Planned Parenthood Federation of America, No. 1592.

Teevan, J. J., Jr. "Reference Groups and Premarital Sexual Behavior." *Journal of Marriage and the Family* 34 (May 1972):283–91.

Thiebaux, H. J. "Self-prescribed Contraceptive Education by the Unwilling Pregnant." *American Journal of Public Health* 62 (May 1972):689–94.

Toolan, James. "Adolescent Concerns About Being 'Normal' Sexually." *Medical Aspects of Human Sexuality*, October 1975.

Toward Informed Consent. National Clearinghouse for Family Planning Information Health Education Bulletin, March 1978.

"True Story of a Pregnant Teenager." *Parents' Magazine & Better Homemaking* 49 (August 1974):38–39 + .

Tyrer, Louise B. "Advantages and Disadvantages of Nonprescription Contraceptives." *Medical Aspects of Human Sexuality*, July 1977.

Uddenberg, N. "Mother-father and Daughter-male Relationships: A Comparison." *Archives of Sexual Behavior* 5 (January 1976):69–79.

Ullmann, H. "You Are Nearly a Woman." *Saturday Evening Post* 243 (Fall 1971):93 + .

"Unintended Teenage Childbearing—United States, 1974." *Morbidity and Mortality Weekly Report* 27 (21 April 1978).

"Unsexual Politics: American Virgin Liberation Front." *Esquire* 77 (May 1972):122–123.

"Update: American Attitudes Toward Premarital Sex." *Sexuality Today* 2 (26 March 1979).

"Using Teens as Peer Birth-control Counselors." *Sexuality Today* 1 (16 October 1978):1.

Vadies, Gene. "Children Bearing Children." *Engage/Social Action*, April 1978.

Vadies, Gene, and Machlowitz, Marilyn M. "Hotlines: A New Ally to Family Planning." *Journal of Clinical Child Psychology*, Fall-Winter 1974.

Vadies, Gene, and Pomeroy, Richard. "Out of Wedlock Pregnancy Among American Teenagers." *Journal of Clinical Child Psychology*, Fall-Winter 1974.

Van Gelder, Lindsy. "Cracking the Women's Movement Protection Game." *Ms.*, December 1978.

"VD: The Epidemic." *Newsweek* (24 January 1972):46–50.

"VD Fact Sheet 1976." U.S. Department of Health, Education and Welfare, *Publication No. (CDC) 77-8195.*

"V.D. Is for Everybody: Television Presentation." *Medical Aspects of Human Sexuality*, January 1974.

Vener, A. M., and Stewart, C. S. "Adolescent Sexual Behavior in Middle America Revisited: 1970–1973." *Journal of Marriage and the Family* 36 (November 1974):728–35.

Vener, A. M., et al. "Sexual Behavior of Adolescents in Middle America: Generation and American-British Comparisons." *Journal of Marriage and the Family* 34 (November 1972):696–705.

Vital Statistics Report. National Center for Health Statistics, Vol. 25, No. 10. 30 December 1976.

Wallace, Helen M. "Venereal Disease in Teen-agers." *Clinical Obstetrics and Gynecology*, 14 June 1971, p. 432.

Warren, C. L., et al. "Sources and Accuracy of College Students' Sex Knowledge." *Journal of School Health* 43 (November 1973):588–90.

Watts, Mary E. "Trends and Developments in Social Services for Teen-age Unmarried Mothers." *Clinical Obstetrics and Gynecology*, 14 June 1971, p. 457.

Wax, J. "Abortion Controversy: What's It All About?" *Seventeen* 34 (November 1975):118–19 + .

Weed, J. A. "Age at Marriage as a Factor in State Divorce Rate Differentials." *Demography* 11 (August 1974):361–75.

Weiss, Brian. "Clash Between Culture and Biology: Earlier Menstruation, Longer Adolescence." *Psychology Today* 8 (November 1974):59.

Werner, Arnold. "Sex Questions Asked by College Students." *Medical Aspects of Human Sexuality*, May 1975.

———. "Sexual Dysfunction in College Men and Women." *American Journal of Psychiatry* 132 (February 1975):2.

"What Sexual Literature Do You Advise Patients to Read?" *Medical Aspects of Human Sexuality*, August 1974.

Whelan, E. M. "What's Wrong with Teenage Sex." *Parents' Magazine & Better Homemaking* 50 (February 1975):44–45 + .

"When Oral Contraceptives Talk Back." *Patient Care*, 1 October 1975.

Whitehurst, Robert N. "Loss of Virginity in College Women." *Medical Aspects of Human Sexuality*, November 1978.

Wigfield, A. S. "Attitudes to Venereal Disease in a Permissive Society." *British Medical Journal* 4 (6 November 1971):342–45.

Wilms, John H. "New Strains on Youth Due to Sexual Liberation." *Medical Aspects of Human Sexuality*, 1978.

Wilson, J. R. "Jumping the Generation Gap with Sixth, Seventh and Eighth Grade Boys." *Pediatrics* 50 (September 1972):459–61.

Wolfish, M. G. "Adolescent Sexuality: Counseling, Contraception, Pregnancy." *Clinical Pediatrics* 12 (April 1973):244–47.

———. "Adolescent Sexuality." *Practitioner* 210 (February 1973):226–31.

Woodbury, R. "Help for High School Mothers." Citrus High, Azusa, Calif. program. *Life* 70 (2 April 1971):34–41.

Woods, N. F., et al. "Changes in Students' Knowledge and Attitudes Following a Course in Human Sexuality." Report of a pilot study. *Nursing Research* 24 (January-February 1975):

———. "Why Young People Are Turning away from Casual Sex." *McCall's* 101 (April 1974):83 +.

Woody, J. D. "Contemporary Sex Education: Attitudes and Implications for Childrearing." *Journal of School Health* 43 (April 1973):241–46.

Wylie, E. M. "Ups and Downs of Young Marriages." *Seventeen* 30 (August 1971):236–37 +.

Yankelovich, Daniel. *The New Morality: A Profile of American Youth in the 70's.* New York: McGraw-Hill, 1974.

Youcha, G. "Awakening to Adolescence." *Parents' Magazine & Better Homemaking* 48 (April 1973):42–43 +.

Young, A. T., et al. "Parental Influence on Pregnant Adolescents." *Social Work* 20 (September 1975):387–91.

Young People, Sex and the Law. Children's Rights Report, Vol. 2, No. 7. April 1978.

"Your Patient from Puberty to Maturity." *Patient Care*, 15 October 1978.

Youth Values Project. The Population Institute. Washington DC, 1978.

Zackler, Jack, and Brandstadt, Wayne, eds. *The Pregnant Teenage Girl.* Springfield, IL: Charles C. Thomas, 1975.

Zelnik, Melvin, and Kantner, John F. "Contraceptive Patterns and Premarital Pregnancy among Women Aged 15–19 in 1976." *Family Planning Perspectives* 10 (May-June 1978):135–42.

———. "First Pregnancies to Women Ages 15–19: 1976 and 1971." *Family Planning Perspectives* 10 (January-February 1978).

Zelnik, Melvin, et al. "Some Preliminary Observations on Pre-adult Fertility and Family Formation." *Studies in Family Planning* 3 (April 1972):59–62.

Zongker, Calvin E. "The Self Concept of Pregnant Adolescent Girls." *Adolescence* 12 (Winter 1977):477–88.

Zuckerman, M., et al. "Sexual Attitudes and Experience: Attitude and Personality Correlates and Changes Produced by a Course in Sexuality." *Journal of Consulting and Clinical Psychology* 44 (February 1976):7–19.

Index